CLAIMS TO TRACEABLE PROCEEDS

Claims to Traceable Proceeds

Law, Equity, and the Control of Assets

DR ARUNA NAIR
Lecturer in Law, King's College London

OXFORD
UNIVERSITY PRESS

OXFORD
UNIVERSITY PRESS

Great Clarendon Street, Oxford, OX2 6DP,
United Kingdom

Oxford University Press is a department of the University of Oxford.
It furthers the University's objective of excellence in research, scholarship,
and education by publishing worldwide. Oxford is a registered trade mark of
Oxford University Press in the UK and in certain other countries

First Edition published in 2018

Published in the United States of America by Oxford University Press
198 Madison Avenue, New York, NY 10016, United States of America

British Library Cataloguing in Publication Data
Data available

Library of Congress Control Number: 2017960270

ISBN 978–0–19–881340–8

Preface

Tracing has attracted considerable scholarly attention over the last thirty years, notably as a result of the pioneering work of Peter Birks and Lionel Smith. The challenge has been to define the actual function of the tracing doctrine, given the highly metaphorical language in which it has been traditionally described, and to address how this traditional doctrine can be adapted to meet the challenges of modern forms of fraud, transaction, and payment system. This book argues that tracing has traditionally aimed to protect claimants who are vulnerable to the decision-making control of defendants over their assets, while still respecting the autonomy of these defendants. This approach, while explaining the existing authorities, can also enable the law to flexibly cope with new situations in a principled way. The law is stated as at 24 November 2017.

This project began as a doctoral thesis, completed at the University of Oxford under the supervision of William Swadling. I am grateful to him for his support and guidance as my doctoral supervisor, for first introducing me to the study of law as an undergraduate, and for consistently helping me to ask better questions about the law. At different stages, I have also benefited from discussions with Andrew Burrows, Elizabeth Cooke, Robert Chambers, James Edelman, David Foster, Ying Liew, Eva Lomnicka, Ben McFarlane, Charles Mitchell, John Mee, Irit Samet-Porat, Lionel Smith, and Eva Pils. All errors are, of course, my own.

Contents

Table of Cases

Table of Legislation

1

The Peculiarities of Tracing

This chapter introduces the concept of 'tracing', and identifies some characteristics of the law of tracing that do not make immediate sense on a first encounter with the cases. Tracing is a term that describes the mechanism by which the courts identify one asset as the product or substitute of another, for the purpose of enabling a claimant entitled to the original asset to make claims to the so-called substitute. There are three aspects of the law that call for explanation. 1.01

First, it is not clear why the law uses the concept of tracing, in its current transactional form, to do this work. That is, it is not clear why tracing is necessary in the first place. Secondly, and as a necessary corollary, the rational basis of specific rules of tracing is not obvious from the case law. Ideas like backwards tracing, the lowest intermediate balance rule, and 'cherry-picking' determine when an asset apparently held by one person is to be treated as the product or substitute for an asset held by another; the exact scope of these concepts, and their underlying justification, is not very clear. Finally, both problems are underpinned by a third and more fundamental problem; this is the absence of any settled definition of the key concept of a 'substitution'. Tracing, in the current law, depends entirely on the identification of particular transactions as involving a substitution of some other asset for the original asset that is being 'traced'. But it is not easy to define the characteristics of a substitution, or to explain why the existence of a transaction of this kind matters so much for the purposes of tracing. 1.02

This is not merely a problem of semantic clarity or accessibility of language. There are some legal terms—for example, 'fee simple absolute in possession'—that may be mostly unfamiliar outside the legal profession, but whose meaning can readily be elaborated in terms that allow anyone to understand what is at stake in the use of the term. It is not difficult to understand the implications of a right to possession of land, which goes on forever and which will not either arise only once some condition is met or terminate on some other condition. Having understood that it is this kind of right that English law recognizes when it recognizes the fee simple absolute in possession, we are then in a position to evaluate the reasons why English law might recognize rights that have this content. The terms 'substitution' and 'tracing', on the other hand, are harder to unpack. They do not make it clear what, if any, normative principle or empirical reality is described by calling A's sale of B's shares, for example, a 'substitution'. To some extent, the language used is circular: tracing allows us to determine whether a substitution has occurred; a substitution is a transaction of the kind through which tracing is possible. The linguistic problem, therefore, 1.03

also becomes a problem of a lack of moral transparency. In seeking to identify the principle that justifies a judicial decision on the facts of some case—for example, a decision to order A's bank to pay the credit balance of A's bank account to B—we are obliged to go beyond the language used by the judge in the case itself.

1.04 The goal of this chapter is to describe the analytical difficulties raised by the tracing concept, and the tracing rules, and the problems of justification that arise as a result. A leading response to those problems—the 'value' model developed by Peter Birks and Lionel Smith and adopted by the courts to some extent in some cases—will be evaluated in Chapter 2.

1.1. Why is Tracing Necessary?

1.05 Lionel Smith defines tracing as a process which:

> ... allows a status or claim to be transferred from one subject matter to another. The nexus between the original subject matter and the new subject matter is substitution: the one was acquired as a substitute for the other. This requires an exchange or an analogous transaction.[1]

1.06 This captures three important aspects of the concept of tracing: when it matters; what it requires; and the problem of defining the exact range of transactions that satisfies its requirements. According to Smith, tracing plays a role in any situation where the law attributes a legal status to a thing that can be transmitted to other things. The status of a thing as the object of a private law claim is only one such status. Other examples include the status of the proceeds of a crime,[2] or of separate or community property of a spouse, in a jurisdiction that recognizes a matrimonial property regime.[3]

1.07 Secondly, this transmission of status is achieved by an event called 'substitution'. Tracing allows a legal status to be transmitted from one thing to another where, and only where, a transaction that counts as a substitution has taken place. The paradigm case of substitution is exchange. For example, suppose A is B's agent and wrongfully sells B's car to C, receiving £500 in cash in exchange. This is a substitution for the purposes of tracing, with the cash representing the proceeds of the car. Contrast a case where A wrongfully makes use of B's car in her travels, and so saves £500 in taxi fares; her existing bank account remains in credit to this amount. In both scenarios, A now has £500 that she would not have had if she had not misappropriated B's car. In both scenarios, therefore, it could be said that the £500 represents the 'proceeds' of the misappropriation of the car in one sense: it represents money that A would not have had if she had not wronged B. But the law of tracing sharply distinguishes the first scenario from the second. There is a substitution in the case where the car is sold; there is no substitution in the case where the car is not sold but a saving of money is made.[4] As a result, B has the prospect of invoking the tracing concept to claim the £500 in cash in the first scenario; in the second, there is no such prospect of a claim

[1] Lionel Smith, *The Law of Tracing* (Clarendon Press 1997) 18. [2] Smith (n 1) 43–45.
[3] Smith (n 1) 38–40. [4] *Re Hallett & Co* [1894] 2 QB 237.

to the bank account. A central question about tracing is why, in the face of various alternative mechanisms for identifying the 'proceeds' of some act or event involving the use of a thing or asset, it focuses so tightly on substitutions.

1.1.1. Tracing and the identification of proceeds of crime

The significance of the difference made by this focus on substitutions can be explained by reference to the Proceeds of Crime Act 2002, which envisages two methods by which the state may recover the 'proceeds' of a crime in the hands of a defendant: confiscation and civil recovery. The substitution concept, which dominates tracing in the private law context, plays a very different role in these different contexts. 1.08

Confiscation orders, under part 2 of the Proceeds of Crime Act 2002, may be made by a court against a defendant who has benefited from a criminal offence of which he has been convicted. As Lord Philips said in *Serious Organised Crime Agency v Perry*,[5] 'confiscation' is a misnomer in this context. No order to confiscate any specific thing or asset held by the defendant can be made under the provisions of Part 2 of the Act.[6] Rather, a confiscation order takes the form of an order that the defendant pay a money sum, which is treated like any other judgment debt for the purposes of enforcement and the accrual of interest due.[7] 1.09

In deciding whether to make a confiscation order, and in quantifying the amount due under such an order, the key question is whether the defendant has benefited from his criminal conduct in the causal sense: is he financially better off than he would have been if the crime had never taken place? Section 76 of the Act provides that a person benefits from conduct if he obtains either property or a pecuniary advantage 'as a result of or in connection with' that conduct.[8] In order to satisfy this test, the prosecution must prove, on the balance of probabilities,[9] that there is a causal connection between acquisition of the property or pecuniary advantage and the crime itself.[10] 1.10

Once the court finds that the defendant has benefited from his criminal conduct,[11] in this sense, it must calculate, and order him to pay, an amount referred to as the 'recoverable amount'. This is defined as an amount that is either 'equal to the defendant's benefit from the conduct concerned'[12] or, where this is lower, the 'available amount'. The available amount describes the value of all the 'free property'[13] held by the defendant at the date of trial, less the value of 1.11

[5] [2012] UKSC 35, [31].

[6] Although there is a power to appoint a receiver in the event that the defendant does not comply with the confiscation order: Proceeds of Crime Act 2002 (hereafter PCA 2002), s 50. The receiver will then have wide powers to deal with the 'realisable property' of the defendant: PCA 2002, s 51.

[7] PCA 2002 (n 6) s 12(2).

[8] PCA 2002 (n 6) ss 76(4) and (5).

[9] PCA 2002 (n 6) s 6(7).

[10] *R v Jennings* [2008] UKHL 29.

[11] PCA 2002 (n 6) s 6.

[12] PCA 2002 (n 6) s 7(1).

[13] All property held by the defendant that is not already the subject of an order under various criminal statutes: PCA 2002 (n 6) s 82.

previous criminal fines due and of the debts he owes to preferential creditors,[14] but including the value of any 'tainted gifts'[15] that he has made.

1.12 'Value' in the 2002 Act is market value.[16] Since the market value of any asset may fluctuate with time, the question of quantification turns, in part, on the date at which the value falls to be assessed. The extent of the value obtained by the defendant from his crime is calculated as the greater of two figures: either the value of the property on the date obtained or, where this is greater, the value of 'property found' in the hands of the defendant at the date of trial.[17] Section 80(3) of the Act provides that 'property found' may refer to the original property obtained as a result of the crime, part of that property, or 'property that directly or indirectly represents it.' In *R v Waya*,[18] it was said that this subsection operated by analogy to tracing in the context of trusts, although this was not to say that the provision was 'intended to bring in the whole panoply of rules as to tracing in equity'.[19]

1.13 In other words, in asking whether the defendant has property that directly or indirectly represents the property obtained as a result of his crime, we ask a question similar to the one we ask in relation to private claims to traceable proceeds: has there has been a substitution? The justification for asking the question in the context of confiscation orders is that it provides a helpful guide to quantification of the benefit obtained by the crime. If the defendant has swapped the property he obtained for other property, it is possible that he is better off as a result of the crime than he would have been if there had been no swap. Or not; if he has made a bad bargain, and the new property is worth less than the original property, section 80 then instructs us to ignore the substitution as irrelevant and take the market value of the original property, at the date obtained, as a better guide to the task of quantifying the overall benefit obtained as a result of the crime.

1.14 In the context of confiscation proceedings, then, the search for the 'proceeds' of a crime involves two key inquiries, both of which are essentially evidential in character: proof of a causal link between a benefit obtained and a crime committed, and proof of the market value of the relevant benefit. In answering the quantification question—how much has the defendant actually benefited as a result of the crime—substitutions play a modest evidentiary role. They offer a guide to whether the defendant has managed to increase the amount of value at his disposal at the date of the trial, by entering into some profitable transaction using the benefit originally obtained as a result of the crime.

1.15 Contrast the work done by the substitution concept in the context of the civil recovery provision of the same Act, found in Part 5. As the phrase 'civil recovery' implies, a person may be vulnerable to claims under this Part, even where she has

[14] PCA 2002 (n 6) s 9(1)(a). These are debts that would have priority in the event of the defendant's insolvency and are defined by reference to the Insolvency Act 1985, s 386.

[15] PCA 2002 (n 6) s 9(1)(b). A tainted gift is any gift made by a defendant who has a criminal lifestyle after the relevant date or any gift of property obtained by particular criminal conduct at any date: PCA 2002 (n 6) s 77. For the meaning of a criminal lifestyle, see PCA 2002 (n 6) s 75.

[16] PCA 2002 (n 6) s 145.

[17] PCA 2002 (n 6) s 80.

[18] [2012] UKSC 51.

[19] *R v Waya* (n 18) [57] (Lord Walker SCJ).

not been convicted of any crime. Under section 243, an enforcement authority[20] may bring proceedings against any person on the basis that she holds 'recoverable property'—that is,[21] property obtained by or in return for unlawful[22] conduct. In the absence of a criminal conviction, the court can make a civil recovery order if it finds as a fact, on the civil standard of proof, that the property was obtained in return for unlawful conduct.[23] Importantly, it is not necessary to show that the particular defendant obtained the property by her own criminal conduct.[24] It is enough that she now has property that was once obtained by this means. She will only be protected from the civil recovery order if the property has ceased to be recoverable in her hands under section 308, or if she has a defence under section 266. Section 308 protects recipients in good faith, for value and without notice of the status of the property as recoverable, as well as those who have themselves recovered it in civil proceedings based on the defendant's unlawful conduct. Section 266 gives the court discretion to modify its order in favour of a defendant who received the property in good faith, without notice of its status as recoverable, and who has relied to her detriment on its receipt.

Against this background, section 305(1) provides that recoverable property includes not only property obtained through unlawful conduct but, also, property that 'represents' that original property. Section 305(2) goes on to define property that represents the original property in the following terms: 1.16

> If a person enters into a transaction by which—
>
> (a) he disposes of recoverable property, whether the original property or property which (by virtue of this Chapter) represents the original property, and
>
> (b) he obtains other property in place of it,
>
> the other property represents the original property.

In this context, then, what matters is either identification of the very asset obtained by or in return for the crime, or identification of its traceable product. Whether an asset counts as a product depends on whether there has been a substitution: a transaction whereby the holder of the original asset disposed of it and obtained another right in place of it. Differently to confiscation proceedings, it is not sufficient to show that the defendant, who once held recoverable property, still has the benefit of other property that has the same market value. Substitution, in the context of civil recovery orders, is not merely a guide to answering an evidential question about the benefit obtained as a result of unlawful conduct, which could be disregarded on the

20 In England and Wales, this now means the National Crime Agency (NCA) the Director of Public Prosecutions, or the Director of the Serious Fraud Office: PCA 2002 (n 6) s 316(1)(a), as amended by the Crime and Courts Act 2013.

21 PCA 2002 (n 6) s 304.

22 Unlawful, in this context, means criminal: PCA 2002 (n 6) s 241.

23 PCA 2002 (n 6) s 241(3). From a date yet to be appointed, an asset will be presumed to be recoverable property for these purposes if the court has made an 'unexplained wealth order' requiring an individual to explain the means by which that asset was acquired and he or she has failed to comply with the order: see the Criminal Finances Act 2017, s 1, inserting new ss 362A–362I into the PCA 2002.

24 See, for example, *National Crime Agency v Azam* [2016] EWCA 1234, in which a civil recovery order was made against a wife who had received recoverable property from her husband as a wedding gift.

grounds of contrary evidence. It determines when such an order will be available against any person who does not have the original property.

1.17 Contrasting the civil recovery provisions with the confiscation order provisions of the 2002 Act, Kennedy has noted that civil recovery is expensive, often calling for 'a forensic accounting exercise.'[25] Confiscation, he says, is a comparatively less expensive mechanism.[26] It is not difficult to see why this might be; transactional tracing involves both factual and legal complexity, and the processes of solving the problems generated by its demands take a good deal of legal as well as forensic energy.

1.18 As explained, transactional tracing depends on proof of a series of transactions that link the asset now held by the defendant to the original asset. If the original property is some cash obtained by drug trafficking, tracing requires us to find out what was obtained with that cash, and then what was obtained with the exchange product of the cash, and so on until we arrive at, for example, the car now held by the defendant. Even where the defendant has made no deliberate attempt to hide what he did with the cash, the number of transactions that may be involved and the necessity of identifying each of them may create difficult evidential problems.[27] By contrast, it is likely to be simpler to prove that the defendant once obtained some cash as a causal consequence of drug trafficking and that the car he now has is worth as much, or more, than that cash; if the law does not take an interest in the precise chain of events in between, evidence about each successive transaction is unnecessary.

1.19 A focus on substitution creates problems, therefore, even where the only transactions entered into by a defendant are a series of direct swaps of one asset for another. In addition, however, the law must often cope with transactions that are more complex than a direct sale or barter of one asset for another. The defendant may have used the cash obtained by drug trafficking to pay for improvements to his home; he may have paid it into a bank account into which all his wages also go; or he may have spent it in paying off a debt, or in satisfying obligations under a more complex contract than one of sale.[28] This relates to the third element of Smith's definition, which describes substitution as an exchange 'or an analogous transaction'. Is payment of money into an existing bank account analogous to an exchange? What about payment for building works that improve the value of one's current home? Rules are necessary to determine whether tracing is possible through any particular type of transaction. As will be explained,[29] the current law on these rules is complex and uncertain around its edges.

1.20 As Kennedy has noted, the application of these rules in the civil recovery context is expensive. The same is true in the context of private claims to traceable proceeds.

[25] A Kennedy, 'An Evaluation of the Recovery of Criminal Proceeds in the United Kingdom' (2007) 10 Journal of Money Laundering Control 33, 38.

[26] Kennedy (n 25).

[27] For the methods by which English law practically manages these evidential difficulties, see Chapter 4, Section 4.1 this volume.

[28] Such as the life insurance contract in *Foskett v McKeown* [2001] 1 AC 102. See paras 1.28–1.32 this chapter.

[29] See paras 1.42–1.77 this chapter.

For example, after the collapse of Lehman Brothers International (Europe), certain creditors attempted to claim the traceable proceeds of their assets in the hands of the administrators. In the High Court, Briggs J said that, even if the creditors did have the right to any traceable proceeds of these assets, identification of the proceeds was likely to involve a 'difficult, time consuming and contentious process'.[30] In their progress report of March 2011, the administrators of Lehman Brothers echoed this concern, describing the applicable legal tests as 'complex' and noting that, if tracing was necessary, they were 'likely to require guidance from the UK High Court as to the correct legal principles to be applied'.[31]

However, in *Re Lehman Brothers* itself, Briggs J was not criticizing the tracing requirement when he described it as 'prohibitively slow and expensive'.[32] The tracing rules, he said, represent 'the fruits of equity judges' and lawyers' endeavours over very many years to find and refine techniques of identifying and recovering trust property'. Their ultimate aim of helping, rather than hindering, claimants was constrained only by 'the unavoidable requirement to identify property to which it is appropriate to attach a proprietary claim'.[33] 1.21

This account implies that we need tracing to support proprietary claims, because proprietary claims require the identification of specific things or assets to which they can attach. Confiscation orders, as has been explained, impose personal obligations to pay an abstract amount of money; as such, we can quantify the amount that ought to be paid by reference to the relatively straightforward question of the market value of anything obtained as a result of a crime. Civil recovery orders, on the other hand, require identification of some specific asset or thing as the subject matter of the order. Quantifying the amount of the benefit obtained by the defendant will not, itself, tell us anything about which specific asset or thing should be recoverable under the regime. This is important because these orders share the core characteristic of proprietary claims—they are enforceable against third-party recipients of the relevant thing or asset—and their impact on individuals is, therefore, shaped by the characteristics of the thing or asset in question.[34] 1.22

Civil recovery orders, like other regimes that generate claims that have this proprietary structure, therefore require some process that yields an answer in the form, '*this* [bank account/car/thing] represents the proceeds of the crime'; 'the proceeds of the crime are £100,000' or some other abstract amount, which is good enough for the purposes of confiscation, would not suffice. On this basis, the necessity of tracing can be justified as a matter of logic. As Briggs J says, it is an unavoidable 1.23

[30] *In Re Lehman Brothers International (Europe)* [2009] EWHC 3228 (Ch), at [193], overruled on the relevance of tracing on the facts by the Supreme Court at [2012] UKSC 6.

[31] PriceWaterhouseCooper, Lehman Brothers International (Europe)—In Administration, Joint Administrators' progress report for the period 15 March 2011 to 14 September 2011 (13 October 2011) p 25. The report is available at http://www.pwc.co.uk/en_uk/uk/assets/pdf/lbie-6th-progress-report.pdf, last accessed on 9 November 2017.

[32] *In Re Lehman Brothers International (Europe)* (n 30) [198].

[33] *In Re Lehman Brothers International (Europe)* (n 30).

[34] Cf B McFarlane and S Douglas, 'Defining Property Rights' in J Penner and H Smith (eds), *Philosophical Foundations of Property Rights* (OUP 2013) 219–43.

requirement that a property right must have some subject matter; the nature of the right requires it.[35] You cannot have a right that imposes correlative liabilities on anyone who interferes with its subject matter unless you know what that subject matter is. If we are going to allow proprietary claims to assets in circumstances where no one has made an express grant identifying the subject matter of the claim, but instead because the asset represents the 'proceeds' of another asset that has been used or misappropriated in some way, we need some mechanism to determine which assets count as proceeds in this sense, and which do not.

1.24 However, this explanation does not tell us why transactional tracing is the best or only mechanism suited to this task. There are rival approaches that have the potential to be less complex. The argument that we must have some mechanism for identifying the subject matter of a proprietary claim, and that transactional tracing is as good as any other, does not, therefore, hold. A positive justification for the requirement of substitutions must be found.

1.25 Two alternatives to transactional tracing have been proposed in the academic literature: a causal approach,[36] and, relatedly, a 'swollen assets' approach.[37] Both have been firmly rejected by the English courts, in terms that do not, however, provide an unequivocal positive justification for the requirement of substitutions.

1.1.2. The 'causal links' alternative to tracing

1.26 Under a straightforwardly causal approach, an asset would count as the traceable product of the claimant's asset if, and only if, the defendant would not have it but for his misappropriation of the claimant's asset.

1.27 The difference between this approach and the transactional approach can be explained by reference to Oesterle's example of a thief who saves a necessary expense as a result of his theft. Suppose A's food bills always amount to $100, and he has exactly $100 in gold coins. He then steals a $100 bearer bond from B, and uses it to buy food, keeping the gold coins he already had. In Oesterle's view, a rational law of tracing would allow B to claim the gold coins, because A has 'retained the coins only because he stole the bond.'[38] Contrariwise, he argues,[39] it should not be possible to trace through a transactional connection that is not a causal connection. For example, suppose A habitually buys a £1 lottery ticket every Friday. With £100 of his own cash in his pocket, he decides to steal £1 from A and happens to use that particular coin to buy a—winning—lottery ticket the next day. Transactional tracing would allow B to identify A's lottery ticket, and the associated winnings, as the traceable proceeds of B's £1. On Oesterle's causal approach,[40] since A would have had the means and the motivation to buy the lottery ticket whether or not the

[35] Cf *Re Goldcorp Exchange Ltd* [1995] 1 AC 74, [90] (Lord Mustill): the requirement of ascertained subject matter is not justified 'by some arid legal technicality but by . . . "the very nature of things."'

[36] D Oesterle, 'Deficiencies of the Restitutionary Right to Trace Misappropriated Property in Equity and in UCC 9-306' (1983) 68 Cornell LR 172.

[37] S Evans, 'Rethinking Tracing and Restitution' (1999) 115 LQR 469.

[38] Oesterle (n 36) 175.

[39] Oesterle (n 36) 199.

[40] Cf J Edelman, 'Understanding Tracing Rules' [2016] QUT Law Review 1, 10, also invoking the example of the thief who buys a lottery ticket she would have bought in any event.

theft had taken place, B would not be able to treat the ticket as the product of his money in this scenario.

1.28 In *Foskett v McKeown*,[41] the majority of the House of Lords categorically rejected this argument based on causation. In that case, a Mr Timothy Murphy had made unauthorized withdrawals from bank accounts that he held on express trust for Mr Foskett and 220 other claimants. Although it was not clear what had become of most of the money, the claimants could show what Mr Murphy had done with £20,440 of it: he had used it to pay at least two out of the five of the insurance premiums due on a life insurance policy he held with Barclays Life Assurance Ltd. The question was whether this meant that, after his suicide, the claimants could claim a proportionate share of the £1m death benefit paid by Barclays to his wife, on trust for his children, as the traceable proceeds of the trust money. The argument on this issue turned, in part, on the relevance of causation.

1.29 Mr Murphy had entered into the relevant life insurance contract with Barclays in November 1986. The contract provided that Mr Murphy would pay Barclays a £10,220 premium on the 6th of November each year for the rest of his life, and that Barclays would pay a death benefit to the policyholder nominated by Mr Murphy on his death. If he failed to pay the first two premiums, the policy would lapse after a one-month grace period, ie on the 6th of December of the relevant year. There was, therefore, a straightforward causal link between these two first premiums and the death benefit eventually paid. Had Mr Murphy not paid the first two premiums within a month of them falling due, the death benefit would not have been payable. If he had used the trust money to pay the first two premiums under the contract, therefore, and had not had the resources to pay using his own assets, Oesterle's causal model and the traditional transactional tracing model would supply the same answer. The death benefit would have represented the product of the trust money, and the claimants would have been entitled to recover it from Mr Murphy's children.

1.30 However, the position is complicated by the fact that Mr Murphy did have the resources to pay these first two premiums out of his own pocket and, in fact, did so, in 1986 and 1987. Under the terms of the contract with Barclays, payment of later premiums had a somewhat different and more complex effect than that of the initial payments. Each premium paid, after the first, was used to allocate units linked to the value of an existing investment fund to the policy. The second premium 'bought' units worth £8,687, while each subsequent premium was deemed to buy £10,220 worth. These were not genuine rights in the fund in question but only units of account, measuring the amount potentially due under the policy. If, at the date of Mr Murphy's death, the aggregate value of the units in the fund notionally 'purchased' exceeded £1m, this higher amount would constitute the death benefit payable. If he paid every premium but died before 'units' worth more than £1m were purchased, the death benefit would be £1m. If he failed to pay any premium after the second, the immediate effect would be to convert the policy to a paid-up one, entitling the policyholder to a lump sum of £1m on Mr Murphy's death.

[41] *Foskett* (n 28).

The units already allocated to the policy would be cancelled as needed to 'pay the cost of life assurance', calculated in accordance with what Sir Richard Scott V-C in the Court of Appeal called 'a fairly complex formula'.[42] The policy would lapse only after there were no longer enough allocated units to match the cost.

1.31 Having paid the first two premiums out of his own funds,[43] Mr Murphy drew on the trust bank accounts to pay the fourth and fifth premiums, misappropriating at least £20,440 of the trust money for this purpose. On 6 March 1991, he committed suicide. A few months later, Barclays paid the death benefit due on the insurance policy into a bank account in the name of Mrs McKeown, Mr Murphy's widow, and a co-trustee, who held it on trust for his children. At the date of Mr Murphy's death, the units allocated to the policy did not exceed £1m in value, so this was the amount paid.

1.32 It was agreed as a fact by both parties[44] that £1m would have been payable even if Mr Murphy had not paid the final two premiums. This was because the payment of the first three premiums had led to enough units being allocated to the policy to prevent it from lapsing before March 1991, and because the payment of the additional premiums did not increase the value of the units allocated to above £1m. On this basis, Mr Murphy's children argued that the claimants had no right to a proportionate share of the death benefit, even though some of the trust money had been used to pay the insurance premiums. In the House of Lords, Roger Kaye QC argued on their behalf that these payments 'were not made in *exchange* for anything since they did not increase the value of the policy or policy moneys. The same sum would have been paid out on M's death whether or not those premiums had been paid'.[45] In other words, there was no causal link between the payment of the death benefit and the misappropriation of the trust money. The children were in the same position as the thief (or the children of the thief) who had used stolen money to buy a lottery ticket that he could afford and would have bought anyway.

1.33 This is the point on which the causal model and the traditional transactional model diverge. While the payment of the later insurance premiums could arguably be seen as a substitution or exchange of the trust money for the rights under the life insurance contract (and this is the view the House of Lords eventually took), those payments clearly were not causally necessary for the payment that represented the ultimate realization of those rights. The majority of the House of Lords—Lord Millett, Lord Browne-Wilkinson, and Lord Hope—rejected the idea that any causal link was necessary. Lord Millett said that:

> [T]he question is one of attribution not causation. The question is not whether the same death benefit would have been payable if the last premium or last few premiums had not been paid. It is whether the death benefit is attributable to all the premiums or only to some of them. The answer is that death benefit is attributable to all of them because it represents

42 [1998] Ch 265, 275.

43 There was an unresolved evidential dispute about the third premium, due in 1988. See Chapter 4, para 4.36 this volume on this aspect of the case.

44 *Foskett* (n 28) [114] (Lord Steyn).

45 *Foskett* (n 28) 105 (emphasis in the original).

the proceeds of realising the policy, and the policy in turn represents the product of all the premiums.[46]

In this passage, Lord Millett describes the alternative to causation as 'attribution'. Instead of asking whether one asset is the product of a misappropriation of another, in the sense that there is a causal link between the misappropriation of the original and the acquisition of the product, we should ask whether the acquisition of the substitute is 'attributable' to the original asset. It is so attributable if the substitute represents the proceeds of the original. On the face of it, there is some circularity here: tracing depends on attribution, not causation, but attribution itself is explained in terms that depend on tracing. Elsewhere in his judgment, Lord Millett describes tracing as being about the movement of the value of the original asset into the substitute asset; 'where one asset is exchanged for another, a claimant can elect whether to follow the original asset into the hands of the new owner or to trace its value into the new asset'.[47] However, it is not clear from the judgment itself why 'attributing' one asset to another—or attributing the value of one asset to another—necessitates a transactional link.

In *Foskett v McKeown*, therefore, the majority of the House of Lords made a clear choice in favour of transactional tracing, rejecting the causal alternative in terms. But the reasons why transactional tracing is to be preferred are somewhat opaque. The arguments for Murphy's children are relatively straightforward to understand. The implicit premise is that A should only be entitled to claim some asset in B's hands if B's acquisition of the asset was *caused by* a previous misappropriation of A's assets. This argument was rejected on grounds that are harder to understand, because they depend on the use of the undefined term, 'attribution'. We do know from the general law of tracing that the concept of attribution, here, depends on the existence of a substitution or a chain of substitutions. But we are still left in the dark about why substitutions matter more than causation, or matter at all. 1.34

1.1.3. The swollen assets alternative to tracing

Like Oesterle's causal links, a 'swollen assets' approach to tracing also defines 'proceeds' in causal terms, but goes one step further in eliminating the need for any link, causal or transactional, to any particular asset held by the defendant. On the augmentation version of that approach,[48] favoured by Evans, it is sufficient to prove that the defendant has been enriched by the misappropriation—for example, because it has enabled him to discharge a debt—and that he has not 'dissipated the enrichment',[49] in the sense of being no better off than he would have been if he had not received it. If this can be proved, and further conditions ensuring that the defendant's creditors are not disadvantaged in the event of his insolvency are 1.35

46 *Foskett* (n 28) 137.
47 *Foskett* (n 28) 127.
48 For the distinction between weak, strong, and 'augmentation' versions of the swollen assets model, see Smith (n 1) 270–74.
49 Evans (n 37) 503.

met, Evans suggests that we can then identify the proceeds of the claimant's assets 'in the defendant's general assets',[50] without needing to point to any one asset that represents those proceeds. The objection based on the need for property rights to have a specific subject matter can be overcome by treating *all* the defendant's assets as the subject matter of the claimant's property right: this can be done by subjecting those assets to an equitable charge, securing repayment of the abstract amount representing the defendant's gain from the misappropriation.

1.36 In *Space Investments Ltd v Canadian Imperial Bank of Trust Co (Bahamas) Ltd*, Lord Templeman appeared to adopt a version of swollen assets tracing.[51] He suggested, obiter,[52] that where a bank trustee had made an unauthorized use of trust assets for its own purposes, the beneficiaries under the trust could trace into *all* the assets of the bank, which would become the subject matter of an equitable charge in their favour. A similar approach is found in the judgment of Hobhouse J in his first instance decision in *Westdeutsche Landesbank Girozentrale v Islington LBC*.[53] However, later cases have made clear that English law does not recognize any such principle, but requires a clear transactional link between the original asset and another particular asset in order for tracing to be possible.[54] As with the rejection of the causal links model, however, the justification for this emphatic preference for transactional tracing is not obvious.

1.37 For example, the Court of Appeal rejected an attempt to invoke a 'swollen assets' approach to tracing in *Serious Fraud Office v Lexi Holdings plc*.[55] The Director of the Serious Fraud Office had obtained a restraint order against the second defendant, 'M', under section 41 of the Proceeds of Crime Act 2002, which prohibited him from dealing with any of his assets, including bank accounts at two banks and his matrimonial home. Lexi Holdings plc applied to vary this order on the basis that M had received unauthorized payments from its director and that some of the frozen assets represented its money that had been paid out in this way. It was clear on the facts that some of the Lexi Holdings money had been paid into the two bank accounts, but M failed to disclose what he had done with the rest of it. It was argued that, in the light of this failure to explain what he done with the money, despite a judicial order for disclosure, the court ought to find that Lexi Holdings could trace into all his existing assets, and assert an equitable charge over them in the amount due.

1.38 The Court of Appeal rejected this argument. Keene LJ, delivering the judgment of the court, said that there had to be a 'nexus' between the assets affected by the charge and the misappropriated company funds; the charge could only affect assets

[50] Evans (n 37). [51] [1986] 3 All ER 75, 77.

[52] The suggestion was obiter because, on the facts of *Space Investments Ltd*, the transaction carried out by the bank trustee was authorized: *Space Investments Ltd* (n 51) 78. As a result, it had the effect of overreaching the beneficiaries' interest in the money paid and, therefore, any claims they might have had to its proceeds.

[53] [1994] 4 All ER 890, overruled by the House of Lords on another point at [1996] AC 669.

[54] *Bishopsgate Investment Management Ltd v Homan* [1995] Ch 211; *Moriarty v Atkinson* [2008] EWCA Civ 1604; *Serious Fraud Office v Lexi Holdings plc* [2008] EWCA Crim 1443.

[55] [2008] EWCA Crim 1443.

that 'derive[d]' from those funds. Tracing, therefore, was a 'vital process': 'it is by that process that the necessary nexus is established and the proprietary remedy, be it by way of constructive trust or equitable charge, made effectual'.[56] He pointed out that M's receipt of the misappropriated money occurred in 2006, while he had purchased the matrimonial home in 1998. It was impossible, therefore, that there was any transactional link between the purchase of the house and the misappropriated funds. The argument that a charge might nevertheless be imposed upon the house went 'against the whole rationale of tracing'.[57]

On Evans' approach, however, the chronology of acquisition of particular rights would not matter. If M could not show that he had dissipated the Lexi Holdings money—and his refusal to disclose what had become of it suggests that he could not—then his general assets should be treated as 'swollen' by the amount misappropriated. The matrimonial home as such may not have increased in value as a result of the misappropriation, but this is the wrong question to ask, if Evans is right; the total fund of marketable assets at the defendant's disposal has been increased by the Lexi Holdings money and Lexi Holdings should, therefore, be able to identify a fraction of the market value of every asset held by him as the product of its money. 1.39

Whatever one makes of this view on the merits, the argument is at least clear. We can understand what it means to say that, if a defendant is better off as a result of a misappropriation of assets, the claimant affected by the misappropriation should be able to attach her claim to every asset held by the defendant, to the extent of the defendant's enrichment. In reply to this argument, the courts assert the necessity of a 'nexus' between the misappropriated asset and the assets claimed, and a requirement that the substitute be 'derived' from the original asset. Again, we are met with a strong judicial commitment to the requirement of specific transactional links from one particular asset to another, but a lack of analytical clarity in the justification offered for that requirement. It is just asserted that tracing is necessary, and presupposed that tracing requires substitutions and not, for example, an inquiry into whether the defendant's assets remain swollen by the amount of the misappropriation. 1.40

This lack of clarity is problematic from a rule of law perspective. If the reason for a judicial decision is described in terms that are analytically unclear, so that it is hard to reach an agreement on what those terms mean, this makes it more difficult for subjects of the legal system to understand how that decision is meant to guide their future conduct.[58] Suppose A's father were to misappropriate B's assets and, some years later, bequeath his entire estate to A. Following *Foskett v McKeown*, how can A know which of the assets she has received from her father, if any, she ought to give up to B on demand? The question, 'which of the assets I now have is *attributable* to the asset misappropriated from B?' is not easy to answer, without some clear explanation of what it practically means to say that the first asset is attributable to the second. 1.41

[56] *Lexi Holdings plc* (n 54) at [50]. [57] *Lexi Holdings plc* (n 54) at [53].

[58] L Fuller, *The Morality of Law* (Yale University Press, revised edn 1977) 63.

1.2. What Does Tracing Require?

1.42 One possible answer to this question is that A need not know anything about the justification for the requirement of substitutions in order to know what that requirement entails. If she knows she has a teapot that her father bought with £50 stolen from B, she can be expected to know that this teapot should be given up to B as the traceable product of B's £50. She does not need to know why the law treats the teapot as the substitute for the £50, as long as she can find out that it does. It is arguable that the requirements of the rule of law can be met by bright-line legal rules, even when those rules appear to have no obvious principled basis but impose arbitrary but clear norms of behaviour.[59] If we accepted this very modest account of the demands of the rule of law, we might say that the answer to the question of justification—*why* substitution—does not matter, provided that it is always clear whether or not a given transaction is, in fact, a substitution.

1.43 However, even if we considered the requirements of the rule of law to be satisfied by predictability without transparent rationality, tracing would remain problematic because the rules of tracing are not wholly predictable in their operation. As the facts of *Foskett v McKeown* themselves illustrate, the paradigm of a direct exchange transaction captures only a limited range of the fact situations to which the law of tracing may potentially apply. The existing cases that deal with the scope of tracing, outside the core—and relatively rare—scenario of a series of simple swaps, share the problem that the justification for their approach is not self-evident from the judicial reasoning. As a result, without an account of the justificatory principle requiring substitution in the first place, it becomes difficult to determine the scope of those rules or to answer questions that are uncertain as a matter of authority.

1.44 The relevant cases can be classified as answering three questions. First, what sort of right, thing, or benefit is capable of being a 'substitute' received under an exchange transaction: ie what counts as an asset for these purposes? A swap of a £50 note for a teapot is a relatively clear case. What if the £50 is exchanged for information, the release of a debt, the provision of a service, or the improvement of some asset already belonging to the defendant? The law in this field is relatively underdeveloped, and the few authorities that exist offer limited guidance on the governing principles.

1.45 Secondly, what happens when assets belonging to several people are swapped for a single substitute? If A buys a teapot for £100, using a £50 note belonging to B and a £50 note belonging to C, does the teapot still count as a substitute for either person's money? If both B and C can treat A's title to the teapot as a substitute for their money, what happens when further transactions involving that title take

[59] Although such a theory seems inconsistent with Fuller's account of the values underpinning the rule of law, which reflect due respect for a subject of law 'as a responsible agent, capable of *understanding and* following rules': see Fuller (n 58) 162. It is doubtful if a rule requiring blind obedience to an incomprehensible norm (which cannot be made sense of in its own terms but only as a prediction of what a judge is like to do in a particular fact situation) satisfies this broader demand for respect for the dignity of the legal subject as a responsible agent.

place? This is the problem of dealing with so-called 'mixed substitutions'. It raises particularly acute issues when the substitute is an asset, like a bank account, which (unlike a teapot) is frequently dealt with in consideration for the acquisition of further assets. How are these subsequently acquired assets to be shared between the different contributors to the acquisition of the first substitute? The law in this area is relatively stable and predictable, but there are questions about the circumstances in which it applies, and about when the rules that conventionally apply can be displaced by other factors.

Finally, what happens when the defendant's acquisition of a new right or asset does not depend on a simple swap, but instead affects her pre-existing legal relations with other people? For example, A may have borrowed £50 from X to buy a teapot and may then have used B's stolen £50 to pay off the debt. In this situation, can B trace 'backwards' in time, through the debt incurred for the purpose of buying the teapot, and argue that the teapot is the substitute for his stolen £50, even though it was acquired before the theft? The law in this area is deeply uncertain, and there is relatively little guidance on offer on the justification for either permitting or refusing backwards tracing of this kind. This poses a particularly acute practical problem, because transactions involving bank transfers through the clearing system will normally, in fact, involve an adjustment of the pre-existing legal relations of various parties; we need to know if chronology matters, and how much, in order to apply the principles that govern the simple case of the swapped teapot to these more complex, and common, scenarios. 1.46

1.2.1. Which rights, benefits, or things can be substitutes?

In the modern law, it is clear that the acquisition of a new assignable legal right—from a legal title to land[60] to a right to be paid a sum of money[61]—can be a substitution. There are other types of benefit, however, that can be acquired by the exploitation of another person's assets, and here the law is less clear. 1.47

Particular attention has been paid to the situation where the defendant spends the claimant's money on services, such as building works, which physically alter land that she already owns. In such a situation, can the physical improvements to the land represent a substitute for the money, generating some kind of right affecting the defendant's title to her land? 1.48

In *Re Diplock*,[62] the Court of Appeal rejected the argument that money could be traced in this way, through a payment for services, into an existing title to land. In that case, various charities had been paid money out of the estate of Caleb Diplock to which they were not entitled, as a result of the executors' mistaken belief that the bequests made in Diplock's will were valid. Five of the charities spent the money on 1.49

[60] *Lane v Dighton* (1762) Amb 409; 27 ER 274.

[61] *Burdett v Willett* (1708) 1 Eq Ca Ab 370; 23 ER 1017.

[62] [1948] Ch 465, affirmed by the House of Lords as *Ministry of Health v Simpson* [1951] AC 251 on a different point.

improvements to their existing land, including the building of a new hospital and the renovation of two children's wards in an existing hospital.[63]

1.50 Having held that Diplock executors were entitled to claim the traceable proceeds of the money in the hands of the charities, on behalf of his next of kin, the Court of Appeal went on to consider whether title to the new and renovated buildings should be treated as traceable proceeds. Lord Greene MR, giving the judgment of the court, noted that there would have been no issue if the charities had mixed the Diplock money with their own, for example, in a single bank account, and had then used the mixed fund to buy land. In this case, their title to the land would represent the proceeds of both their own money and the Diplock money, and they would have held it subject to an equitable charge in favour of the Diplock contributors, securing repayment of the amount of their involuntary contribution to its acquisition.

1.51 However, the court held that the case of payment of money to improve existing land was importantly different from the case of payment of money into an existing bank account. It was not possible to identify the proceeds of the Diplock money once spent in this way; in addition, even if it were possible, it would be unjust and inequitable to award the remedy of an equitable charge, compelling the landowner to put his land at risk of sale when he had no intention of taking such a risk and when he himself was not a wrongdoer.[64]

1.52 Two arguments are offered to explain why tracing fails at the point when the money is spent on improving the physical land. First, there was no guarantee that such 'improvements' would actually increase the market value of the land. The court offers the example of a trustee who uses trust money to add an idiosyncratic extension to his house, which 'adds not one penny'[65] to its market value. However, this can hardly be the *ratio* of their decision, as the court made no investigation into whether the building works carried out by the charities had actually improved the market value of their land, and it seems improbable that the building of a new hospital, for example, could have had no positive impact on the market value of the land.

1.53 It is the second argument put forward by the Court that seems, therefore, to represent the real *ratio* of the decision. This was the view that, regardless of any increase in the market value, the land just could not sensibly be identified as the product of the money. Tracing money into its substitute presupposed 'the continued existence of the money either as a separate fund or as part of a mixed fund or as latent in property acquired by means of such a fund'.[66] If the charities had mixed the Diplock money with their own, and then used it to buy some asset, such as land, the Diplock money would have been 'necessarily present throughout the existence of the asset in an identifiable form'.[67] In the case where, on the other hand, they had used the money to improve their existing land 'it by no means necessarily follows that the money can be said to be present in the adapted property'.[68]

1.54 It has been suggested, *obiter*, in later cases,[69] that it should be possible, at least in some situations, for a claimant to trace through a defendant's improvements of

[63] *Re Diplock* (n 62) 545. [64] *Re Diplock* (n 62) 548. [65] *Re Diplock* (n 62) 547.
[66] *Re Diplock* (n 62) 521. [67] *Re Diplock* (n 62) 546 [68] *Re Diplock* (n 62).
[69] *Boscawen v Bajwa* [1996] 1 WLR 328, 355 (Millett LJ); *Foskett* (CA) [1998] Ch 265, 282 (Sir Richard Scott V-C), overruled by the House of Lords on a different point at *Foskett* (n 28).

his physical land into his title to the land itself, subjecting it to an equitable charge securing the amount spent. The judgment in *Re Diplock* implies it may be relevant whether or not the market value of the land is actually improved by the changes. However, it is difficult to square the requirement of an actual increase in market value with the general approach of the law of tracing, as seen in *Foskett v McKeown*, as well as with the outcome on the facts of *Re Diplock* itself. Beyond this, *Re Diplock* tells us that the question is whether the money can still be identified as 'latent' in the land, or whether it has lost its identity after being used to pay for services that improve the value of the land.

Generalizing from this, we might say that a right, thing, or benefit can be a substitute only when it can be distinguished from the other rights, things, or benefits belonging to the defendant. The question then becomes how we make this distinction. A very sharp line might have been drawn between pre-existing assets of the defendant and assets freshly acquired by the act of dealing with the original asset itself: it might have been decided that any asset already held by the defendant, before she made the disposition of the original asset that is being characterized as a substitution, should be 'off limits' for the purposes of tracing. The effect of such a principle would be that English law would only recognize tracing through 'clean' substitutions. Direct swaps of assignable rights would be in the category. Every benefit linked to the enjoyment of a pre-existing right—whether this means physical improvement of land or increasing the credit balance of an existing bank account—would be excluded. However, English law has not taken this view, at least not in all cases. This is another area where the law is uncertain. 1.55

1.2.2. When is it possible to trace into a mixed substitution?

As a matter of legal history, it is clear that some courts[70] have held that English law recognizes two distinct sets of 'rules of tracing': one set applies in equity, is available only to principals in fiduciary relationships, and can cope with mixed substitutions. The other applies at common law, is available to other types of claimant, and is defeated when 'the subject is turned into money and mixed and confounded in a general mass of same description',[71] rather than being earmarked and kept in a bag. In modern cases, this has been taken to mean that the common law can trace into the acquisition of a new asset, but cannot trace into a mixed substitution, while equity can do both.[72] The effect is that, when a trustee pays £100 of trust money into her existing bank account, which is already in credit by £100, the beneficiary under the trust can say that half the credit balance of the bank account represents the traceable proceeds of the trust money. When a thief pays £100 of stolen money into 1.56

[70] Cases acknowledging such a distinction include *Banque Belge pour l'Etranger v Hambrouck* [1921] 1 KB 321, 330 (Scrutton LJ) and 329 (Bankes LJ); *Re Diplock* (n 62); *Trustee of FC Jones v Jones* [1997] Ch 159; *Agip (Africa) Ltd v Jackson* [1991] Ch 547; and *Lipkin Gorman v Karpnale Ltd* [1991] 2 AC 548.

[71] *Taylor v Plumer* (1815) 3 M & S 562, 575; 105 ER 721.

[72] *Agip (Africa) Ltd v Jackson* [1990] Ch 265 (HC), 285 (Millett J), affirmed on this point by the Court of Appeal in [1991] Ch 547, 566.

his existing bank account, on the other hand, the victim of the theft[73] cannot say that the credit balance of the account represents the traceable proceeds of her money.

1.57 As a matter of authority, it is doubtful whether there still are special rules of tracing for common law claimants. In *Foskett v McKeown*,[74] Lord Steyn and Lord Millett emphatically rejected the idea that there was any justification for maintaining separate rules of tracing at law and in equity. However, these statements were *obiter dicta*, and cases can be found that both affirm[75] and reject[76] the distinction. Further, there are *dicta* in favour of the distinction as well as against it. In *Re Diplock*,[77] the Court of Appeal took the view that there is a genuine principled difference between common law and equitable tracing, which rests on a difference in the underlying justification for the recognition of claims to traceable proceeds in the two jurisdictions. Common law tracing, the court said, depends on some version[78] of ratification: the common law 'proceeded on the basis that the unauthorized act of purchasing was one capable of ratification by the owner of the money'.[79] By contrast, the 'metaphysical approach of equity'[80] allowed it to perceive a mixed asset—such as the bank account—'as an amalgam constituted by the mixture of two or more funds each of which could be regarded as having, for certain purposes, a continued separate existence'.[81] The common law, not sharing this metaphysical approach, could not adopt the same perspective on a mixed asset.

1.58 Lord Millett in *Foskett v McKeown* took the opposite view. Having distinguished tracing from claiming,[82] he said that there was 'nothing inherently legal or equitable about the tracing exercise';[83] while the distinction between law and equity may have a bearing on the rights to the product that the claimant might eventually assert, this had nothing to do with the process of identifying the product in the first place.

1.59 In order to understand what is at stake in this debate, it is necessary to determine what is meant by the distinction between tracing and claiming, and how it relates to the language of ratification, and of defining the boundaries of a fund, which show up in the case law. A victim of theft might argue that it is absurd that a beneficiary under a trust has superior remedies, allowing her to identify trust property in circumstances where stolen property cannot be identified. However,

[73] Assuming, as has often been asserted, that a victim of theft is the paradigm common law claimant who may rely on tracing. See Chapter 8 this volume.

[74] *Foskett* (n 28).

[75] Eg *Shalson v Russo* [2003] EWHC 1637 (Ch), [2005] Ch 281, [103]–[104] (Rimer J); *LAH v Lee* [2007] EWHC 2061 (Ch), [256]–[257] (Etherton J).

[76] Eg *Bracken Partners Ltd v Gutteridge* [2003] EWHC 1064 (Ch), [31] (Peter Leaver QC); *Barros Mattos Junior v MacDaniels Ltd* [2005] EWHC 1323, [135] (Lawrence Collins QC).

[77] *Re Diplock* (n 62).

[78] It cannot depend on ratification in the usual sense used in the law of agency, because of the rule that an undisclosed principal cannot ratify an unauthorized transaction: *Keighley, Maxsted & Co v Durant* [1901] AC 240. In most cases of common law tracing, the defendant receives assets from a third party who believes he is dealing with the defendant as a principal and has no idea of the claimant's rights. For a more detailed discussion of the origins of the language of ratification as used in cases like *Re Diplock*, see Chapter 3 in this volume, Section 3.3.1.2.

[79] *Re Diplock* (n 62) 519.

[80] *Re Diplock* (n 62) 520.

[81] *Re Diplock* (n 62).

[82] See Chapter 2 this volume.

[83] *Foskett* (n 28) 128.

it might be replied that the victim of theft has rights in respect of the stolen money very different from the rights of the beneficiary under the trust. It is equity that tends to characterize assets vested in A as a 'fund', capable of being affected by rights vested in B;[84] if the ability to trace into mixtures is linked to this characterization and to the fund structure, the limitation on common law tracing may be a reasonable one.

This issue ultimately depends on what a thief is doing when he pays stolen money into his existing bank account, and whether this is the same kind of thing that a trustee does when she pays trust money into her existing bank account: are both events substitutions, or not? As in the case of the trustee improving her land by spending trust money on building works, we can only answer this question if we identify the justification for the law's focus on substitutions in the first place. We can then determine whether the thief's act, the trustee's act, and the improvement of land all share the characteristics that render an exchange transaction of such significance to the identification of traceable proceeds. **1.60**

1.2.3. How are payments out of a mixed substitution to be attributed?

It has been explained that a beneficiary under a trust, B, can trace into a bank account into which the trustee, T, has also paid someone else's money. The effect is that T holds the bank account subject to B's rights in proportion to B's contribution. If she had paid in £100 of her money and £100 of trust money, she will hold for herself as to a half-share and for B as to the other half. A similar principle applies if the other payment represents £100 of the money of a beneficiary under a different trust, B2; in this case, T will hold on trust for B and B2 in half-shares. **1.61**

Having accepted this possibility, the law then has to deal with what happens when T begins to draw on the account to acquire new assets. Suppose, for example, that she draws £50 from the mixed account in cash and uses it to buy a title to a painting. For whose benefit does she hold this title to the painting, and for whose benefit does she hold the £150 remaining credit balance of the bank account? The issue may make a considerable practical difference if, for example, T has made an exceptional bargain and the title to the painting is worth £500 or, conversely, if she has made a terrible bargain and it is worth only £5. After some hesitation,[85] English law has chosen to sharply distinguish between the case where T is the other contributor to the account and the case where B2, an innocent third party, is the other contributor. **1.62**

[84] J Penner, 'Duty and Liability in Respect of Funds' in J Lowry and M Loukas (eds), *Commercial Law: Perspectives and Practice* (Lexis Nexis Butterworths 2006) 207.

[85] Eg *Pennell v Deffell* (1853) 4 De G M & G 372; 43 ER 551, where the Master applied the 'cherry-picking' approach to payments out of a bank account but the Court of Appeal overturned this approach and applied the 'first in, first out' approach instead. See, also, *Brown v Adams* (1869) LR 4 Ch App 764.

1.2.3.1. Cherry-picking and the lowest intermediate balance rule

1.63 So far as a wrongdoer like T is concerned, the law applies what Rimer J in *Shalson v Russo* called a 'cherry picking'[86] approach. If the painting has appreciated in value, while the £150 in the bank account has been untraceably spent on food and drink, B is entitled to say that T used his money to buy the painting and dissipated her own.[87] On the other hand, if the painting has depreciated in value, while the money in the bank remains intact, B is entitled to say, instead, that T spent her own money on the painting, leaving B's money intact as the credit balance of the account.[88]

1.64 There are limits, however, to this 'cherry picking'. If T withdraws £190 of the money in the account to spend on an expensive dinner, leaving a credit balance of only £10, this £10 will be the traceable product of B's money. If T then credits the account with £190 from another source, this money will be held for her own benefit,[89] not B's. Thus, if the total credit balance of the account has fallen to a certain amount, that amount represents the maximum interest that B can have in the account, regardless of any later fluctuations in the balance. This is the so-called 'lowest intermediate balance rule'. Despite attempts to argue that the logic of cherry picking should extend to this situation, entitling B to assert that the £190 dissipated on dinner belonged to T and the £190 later paid in belongs to him, the courts have refused to accept the argument.[90]

1.65 In *James Roscoe (Bolton) Ltd v Winder*,[91] James Roscoe (Bolton) Ltd had sold its business to a Mr William Wigham. The agreement for sale provided that he would collect the company's book debts and pay them all money received on account of debts due before the 1st of March 1913. Wigham began to collect money from the company's creditors and paid a total of £455, 18s and 11d of this money into his personal bank account. On the 21st of May 1913, the credit balance of the account fell to £25, 18s. However, Wigham then paid in and drew out more money; at the time of his death, insolvent, on the 20th of June 20 1913, the account was in credit to the tune of £358, 5s and 5d.

1.66 The liquidator of the company brought a claim against Wigham's trustee in bankruptcy, claiming a lien or charge over the bank account, as security for the debt of £455, 18s and 11d owed to them. Without admitting liability, the trustee paid £25, 18s into court and contended that no more was due. Sargant J agreed. Although he held that the agreement had created a trust of the book debts, entitling the company to their traceable proceeds, he held that the company could not trace into the whole credit balance of the account at the date of Wigham's death. Instead, it could only recover the £25, 18s, that represented the lowest balance the account

[86] *Shalson* (n 75) [144].

[87] *Re Oatway* [1903] 2 Ch 356. She also has a choice as to the content of her right: depending on the value of the painting, she may claim that it is held on trust for her or claim an equitable charge over it.

[88] *Re Hallett's Estate* (1880) 13 Ch D 696.

[89] That is, although her breach of trust may mean that she personally owes B a debt of £100, she is not obliged to pay him more than £10 out of this particular bank account. This will normally matter where she is insolvent and, therefore, unable to pay all her debts out of the total pool of her assets.

[90] *Re Goldcorp Exchange Ltd* (n 35); *Bishopsgate Investment Management Ltd* (n 54).

[91] [1915] 1 Ch 62.

had reached after the company's money had been paid in. The cherry-picking rule did not mean that Wigham's subsequent payments into the account were to be attributed to the claimant company, in the absence of any evidence that he positively intended such an attribution. Distinguishing *Re Hallett's Estate*, the leading case on the cherry-picking principle, he said that the principle in that case could only apply where you could 'put your finger on some definite fund which either remains in its original state or can be found in another shape. That is tracing, and tracing, by the very facts of this case, seems to be absolutely excluded except as to the 25*l* 18*s*.'[92]

Again, this invites us to ask why. What does it mean to say that the court is trying to identify 'some definite fund'? And why is it that such a fund will continue to exist in identifiable form where there has been a chain of clean substitutions, however long, but cannot be said to survive the exhaustion of a bank account as in *James Roscoe*? The law permits tracing where A swaps B's £50 for a teapot and then swaps the teapot for a car and swaps the car for a painting (a chain of clean substitutions). The cherry-picking rule then treats this as essentially analogous to the case where A pays B's £50 into his existing bank account and then, after several unprofitable withdrawals that reduce the balance of the account to £50 exactly, withdraws the final £50 to buy a painting (mixed substitution). However, the lowest intermediate balance rule says that both these situations are completely different from the case where A pays B's £50 into his existing account, reduces the whole balance to £0, pays another £50 in, and then withdraws £50 to buy a title to a painting. In this final case, tracing is 'absolutely excluded'; the purchase of the painting is not a substitution. In order to put these rules on a principled footing, and to evaluate the basis for both cherry-picking and for the limitation on cherry-picking represented by the lowest intermediate balance rule, it is necessary to understand the basis for calling one set of transactions a series of substitutions and denying that status to another set. 1.67

1.2.3.2. The rule in Clayton's Case *and its alternatives*

When the issue of attribution of payments arises between innocent contributors to a mixed asset, the position[93] is different. Innocent contributors are not entitled to cherry pick against each other. In the current state of the law, the attribution of payments between them seems to depend on whether the mixed asset is a bank account or not. 1.68

If it is a bank account, as in the example above, the nineteenth-century courts held that payments out of the account should be attributed on a 'first in, first out' basis;[94] this mirrors the way the law attributes payments in (debts owed by the bank) to payments out (debts satisfied by the bank) as between the account-holder and the bank, under the rule established in *Clayton's Case*.[95] So, if T paid £100 held on 1.69

[92] *James Roscoe (Bolton) Ltd* (n 91) 68–69.

[93] Also addressed in *Re Hallett's Estate* (1880) 13 Ch D 696 (n 88). See Section 5.1 this volume.

[94] Dicta of Baggallay LJ in *Re Hallett's Estate* (n 88), 732, affirming *Pennell* (n 85), 43 ER 551 on this point, and followed by North J in *Re Stenning* [1895] 2 Ch 433 and the Court of Appeal in *Re Diplock* (n 62). See Section 5.1 this volume.

[95] (1816) 1 Mer 572; 35 ER 781.

trust for B into the account on Monday and paid in £100 held on trust for B2 on Tuesday, this approach dictates that the first £100 paid out of the account should be attributed to B alone. If T were to withdraw £100 in cash to buy a title to a painting on Wednesday and then to withdraw £90 to buy a meal or pay for a holiday on Thursday, B would be better off than B2. The title to the painting would be the traceable product of her money, while £10 credit balance of the bank account would be the sole traceable product of B2's money.

1.70 However, unlike the attribution of payments under the cherry-picking rule, this favourable outcome for B would depend on luck, rather than the law preferring the interests of the person whose asset was first misappropriated. B would only be better off if it so happened that T's earliest investments were the better ones. If, instead, T had first spent £90 on the expensive dinner and had only later spent £100 on the painting, it would be B2 who would be better off. The application of this rule has been criticized by modern courts,[96] and it has been held that it will be applied only where it is not unjust or impracticable to do so.[97] In cases where it is unjust or impracticable, withdrawals from bank accounts in these situations will be treated in the same way as withdrawals from any other type of mixed pool of assets.

1.71 In relation to such assets, the rule appears to be that withdrawals from the pool will be attributed to innocent contributors in proportion to their contribution.[98] This could mean one of two things. It could mean that each individual payment is to be attributed to all the right-holders, in shares proportionate to their contribution at the time of the transaction. This is the so-called North American or 'rolling charge' solution.[99] Alternatively, it could mean that, at the date when the issue arises for determination, all assets acquired using the pool, or left in the pool, will be attributed to the parties in proportion to their total contribution to the original pool. The distinction would make a difference in a case where the contributions made by B and B2 to the pool had varied over time, so that each party's proportionate share at the time of a particular transaction might differ from their proportionate share of the overall pool. In this jurisdiction, the North American solution has not yet been applied, but Woolf LJ suggested in *Barlow Clowes v Vaughan* that it might be the most just approach[100] in a case where it would not be too impracticable to apply.

1.72 The question whether *Clayton's Case* ought ever to apply to the attribution of payments between innocent contributors to a mixed bank account depends on the extent to which the legal relationship between account-holder and bank ought to affect the relationship between the contributors. From the perspective of the bank, it might be said that the result of T paying it B's money on Monday was that it immediately incurred a debt of £100 to T. On Tuesday, when it in turn paid £50 in

[96] *Barlow Clowes International Ltd v Vaughan* [1992] 4 All ER 22.

[97] *Russell-Cooke Trust Co v Prentis* [2002] EWHC 2227 (Ch), [2003] 2 All ER 478; *Commerzbank Aktiengesellschaft v IMB Morgan plc* [2004] EWHC 2771 (Ch), [2005] 2 All ER (Comm) 564.

[98] *Pinkett v Wright* (1842) 2 Hare 120; 67 ER 50, affirmed by the House of Lords as *Murray v Pinkett* (1846) 12 Cl & F 764; 8 ER 1612; *Re Diplock* (n 62).

[99] So referred to by the judges in *Barlow Clowes International Ltd* (n 96), 27 (Dillon LJ) and 29 (Woolf LJ).

[100] [1992] 4 All ER 22, 35.

cash to T, *Clayton's Case* implies that the bank paid off part of this very debt ('first in, first out'). Does this imply that it must be that £50 which represents the substitute for B's £100, because there is a transactional link between the debt owed to T and the money used to satisfy part of that debt? The objection is that this is an overly formalistic way of understanding the question of transactional links, and its effect is to make the legal position of B and B2 turn on an issue that has nothing to do with the ultimate justification for their claims. There is no reason, it might be suggested, why the chronology of T's dealings with the bank should diminish one person's rights and preserve another's.

However, as we have seen in the context of the rejection of the swollen assets model of tracing, the chronology of transactions does matter, to some extent, in tracing. As the Court of Appeal held in *Serious Fraud Office v Lexi Holdings plc*, a house acquired in 1998 cannot, without more, be the traceable product of money misappropriated in 2006. This is true even if the defendant would have lost the house if he had not taken the money. The question, then, is not whether chronology ever matters in tracing, but rather *why* it matters, and to what extent. 1.73

1.2.4. Backwards tracing?

This raises the problem of 'backwards tracing', the area of English law where there is currently the most uncertainty. It is generally accepted that, when money is used to satisfy a debt, it has no traceable proceeds.[101] For example, suppose that A uses B's money to pay off the overdraft on her existing bank account. This will not give B any interest in the bank account, once A has used further payments to put it back in credit again. She may be subrogated to the bank's right to recover the debt represented by the overdraft, but this will not entitle her to claim other assets acquired by A using the bank account itself. 1.74

On the other hand, suppose that, before she misappropriated B's money, A had drawn on her overdraft to buy a title to a computer. She then used B's money to pay off the overdraft. Does this change the situation, so that B can trace 'backwards' in time and identify title to the computer as the traceable product of his money? English law is currently unclear on the point; there are a number of authorities that can be interpreted as permitting or rejecting the possibility.[102] 1.75

In *Federal Republic of Brazil v Durant International Corporation*,[103] the Privy Council held that it should sometimes, but not always, be possible to disregard chronology in the context of tracing. In that case, the mayor of Sao Paulo, a Mr Maluf, had taken bribes in connection with a major road-building contract, and the Municipality of Sao Paulo was seeking to recover the traceable proceeds of these 1.76

[101] Although the claimant may be subrogated to the rights of the creditor whose debt was satisfied: *Boscawen* (n 69).

[102] These authorities have most recently been surveyed by M Conaglen, 'Difficulties with Tracing Backwards' (2011) 127 LQR 432. See also L Smith, 'Tracing into the Payment of a Debt' (1995) 54 CLJ 290. For a more recent treatment of the authorities, see K Bloomfield, 'An Exploration of Backwards Tracing: Doctrine, Theory and Practice' (2017) 23 Trusts and Trustees 227.

[103] [2016] AC 297.

bribes from Durant International Corporation and another company registered in the British Virgin Islands. A dollar amount of over $10.5m, representing these bribes, was paid into the New York bank account of Mr Maluf's son; this was achieved by a series of payments over a period of just under a month, ranging from 9 January to 8 February 1998. Between 14 January and 26 January 1998, a total of $13m was debited from the son's New York account and credited to the Jersey bank account of Durant; over the following ten days, a similar sum was debited from Durant's account and credited to the account of the other company.

1.77 Three of the bribe payments to the son's account, totalling just under $3m, were made after 26 January; that is after the last of the payments in favour of Durant. Durant argued, therefore, that the money it had received could not represent the full $10.5m, since its receipt was earlier in time than the son's acquisition of the final tranche of the bribe money. The Privy Council rejected this argument on the basis that all these payments had been 'part of a co-ordinated scheme',[104] the 'overall purpose and effect'[105] of which was to ensure that the bribe money ended up in the hands of Durant. However, they rejected the broad proposition that backwards tracing should, in general, be possible whenever the debt satisfied debt was incurred in order to acquire an asset.[106] Instead, they said, the chronology of transactions would be disregarded where the claimant could establish:

> a co-ordination between the depletion of the trust fund and the acquisition of the asset which is the subject of the tracing claim, looking at the whole transaction, such as to warrant the court attributing the value of the interest acquired to the misuse of the trust fund.[107]

The principle, then, seems to be that backwards tracing will be possible where 'the transaction as a whole' warrants the court 'attributing the value' of the newly acquired asset to the misappropriation of the original asset. We can solve the problem of backward tracing by asking whether a series of apparently chronologically separate transactions are actually a single transaction: a single substitution, for the purposes of tracing. If so, it will be possible for the court to attribute the value of the interest acquired under that/those transaction(s) to the value of the misappropriated asset. But in order to know when to do this, we need to know whether there is enough of a connection, or co-ordination, between the use of the original asset and the acquisition of the substitute to warrant the conclusion. We need to know, in other words, what makes a transaction a substitution.

1.3. What is a Substitution?

1.78 At first glance, the concept of substitution seems to equate with the intuitively clear and common sense idea of a swap. A trustee sells shares that he holds on trust, and

[104] *Federal Republic of Brazil* (n 103) [38] (Lord Toulson SJC).
[105] *Federal Republic of Brazil* (n 103).
[106] *Federal Republic of Brazil* (n 103) [33] (Lord Toulson SJC).
[107] *Federal Republic of Brazil* (n 103) [40] (Lord Toulson SJC).

receives £1000 in cash from the purchaser as their price;[108] an employee embezzles funds from his employer, and uses the money to buy some shares in a company;[109] a thief steals the claimant's car and sells it, and then uses the proceeds of sale to buy another car;[110] a car is exchanged for a boat, or a cow for a goat, or £1,000 in cash for a picture;[111] and so on. In each example, A has something—it is immaterial whether this is a set of shares, access to a bank account, a boat, or a goat—and he then gives that something to another person, C, and gets something else (shares, cash, a car, a cow) in return. If the thing swapped belonged to a third person, B, this transaction constitutes a swap or exchange of B's thing for the thing received from C. This account implies that the core concept of a substitution is relatively straightforward, and the only problem is in dealing with edge cases, such as the improvement of land or the satisfaction of debts.

However, this apparent simplicity is misleading. The similarity between the textbook cases described here is obvious only if we disregard the legal position of the parties and focus exclusively on the idea of physical changes in the location of tangible things. From this perspective, the exchange of a car for a boat looks like a similar sort of event to the exchange of a cow for a goat or a car for some cash. In each case, by the act of a person, one thing comes to occupy the physical space that was previously occupied by another thing. The particular identity of the person who has brought about this spatial change, and the legal relations in which that person stands, make very little difference to our idea of what has happened. 1.79

However, a perspective that focuses on changes in the physical location of a tangible thing cannot offer us any explanation of what is happening in the examples where the 'thing' swapped is a share in a company or the credit balance of a bank account. In these cases, there is no physical object that has moved from one place to another, or from the possession of one person into the possession of another. If anything at all has changed in a case where an employee has drawn on his employer's bank account in order to buy shares in his own name, it is surely the *legal* position of the employee, the employer, and/or the bank: to say that the credit balance of the employer's bank account has fallen, or that shares in the company are now vested in the employee, is to describe a change in legal relations. 1.80

As Smith has argued, even in cases involving the sale or barter of chattels, it is a mistake to characterize the event of exchange as merely involving a change in the physical control or possession of the original chattel and the substitute respectively.[112] This is because it is not possession that is transferred by a sale, but the title to the chattel held by the vendor. Possession, in fact, need not be transferred immediately in order for the vendor's title to pass.[113] In a case where there is a delay between the transfer of title and delivery of possession, therefore, there is a necessity for choice in deciding when the substitution has taken place. Has it taken place once title to the original chattel has vested in the purchaser, and title to the purchase price 1.81

[108] J Penner, *The Law of Trusts* (OUP 2016) 45. [109] Smith (n 1) 3.
[110] G Virgo, *Principles of the Law of Restitution* (OUP 2015) 613.
[111] A Burrows, *The Law of Restitution* (3rd edn, OUP 2011) 123. [112] Smith (n 1) 16.
[113] Title passes when the parties to a contract of sale intend it to pass: Sale of Goods Act 1979, s 17.

has vested in the vendor, or has it taken place only when the cash and the chattel have been physically delivered to their new owners? Given that the majority of the tracing cases concern rights that are incapable of physical delivery, it seems improbable that physical delivery is relevant in itself, apart from in those instances where it coincides with the passing of title.

1.82 Thus, we are obliged to bring the legal relationships between the parties into the picture in order to make sense of the concept of an exchange transaction or substitution. This is the only basis on which we can accommodate the majority of the cases, where apparent transfers or variations of rights with no material subject matter—bank accounts,[114] shareholdings,[115] and other choses in action[116]—do take place at some stage during the chain of substitutions.

1.83 However, once we think of substitution as entailing an alteration in legal rights, rather than merely in the physical location of things, the similarities between different examples of exchange begin to look less obvious. In particular, it becomes difficult to explain in what sense each example represents an instance of the *claimant's* rights being exchanged, or substituted, by the defendant.

1.84 This point can be illustrated by reference to McFarlane's discussion of the law of tracing in his textbook, *The Structure of Property Law*.[117] McFarlane introduces the concept of tracing by reference to a series of examples, which are presented as typical of the kind of exchange transaction found in the case law. He then offers a systematic legal analysis of each example in turn, seeking to demonstrate the features that they have in common. The complexities that are generated by this close analysis are revealing.

1.85 McFarlane makes use of three examples. The first involves a set of transactions carried out by a thief, A, who has stolen a bicycle to which B has a legal title ('Ownership', in McFarlane's terminology).[118] A then 'swaps that bike for C's car': that is, McFarlane elaborates, 'in return for giving *his* Ownership of the bike to C, A receives C's Ownership of the car'.[119] In this situation, it is said, tracing enables B to 'identify A's Ownership of the car as a product of *B's* initial right: *B's* Ownership of the bike'.[120]

[114] Eg *Small v Attwood* (1831–1832) You 407; 159 ER 1051; *Pannell v Hurley* (1845) 2 Coll 241; 63 ER 716; *Trench v Harrison* (1849) 17 Simons 111, 60 ER 1070; *Pennell* (n 85); *Frith v Cartland (*1865) 2 H & M 417; 71 ER 525; *Re Hallett's Estate* (n 88); *Cave v Cave* (1880) 15 Ch D 639; *Banque Belge pour l'Etranger* (n 70); *Re Tilley's WT* [1967] Ch 1179; *Re Leslie* [1976] 1 WLR 292; *Agip (Africa) Ltd v Jackson* (n 70); *Trustee of FC Jones* (n 70); *Foskett* (n 28); *Shalson* (n 75); *Dyson Ltd v Curtis* [2010] EWHC 3289; *Relfo Ltd (In Liquidation) v Varsani* [2014] EWCA Civ 360.

[115] Eg *Lord Chedworth v Edwards* (1802) 8 Ves Jun 47; 32 ER 268; *Harrison v Harrison* (1740) 2 Atk 121; 26 ER 476, reported as *Harrison v Pryse* (1740) 2 Barn Ch 324; 27 ER 664; *Lane* (n 60); 27 ER 27; *Liebman v Harcourt* (1817) 2 Mer 512; 35 ER 1036; *Marsh v Keating* (1834) 1 Bing (NC) 198; 131 ER 1094; *Murray v Pinkett* (1846) 8 ER 1612; *Great Eastern Railway Co v Turner* (1872) LR 8 Ch App 149; *Roadchef (Employee Benefit Trusts) v Hill* [2014] EWHC 109.

[116] Eg *Burdett* (n 61), 23 ER 1017; *Trustee of FC Jones* (n 70); *Foskett* (n 28).

[117] B McFarlane, *The Structure of Property Law* (Hart Publishing 2008).

[118] See McFarlane (n 117) 140, defining 'Ownership' as 'a right to immediate exclusive control of a thing forever'. This definition is intended to capture any legal title to a chattel, including a possessory title capable of being defeated by the better title of another: McFarlane (n 117), 144–46.

[119] McFarlane (n 117) 323 (emphasis added).

[120] McFarlane (n 119) (emphasis added).

The second example varies these facts by making A into a trustee, rather than a thief. He holds his title to the bike on trust for B, and then 'swaps that bike for C's car'.[121] In this scenario, McFarlane explains, A's title to the car is 'a product of the right initially held on trust for B: *A's* Ownership of the bike'.[122] 1.86

The final example is a simplified variation on the facts of *Lipkin Gorman v Karpnale Ltd.*[123] B becomes B Co, a firm that has a bank account with Z Bank, while A becomes a partner of the firm who, in accordance with the terms of the contract between B Co[124] and Z Bank, may validly withdraw funds from that account. A makes an unauthorized withdrawal of £5,000 from B's account with Z Bank, and uses this money to buy C's title to the car. Both transactions count as substitutions, in accordance with the rules of tracing: that is, A's title to the £5,000 in cash received from Z Bank, and his title to the car bought using that money, are both products 'of *B Co's* initial right: its personal right against Z Bank'.[125] 1.87

According to McFarlane, each of these examples counts as an obvious case of a substitution. In each case, he says, 'A clearly used B's right in order to acquire Ownership of the car'.[126] In fact, however, this analysis holds in rather different senses in each of the three scenarios. 1.88

In the first case, the case of the thief who has sold a stolen bicycle, A has transferred his own possessory title to the bicycle to C, receiving C's title to the car in exchange. This transaction will have had no legal effect at all on B's independent title to the bicycle, which will remain vested in him unless C, for some reason, has a defence capable of defeating that title.[127] The only legal consequence of the transaction for B would be that, in addition to his claim in conversion against A, he might also gain a claim in conversion against C.[128] Here, it is unclear how A could be said to have used B's *right* in respect of the bicycle in order to acquire title to the car, since A and B have two distinct and free-standing rights[129] in respect of the bicycle and A has 1.89

[121] McFarlane (n 119). [122] McFarlane (n 119) (emphasis added).

[123] *Lipkin Gorman* (n 70).

[124] Ie between the partners in B Co jointly and Z Bank. In England and Wales, a firm is not, itself, a legal person capable of entering into contracts, but a collective term describing persons who are in partnership with each other and who are jointly bound and benefited by contracts entered into in the name of the firm.

[125] McFarlane (n 117) 324 (emphasis added). [126] McFarlane (n 125).

[127] Since the abolition of market overt in 1994, no such defence would exist in favour of a purchaser of title to a chattel from an ordinary thief like A: see the Sale of Goods (Amendment) Act 1994, repealing the Sale of Goods Act 1979, s 22. The position would be different if A had entrusted B with possession of the bicycle in circumstances that engaged one of the limited statutory exceptions to the *nemo dat quod non habet* principle: for an overview of these defences, see, generally, M Bridge, 'Transfer of Title by Non-Owners' in M Bridge and others, *Benjamin's Sale of Goods* (9th edn, 2014) paras 7-001 to 7-115.

[128] *Hollins v Fowler* (1874-75) LR 7 HL 757.

[129] This analysis depends on the assumption that a thief does not, by virtue of his theft, become a trustee of his possessory title for the benefit of his victim. In *Westdeutsche Landesbank Girozentrale v Islington LBC* [1996] AC 669, 716, Lord Browne-Wilkinson expressed the obiter view that a thief of money would become a trustee of (presumably) his title to the stolen money. If this is right, McFarlane's first example would be open to alternative analysis as an instance of his second example (a trustee sells the trust asset). However, it has sometimes been asserted that a holder of common law title to a chattel is, by virtue of that title and apart from the existence of any beneficial interest, entitled to claim the traceable proceeds of the stolen chattel in the hands of a thief at common law: see Chapter 8 this volume. As such, it is necessary to analyse the implications of this example separately.

used his own title, not B's, in order to acquire title to the car. The only link between A's act and B's 'rights' arises out of the fact that A, in selling his title to the bicycle to C and delivering possession of that bicycle to C, may have committed the tort of conversion; as such, the act of sale itself could be a breach of a duty owed to B and thus an interference with the rights of B. In this rather loose sense, it could be said that A has 'used' B's rights to acquire title to the car, since the acquisition of the title to the car is a causal consequence of a violation by A of B's rights.

1.90 In the second scenario, where A is a trustee, it is equally true that the title to the car is acquired in circumstances that constitute a breach of a duty owed by A to B. Assuming that the sale of A's title to the bicycle is unauthorized, or that the acquisition of the car is intended to be for A's own benefit, A will have committed a breach of trust by entering into this sale with this motive.

1.91 In addition, however, there is a further sense in which it could be said that A has 'used B's right' in order to acquire the car on the facts of this example. Unlike a thief and his victim, a trustee and his beneficiary do not hold two distinct and independent titles to a chattel held on trust: the orthodox analysis[130] is that the trustee holds his own title to the chattel on trust for the beneficiary, whose claims in respect of the chattel are contingent on the continued existence of that title,[131] either vested in the trustee or in a successor in title to the trustee. By contrast, a thief and his victim can be said to have two distinct entitlements to the stolen chattel, each of which exists independently of the other: if one title is destroyed,[132] the other title can continue to exist.

1.92 This structural feature of a trust thus produces a distinct sense in which it could be said that A has acquired his title to the car 'by using B's right', regardless of whether the sale of the bicycle constituted a breach of a duty owed to B. Even if the transaction had been an authorized one, entered into for B's sole benefit, it would still be true to say that A had acquired the title to the car using the very right that he held on trust for B. Unlike the victim of theft, the beneficiary's entitlements are mediated via the rights held by the trustee; as a result, any exercise of those rights by the trustee could meaningfully be described as a use of '[the subject-matter of] the beneficiary's rights.'

1.93 Finally, there are the *Lipkin Gorman v Karpnale Ltd* facts. Two substitutions are said to have taken place in this scenario: first, A has substituted title to £5,000 in cash for B Co's personal claim against Z Bank and, next, A has substituted C's title to the car for his title to the £5,000 in cash. The effect of the unauthorized withdrawal from B Co's bank account depends on the terms of the banking contract between

[130] Eg FWB Maitland, *Equity* (CUP 1929) 112–21.

[131] See, for example, *Bolling v Hobday* (1882) 31 WR 9, holding that the extinction of a freehold title by adverse possession will also extinguish any trusts affecting the title. The Limitation Act 1980, s 18, preserves trusts of unregistered land by preserving the underlying title until the claims of all the beneficiaries have accrued and also been extinguished by the passage of time. See the Land Registration Act 2002, sch 6 para 12, for the equivalent protection in registered land.

[132] For example, by the passage of time under the Limitation Act 1980, s 3. Where a chattel has been obtained by actual theft, in the criminal law sense, time will not begin to run until the chattel comes into the hands of a good faith purchaser for value without notice of the theft: Limitation Act 1980, s 4.

the partners in B Co and Z Bank.[133] In withdrawing money from the account for his own private purposes, A will be acting beyond the scope of his actual authority as an agent of his partners.[134] As such, the general rule is that Z Bank will not have satisfied the debt owed by it to B Co by paying £5,000 to A individually;[135] unless Z Bank has inserted an express term into the contract with B Co, restricting its liability in such cases, B Co will be entitled to demand that the £5,000 be re-credited to the account. However, if A had apparent authority to draw on the account—for example, if he is an authorized signatory and the account is one that partners regularly draw on in their own names, without the consent of the others, for the purposes of their business—the position will be different. In such a case, A's withdrawal from the account will be a transaction binding on his principals[136] and will have the legal effect of reducing Z Bank's liability to B Co. If so, in paying the £5,000 in cash to A, Z Bank will have satisfied the debt in that amount that it previously owed to B Co and will be under no obligation to re-credit the account or compensate B Co for its losses.[137]

In the case of this example, then, A has not only gained his title to the £5,000 as a result of committing a wrong against his partners in B Co, although this is undoubtedly also an available characterization of the facts. In addition, A has either obtained his title to the £5,000 in cash by directly varying B Co's rights against Z Bank or by leaving those rights entirely unaffected by his act. Unlike both thief and trustee, there is no sense in which he can be said to have altered his own rights to the bank account, quite apart from the impact of the transaction on his partners in B Co. This is because, on the facts of the scenario, A has no such rights in his personal capacity, ie apart from in his role as a partner in the firm. The £5,000 is owed by Z Bank to the partners in B Co jointly. Either A's unauthorized withdrawal of this amount from the account is simply a nullity so far as the bank account is concerned, so that Z Bank remains liable to the partners in that amount, or the transaction validly extinguishes the debt. There is no mediating entitlement held by A in his own right, which he might have transferred or varied in consideration for his title to the £5,000. **1.94**

Thus, the three examples generate different definitions of the 'exchange transaction' or 'substitution' carried out by A; in each case, A has 'used B's rights' in a different sense. It could be said, in order to accommodate the theft case, that A has substituted the subject matter of B's rights in any case where he has obtained a right by transferring a right of his own, in circumstances where that transfer is **1.95**

[133] See *Tai Hing Cotton Mill Ltd v Liu Chong Hing Bank Ltd* [1986] AC 80, rejecting the relevance of a potential duty of care in the law of tort as between banker and customer in this context.

[134] Partnership Act 1890, s 5.

[135] See, generally, EP Ellinger, E Lomnicka and CVM Hare, *Ellinger's Modern Banking Law* (5th edn, OUP 2011) 332–34.

[136] *Freeman & Lockyer v Buckhurst Park Properties Ltd* [1964] 2 QB 480.

[137] As in *Lipkin Gorman v Karpnale Ltd* itself, where the Court of Appeal held that Lloyds Bank plc had acted within the terms of its mandate in paying cash to the wrongdoing partner and debiting the firm's client account accordingly: [1989] 1 WLR 1340, overruled by the House of Lords on a different point, *Lipkin Gorman* (n 70).

also a wrong against B. Alternatively, and more narrowly, it could be said that a substitution takes place where A has obtained a right by transferring a right of his own, in circumstances where the right transferred is itself the subject matter of an equitable interest vested in B. Finally, in order to accommodate the case of the unauthorized withdrawal from the bank account, it could be said that a substitution takes place where A obtains a right by acting in such a way as to directly alter B's own rights. In order to know what a substitution is, we need to know exactly when it is true to say that A has 'used B's rights' to acquire a right for himself in the sense dictated by the tracing rules.

1.4. Conclusions

1.96 One possible answer to the questions raised in this chapter is that the focus on 'substitutions' as such, as events to which the law responds is misguided. The real question is not about substitution, but about value; the law requires substitutions because they provide evidence that the value of the original asset is now to be located in the substitute, and we can understand which transactions count as substitutions by asking whether they represent a use or exchange of the value of the original asset for the value of the substitute. On this view, the Privy Council reasoning in *Durant* needs to be turned on its head. It is not that carefully examining a transaction, to see if it is a substitution, will tell us whether to attribute the value of one asset to the value of another. Rather, we can ask directly if the value of one asset has been used to acquire another, and define a substitution merely as a kind of evidence that this has taken place.

1.97 This argument rests on the work of Peter Birks and Lionel Smith, and underpins the language of value that is now used in many of the post-*Foskett* cases that apply the tracing rules. Chapter 2 examines the extent to which this 'value' account can tell us why tracing in its current form is necessary, justify its current requirements, and enable us to understand the concept of substitution.

2

Value and Other Metaphors

Tracing, Claiming, and Following

2.01 Chapter 1 presented the law of tracing as a self-contained body of legal rules organized around the central idea of substitution. I have suggested that tracing, seen from this perspective, raises some puzzling questions; these ultimately reduce to the question what a substitution actually is, and why proving that a substitution has taken place matters so much in the context of claims to traceable proceeds.

2.02 Modern accounts of tracing tend to answer these questions in two ways by adopting an approach developed by Lionel Smith[1] and Peter Birks.[2] First, tracing is explained by bringing it into relation to two other ideas: following and claiming. Following refers to the identification of the claimant's original asset, either as it moves from person to person or as it undergoes changes in physical appearance or form. Claiming refers to the principles that explain the source of the claimant's right to an asset, the content of the right, and the remedies that are available to the claimant because of it. These distinctions provide a kind of negative definition of tracing, by reference to what is not. Tracing is not following, but (like following) it is not claiming either.

2.03 Secondly, the focus on substitution is explained as a proxy for a different organizing idea—that of value. The goal of tracing is to identify substitutions, but this is because substitutions allow us to locate the value of the original asset in the form of the substitute. This explanation supplies the basis for the distinctions emphasized by Birks and Smith between tracing, claiming, and following. Tracing is

[1] L Smith, *The Law of Tracing* (Clarendon Press 1997); see also 'Tracing' in A Burrows and Lord Rodger of Earlsferry (eds), *Mapping the Law: Essays in Memory of Peter Birks* (OUP 2006) 119.

[2] *An Introduction to the Law of Restitution* (rev edn, Clarendon Press 1989) 358–401; 'Mixing and Tracing: Property and Restitution' (1992) 45 3CLP 69; *Restitution – The Future* (The Federation Press 1992) 106–22; 'Trusts in the Recovery of Misapplied Assets: Tracing, Trusts, and Restitution' in E McKendrick (ed), *Commercial Aspects of Trusts and Fiduciary Obligations* (Clarendon Press 1992) 149; 'Overview: Tracing, Claiming and Defences' in P Birks (ed) *Laundering and Tracing* (Clarendon Press 1995) 289; 'Tracing, Subrogation and Change of Position (*Boscawen* v *Bajwa, Abbey National plc* v *Boscawen*)' (1995) 9 Trust Law International 124; 'Tracing Misused (*Bank Tejarat* v *Hong Kong and Shanghai Banking Corp*)' (1995) 9 Trust Law International 91; 'Property and Unjust Enrichment: Categorical Truths' [1997] NZLR 623, 659–65; 'On Taking Seriously the Difference Between Tracing and Claiming' (1997) 11 Trust Law International 2; 'Mixtures' in N Palmer and E McKendrick (eds), *Interests in Goods* (2nd edn, LLP 1998) 227; 'The Necessity of a Unitary Law of Tracing' in R Cranston (ed), *Making Commercial Law: Essays in Honour of Roy Goode* (Clarendon Press 1999) 239; 'Property, Unjust Enrichment and Tracing' (2001) 54 CLP 231.

not following, because identifying an asset and identifying its value in its substitutes are different exercises. However, tracing and following share the characteristic of being mere exercises in identification. In the same way that finding the current location of a pair of candlesticks tells us nothing about who owns them, finding the current location of the value of the candlesticks—say, in the form of the credit balance of a bank account—tells us nothing about any rights to that value.[3] Hence, tracing must be distinguished from claiming, as well as from following.

2.04 This terminology—tracing, claiming, following, value—was endorsed by the House of Lords in *Foskett v McKeown*;[4] it is now ubiquitous in descriptions of tracing across the common law world. However, because of its dependence on the ambiguously defined concept of value, its explanatory force has been called into question.[5] What does it actually mean to say that the rules of tracing aim to locate value? What, if anything, does this tell us about the supposed difference between tracing and claiming, or about the supposed analogy between tracing and following by reference to which that difference is explained?

2.05 This chapter argues that the value account is best understood as the latest in a long series of useful metaphors that describe why substitutions matter. Traditional descriptions of the claimant searching for his thing, and identifying it despite changes in its form, have been replaced by the more helpful metaphor of the claimant searching for his value and identifying it despite changes in its location. Both metaphors reify the actions of the defendant, imagining that some underlying object—a thing, a fund, some value—survives all his acts and represents the stable subject matter of the claimant's rights. Both are often expressed in counter-factual terms, denying that what the defendant has done can have any effect on the rights of the claimant. I argue that this is because both metaphors point to the law's aim of protecting the claimant from the impact of acts by the defendant that inevitably, though wrongfully, alter the claimant's pre-existing legal position.

2.06 However, the metaphor of locating value represents an improvement on the older metaphor of physical metamorphosis in two respects. First, it allows the special justificatory questions raised by substitution to be disentangled from the analogous, but distinct, problems raised by the law's approach to the event of physical mixture or transformation. Secondly, the metaphor links the tracing idea to a particular legal structure, by which it can be said that the power to dispose of assets is vested in one person, while a right to the *value* of those assets is vested in another. Understanding tracing in these terms allows us to arrive at a preliminary definition of a substitution—the exercise of a power to realize the value of an asset—and gives us a starting point for understanding its normative significance. This, in turn, makes it possible to identify the principles that underpin the substantive law of tracing, as it has developed to deal with various situations, and to address hard cases. Identifying those principles is

[3] Birks, 'The Necessity of a Unitary Law of Tracing' (n 2) 239, 244.

[4] [2001] 1 AC 102, 129 (Lord Millet); [2001] 1 AC 102, 113 (Lord Steyn).

[5] Eg C Rotherham, 'The Metaphysics of Tracing' (1996) 34 Osgoode Law Journal 321; T Cutts, 'Tracing, Value, and Transactions' (2016) 79 MLR 381; J Edelman, 'Understanding Tracing Rules' (2016) 16 QUT Law Review 1.

not, as the usefulness of the value metaphor shows, a matter of throwing out all the traditional metaphors and fictions, and identifying a fresh explanation of the function of tracing that has no relation to the figurative language used by the judges. Rather, it involves taking the figures of speech seriously as such, with the aim of discovering the normative principles that motivate the judges' embrace of them. Chapter 3 takes up this task in more detail.

2.1. The Value Model of Tracing and its Roots in the Case Law

The sixteenth edition of *Lewin on Trusts*, published in 1964, introduced the section on tracing as follows: 'If the trust estate has been wrongfully disposed of by the trustee, the beneficiaries may attach and *follow* the property that has been substituted for the trust estate, so long as the metamorphosis can be *traced*'.[6] The authors then go on to address the situation where trust money 'is mixed in the same heap with the trustee's money'; they note that the beneficiary must have a lien on the mixture in such a case, because he has a lien in the analogous situation where the trustee has used his own money and the trust money to buy a single estate in land.[7] The two situations are analogous, it is said, because 'it cannot be predicated of any particular part of the estate that it was purchased with the beneficiary's money';[8] in the same way, the beneficiary cannot point to 'the identical pieces of coin'[9] in the 'general heap' of cash with which the trustee has mixed his money. 2.07

This analysis is typical of traditional explanations of tracing throughout the nineteenth and twentieth centuries. 'Tracing' and 'following' are used as interchangeable terms, describing the process by which a beneficiary shows that some asset is trust property, held for her benefit. The event of substitution is described as a kind of metamorphosis and presented as similar to the event of physical mixture; buying an estate in land with my money and your money is the same kind of event as mixing two sacks of cash together in a heap or chest, and the principles that apply to the former situation must apply to the latter. The language of metamorphosis can be found in the first edition of Lewin's treatise on the law of trusts, published in 1837: a trust arises, he says, 'whenever the estate is converted by the trustee from one species of property to another', and he goes on to describe this as a 'change of [the] form' of the trust property.[10] By the third edition, published in 1857, the problem of money mixed in a heap of the trustee's own money has made its appearance, and the analogy with the purchase of land has been invoked to explain why the beneficiary should have a lien in the former case, as in the latter;[11] this analogy, once introduced, 2.08

[6] J Mowbray and others, *Lewin on Trusts* (16th edn, Sweet & Maxwell 1964) 650 (my emphasis).

[7] The idea that the beneficiary is confined to a lien in such a case arises from a dictum of Jessel MR in *Re Hallett's Estate* (1880) 13 Ch D 696, which has since been disapproved by the House of Lords in *Foskett* (n 4) 131 (Lord Millett).

[8] J Mowbray and others (n 6) 650. [9] Mowbray and others (n 6) 650.

[10] T Lewin, *A Practical Treatise on the Law of Trusts and Trustees* (A Maxwell & Co, London 1837) 201.

[11] T Lewin, *Practical Treatise on the Law of Trusts and Trustees* (3rd edn, W Maxwell & Co, London 1857) 601.

survives in all the successive editions of *Lewin* and persists into the sixteenth edition, published in 1964.

2.09 This continuity is, however, disrupted in the seventeenth edition, published in 2000, some months after the House of Lords decision in *Foskett v McKeown*.[12] In that edition, the discussion of tracing begins with a section introducing 'some basic concepts and terminology': these include 'tracing', 'following', 'claiming', 'mixed substitution', and 'clean substitution'.[13] In post-*Foskett* editions of *Lewin*, the language of following is scrupulously distinguished from that of tracing, and the exercise of tracing trust assets is distinguished from that of asserting claims over them.[14] The analogy between the mixed heap of coins and the land purchased using funds from two sources disappears, as do all references to metamorphosis; where Lewin himself described property as changing its form, the current authors say that 'the value that was to be found in the old asset is now to be found in the value inherent in the new one'.[15]

2.10 These changes mirror a corresponding change in judicial language. For Thomas Lewin, writing the first edition of his treatise, the leading case on tracing was *Taylor v Plumer*.[16] In that case, Lord Ellenborough CJ justified his conclusion that Sir Thomas Plumer was entitled to the assets purchased by his agent, Walsh, using his money,[17] because 'if the property in its original state and form was covered with a trust ... no change of that state and form can divest it of such trust'.[18] When Walsh exchanged Sir Thomas' cheque for cash at his bank, and then exchanged the cash for gold and share certificates obtained from various third parties, Lord Ellenborough CJ characterizes these acts as changes in the 'form' of Sir Thomas' property that made no difference to his rights: 'it makes no difference in reason or law into what other form, different from the original, the change may have been made ... for the product of or substitute for the original thing still follows the nature of the thing itself, as long as it can be ascertained to be such[.]'.[19]

2.11 When Lewin, in 1857, described the problem raised by a mixture of coins in a heap as analogous to a problem raised by a mixed substitution, he was also being faithful to the language of the courts. One of the earliest cases to confront the problem of the mixed bank account was *Pennell v Deffell*.[20] The trustee, Mr Green, had paid money that he received on various different trusts into two personal bank accounts, into which he also paid his own money; he died insolvent. The question was whether the beneficiaries under the trusts could trace into these personal bank accounts and, if so, how payments out of them should be attributed as between the several beneficiaries and as between the beneficiaries collectively and Mr Green's

[12] According to the preface to this edition, the law is stated as at 23 November 2000: J Mowbray and others, *Lewin on Trusts* (17th edn, Sweet & Maxwell 2000) xi. The House of Lords handed down its decision in *Foskett v McKeown* on 18 May 2000.

[13] Mowbray and others (n 12) 41-002.

[14] L Tucker and others, *Lewin on Trusts* (19th edn, Sweet & Maxwell 2015) 41-002-41-007.

[15] Tucker and others (n 14) 41-005.

[16] (1815) 3 M & S 562,105 ER 721.

[17] For a detailed account of the facts of the case, see Chapter 3 this volume, Section 3.3.1.

[18] (1815) 3 M & S 562, 574–75; 105 ER 721, 725–26.

[19] (1815) 3 M & S 562, 574–75; 105 ER 721, 725–26.

[20] (1853) 4 De G M & G 372, 43 ER 551.

creditors. Knight-Bruce LJ began his analysis of this problem by asking himself a hypothetical question: suppose, he said, 'the very coins and the very notes received by [Mr Green] on account of the trusts . . . had been placed by him together in a separate repository—such as a chest—mixed confusedly together among themselves'.[21] The principles that would govern the attribution of withdrawals from this chest of money, he suggested,[22] must equally govern the attribution the payments out of the bank accounts. The same analogy between payment into a mixed bank account and a physical mixture of coins also appears in a number of other nineteenth-century cases, including *Frith v Cartland*[23] and *Re Hallett's Estate*.[24]

For the authors of the current edition of *Lewin on Trusts*, however, the leading case is *Foskett v McKeown*.[25] In that case, Lord Millett began his judgment with an extended analysis[26] of tracing, as distinguished from following and from claiming. Mr Murphy's action in using the claimants' money to pay some of the premiums on his life insurance policy[27] is not, like Walsh's use of Plumer's money to buy gold, described as a change in the form of the money. It is, instead, 'a textbook case of . . . mixed substitutions'.[28] Instead of seeking 'to follow the money any further once it reached the bank or insurance company', the claimants had 'chosen at each stage to trace the money into its proceeds'.[29] The difference between the exercise of following the original asset and tracing into the substitute is emphasized. What is being traced is not 'the physical asset itself but the value inherent in it'.[30] 2.12

Once tracing is completed, and the value inherent in the original asset is identified in its proceeds, the question what claims to those proceeds can be made arises. Tracing itself merely 'enables the claimant to substitute the traceable proceeds for the original asset as the subject matter of his claim';[31] 'it does not affect or establish his claim,'[32] the content of which will depend on various other factors. It follows from this that 'there is nothing inherently legal or equitable'[33] about tracing, and that the rules of tracing must be the same, whatever the basis for the claimant's claim to the original asset or the content of the claim he eventually makes to the substitute.[34] 2.13

[21] *Pennell* (n 20) 381; 43 ER 551, 555.

[22] *Pennell* (n 20) 382–83; 43 ER 551, 556: 'If these propositions [concerning the chest of money] . . . are true . . . , can the Plaintiff be wholly wrong in his actual contention? I apprehend not'.

[23] (1865) 2 H & M 417; 71 ER 525, 2 H & M 417, 421; 71 ER 525, 528 (Page-Wood VC): 'If a man has £1000 of his own in a box on one side, and £1000 of trust property in the same box on the other side, and then takes out £500 and applies it for his own purposes, the Court will not allow him to say that that money was taken from the trust fund. . . . So here, Edwards could not be allowed to say that the £284 deposited in the Bank of England was his own, and that the trust portion of the fund was that which he took abroad with him, and from which he drew as he required for his own purposes'.

[24] (1880) 13 Ch D 696, 711 (Jessel MR): 'Supposing the trust money was 1000 sovereigns, and the trustee put them into a bag, and by mistake, or accident, or otherwise, dropped a sovereign of his own into the bag. Could anybody suppose that a Judge in Equity would find any difficulty in saying that the *cestui que trust* has a right to take 1000 sovereigns out of that bag? It would make no difference if, instead of one sovereign, it was another 1000 sovereigns; but if instead of putting it into his bag, or after putting it into his bag, he carries the bag to his bankers, what then?'

[25] *Foskett* (n 4).

[26] *Foskett* (n 4) 127–34.

[27] See Chapter 1, paras 1.28–1.33 this volume for the facts of the case.

[28] *Foskett* (n 4) 127.

[29] *Foskett* (n 4).

[30] *Foskett* (n 4) 128.

[31] *Foskett* (n 30).

[32] *Foskett* (n 30).

[33] *Foskett* (n 30).

[34] *Foskett* (n 30).

2.14 Later in his judgment, Lord Millett went on to analyse the rules that determine when tracing through a mixed substitution is possible. In this context, he said that the tracing rules 'correspond to the common law rules for following into physical mixtures (though the consequences may not be identical)';[35] in both contexts, the law adopts the principle that 'the interests of the wrongdoer who was responsible for the mixing and those who derive title under him otherwise than for value are subordinated to those of innocent contributors'.[36] He cited *Jones v De Marchant*,[37] a Canadian case involving the use of beaver skins belonging to two different contributors as another instance of the same principle in operation: while 'the coat was a new asset manufactured from the skins and not merely the product of intermingling them',[38] the same principle of subordinating wrongdoers applied to determining its ownership as applied to cases of physical mixture and to mixed substitutions.

2.15 Lord Millett's approach in *Foskett* is thus underpinned by four substantive propositions about the law of tracing.

2.16 First, tracing is not following: identifying the traceable proceeds of the claimant's asset is importantly different from identifying the asset itself, either in new hands or despite some change in its physical location or structure.

2.17 Secondly, however, there is some kind of overlap or analogy between the rules of tracing and the rules of following. The rules that govern the attribution of transactions out of a mixed substitution are similar to the rules that govern the attribution of withdrawals from a physical mixture; they also overlap with the law's handling of problems like that of physical transformation or the manufacture of new things using other people's property.

2.18 Thirdly, tracing is not claiming. A claimant who succeeds in showing that some asset is the traceable product of some other asset has not done all she needs to do to obtain a remedy from a court. The rules that she can invoke to show that some asset is indeed the traceable product of some other asset are not dependent on the specific content of her pre-existing rights to the original asset, if any; they are neither legal nor equitable.

2.19 Finally, tracing is about locating the value of assets. It is this positive definition of tracing that explains the distinction between tracing and following and the distinction between tracing and claiming. Tracing is not following, because it is about locating the value of an asset, not the asset itself. However, it is not claiming because locating the value of an asset is not the same thing as proving that one has a right to that value, any more than locating an asset is the same as proving that one has a right to that asset. The rules of tracing are analogous to the rules of following because the law uses similar principles to handle difficulties in locating physical things and difficulties in locating value.

2.20 These propositions originate in the scholarly work of Peter Birks[39] and Lionel Smith.[40] This scholarship emphasizes the existence and importance of the

[35] *Foskett* (n 4) 132. [36] *Foskett* (n 35)

[37] (1916) 28 DLR 561, discussed in *Foskett* (n 4) 132–33. [38] *Foskett* (n 4) 133.

[39] Birks 'The Necessity of a Unitary Law of Tracing' (n 2) 239, cited with approval in *Foskett v McKeown* by Lord Steyn at (n 4) 113, and Lord Millett at (n 4) 128–29.

[40] Smith (n 1), cited with approval in *Foskett v McKeown* by Lord Millett at (n 4) 129, 143, as well as by Lord Hope at 119.

distinctions between tracing, following, and claiming, and uses the language of value to explain these distinctions. As such, it represents a reaction to the approach of older cases, which is summed up in the pre-*Foskett* editions of *Lewin*. Its central argument is that we cannot make sense of what is going on in those older cases unless we depart from the traditional language used by the judges who decided them and instead use new analytical tools—tracing, following, claiming, value—to clarify what they are really doing. In determining what these four propositions have to tell us about tracing, therefore, it is helpful to examine each in the context of the case law to which it responds.

2.1.1. Tracing is not following: substitution is not transformation

The idea that tracing addresses a problem arising from a change in the 'form' of the claimant's asset is ubiquitous in the case law. For example, in *Banque Belge pour l'Etranger v Hambrouck*,[41] Scrutton LJ said that an owner of property was entitled to recover it in the common law courts provided that 'the property was capable of being traced, whether in its original form or in some substituted form'.[42] In *Boscawen v Bajwa*,[43] Millett LJ described the remedies of a claimant who 'succeeds in tracing his property, whether in its original or in some changed form'.[44] In *Re Diplock*, the Court of Appeal said that equity could identify money in a mixed fund but that its forms of relief 'pre-suppose the continued existence of the money either as a separate fund or ... as latent in the property acquired by means of such a fund';[45] here, the possibility of tracing through the use of one's money to buy a new asset is made to depend on the idea that the money somehow exists *in* that new asset, albeit in a latent form. 2.21

At the heart of this language is the proposition, crystallized by Lord Ellenborough CJ in *Taylor v Plumer*, that a substitution 'makes no difference in reason or law'[46] to a claimant's rights. Substitution, Lord Ellenborough suggests, changes the 'form' of the claimant's thing but not its 'nature'. Since the nature of the claimant's thing remains the same, persisting into its product or substitute, there is no reason why the claimant's rights should not also remain the same. Lord Denning, writing extra-judicially, offers a similar account of the implications of characterizing substitution as a change in form: '[money] might change its form from coins to cash at bank, or from cheques to notes', he says, but 'whatever its form and into whomsoever hands it came, the plaintiff to whom it belonged had [the action for money had and received] to recover it *back*[.]'.[47] If A steals a wallet full of cash from B, and swaps the cash for a bank account, B's demand that A pay her the credit balance of the account is simply an assertion of her original right to the cash—or rather to the money that happened to exist in the form of cash at the time. The form of B's money has changed, from a 2.22

[41] [1921] 1 KB 321. [42] *Banque Belge pour l'Etranger* (n 41) 330.
[43] [1995] 4 All ER 769. [44] *Boscawen* (n 43) 777. [45] [1948] Ch 465, 520.
[46] See text to (n 19).
[47] AT Denning, 'The Recovery of Money' (1949) 65 LQR 37, 39 (emphasis added).

stack of banknotes in her wallet to a debt owed by a bank to A, but this has no effect on her rights.

2.23 At face value, there is something counter-factual about this analysis. B's title to a stack of banknotes, for example, involves certain rights that cannot be exactly mirrored in relation to a bank account. She might have been entitled to physical possession of the notes, for example, in the sense that others owed her a duty not to touch or take them without her consent. It is impossible, without the aid of a metaphorical sleight of hand, to say that she has *identical* rights in respect of a debt owed by a bank to A. She cannot be entitled to physical possession of the debt, because there is no tangible object there to possess. To say that no one should touch or take the debt, assuming any such general duty exists,[48] is to invoke a metaphor: it must mean that some other kind of action—say, forging A's signature to a cheque and so bringing about a reduction in the credit balance—should be avoided, because it is analogous to physically touching or taking banknotes belonging to another person. Similarly, before A stole the cash from B, B stood in no special legal relation at all to the bank; it owed her only the same negative duty as the rest of the world, not to touch or take the banknotes without her consent. Now she is arguing that a debt owed by the bank is held by its creditor for her benefit, with various potential legal consequences for the bank itself,[49] as well as for other third parties. So substitution, by changing the subject matter of the claimant's right, does seem to inevitably involve some kind of change in the content of those rights as well. The rival view depends on what Peter Birks described as the leech theory[50] of property rights—a theory that, like leeches, such rights latch onto whatever victim/subject matter they come across, without changing their essential nature—and this view is difficult to defend, given the way in which the content of any given property right is shaped by its subject matter.

2.24 Nevertheless, the judges in some cases do treat tracing as involving a counter-factual denial that anything has happened as a result of the defendant's actions. In *Lane v Dighton*, for example, the claimant beneficiaries succeeded in tracing through a sale of trust shares into a purchase of some land in Oxfordshire, known as Sherborne Woods. Sir Thomas Clarke MR is reported to have declared that

[48] On the question whether intangible assets, like bank accounts, can be protected by the imposition of any duty of non-interference analogous to that which relates to tangible things, see *OBG v Allan* [2007] UKHL 21, and criticisms of that decision in S Green and J Randall, *The Tort of Conversion* (Hart Publishing 2009) 107–46.

[49] For example, where the cash paid into the account is trust money, a bank with knowledge of the trust may be prevented from setting off the debt that it represents against a separate debt owed to it by the trustee personally: see *Pannell v Hurley* (1845) 2 Coll 241, 63 ER 716; *Bodenham v Hoskins* [1843–60] All ER Rep 692; *Thomson v Clydesdale Bank* [1893] AC 282; *Coleman v Bucks and Oxon Union Bank* [1897] 2 Ch 243; *Baden v Société Générale Pour Favoriser le Developpement du Commerce et de L'industrie en France S.A* [1993] 1 WLR 509. Where the cash is simply stolen from its legal owner and paid into a bank account, it has been suggested that the bank may come under a direct liability to account for the credit balance of the account to the victim: *Trustee of FC Jones v Jones* [1997] Ch 159, 167 (Millett LJ). For problems arising from this analysis, and an alternative account of the victim's remedy in such a case, see D Fox, *Property Rights in Money* (OUP 2008) 192–95 and Chapter 3 this volume, paras 3.116–3.119.

[50] Birks, 'Property, Unjust Enrichment and Tracing' (n 2) 233, 244.

'it appearing that ... part of the trust money or funds ... was invested ... in the purchase of the Sherborne Woods estate ... the same ought to be considered as in the same plight or condition as if the same had not been invested[.]'[51] This must mean that the land should be treated as being in the same plight or condition as the money would have been, if it had not been invested: that is, as the judge went to say,[52] the land was held on the same trusts as the shares had been. However, the phrasing obscures the difference between the money and the land. Both are 'the same'.

It is against this background that Smith and Birks object to the language of 'changes of form', as applied to substitution, and insist on a distinction between tracing and following. Smith, for example, criticizes Lord Denning's suggestion that payment of cash into a bank account is merely a change in the 'form' of the cash,[53] on the basis that it depends on a false analogy. He points out that payment of money into a bank account is not a change in the physical identity of the cash but, instead, a change in the legal relationship between the account holder and the bank. Meanwhile, nothing has happened to the cash itself: 'it goes into a drawer at the bank'.[54] If the claimant wished to discover the fate of the cash—to identify the precise drawer at the bank where the notes had gone, and to distinguish her own money from other notes in the same drawer—this would be following, in Smith's terminology. On the other hand, identifying the bank account as the substitute for the cash is tracing. 2.25

Following, then, is identifying an original 'thing' in the hands of a new person, or in a new location, or despite some change in its appearance or other physical characteristics. A claimant who points out that his car is now sitting in the defendant's garage, and argues that it remains the same car even though she has applied a layer of paint to it, is following.[55] If he asserts his title to the car, and sues the defendant for refusing to return it to him, he is not asserting any new right that arises from the event of the car having been painted. He is only enforcing the right to the car that he already had against a new person, and saying the painting 'makes no difference in reason or law' to that right. The point at which an act of physical transformation might make a difference—where the law considers that the car has been transformed into a new thing, which does not belong to the claimant[56]—is the point at which following ends.[57] When one traces, by contrast, one brings a new thing into the picture, not a new person.[58] The claimant who traces her cash into a new bank account and demands that the account-holder pay her the balance is not simply 2.26

[51] (1762) Amb 409, 413–14; 27 ER 274, 275–76.
[52] (1762) Amb 409, 414; 27 ER 274, 276.
[53] Smith (n 1) 7, responding to the passage quoted above at text to (n 47).
[54] Smith (n 1) 7. [55] For the example of the painted car, see Smith (n 1) 7.
[56] As, eg in *Borden (UK) Ltd v Scottish Timber Products Ltd* [1981] Ch 25.
[57] Smith (n 1) 7.
[58] Smith (n 1) 8: 'Following ... is always concerned with the *original thing*, and it can bring into the picture a *new person*. ... Tracing ... always brings into the picture a *new thing*, acquired by the *original holder*. It does not bring a new person into the picture; it focuses on a single person' (emphasis in the original).

enforcing her old rights to the cash against a new person. Instead, she is enforcing new rights—or, at least, rights to a new thing—against a person previously bound by her right to the cash.

2.27 The importance of this distinction, in the work of both Birks and Smith, does not depend merely on the insight that there is a factual difference between painting a car and selling it for cash. It also depends on the argument that even an analogy between these two events is misleading, because they raise such different justificatory questions. The 'idea that a substitution is *like* a change in form will not stand up to scrutiny,'[59] Smith argues, because 'a claim in relation to the [substitute asset] ... cannot be justified on the same basis that permits a claim in relation to a car even when it has been painted'.[60] Birks expresses the same point in the language of causative events: 'The new asset implies a new right ... The new right has to be referred to a causative event. ... The metaphor of hunting for things has concealed even the need for that explanation'.[61]

2.28 There is, therefore, an irony in Lord Millett's adoption of the conclusions of this scholarship in his majority speech in *Foskett v McKeown*. As Birks notes,[62] the majority judges in *Foskett* did not, in terms, describe the event of substitution as a distinctive causative event that gives rise to new rights in new things. Lords Millett,[63] Hoffmann,[64] and Browne-Wilkinson[65] all described the claim to the product as one that vindicated the claimants' existing property rights; none of the judges suggested that these property rights themselves arose, anew, in response to the distinctive event of substitution. Only Lord Steyn described the claimants' case as a demand that the court recognize a new property right, and this seems to be because he dissented from the majority on the question whether they could trace at all. Thus, he said that, since their claim was not underpinned by 'any considerations of fairness or justice',[66] 'there [was] no justification for creating *by analogy with cases on equitable interests in mixed funds* a new proprietary right to the policy moneys in the special circumstances of the present case'.[67] By contrast, Lord Browne-Wilkinson, in the majority, expressly denied that there were any new rights in the case. He emphasized that no new trust—resulting or constructive—was at issue, but that the beneficiaries were simply enforcing their rights under the original express trust in relation to new assets.[68]

2.29 On this view, the fact that tracing involves new things does not mean it involves new rights. If so, the essence of Lord Ellenborough's analysis in *Taylor v Plumer*—that substitution makes no difference to the rights of a claimant, even though it may alter the subject matter of those rights—seems to survive *Foskett v McKeown*. The formidable analytical objections to that position, articulated by Birks and Smith as

[59] Smith (n 1) 7. [60] Smith (n 1) 8 (emphasis added).

[61] Birks, 'Establishing a Proprietary Base (*Re Goldcorp*)' [1995] RLR 83, 92.

[62] Birks, 'Property, Unjust Enrichment and Tracing' (n 2) 233.

[63] *Foskett* (n 28) describing the claimants as having a '*continuing* beneficial interest' in the traceable proceeds and justifying this claim on the basis that such a claimant 'succeeds if at all by virtue of his own title, not to reverse unjust enrichment'.

[64] *Foskett* (n 4) 115. [65] *Foskett* (n 4) 108. [66] *Foskett* (n 4) 115.

[67] *Foskett* (n 66). [68] *Foskett* (n 65).

the rationale for distinguishing tracing and following, remain. These objections boil down to the necessity, in Birks' terminology, of referring new rights to new causative events.

2.30 When the owner of a car points to her car in another person's garage, we can understand what she is doing without reference to the idea that she is proving that some specific causative event has taken place. The fact that someone has taken the claimant's car from her garage and put it elsewhere is not, in itself, the event that gives rise to her title to that car; it need not even, necessarily, be the event that gives rise to the particular claim she is making in the context of litigation. Proving that a change in location has happened—following—is just an evidential process that may make it practically easier for her to succeed in such a claim in a number of circumstances. For example, suppose she had lent her car to a friend, and the defendant stole it from the friend's garage. In this situation, the claimant might be suing the defendant in the tort of conversion; the causative event that gives rise to the claim is the wrong of interfering with the possession of the car. In order to show that this claim is available, the claimant must show, inter alia, that the particular car taken by the defendant is the very one that she, for example, purchased from a retailer and to which she therefore has a superior title. Following plays a subordinate role in this story, as evidence of a fact that is relevant to proving the causative event—it allows her to prove that it was *her* car that the thief took—but the fact that it enables the claimant to prove is not a causative event in itself.

2.31 By contrast, where a claimant points to some shares that are apparently vested in a defendant, and characterizes these as the traceable product of her cash, it is less clear what she is saying has happened and what bearing it has on any rights that she may be asserting. To understand her right to the shares, we need to understand the causative event that generates that right. Given that she could not have had any right to the shares prior to the substitution, this means that we have to define the event of substitution itself as a causative event or as an element of a causative event. As Birks and Smith use the distinction between tracing and following to demonstrate, we cannot ignore the fact of substitution and pretend that the claimant is simply asserting a right to the shares that she had all along. Instead, we must pose the question which, as Birks says, was concealed by the courts' use of the metaphor of hunting for things: what fact or other conclusion is the claimant actually proving, when she shows that there is a transactional link, or a chain of such links, between the shares held by the defendant and the cash misappropriated from her?

2.32 The answer, according to Birks and Smith, and according to Lord Millett in *Foskett v McKeown*, is that she is proving that the value of her cash is now located in the shares. Birks goes on to answer the causative event question that he raises by reference to this idea of value: the causative event of 'non-consensual substitution' occurs when 'an asset has been acquired by a person through his application to that end of the value of an asset in which the other has a proprietary interest'.[69] But Lord Millett in *Foskett v McKeown*, although he picked up and used the language of

[69] Birks, 'Property, Unjust Enrichment and Tracing' (n 2) 233, 245.

value, did not use the language of causative events. He said that the claimant who traces through a substitution is locating her value, but he did not address the precise character of the difference between this project of locating one's value and the project of locating one's original thing or asset in the hands of someone else. Instead, we still find the key idea of vindicating one's rights to the original asset at the heart of Lord Millett's analysis, as it was at the heart of Lord Ellenborough CJ's analysis in *Taylor v Plumer*. The difference is that, where Lord Ellenborough said the claimant was identifying his original *thing*, despite a change in its form, Lord Millett implied that the claimants were identifying their original *value*, despite a change in its location. One of the central insights that Birks and Smith offer—that, at the level of justification, the law's response to the location of things must be importantly different from its response to the location of value—is not commented on. In Lord Millett's analysis, the idea of a movement of value steps into the place of the older idea of the transformation of things. The idea that neither makes a difference to the assertion of the claimant's rights is not challenged.

2.33 Like the older cases, therefore, *Foskett v McKeown* raises the question of the basis of the analogy between tracing and following. The now-dominant view that tracing is about locating value, whereas following is about locating things, establishes a distinction between the two processes but does not, in itself, tell us how similar these two processes nevertheless are. Must we still say, post-*Foskett*, that the claimant who traces his value is like the claimant who follows his thing, in that he is simply vindicating his pre-existing right to that value? Alternatively, do we follow Birks in saying that the person who follows his thing through a change in its form—as where paint is applied to his car—is simply asserting his rights to his pre-existing thing, whereas the person who argues that the value of his asset has been applied to the end of acquiring another asset is asserting a new right, arising from a distinctive causative event that is quite different in principle from events like the application of paint to a car?

2.34 In this way, the value model highlights the distinction between substitution and physical transformation, and raises the question whether there might be any basis for treating these events as somehow similar. That question is important, and not only because of the prevalence of metaphors of transformation in judicial descriptions of substitution. It is also significant because of the overlap between substantive rules of tracing and the rules that govern the law's response to physical transformations and mixtures.

2.1.2. Rules of tracing are analogous to rules of following

2.35 The association between the law of tracing and the law governing physical mixtures of chattels—particularly chattels with the status of money—is an ancient one. *Kirk v Webb*,[70] for example, is one of the earliest reported cases in which an English court contemplated the possibility of tracing, and the analogy of physical mixture appears

[70] (1698) Prec Ch 84; 24 ER 41. Also reported at (1698) 2 Freem Ch 229, 22 ER 1177.

already in counsel's arguments in that case. It recurs throughout the subsequent case law, and Lord Millett affirmed its validity in *Foskett v McKeown*. However, the factual differences between physical mixture and mixed substitution, highlighted by Smith and Birks, raise questions about the scope and justification of this analogy.

We find the comparison between tracing through a substitution and following into—and out of—a mixed heap of fungible things in two contexts. First, as in *Kirk v Webb* itself, it is used to explain how factual uncertainties regarding the transactional history of an asset can be overcome with the help of a presumption against a wrongdoer. In this context, the courts have drawn an analogy to situations where the proportion or quality of fungibles contributed to a mixture by the various parties is uncertain, because of the decision of a wrongdoer to bring about the mixture. In these cases, uncertainty is resolved against the wrongdoer. Similarly, when the transactional history of an asset is unknown or unclear, because of the failure of a wrongdoer to keep accurate accounts, that uncertainty is also resolved against the wrongdoer. Both rules represent an application of the principle in *Armory v Delamirie*,[71] which resolves factual uncertainties against wrongdoers responsible for the absence of the relevant evidence in a wide range of contexts. 2.36

Secondly, in cases like *Frith v Cartland*[72] and *Re Oatway*,[73] the analogy to physical mixture is used to explain the rules that govern the attribution of payments out of a mixed fund. Where a wrongdoer brings about a physical mixture of his own things and those of the claimant, he is treated as withdrawing his own property first and making inroads into that of the claimant only once his own share is exhausted.[74] Where a wrongdoer creates a mixed fund by substitution, he is treated as making prudent investments on behalf of the claimant and untraceably spending his own assets.[75] In both contexts, the lowest intermediate balance of the mixture provides a cap on the innocent contributor's claim; once the balance has fallen below a particular level, fresh additions to the physical mixture, or fresh payments into the mixed fund, will not be treated as replenishing the share of the claimant rather than the defendant,[76] unless the defendant has a positive intention to do this. 2.37

2.1.2.1. *Inferences from missing evidence: physical and accounting confusions*

In *Kirk v Webb*,[77] a trustee had taken possession of trust land in the mistaken[78] belief that he had become a beneficiary under the terms of the settlement. He was alleged 2.38

[71] (1722) 1 Stra 505; 93 ER 664.
[72] *Frith* (n 23) 420; 527.
[73] [1903] 2 Ch 356.
[74] *Glencore International AG v Metro Trading International Inc* [2001] 1 All ER (Comm) 103, 173 (Moore-Bick J).
[75] *Re Hallett's Estate* (1880) 13 Ch D 696; *Re Oatway* (n 73); *Shalson v Russo* [2003] EWHC 1637 (Ch).
[76] *James Roscoe (Bolton) Ltd v Winder* [1915] 1 Ch 62; *Glencore International AG v Metro Trading International Inc* [2001] 1 All ER (Comm) 103, 173 (Moore-Bick J).
[77] *Kirk* (n 70).
[78] See Chapter 3 this volume, paras 3.15–3.17, for a more detailed account of the facts of the case.

to have used its rents and profits to buy more land, which he subsequently left to the executor of his will, Webb. Kirk, the widower of the actual beneficiary, sought to have this land sold and the proceeds paid over to him. It was argued, on his behalf, 'that the land purchased with the profits should go in the same manner as the profits themselves would have gone'.[79]

2.39 However, as counsel conceded, it was not actually clear on the facts that the land *had* been purchased exclusively with the profits from the trust land. The trustee, believing himself to be the life tenant and to have received the rents and profits in his own right, had not kept an account. Counsel argued[80] that Kirk was entitled to the land anyway since this gap in the evidence—the absence of a clear record of the source of the funds used to buy the land—arose 'through the trustee's own fault, whose part it was to have kept the account': 'and it was compared to the case where a man mixes his money with another man's heap, he shall lose his own money[.]'[81]

2.40 The principle that money mixed in a heap will be lost to the person who brought about the mixture was acknowledged in *Warde v Aeyre*,[82] a decision of the Court of King's Bench in 1615. The reported facts of that case are that the claimant and defendant 'being at play, the [claimant] thrust his money into the defendant's heap and so intermingled them together', whereupon 'the defendant kept all'. As a result of their 'striving together for the money', the claimant brought an action for trespass to the person as well as an action to recover his five marks. Coke CJ held that, having wrongfully mingled his money with the defendant's, he could not recover it. The reason he gave for refusing the claim explains why counsel in *Kirk v Webb* saw an analogy between this dispute and the otherwise rather different facts of that case: 'for that [the claimant's] own proper money ... *cannot now be known*, and therefore by this his intermingling, being his own act, and of his own wrong, by the law he shall lose all'.[83]

2.41 The argument is that, in both cases, the court is faced with an evidential difficulty which arises as a result of the wrongful conduct of one party to the litigation, and which, therefore, should be resolved against that wrongdoer. This principle, which was applied to a different evidential problem in *Armory v Delamirie*,[84] was recognized as the basis of the rule in cases like *Warde v Aeyre* by Lord Eldon in *Lupton v White*.[85] In *Indian Oil Corporation Ltd v Greenstone Shipping SA*,[86] Staughton J affirmed this interpretation, holding that the court will apply the effectively confiscatory rule in *Ward v Aeyre* only where there is genuine doubt about the quantity or quality of the respective contributions of the wrongdoer and the innocent contributor, and the wrongdoer cannot distinguish his own share.

2.42 In *Lupton v White*, Lord Eldon associated this principle with cases concerned with evidential difficulties in tracing. *Lupton v White* itself addressed a problem of following. Lupton and White were owners of adjoining lead mines in Yorkshire. Lupton's title to his mine, 'Little Ing', had been disputed by White, who owned

[79] *Kirk* (n 70) 87; 42.
[80] For the actual decision in the case, see Chapter 3 this volume, para 3.18.
[81] *Kirk* (n 79) 87; 42.
[82] (1615) 2 Bulst 323.
[83] *Warde* (n 82) 324.
[84] *Armory* (n 71). See para 2.45 this chapter.
[85] (1809) 15 Ves Jun 432; 33 ER 817.
[86] [1987] 1 QB 345.

the neighbouring 'Prosperous Mine'. Lupton obtained an injunction forbidding White from mining Little Ing until his title had been determined. However, the injunction was lifted because White promised the court that he would ensure his agents would keep the ore from the two mines separate and account to Lupton, if his title were proved, for the proceeds of sale of the ore from Little Ing. In breach of this undertaking, White's agents deliberately mixed the ore from the two mines, ensuring that they were 'smelted together at the same hearth, and marked with the same mark and letter'.[87] They also made it impossible to estimate how much ore could have been got out of Little Ing, by 'deliberately permit[ing] some of the workings to fall in', 'fill[ing] up other parts with rubbish', and 'drowning the lower part'.[88]

Lord Eldon ordered White to account to Lupton for the proceeds of sale of all the ore sold after the date of his undertaking in court, unless he could positively identify which ore was mined from his own mine. The case, he said, was governed by 'the great principle, familiar both at law and in equity', that where a person who has 'undertaken to keep the property of another distinct' 'mixes it with his own', the whole mixture will belong to that other until 'the former puts the subject under such circumstances that it may be distinguished'.[89] As authority for this principle, he cited 'the cases in the old law of a mixture of corn or flour'.[90] But he did not confine himself to these cases, or to other instances of physical mixture. He also cited *Panton v Panton*[91] and his own decision in *Lord Chedworth v Edwards*,[92] cases where there was no physical mixture, but only a gap in the accounts that made tracing difficult. 2.43

In *Lord Chedworth v Edwards*, a steward had used the rents of his employer's land, and the proceeds of sale of his timber, to buy stocks and increase the credit balance of a bank account. Since he had failed to keep proper accounts, it was unclear which stocks had been obtained using the employer's money and which by the steward's own funds, or how much of the credit balance of the account was attributable to the employer's money. Lord Eldon granted the employer an injunction restraining the steward from disposing of the stock until he could show how much of it was purchased with his own money.[93] Unlike *Lupton v White*, there was no suggestion of an actual physical confusion of things in this case, only of confusion in the accounts. The steward had sold his employer's timber, just as White's agents had sold Lupton's lead, but there was no suggestion that, like them, he had previously mingled it with logs of his own timber. *Panton v Panton* is unreported elsewhere, but—according to Lord Eldon's account of the case in *Lupton v White*—it concerned wholly dematerialized assets, securities, and could not, therefore, have involved any physical mixture. 2.44

Lord Eldon characterized all these cases as governed by the same principle, ie the principle in *Armory v Delamirie*. *Armory v Delamirie* concerned a chimneysweeper's boy who had found in a ring in a chimney and taken it to a jeweller to be valued. The jeweller's agent removed the jewel from the socket of the ring, and declined to 2.45

[87] (1808) 15 Ves Jun 432, 434; 33 ER 817, 819. [88] *Lupton* (n 87).
[89] *Lupton* (n 85) 439; 820. [90] *Lupton* (n 85) 442; 821.
[91] Unreported elsewhere. [92] (1802) 8 Ves Jun 47, 32 ER 268.
[93] *Lord Chedworth* (n 92).

return it. Having held that the boy had a better title to the ring than the jeweller, Pratt CJ directed the jury 'that unless the defendant did produce the jewel and show it not to be of the finest water, they should presume the strongest against him and make the value of the best jewels the measure of damages'.[94] Lord Eldon explained this decision as follows:

> If a man by his own tortious act, makes it impossible for another to ascertain the value of his property . . . is the argument to be endured that, as the party so injured cannot distinguish his property, therefore he shall have nothing? That is not the law of this country.[95]

2.46 On this basis, he said, obiter, that a defendant who mixed his corn or flour with that of a claimant would not lose his share of the mixture if 'they were of equal value'.[96] He would be unable to claim any portion of the mixture only if 'articles of different value are mixed, producing a third value . . . and . . . through the fault of the person mixing them, the other person cannot tell what was the original value of his property'.[97] In *Indian Oil Co v Greenstone SA Indian Oil Corporation Ltd v Greenstone Shipping SA (Panama)*,[98] Staughton J applied this dictum. He said that, where known quantities of oil of the same value were mixed, the respective contributors become co-owners of the total mixture. It was only where some fact—such as the total quantity contributed, or the value of either party's contribution—was genuinely unknown that *Armory v Delamirie* should be invoked against a wrongdoer.

2.47 Thus, the principle in *Armory v Delamirie* applies when the value of a thing cannot be ascertained because of the wrongdoing of the defendant. The principle is not, however, confined to the task of quantifying the value of things. It also applies when the answer to other questions of fact cannot be ascertained as a result of the wrongdoing of one of the parties. In *Keefe v The Isle of Man Steam Packet Co*,[99] for example, the principle justified a finding that the claimant seaman's deafness was caused by the excessive noise to which his employer, the defendant, had negligently exposed him on board its ships. There was no positive evidence that the level of noise was such that it would have caused deafness, but this was because the employer—in breach of duty—had failed to keep any record of the noise levels on its ship. Given this breach of duty, the judges drew the inference that the noise levels had been excessive. Longmore LJ said that 'a defendant who has, in breach of duty, made it difficult or impossible for a claimant to adduce relevant evidence must run the risk of adverse factual findings',[100] citing *Armory v Delamirie* as authority for this principle.[101]

2.48 In the context of tracing, such adverse factual findings are often made where the claimant cannot adduce relevant evidence of the transactional history of an asset, but where this is because of the defendant's wrongdoing. Where a wrongdoer has undoubtedly misappropriated the claimant's assets, and is unwilling or unable to tell the court what he has done with them, the court will often draw the inference that

[94] *Armory* (n 71) (Pratt CJ). [95] *Lupton* (n 90). [96] *Lupton* (n 90).
[97] *Lupton* (n 90). [98] [1987] 1 QB 345. [99] [2010] EWCA Civ 683.
[100] *Keefe* (n 99) [19]. [101] *Keefe* (n 99) [20].

some of the assets now vested in him were acquired—unless proved otherwise—using the misappropriated assets.[102]

2.49 However, there are limits to the scope of the principle. In *Gulati v MGN Ltd*,[103] Mann J said that the principle in *Armory v Delamirie* did not mean that 'the court will ignore the evidence that is available, or will make purely speculative or fanciful findings';[104] the actual evidence must be taken into account, and 'any assumptions made against the wrongdoing party must be realistic'.[105] Thus, in the context of tracing, it remains open to a defendant to displace the operation of the principle by showing that some particular asset cannot realistically be transactionally linked to the claimants' misappropriated asset. Courts have declined to permit tracing into an asset where a defendant can point to the precise source of the funds used to acquire that particular asset,[106] where he can show it was acquired long before the relevant misappropriation,[107] or where they simply find the inference of a transactional link implausible. These principles are not peculiar to either tracing or following, but rather represent a general approach to a problem—solving evidential difficulties, created by wrongdoers—that often arises in the context of both projects. As such, these principles tell us relatively little about tracing or following, or about the relationship between them.

2.1.2.2. Subordinating wrongdoers: mixed substitutions and physical mixtures

2.50 However, we also find a strong analogy between tracing and following in a context where the relevant legal rules are more distinctive. These rules—cherry-picking, subordination of wrongdoers, the lowest intermediate balance rule—apply in situations where the problem before the court is how to distinguish the rights of different parties as they affect a mixed fund or physical mixture, where the actual contributions of the parties to the mixture are known but where pro rata division is incapable of satisfying the claims of all parties in full. Typically, such situations arise where subsequent transactions have depleted the initial physical mixture or mixed fund, and the law must determine the effect of these transactions on the different contributors. Lord Millett suggested, in *Foskett v McKeown*,[108] that some cases that respond to physical transformation—the accession of chattels to other chattels, or the manufacture of a new object using another person's chattels—can also be understood as instances of the same principle in operation.

[102] Eg *Lane v Dighton* (1762) Amb 409, 412, 27 ER 274, 275; *Harford v Lloyd* (1855) 20 Beav 309, 52 ER 622; *Cook v Addison* (1869) LR 7 Eq 466, 470; *Harris v Truman* (1882) 9 QBD 264; *El Ajou v Dollar Land Holdings plc (No 1)* [1993] 3 All ER 717, overruled by the Court of Appeal at [1994] 2 All ER 685; *Islamic Republic of Pakistan v Zardari* [2006] EWHC 2411 (Comm); *Sinclair Investments (UK) v Versailles Trade Finance Ltd* [2010] EWHC 1614 (Ch), [145]–[155]. See Chapter 4 this volume, Section 4.1.1.

[103] [2015] EWHC 1482 (Ch). [104] *Gulati* (n 103) [88]. [105] *Gulati* (n 104).

[106] As in *Sinclair Investments (UK) Ltd v Versailles Trade Finance Ltd* [2010] EWHC 1614 (HC), affirmed by the Court of Appeal at [2011] EWCA Civ 347.

[107] As in *Serious Fraud Office v Lexi Holdings plc* [2008] EWCA Crim 1443.

[108] *Foskett* (n 4) 132–33.

2.51 For example, suppose that A has wrongfully mixed fifty barrels of his own oil with fifty barrels of B's. If the quantity of the contributions made by each party are known, the result is that A and B are both entitled to 50 per cent of the mixture at this stage; it is frequently said[109] that they have become tenants in common of the mixture, although Smith suggests[110] that this is only an inaccurate way of describing the survival of their individual rights to their original oil in the mixture. Suppose that A then withdraws and sells 50 per cent of the mixture, untraceably dissipating the proceeds. It is necessary to determine the effect of this diminishment of the mixture on B's rights: is he now entitled to only 50 per cent of the remaining mixture (ie, 25 barrels) or can he take all of it? A parallel problem arises in the tracing context, where A, for example, wrongfully pays £50 he holds on trust for B into a bank account into which he has paid £50 of his own money. In this situation, A holds his right to be paid £100 by the bank for himself and B, with an obligation to pay £50 of the balance to B. If, in this situation, A withdraws £50 from the bank account and spends it, what is the impact on B's rights? Is he now entitled to only 50 per cent of the remaining credit balance of the account—so that A now has a duty to pay him £25—or can he say that the remaining £50 is now held for him alone?

2.52 In both these situations, the same principle applies. As Lord Millett put it in *Foskett v McKeown*, B, the innocent contributor, 'is entitled to locate his contribution in any part of the mixture and to subordinate [the claims of a wrongdoer responsible for the mixture] to share in the mixture until his own contribution has been satisfied'.[111] Thus, in the example above, B can say that A sold all of his own oil before resorting to B's oil and that, therefore, he, B, is solely entitled to the remaining 50 barrels of oil. Similarly, in the case of the mixed bank account, B can either choose to be satisfied in full from the remaining balance of the account or, if this is to his advantage, treat anything particularly valuable purchased by A, using the withdrawn £50, as purchased exclusively with his money. This principle of subordinating wrongdoers is limited only by the rule that the claimant cannot assert an entitlement to anything more than the lowest balance reached by the mixed fund[112] or physical mixture[113] after the date of the mixture. Thus, if the total amount of oil in the mixture dips to forty barrels, or the total credit balance of the bank account drops to £40, this becomes the maximum cap of the claimant's entitlement even if the defendant later replenishes the fund or mixture.

2.53 Following and tracing are, thus, treated as raising strictly parallel questions, to be solved by the application of the same principles, in these contexts. The parallel in the minds of the judiciary is very clear. The judges explicitly invoked the analogy of physical mixture when they developed the rules applicable to mixed substitutions;[114] conversely, the tracing rules have been used as guidance in developing the rules

[109] See RWJ Hickey, 'Dazed and Confused: Accidental Mixtures of Goods and the Theory of Acquisition of Title' (2003) 66 MLR 368, and authorities cited therein.

[110] Smith (n 1) 71, 75–76. [111] *Foskett* (n 4) 132.

[112] *James Roscoe (Bolton) Ltd v Winder* [1915] 1 Ch 62, and see para 2.34 this chapter.

[113] *Glencore International AG v Metro Trading International Inc* [2001] 1 All ER (Comm) 103, 173 (Moore-Bick J).

[114] Eg *Pennell v Deffell* (n 20); *Frith v Cartland* (n 23).

applicable to physical mixture.[115] The question is the basis of that parallel, given the factual differences between following and tracing that have already been discussed.

As Birks and Smith have pointed out, finding out what has become of a £50 note is very different from finding out what has become of the value of that note; following the note into a physical mixture in a box or drawer is very different from tracing its value into the credit balance of a bank account. Why, then, does the law treat these questions as apparently similar, to be solved by the application of a similar principle? 2.54

Smith[116] and Birks[117] argue that these rules, like the rule in *Lupton v White*, represent an application of the evidential principle in *Armory v Delamirie*. When attributing withdrawals from a physical mixture, they suggest, the courts are solving an evidential problem. The rights of the contributors to the mixture depend on identifying the actual units of oil, or other fungible thing, contained in each withdrawal as belonging to one or other of the contributors. Since the physical evidence needed to answer this question of fact is unavailable, as a result of the wrongdoing of one contributor, *Armory v Delamirie* can be invoked against him: the court draws the inference that it is his contribution that has been withdrawn and the innocent contributor's contribution that has been preserved. 2.55

In the case of a mixed substitution, Birks and Smith argue, a similar factual problem is solved in the same way. The rights of the contributors to a mixed fund depend on locating the actual value belonging to each person that has been used in each transaction drawing on the fund. Since the evidence needed to answer this question is unavailable, as a result of the wrongdoing of one contributor, *Armory v Delamirie* can be invoked against him: the court draws the inference that it is his value that has been untraceably dissipated and the innocent contributor's contribution that has been preserved or profitably invested. 2.56

On this view, the lowest intermediate balance rule exists because the rule in *Armory v Delamirie* allows a claimant to assert that evidential difficulties should be resolved in her favour, but does not allow her to assert that the court should draw a conclusion that is contrary to the known facts.[118] In a case of physical mixture, the claimant can assert that all the units of the mixture remaining after a withdrawal are hers, but she can only assert that none of the units withdrawn were hers if the total amount withdrawn does not exceed her initial contribution. Thus, suppose A wrongfully mixes fifty barrels of B's oil with fifty barrels of his own. When A withdraws ten or twenty or fifty barrels, it is impossible to say whether or not any of this oil represents B's oil. It is theoretically possible that all of it is A's, and the law draws that inference against him as a wrongdoer. By contrast, if A withdraws sixty barrels, it is no longer even theoretically possible that all of it is A's. At minimum, at least ten barrels of 2.57

[115] As in *Glencore International AG v Metro Trading International Inc* [2001] 1 All ER (Comm) 103, where *James Roscoe (Bolton) Ltd v Winder* [1915] 1 Ch 62 was cited as authority for the lowest intermediate balance rule, which was then applied to a case of physical mixture of oil.

[116] Smith (n 1) 77–85 (on following), and 177–81 (on tracing).

[117] Birks (n 2) 358–401; 'Mixing and Tracing' (n 2) 69; 'Mixtures' (n 2) 227; 'The Necessity of a Unitary Law of Tracing' (n 2) 239.

[118] Smith (n 1) 202.

the sixty must belong to B, since there is no other possible source for the additional barrels. A subsequent addition of oil to the mixture by A has no bearing on the question whether ten barrels of B's oil have already been withdrawn; thus, B's claim is capped at the lowest intermediate balance of the mixture, forty barrels.

2.58 The same analysis holds, according to Smith, in the case of tracing into a mixed fund. He proposes an example in which a wrongdoer pays £100 of the claimant's money into a mixed bank account, the credit balance of which subsequently drops to £60 because of the wrongdoer's withdrawals. It is impossible to know whether or not this £60 represents the claimant's money, rather than the wrongdoer's, so the law concludes in the claimant's favour that it is all hers. But this is the best that can be done: so far as the other £40 is concerned, 'we know that it was withdrawn, since the balance was only £60. It cannot be in the account any longer'.[119] This analysis clearly proceeds on the basis that there is a strict analogy between units of money—or rather value—in a bank account and units of oil in a physical mixture. Once the balance of a mixed fund has fallen below a certain level, the amount of value in it has also fallen to that level; later events may increase the size of the fund, but this new value must be distinguished from the old value that was previously in the mixture and has been exhausted by withdrawals.

2.59 According to Birks and Smith, these are evidential problems, similar to problems that might arise because the amount contributed to a mixture is unknown or because the quality of a stolen jewel cannot now be determined, which the law solves in the same way that it solves all such problems created by wrongdoers—by reference to the principle in *Armory v Delamirie*.

2.60 However, as Smith notes, the law's response to these problems is rather more distinctive than its response to simple gaps in the available evidence in other contexts, which are solved by drawing plausible negative inferences against a wrongdoer. Unlike the principle in *Armory v Delamirie* as it operates in other contexts, the conclusions produced by the principle of subordinating wrongdoers are not open to attack on the grounds that they are implausible inferences from the known facts. As has been explained, *Armory v Delamirie* enables the court to draw inferences of fact against a wrongdoer who is responsible for the absence of relevant evidence, but these inferences are open to attack by the introduction of contrary evidence or by attacks on their plausibility, given the evidence that actually exists. Thus, as Mann J said in *Gulati v MGN Ltd*,[120] the principle could not have been used in *Armory v Delamirie* itself to show that the jeweller had converted 'something the size of the original Koh-i-Noor'.[121] The size of the mount provided a starting point for assessing the plausible value of any jewel that could have fit the ring. Even if evidence of the size of the ring was unavailable, plausibility provided a constraint: the principle could not have justified the jury in finding 'that a diamond of that size was missing, because no other diamond of that size was known and it would be perverse to assume that the ring in that case contained another'.[122]

[119] Smith (n 1) 202–03. [120] *Gulati* (n 103) [121] *Gulati* (n 103) [94].

[122] *Gulati* (n 121). See also *Colbeck v Diamanta (UK) Ltd* [2002] EWHC 616 (QB), in which Field J refused to apply the presumption in *Armory v Delamirie* to the valuation of diamonds whose quality

2.61 By contrast, plausibility is not a constraint on the rules governing the attribution of withdrawals from a mixture. On Smith's analysis, the courts respond to a scenario in which a wrongdoer withdraws some oil from a mixture by inferring that he has withdrawn every molecule of his own oil and left every molecule of the innocent contributor's oil intact; they take this to be the case for every single withdrawal until the moment when the conclusion becomes impossible, because the total quantity of oil has fallen below the amount of his original contribution. As an inference of fact, tested against a standard of probability, this is as perverse as it would have been to find, on the facts of *Armory v Delamirie*, that the ring taken by the jeweller had contained the only other diamond in the world the size of the Koh-i-Noor. Nevertheless, the courts do not engage with the question of plausibility in this context. They draw an inference against the wrongdoer that cannot be challenged on any such grounds.

2.62 Smith suggests that this is because, in these contexts, the courts are not dealing with a mere evidential difficulty but, instead, with what he calls an evidential *impossibility*.[123] In a case where A has mixed his oil with B's, and has deliberately kept no record of their respective contributions, there is a mere evidential difficulty; if A had kept a record of the contributions, the proportions of the mixture contributed by both A and B would be knowable. The court can make a guess at the answer; other evidence, such as B's own records of the total amount of oil that belonged to him before the withdrawal, may be relevant.[124] It is only in the absence of all such evidence that the court will draw the inference, against A, that all the oil in the mixture is B's.

2.63 By contrast, where A has mixed his oil with B's, the question of apportioning a withdrawal between them depends, according to Smith, on identifying the actual units of oil found in each withdrawal and distinguishing the oil of A from that of B within the mixture. This fact is, *ex hypothesi*, completely unknowable. It is not unknowable because A has concealed the relevant evidence in a particular case, but because a physical mixture of this kind necessarily renders the separate identification of each person's contribution impossible. As a result, the law responds by drawing a firmer inference against A than any that could be justified by the physical evidence alone.

2.64 On this analysis, the analogy between tracing and following in this context depends on the characterization of both mixtures and mixed substitutions as creating a problem of evidential impossibility: that is, raising questions of fact that are simply unanswerable on any evidence. In the case of following, the unanswerable question has to do with locating each person's physical thing after a transformative event, such as a mixture of fungibles or use in the manufacture of a new thing.[125] In

was unknown, on the grounds that 'the presumption against the wrongdoer must be consistent with the rest of the facts', and that the facts in that case were not consistent with the diamonds being of the finest quality, given that they had been sold at a relatively low price and no one had ever described them as being of the finest quality.

123 Smith (n 1) 78.

124 *Indian Oil Corporation Ltd v Greenstone Shipping SA (Panama)* [1987] 1 QB 345, 369.

125 As in *Jones v De Marchant* (1916) 28 DLR 561.

the case of tracing through a mixed substitution, the unanswerable question has to do with locating each person's value. Birks' description of the nature of this problem is instructive. When money is paid into a bank account, he says, 'or for that matter, a bucket, if money were often so kept' and there are subsequent drawings out, the same evidential problem arises: 'it is usually not possible to show by evidence exactly when those particular units of value were withdrawn'.[126] Drawing coins or banknotes from a bucket and debiting the credit balance of a bank account are, in this sense, analogous: both involve the withdrawal of units of value from a mixture, and both raise the problem of defining whose units of value are included in a particular withdrawal.

2.65 This account of the tracing rules, therefore, proceeds in two steps. First, the rules that govern tracing through mixed substitution are explained on the basis that they proceed by analogy with the rules that govern following through physical mixtures. The evidence for this is overwhelming; the cases plainly invoke similar principles of cherry-picking and the lowest intermediate balance in handling both types of mixture, and they reason from cases concerning following in solving tracing problems, and vice versa.

2.66 Secondly, both sets of rules are explained as evidential rules, representing a special application of the principle in *Armory v Delamirie*. On this view, the analogy between tracing and following is underwritten by a genuine substantive similarity between the two exercises. While the two projects of identifying things and identifying value are different, they sometimes run into a distinctive form of evidential difficulty—a kind of evidential impossibility—and solve such difficulties by a distinctive variation on the principle in *Armory v Delamirie*. This analysis depends on the underlying thesis that both tracing and following are exercises in the discovery of facts that have been rendered unknowable by events: the identification of physical things in one case, and the identification of value in the other. Its justification depends on the idea that tracing is about the location of value, and the characterization of this task as an evidential one.

2.1.3. Tracing is not claiming

2.67 The analogy between tracing and following, and the characterization of both as evidential processes, also underpins Birks' and Smith's explanation of the distinction between tracing and claiming. Two features of the case law suggest that there is such a distinction. First, in many of the cases, the judges proceed in a two-step fashion, distinguishing the tracing inquiry from the question whether any claims to traceable proceeds are available.[127] Secondly, and more strikingly, it is clear that tracing can be invoked in a number of disparate contexts where the underlying claim or legal status transmitted is very different. [128] Yet, apart from the possible limitations of common law tracing,[129] the rules of tracing are uniform across these contexts.

[126] Birks, 'The Necessity of a Unitary Law of Tracing' (n 2) 239, 254.

[127] Smith (n 1) 12, citing dicta from *Taylor v Plumer* (1815) 3 M & S 562, 105 ER 721; *Sinclair v Brougham* [1914] AC 398; *Re Diplock* [1948] Ch 465; and *Boscawen v Bajwa* [1996] 1 WLR 328.

[128] Smith (n 1) 14. [129] See Chapter 1 this volume, paras 1.56–1.58.

In *Re Hallett's Estate*,[130] the Court of Appeal firmly rejected the view that the rules of tracing might differ based on whether the claimant was a beneficiary under a trust or stood in some other kind of legal relationship to the defendant. Jessel MR held that equity had the ability to trace into a mixed fund through the transactions of an 'express trustee, or an agent, or a bailee, or a collector of rents, or anybody else in a fiduciary position';[131] in *El Ajou v Dollar Land Holdings Ltd plc (No 1)*, Millett J commented that these equitable tracing rules were also available to parties who had been 'simply swindled',[132] such as the victims of a fraudulent misrepresentation. It has already been noted that, in the context of civil recovery orders, the status of an asset as the proceeds of crime depends, at least by analogy,[133] on the application of the tracing concept. This suggests that the work done by tracing is, in some sense, freestanding; the task of identifying the proceeds of an asset is independent of the considerations that determine the scope of the ultimate claim that is being made to those proceeds. 2.68

Birks and Smith suggest that this feature of the law can be explained by analogy with the distinction between *following* and claiming. The distinction between the process of following a thing and actually claiming that thing, once found, is an intuitive one. If B is looking for his car, the kind of evidence that is relevant to its discovery will be the same, whether B's goal is to sue A for taking it or merely to discover whether, having given it to A as a birthday present, A still happens to have it. In either case, he will still need to, perhaps, ask A if he has the car or, failing this, to discover whether A has been photographed driving it or whether some third person has seen it sitting in A's garage. 2.69

If B is trying to prove this fact to a court, in the context of litigation, rather than merely to indulge a private curiosity, certain legal standards will govern what kinds of evidence he can rely on. These are not special 'rules of following'. They are simply the ordinary rules of evidence, which apply to the proof of any fact whatsoever in the context of civil proceedings. The principle in *Armory v Delamirie* is among these rules. Thus, B might be able to invite the court to draw the inference that A took the car in a situation where A has a very similar car in his garage and has deliberately destroyed the licence plates and documentation associated with that car. 2.70

Nevertheless, the project of finding the current location of the car does not take on a special normative character merely because some rules are associated with succeeding in that project in a court of law. Various substantive rules of law may be engaged by the facts proved by the exercise of following—for example, the law governing civil wrongs, or the law of contract, or the bankruptcy rules—and it is these rules that allow a claimant who has conducted a following exercise to make some kind of legal claim in relation to the thing he has found by following. It would 2.71

[130] (1880) 13 Ch D 696. [131] *Re Hallett's Estate* (n 130) 710.

[132] [1993] 4 All ER 717, 734.

[133] In *Serious Organised Crime Agency v Namli* [2013] EWHC 1200 (overruled on a different point by the Court of Appeal, [2014] EWCA Civ 411), Mann J considered, but did not settle, the question whether section 306 of the Proceeds of Crime Act 2002 represented an exhaustive statutory code or whether the common law and equitable rules of tracing applied to determine when proceeds of crime could be identified in, or through, a mixed fund.

be a mistake to argue that a claimant who is looking for a car because, for example, he wishes to show that the defendant has converted it should be entitled to rely on stricter or looser 'rules of following' than a claimant who is doing so for some other purpose: for example, because he wishes to show that he has fulfilled his contract to sell such a car to the defendant or because he is a trustee in bankruptcy who wishes to take possession of the car as the very one belonging to the bankrupt. Following is the same exercise in discovering facts, whatever legal conclusion it is meant to support. As we have seen, Birks and Smith argue that the rules that govern the attribution of withdrawals from a physical mixture, as between innocent contributors or between innocent contributors and wrongdoers, are also rules of evidence that do not alter the purely factual character of the following exercise.

2.72 Both Birks and Smith emphasize that the distinction between tracing and claiming parallels this distinction between following and claiming. Whether a claimant can trace through a given set of transactions is a freestanding question, distinct from whether the claimant has any right in respect of the original asset,[134] the nature of his right to the product, if any, and whether that right entitles him to any remedies against a particular defendant in a given situation.[135] However, Birks and Smith appear to differ from each other on the basis of this analogy.

2.73 In Birks' account, the distinction between tracing and claiming—like the distinction between tracing and following—seems to map to the distinction between questions of law and questions of fact. Identifying the asset that currently represents the value of some money, for example, is a question of fact in the same sense that identifying the current location of a car is a question of fact. He compares it to the task of identifying the history of one's family silver. A person might, 'through diligent research', show through whose hands a set of silver candlesticks had passed and where they could now be found. This would be following. Similarly, he might show that it was by selling those candlesticks that another person 'acquired the Hockney drawing which hangs on [their] wall'. Like following the candlesticks into the hands of their current legal owner, tracing their value through such a substitution, 'entails no rights'. Both exercises 'may satisfy curiosity, but they are compatible with a thousand different stories'.[136] The implication is that tracing through a substitution, like following through a change of hands, is a description of something that one might do without the aid of legal rules, in order to discover facts that are of interest to one for reasons other than litigation.

2.74 Smith's explanation of the analogy between following and tracing, however, is complicated by his insistence that—unlike following—tracing always and inevitably involves the application of legal rules. While following can be 'exclusively factual', tracing cannot: it always 'involves the application of legal rules'.[137] A claimant who wishes to prove that some candlesticks are in a particular place can simply prove that fact. On the other hand, a claimant who wishes to prove that the value of the candlesticks is now in the Hockney painting cannot just prove this: 'she must prove

[134] Smith (n 1) 12–14. [135] Smith (n 1) 121–22.
[136] Birks, 'The Necessity of a Unitary Law of Tracing' (n 2) 239, 244.
[137] Smith (n 1) 11.

certain facts; and it must be the case that *the application to those facts of the rules of tracing* leads to the conclusion that the original asset can be traced into the asset which is now the subject matter of the claim'.[138] On this analysis, you cannot just prove that the value of the candlesticks is in the painting. You must prove something else: the fact of a substitution, a transaction of a particular kind, and then invoke the rules of tracing to show that transactions of that kind do, as a matter of law, transmit value from asset to asset.

Nevertheless, Smith argues, the distinction between those rules and the rules of claiming still holds. Although 'legal rules are inevitably involved' in the tracing exercise, it remains 'just that: an exercise or process that is preliminary to the making of a claim'.[139] He suggests an analogy with the law of contract formation. A claimant who wishes to show that the defendant has breached a contract must show that a contract actually exists. To do this, he must prove certain facts—an offer, acceptance of the offer, consideration—and show that the rules of contract formation apply to those facts and lead to the conclusion that a contract was formed. Proof that a contract exists does not, in itself, entitle a claimant to any remedy from a court. It is just something the claimant is at liberty to do, and must do to get certain remedies in certain situations (eg to succeed in an action for breach of contract). 2.75

This account of the distinction between tracing and claiming clearly does not map to the distinction between questions of law and questions of fact. Proof that a contract exists—and the invocation of the rules of contract formation to show that the events that have happened gave rise to a contract—is proof of a conclusion of law. It is proof that the legal relations of the contracting parties have been altered by events like the making of an offer and its acceptance. By definition, successful invocation of the rules of contract formation cannot be said to 'entail no rights', since it is precisely the creation of a new set of contractual rights that is at stake in the question whether a given set of events counts as the formation of a contract. If the rules of tracing allow a claimant to prove that the value of one asset can be traced into another, and this is a conclusion of law, not fact, they seem inherently different from the rules that might sometimes assist a claimant in proving that some candlesticks that were once in his possession are now to be found in the house of the defendant. 2.76

This element of Smith's work is related to a significant tension between two definitions of tracing offered in *The Law of Tracing*. First, it is a process that allows one asset to stand in the place of another, 'for certain legal purposes'.[140] Secondly, it is a process that enables a litigant 'to prove that the value which used to inhere in one asset has passed into and now inheres in another asset'.[141] It is not obvious how the two definitions are synonymous. If we accept the first definition, and say that the aim of the rules is to discover whether, 'for certain legal purposes', one asset can stand in the place of another, it seems reasonable to infer that their content will only be intelligible by reference to the relevant legal purposes. If we accept the second, on the other hand, we can say that the content of the rules will be intelligible by reference 2.77

138 Smith (n 137).
139 Smith (n 137).
140 Smith (n 1) 3 and 17.
141 Smith (n 1) 24.

to the idea of value being transmitted from one asset to another. If that idea refers to a fact susceptible to proof by ordinary empirical evidence, then the exercise of tracing will be like following—intelligible without reference to any particular legal purpose. While it might be relevant to various different kinds of litigation, it might equally well be conducted outside the context of litigation, for purposes that are not legal. If this is true, it is not clear why tracing must always be a matter of legal rules, as Smith puts it.

2.78 The corollary of these two accounts of tracing is that there are also two possible, and logically distinct, explanations of the distinction between tracing and claiming. First, it could be said that all the legal purposes served by the transmission of a status from one asset to another can be achieved by the application of the set of legal rules known as the rules of tracing. If this were accepted, it would follow that the rules of tracing could be understood independently of the particular differences between the legal purposes that the person tracing was trying to achieve. The principles that enable the transmission of 'proceeds of crime' status would be the same as the principles that enable the transmission of 'subject matter of a beneficial interest under a trust' status. The reason why those principles are the same across the board would then call for explanation; the distinction between tracing and claiming, understood in this sense, would be a positive choice made by the legal system, standing in need of justification in doctrinal terms, by reference to the purposes achieved by the application of the rules in different contexts.

2.79 On the other hand, the argument could be that the distinction between tracing and claiming, like that between following and claiming, maps to the distinction between law and fact. Proof that a factual assertion is true is to be distinguished, as a matter of logic, from the legal response to that fact if proved. If the rules of tracing are genuinely rules of evidence, which enable a fact to be proved to the satisfaction of a court, the distinction between tracing and claiming would not therefore call for doctrinal justification. It would merely reflect the reality that the question whether an event has taken place is different from the question how the legal system ought to respond to that event.

2.80 The choice between these two understandings of the distinction between tracing and claiming depends, once more, on what it means to say—as Birks and Smith both say—that tracing aims to identify value. 'When a person makes a substitution', Smith says, 'value is the only constant that is held by that person before, through, and after the substitution'.[142] Does this mean, as Birks suggests, that substitution is only evidence of the movement of value, and that determining whether such a movement of value has taken place is a factual question? Or does it mean, as Smith suggests, that the idea of the movement of value is inherently linked to the idea of substitution, so that the only way of showing that the value of asset 1 is now found in asset 2 is by proving a transaction that links them and then invoking the rules of tracing to show that the transaction counts as a substitution? Like the distinction between tracing and following, and the analogy between tracing and following,

[142] Smith (n 1) 16.

the distinction between tracing and claiming both supports the conclusion that tracing is about value and raises fundamental questions about the meaning of that conclusion.

2.1.4. Tracing locates value: two conceptions of value in *Foskett v McKeown*

As discussed, Birks and Smith use the value model to make sense of several features of the law that would otherwise be puzzling. It is used to point out the metaphorical character of the judicial language of transformation, which has traditionally been used to justify the possibility of tracing. It is used to clarify the well-established analogy between physical mixture and mixed substitution that underpins the substantive rules of tracing through mixed funds. Finally, it accounts for the distinction in the case law between identifying traceable proceeds and making particular claims to traceable proceeds. However, as discussed, the implications of this characterization of tracing depend, ultimately, on what the term 'value' means in this context. 2.81

Unfortunately, this is the point on which agreement between Birks and Smith, and between the judges in *Foskett v McKeown*, breaks down most radically. In *The Law of Tracing*, Smith offers a definition of value that is sharply different from the usual understanding of value as a factual characteristic of things or assets. The value of a thing, in the factual sense,[143] usually refers to a monetary amount that represents what the thing or asset is worth relative to other things or assets, either to a particular person or under the conditions of a particular market (ie to people in the aggregate).[144] Such claims are statements of fact, describing the amount of money that a particular person, or participants in a particular market, would be prepared to pay to obtain the relevant asset. Market value—the aggregate price that participants in a market would be willing to pay for the asset—is the usual sense in which we use the term 'value' in legal contexts. 2.82

Smith denies that such accounts of value have anything to do with tracing. Value, in the context of tracing, 'does not refer to a fixed monetary amount; it simply reifies that which inheres in an asset and which can be seen as passing into another form when that asset is exchanged for another asset'.[145] He particularly emphasizes the irrelevance of *market* value to tracing. Thus, for example, suppose that A uses a £100 banknote, belonging to B, to buy a painting, and the market value of the painting turns out to be £1000. As this is a clean substitution, the value of A's title to the painting can be attributed wholly to the value of B's cash, despite the disparity in the market value of the two assets.[146] B can say that the value of his £100 banknote is now found in A's title to the £1000 painting, and A cannot challenge his conclusion on the grounds that the title to the painting is worth much more—either to him, 2.83

[143] As distinct from the senses in which the term 'value' is used in the context of moral philosophy. For a discussion of the relationship between value understood as a factual description of aggregate or individual relative preferences and ethical and meta-ethical conceptions of value, see E Anderson, *Value in Ethics and Economics* (Harvard University Press 1995) 141–63.

[144] See Section 2.2.1 this chapter. [145] Smith (n 142). [146] Smith (n 142).

or to people in general, under market conditions—than B's banknote ever was or could be. Smith's comment on this example of the £100 note used to buy the £1000 painting is that 'there are good and bad bargains, and the invocation of "value" as the object of the verb "to trace" does not entail that an asset must have the same market value as the asset used to acquire it'.[147] Tracing is not about the equivalence in value, market or otherwise, between the original asset and the substitute. It is about a transactional connection between the two.

2.84 The question, however, is what 'the invocation of "value" as the object of the verb "to trace"' *does* entail, if it does not entail a focus on the market values of particular assets. One possibility is that the aim of the exercise is not to quantify the value of the original asset, but rather to quantify the amount by which the defendant is enriched as a result of his act of misappropriating that original asset. This is the sense in which Birks seems to understand the focus of tracing. In his *An Introduction to the Law of Restitution*, he argues that the function of the tracing rules is to determine how much of the value that was received by the defendant, at the expense of the claimant, 'survives' in his hands.[148] 'Value' is here synonymous with 'enrichment' in the context of his account of unjust enrichment.[149] A defendant who receives something of value to him[150] is better off because the receipt has increased the total pool of wealth at his disposal: that is, it has increased the aggregate amount of value he could obtain by exchanging all the things or assets in his control. For example, a defendant who misappropriates £100 from the claimant, paying it into his own bank account, now has £100 more at his disposal than he would have had but for the misappropriation. He can afford to acquire more things, assets, or services that he values than he would have been able to obtain in the absence of the misappropriation.

2.85 Identifying how much value the defendant has obtained as a result of a transaction and how much of it has survived, in this sense, is a question of causation. The amount of value obtained as the result of a transaction may be more or less than the abstract monetary worth of the asset that the defendant happened to be dealing with, depending on whether he has made a good or a bad bargain. Thus, the defendant who makes an exceptionally good bargain—who uses the £100 banknote to buy

[147] Smith (n 1) 17. [148] Birks, *An Introduction to the Law of Restitution* (n 2) 83.

[149] Reflected in the fact that, in the index to *An Introduction to the Law of Restitution*, the entry for 'value' says 'see enrichment'. Scholars have recently argued that enrichment in the law of unjust enrichment is not perfectly synonymous with value in the sense used by Birks, but that value is only one kind of enrichment, with legal enrichments (such as the acquisition of legal rights or the release of legal obligations) being the other: see R Chambers, 'Two Kinds of Enrichment' in R Chambers, J Penner, and C Mitchell (eds), *Philosophical Foundations of the Law of Unjust Enrichment* (OUP 2009) 242, and A Lodder, *Enrichment in the Law of Unjust Enrichment and Restitution* (Hart 2012). This does not affect the argument in the text, which considers Birks' view that tracing is concerned with enrichment by the receipt of value.

[150] In the context of a claim in unjust enrichment, determining that a receipt is of value to the defendant will depend on whether it is an incontrovertible benefit (such as money) or, if not, if the particular defendant is known to value it (as where, for example, he has requested it). The quantification of how much value the benefit represents will depend, initially, on its market value, subject to any devaluation necessary to give due regard to the defendant's autonomy: *Benedetti v Sawaris* [2013] UKSC 50. See J Edelman, 'The Meaning of Loss and Enrichment' in R Chambers, C Mitchell, and J Penner (eds), *Philosophical Foundations of the Law of Unjust Enrichment* (OUP 2008) 211.

the £1,000 painting—has increased the aggregate wealth at his disposal by £900 as a result of this transaction. If the £100 never belonged to him, but belonged to B, he has increased his aggregate wealth by £1,000; but for the misappropriation, he would be £1,000 worse off than he now is.

Birks notes that claims to traceable assets, unlike some other claims based on unjust enrichment, assume 'that enrichment survives, not in the level of the abstract fund, but in particular assets in which the value of the original is re-invested'.[151] Nevertheless, the idea that the goal of tracing is to determine whether an enrichment received has 'survived'—whether in the form of new assets or in the form of an increase in the abstract fund of assets at the defendant's disposal—makes it a matter of causation. The question is whether the benefit actually caused by the original receipt, or misappropriation, has led to the acquisition of more benefits or not. Has the defendant 'spent, lost, eaten or destroyed the enrichment', or has he 'invested it with huge success or otherwise caused it to increase'?[152] If the defendant has made a bad bargain, swapping the claimant's £100 for a painting worth £10, he has unprofitably spent £90 of the enrichment that he originally received and now has only £10 worth of enrichment, in the form of his title to the painting. 2.86

As Smith points out,[153] it is the choice between his transactional conception of value and this causal conception that explains the division between the majority and the minority in *Foskett v McKeown*. Lord Steyn, dissenting, refused to allow the misappropriated money to be traced into the insurance payout on the facts of that case[154] because there was no causal link between the misappropriation of the money and the payout. Mr Murphy had, in a sense, made a bad bargain on the facts of the case, having traded the trust money for wealth that would have been available to his children anyway, in the events that had happened. This would have been relevant on a causal approach to the task of locating value. The children gained no value at all as a result of the misappropriation of the trust money; the abstract pool of wealth at their disposal would have been the same if the misappropriation had never taken place. 2.87

The majority, denying the relevance of this argument, 'applied a transactional approach'. They held that the value inherent in the trust money had become inherent in the right to receive the insurance payout and that it did not matter if the exchange of one for the other hand been a good bargain or a bad one. Thus, although Lord Millett expressed his agreement with Lord Steyn on the value conception of tracing, and the distinction between tracing and claiming,[155] *Foskett v McKeown* does not provide clear authority on the meaning of the distinction because the judges differed so fundamentally on the underlying concept of value as it related to the outcome of the case. The *ratio* of the case appears to support a transactional understanding of value—with Lord Millett denying, in terms, that the tracing inquiry has anything 2.88

151 P Birks, *Unjust Enrichment* (OUP 2005) 70.

152 Birks, *An Introduction to the Law of Restitution* (n 2) 76.

153 'Tracing' in A Burrows and Lord Rodger of Earlsferry (ed), *Mapping the Law: Essays in Memory of Peter Birks* (OUP 2006) 119.

154 See para 2.12 this chapter for the facts.

155 [2001] 1 AC 102, 129–30.

to do with causation—but this is complicated by the difficulty in defining what the transactional conception of value actually means.

2.2. Value as a Fact: Problems with the Evidential Model

2.89 As Cutts has persuasively argued,[156] there is a total lack of fit between the transactional focus of the rules of tracing and any kind of evidential project of 'locating value'.

2.90 Locating value might be an evidential project in two senses. First, the term 'value' can be used to describe a factual characteristic of a particular asset; there are factual questions, therefore, that can be asked about defining the value of any given asset. However, it is not clear what it means to say that value in this sense can be transmitted or move from one asset to another. It might mean that the two assets share that characteristic—ie, that they have the same value—but the law of tracing is manifestly uninterested in this question and cannot be sensibly understood as aimed at locating the value of the original asset in this sense.

2.91 Secondly, 'value' may describe the benefit obtained by a defendant as a result of an act of misappropriating or using an asset. In this sense, it describes the aggregate amount of realizable wealth at the disposal of a particular person, and there are factual questions that can be asked about defining the consequences of a given transaction on that pool of wealth. Locating value, in this sense, may refer to an attempt to determine the causal consequences of a transaction, as it affects the wealth of the defendant or the claimant. However, there is no fit between such a project and the law of tracing either.

2.92 This lack of fit has led some authors[157] to argue that the only rational model of tracing is one that wholly jettisons the current law, with its requirement of transactional links, and focuses directly on the question of value, either as a characteristic of a given asset or as a consequence of a given transaction. However, this approach is difficult to justify in the light of the courts' long-standing commitment to the requirement of transactional links.

2.2.1. Value as a factual characteristic of assets

2.93 In ordinary speech, we might describe the value of a thing as having something to do with its intrinsic qualities.[158] In speaking of the value of an apple, for example,

[156] Cutts (n 5).

[157] Eg S Walt and EL Sherwin, 'Contribution Arguments in Commercial Law' (1993) 42 Emory LJ 897; C Rotherham, 'The Metaphysics of Tracing: Substituted Title and Property Rhetoric' (1996) 34 Osgoode Hall LJ 321; S Evans, 'Rethinking tracing and the law of restitution' (1999) 115 LQR 469; DJ Oesterle, 'Deficiencies of the Restitutionary Right to Trace Misappropriated Property in Equity and in UCC 9-306' (1983) 68 Cornell LR 172.

[158] For an example of this usage of 'value', which opposes it to 'price' (what is here described as market value) see GK Chesterton, 'Reflections on a Rotten Apple' in *The Well and the Shallows* (Ignatius Press, San Francisco 2006) 163, 170: 'Price is a crazy and incalculable thing, while Value is an intrinsic and indestructible thing'. Chesterton takes his distinction between price and value from Oscar Wilde's

we may be referring to its edibility, flavour, or ripeness. However, value in this sense cannot be the concern of the law of tracing. It would be nonsensical to talk about the intrinsic qualities of one thing being transmitted to another: a quality intrinsic to an object is, by definition, not transferable away from that object. If an apple is valued, in GK Chesterton's terminology,[159] because of its intrinsic qualities as a thing that is good to eat, that quality is peculiar to the very apple in question. It cannot be transmissible from the apple to a coin obtained in exchange for it, or even to a pear for which the apple is bartered.

If we move away from the notion of intrinsic qualities, then, the value of an asset describes the worth of the asset relative to other things that also have value in the relevant sense. This is what Lodder calls 'relational value': 'an abstract standard for the comparison and exchange of qualitatively heterogeneous things in quantitatively comparable terms'.[160] To speak of value in this sense is, by definition, to abstract from the particularity of a given object—the bundle of rights, powers, duties, and privileges comprised by a person's title to an apple, or the qualities of the apple itself looked at in isolation (eg its colour, kind, or flavour)—and to bring to bear a standard that relates it to other objects, either for the purposes of comparison or for the purposes of exchange. This standard is necessarily relative. To say that two apples are green, or ripe, is not to make a claim about the value of either one; to say that one apple is a brighter green than the other, or is riper, is to treat these characteristics as a standard of valuation that can be used for the purposes of comparison. 2.94

As this example suggests, we might abstract from the particularity of a given object at different levels, for different reasons. A person buying an apple for the purpose of eating it might be more interested in its ripeness than its greenness, while an artist who is buying it for use as a model to produce a still life painting might be more interested in its colour. For the purposes of comparison, it is possible to devise innumerable such standards, at different levels of abstraction, covering a broader or narrower category of comparable things. Thus, if I barter my title to an apple for a title to a pear, I might say that the pear is a lighter green than the apple but is rather less ripe; this is not the kind of comparison I could meaningfully make if I had swapped my apple for cash or some shares in a company. This type of variable and context-specific evaluative standard can serve the purposes of comparison, but does not work as a standard of valuation that can be used for the purposes of exchange. For the purposes of exchange, it is necessary to introduce an evaluative standard that not only allows one object to be related to another, but also allows them to be related in a particular quantitative sense: that is, in the sense that allows us to say 'that an *amount* of *x* is worth the same as another *amount* of *y*, irrespective of the particularities of *x* and *y*'.[161] In other words, if we wish not only to compare *x* and *y*, 2.95

characters in *Lady Windemere's Fan*, citing Lord Darlington's famous definition of a cynic as 'a man who knows the price of everything and the value of nothing'. See O Wilde, *The Importance of Being Earnest and Other Plays* (OUP 2008 reissue) 45.

[159] GK Chesterton, 'Reflections on a Rotten Apple' in *The Well and the Shallows* (Ignatius Press 2006) 163, 172.

[160] Lodder (n 149) 16. [161] Lodder (n 160).

but to introduce a standard by which they can be treated as interchangeable, we will need to express our evaluative standards in the language of units of account.

2.96 As Lodder suggests, we might invent different units of account that serve this function in different contexts: thus, for example, the rules of a game may stipulate that one black marble is worth three white marbles and seven gold ones.[162] However, if we set aside such artificially self-contained systems of valuation, the value of a commodity in a given society can normally be expressed in terms of money. This is because money is the universal denominator of value: by the very definition of 'money', all commodities[163] can be exchanged for it. As a result, the indirect exchange ratios between all commodities in the economic system can be expressed by a sum of money.[164] If an apple is worth ten pears to me, I can express this by saying that I would pay £1 for an apple but only 10p for a pear. This preference of mine may or may not reflect the aggregate preferences of others in the society in which I live. It may be that an apple is worth £1 to me, personally, but I know that I could sell it in a competitive market for only 50p, while I could buy a pear for £1; other participants in the market for fruit do not share my preference for apples over pears. If my interest in the apple is only as a marketable commodity, its value to me will track the market value, whatever it is; it will drop to 50p when the market value drops to that figure, and rise to £1 when the market value rises. However, I might personally value the apple for other reasons—for example, because I wish to eat or paint it—and, in such a situation, my personal valuation of it need not fluctuate with the market value. I might prefer one apple to ten pears, whatever the market says, and therefore refuse to part with my apples at the market price of 50p each.

2.97 Thus, when we speak of value as a factual characteristic of assets, we are really describing a factual characteristic of persons, either individually or in the aggregate. We are describing the relative strength of individual preferences for those assets, either singly (as when we speak of a person's subjective valuation of the asset) or in the aggregate (as where we speak of objective market value). Unlike intrinsic qualities, we can sensibly speak of value in this sense as being transmitted from one asset to another. If I value mangos as much as apples, for example, I might be willing (assuming zero transaction costs) to barter one of my apples for a mango with a market price of £1. It would be an understandable figure of speech to say, in this context, that the £1 unit of value that I had at my disposal, which was previously embodied in the apple, is now to be found in the mango; this might be a metaphor to express the conclusion that I value the two equally, as evidenced by my decision to accept one in exchange for the other. Alternatively, if we are not interested in my personal valuation of the

[162] Lodder (n 149) 34.

[163] This characterization of money depends on defining 'commodity' as an asset that can be exchanged for money. Assets that cannot legally be exchanged for money can still be understood as possessing value, in this sense, if there is an illegal market for their sale. For example, in *R v Islam* [2009] UKHL 30, the House of Lords held that a court could calculate the market value of a consignment of heroin, for the purposes of making a confiscation order under the Proceeds of Crime Act 2002, by reference to the price which a willing buyer would pay to a willing seller in the illegal but well-established market for the sale of that commodity.

[164] Fox (n 49) 8.

apple, but instead in its market value, we might say that the 50p unit of market value that was previously embodied in the apple is now part of the £1 unit of value found in the mango. The two are not of equivalent market value, but I have parted with 50p of the market value at my disposal in order to obtain the £1 market value of the mango. That conclusion that might be expressed by saying that half the value of the mango represents the value that I had at my disposal before the sale of the apple.

The trouble, however, is that these accounts of what it means for value to be transmitted from asset to asset seem to have very little relevance to the operation of the law of tracing. Suppose, for example, that A holds a title to a car on trust for B. A's title to the car is worth £3,000 in terms of its market value; this is the price he is likely to obtain in exchange for it in a competitive market. Meanwhile, B's personal valuation of the car is £5,000; he would not be prepared to part with his beneficial interest in A's title to the car for less than that sum. Suppose that A then sells the title to the car to X, obtaining £4,000 in cash as its price. The £4,000 in cash is, as money, worth exactly £4,000 to both B and to participants in the market for cash generally.[165] In what sense can i be said that either the £3,000 market value of the legal title to the car, or B's £5,000 personal valuation of his own interest in the car, has now *become* the £4,000 value of the cash? The cash is worth more than the market value of the trustee's title to the car, and less than the beneficiary's personal valuation of his own interest in it. The only persons whose valuations of the car could be reflected in the transaction are the parties to it: X and A, who are willing to pay and willing to accept £4,000 to sell and to acquire it respectively. It is not clear why the law of tracing should be attentive to either of these valuations when the question is whether B, the claimant, can say that *his* value has moved from A's title to the car to A's title to the cash, given that A is a wrongdoer and X is a stranger. On an account of value as a factual characteristic of *B's* assets, we should be interested in either the market value of those assets or his personal valuation of them and A's transaction with X need not, and often will not, reflect either. 2.98

As Smith points out, the law of tracing takes no interest in the difference between the value of the asset actually obtained under a transaction and the value of the asset exchanged, understood in either factual sense. It will not allow A to argue that only £3,000 of the cash represents the traceable proceeds of the trust asset,[166] on the basis that this was the market value of his title to the car—the subject matter of 2.99

[165] Setting aside the possibility that the cash might be idiosyncratically valued by one or other party for some quality other than its status as money, eg because one of the notes is a rare one that is no longer in circulation.

[166] In this particular example, A might be liable to give up the extra £1,000 in any case, because it would represent an unauthorized profit made by a fiduciary: *FHR European Ventures LLP v Cedar Capital Partners LLC* [2014] UKSC 45. However, the identification of the full value of the £4000 in cash with the value of the title to the car does not depend on the availability of this remedy, as is evidenced by the fact that the outcome does not change where the defendant does not owe the normal fiduciary duties of loyalty to the claimant, as where she is a recipient of trust assets or a recipient of assets under a rescinded contract. *Trustee of FC Jones* (n 49), discussed at para 2 101 this chapter, is an example of such a case, where the claimant owed no fiduciary duty of loyalty to the defendant but was nevertheless not permitted to invoke the difference in market value between the misappropriated asset and the substitute to limit the operation of tracing from one into the other.

B's beneficial interest—at the time of the transaction. Nor can B argue that she can identify another £1,000 of A's cash as the traceable proceeds of the car, in addition in the £4,000 obtained from X, on the basis that A would have obtained £1,000 more from X if he had sold it only at a price that equalled B's personal valuation of her interest in the car.

2.100 It might be argued that the law does not pay attention to these possible differentials because they are too difficult to deal with on the facts of most real-world situations. That is, it might be argued that it is difficult to quantify the market value of the original trust asset, and even more difficult to calculate the beneficiary's personal valuation of that asset; therefore, the law depends on tracing as a rough-and-ready means of calculating the answer to one or other of these questions, treating any asset obtained under an exchange transaction as approximately equal in value to one or other of these valuations of the original asset. However, the law's radical indifference to such questions cannot be accounted for in this way.

2.101 In *Trustee of FC Jones v Jones*,[167] for example, Mrs Jones received some money from her husband, a bankrupt; he paid her £11,700 in cheques, which she subsequently invested in potato futures. As a result of her transactions, she eventually obtained a payout of £50,760 from the commodity brokers to whom she had paid the £11,700. Her husband's trustee in bankruptcy was able to identify the entire credit balance of the bank account into which the commodity brokers made this payment as the traceable proceeds of the cheques initially paid to her out of the bankrupt's estate. This decision cannot credibly be explained on the basis that it was too difficult for the law to calculate the actual value of two cheques with the face value of £11,700 and the judges, therefore, were prepared to presume that their value was the same as that of a bank account with a credit balance of £50,760. The market value of the cheques would have not been difficult to quantify, and the law does not usually permit individuals to claim that their personal valuation of money differs from its face value.[168] In any case, such an argument based on an idiosyncratic personal valuation could not plausibly have been made by the trustee in bankruptcy on the facts of *Trustee of FC Jones v Jones*; his only interest in the cheques could have been to realize them for the purpose of paying the debts owed to the husband's creditors, and he could hardly have said that he personally would only have parted with them at a price of £50,760.

2.102 As Cutts points out,[169] anyone can see that there is a clear—fivefold—difference between the value of the money initially taken from the bankrupt's estate and the money eventually obtained by Mrs Jones, as a result of her speculations. The transactional link inquiry is not necessary as an aid to making this comparison, and

[167] *Trustee of FC Jones* (n 49).

[168] See *BP Exploration Co (Libya) Ltd v Hunt (No 2)* [1979] 1 WLR 783 (subsequently affirmed by the Court of Appeal [1981] 1 WLR 232, and the House of Lords [1983] 2 AC 352), 799 (Robert Goff J): 'Money has the peculiar character of a universal medium of exchange. By its receipt, the recipient is inevitably benefited; and (subject to problems arising from such matters as inflation, change of position and the time value of money) the loss suffered by the plaintiff is generally equal to the defendant's gain, so that no difficulty arises concerning the amount to be repaid'.

[169] Cutts (n 5) 393.

is positively misleading in the answers it gives to the question of comparative value. Any case that involves tracing the proceeds of money is open to a similar objection. Courts routinely hold that money can be traced into assets that are manifestly worth more than the face value of the money, including other money. It is implausible to suppose that, when they are doing this, their goal is to calculate the value of the money originally misappropriated and compare it to the value of some money or other asset now in the hands of the defendant. Both these tasks are more straightforward than asking for proof of the transactional links that connect the money misappropriated and the asset now held by the defendant. If the only aim of the law is to find some asset now in the defendant's hands that is of equivalent value to the misappropriated asset, therefore, tracing is an irrationally complicated way of achieving that aim.

2.2.2. Value as a factual consequence of transactions

However, it may more plausibly be argued that the law is trying to solve a somewhat more complex factual question, and that tracing does serve as a relatively simple proxy for addressing that question. This is the argument made by Oesterle, Rotherham, and Sherwin, all of whom suggest that tracing serves as 'a complicated facade for a rough doctrine of causation',[170] a 'second-best means'[171] for promoting the law's aims, and an 'objective and mechanical'[172] means of solving an evidential problem that would otherwise be 'too costly and difficult'[173] to prove by direct evidence. This is the question whether the defendant's assets have been swollen as a result of his misappropriation of the claimant's asset. In the language of value, the task can be described as one of quantifying the total amount of value at the defendant's disposal and determining how much of that value arises as a causal consequence of the transaction involving the claimant's assets. 2.103

On this view, tracing is not concerned with value as a characteristic of particular assets but, rather, with value as an abstract description of the situation of a particular person. For example, take a defendant who has ten apples that are worth £1 each to him personally and 50p each on the open market. The total amount of value at his disposal—the value that he can exchange with others, to obtain other items of value—is £5. He may personally value each apple at £1, and therefore consider himself to be in possession of £10 of value, but this is not true from the perspective of the other persons with whom he must engage if he wishes to use his apples to obtain other items of value. It is clear that scholars who adopt this view of tracing are interested in the quantity of market value at the disposal of the defendant, as opposed to other abstract conceptions of value; this is apparent from their focus on 2.104

[170] Oesterle (n 157) 190.

[171] C Rotherham, 'Policy and Proprietary Remedies: Are We All Formalists Now?' (2012) 65 CLP 529, 532.

[172] E Sherwin, 'Constructive Trusts in Bankruptcy' [1989] University of Illinois Law Review 297, 333.

[173] Sherwin (n 172).

the impact of the defendant's transactions on his creditors in insolvency, rather than on him personally.[174]

2.105 If this analysis of tracing is correct, the goal of the tracing rules is to determine whether a defendant would have some valuable asset at his disposal—and thus, whether the value of that asset would be available to his creditors in insolvency—if he had not misappropriated the claimant's assets. The idea that value can move from the misappropriated asset to some substitute would then be a metaphor to express this causal claim: but for the defendant's decision to deprive the claimant of the value of his asset, the defendant would not now have the value of the substitute asset at his disposal. For example, in *Trustee of FC Jones v Jones*, the argument would be that Mrs Jones would not have obtained the £50,760 credit balance of her bank account if she had not received the £11,700 cheques from her husband.

2.106 This is an argument based on causation. It depends on showing that, but for Mrs Jones' acquisition of the cheques from her husband, she would not have invested in potato futures at all and would not, therefore, have obtained the £50,760 from the commodity brokers. Proponents of this version of a value model of tracing argue that a fact of this kind is very difficult to prove—since it depends on a counter-factual hypothesis about what Mrs Jones would have done if she had not taken the cheques—and, therefore, proof of transactional links between the cheques and the bank account serve as a second-best mechanism for proving a direct causal link.

2.107 As a doctrinal interpretation of English law, however, this analysis is difficult to square with the courts' firm rejection of causal arguments in situations where evidence supporting plausible claims about causal links—or their absence—is clearly available. If tracing is about causation, it ought to fail where the defendant can prove that his misappropriation of the claimant's asset has not, as things have turned out, enabled him to obtain any increase in the aggregate value at his disposal at the time of litigation. On the facts of *Foskett v McKeown*, for example, the death benefit would have been paid to the defendants even if Mr Murphy had not misappropriated the trust money. That fact is deducible from the terms of the contract between Barclays and Murphy, without any necessity of posing complex counter-factual questions about broader motives and habits of Mr Murphy. Nevertheless, the majority expressly refused to treat the evidence concerning causation as relevant and compelled the defendants to give up a proportion of the death benefit to the claimants, despite the absence of any causal link between the acquisition of the value of the death benefit and the misappropriation of the claimant's assets.

2.108 If Sherwin is right, judges reach conclusions of this kind because they find the causal question too evidentially difficult to answer in many situations; having substituted the easier transactional link question for the difficult causal question, they then apply the transactional approach 'mechanically' to all cases, without regard to any evidence that might actually support either party's contentions on causation. However, such an approach is difficult to justify in principled terms. If the reason for requiring a defendant to give up an asset is based on arguments about causation,

[174] See, especially, Sherwin (n 172) 297, 305–13.

it seems unfair to prevent the defendant from making the relevant arguments about causation when he has the facts on his side, merely because the facts might be harder to prove in some other situation. This unfairness is particularly pronounced in a case like *Foskett v McKeown*, where the defendants were not liable because of their own wrongdoing, but because they were innocent recipients from a wrongdoer.

Similarly, a claimant would be entitled to object to the exclusion of arguments based on causation in situations where the evidence is on his side. There may well be cases where the claimant can, in fact, prove that the defendant is better off by a particular amount as a result of a misappropriation, and this may have nothing to do with his fortuitous decision to use one bank account rather than another in entering into some enriching transaction, or with the chronological order of his transactions. 2.109

For example, suppose that a defendant trustee pays £1,000 of trust money into her personal bank account, which is already in credit by £1,000. The total market value of all her assets before the misappropriation, including the bank account, was £5,000. If we ask whether she is better off as a result of the misappropriation at this point, the answer is yes: the total amount of value at her disposal has been increased to £6,000, and this increase would not have happened but for the misappropriation. The same conclusion could be as easily reached if, instead of paying the £1,000 into her existing bank account, she had used it to open a new bank account. No special evidential problems apply in the first case that do not apply in the second; increasing the market value of an existing asset is as straightforwardly an increase in the pool of value at the disposal of the defendant as the acquisition of a new asset would be. The supposed evidential problems created by mixed substitutions vanish on this account of what it means to identify value. 2.110

The same is true if the trustee enters into new transactions after the misappropriation. In determining whether she still has extra value at her disposal, and how much, the facts that matter are whether she has made good investments or bad ones, and whether any of those investments—good or bad—would have been made even if she had not misappropriated the trust assets. For example, suppose the trustee in our example withdraws £500 from the £2,000 credit balance of the mixed bank account and uses it to buy a title to a painting with a market value of £400. The effect of this transaction is to reduce her overall wealth by £100; the credit balance of the account is now £1,500 and the title to the painting is worth £400, reducing the value at her disposal from £6,000 to £5,900. 2.111

Does this represent a reduction in the £1,000 increase in her wealth obtained as a result of the misappropriation? That depends on whether she would have bought the painting even without access to the trust money. If she would have made the purchase regardless, she is still enriched by £1,000. But for the trust money, she would have taken £500 from somewhere else—perhaps by reducing the credit balance of her bank account, or perhaps by making use of some other asset—to buy the painting and would have reduced her total wealth to £4,900 by her bad bargain. Thanks to the trust money, she has a total wealth of £5,900 instead, and is still better off by £1,000. On the other hand, if she would not have bought the painting without the extra £1,000 at her disposal, the bad bargain could be said to have reduced the amount of her original gain. But for the misappropriation, her wealth 2.112

would have been £5,000, as she would have left her existing assets alone. As a result of the misappropriation, and the spending causally linked to the misappropriation, her wealth is now £,5900. The value received from the claimant that survives in her hands has thus been reduced from its initial peak of £1,000 to £900.

2.113 The issues are exactly the same in the scenario where the trustee has paid the £1,000 trust money into a new bank account, instead of paying it into her existing account. If she withdrew £500 from this account to buy a £400 painting, this need not necessarily mean that she has diminished her initial £1,000 gain in value. Again, whether she had done so would depend on the context of her transaction, and her motives in entering into it, and not the particular asset she happens to use when entering into that transaction.

2.114 Questions about reductions in overall wealth are, therefore, answerable by an investigation of facts about the context and motives of the defendant's transactions. It is true that, in many situations, these facts may be difficult to investigate; evidence of a person's motives may be elusive and the counter-factual question what the defendant would have done without access to the claimant's wealth may be hard to answer. Where such evidence is unavailable, the presumption against the wrongdoer in *Armory v Delamirie* might be invoked; thus, absent adequate evidence relevant to causation, the court could justify finding that the trustee would have bought the painting using her own money, whether or not she had taken the trust money, and drawn the negative inference that she is still enriched by the trust £1,000. This limited use of presumptions against a wrongdoer, in the absence of relevant evidence, does not explain the law's actual use of the cherry-picking rule in all situations of mixed substitution. Difficulties in proving causal links are not, in Smith's terminology, problems of evidential impossibility. In many situations involving mixed substitutions, relevant evidence might be available and could be used to prove the causal connection—or absence of causal connection—between a misappropriation and a reduction or increase in wealth, to the balance of probabilities standard.

2.115 Take, for instance, cases where a defendant makes a payment under an existing debt or arrangement with a third party, which preceded the act of misappropriation. For example, suppose a trustee owes her landlord £2,000 a month in rent and empties a mixed bank account, which includes £1,000 of trust money, to pay this sum. It is a plausible inference from the facts—the trustee has a legal obligation to pay rent, and a very good practical reason to do so—that she would have used her own resources to pay the rent if the misappropriation had not taken place. Thus, she is still better off by £1,000 because she has taken the trust money, even if she has exhausted a particular bank account at her disposal. A similar argument could be made in the *Lipkin Gorman v Karpnale*[175] scenario of a long-established gambling addiction. A court could be persuaded that, on the balance of probabilities, an addict would have used her own money to gamble even if she had not taken trust money. The converse argument could be made in cases where, immediately after the

[175] [1991] 2 AC 548.

misappropriation, the trustee begins to make extravagant gifts to third parties or to make risky investments of a kind she has never made before. In such cases, it would be possible to persuade a court that the gifts or investments would not have been made but for the misappropriation, and that these payments ought, therefore, to be treated as genuine reductions in value surviving in the trustee's hands.

Thus, this version of the value question makes very little sense of the actual rules of tracing. The evidential impossibility of identifying value in a mixed substitution, which Smith calls on to justify the principle of subordination of wrongdoers, does not exist on this view and the justification for both cherry-picking and the lowest intermediate balance rule drops away at the same time. 2.116

As we have seen, cherry-picking allows claimants to assert—with the benefit of hindsight—that a wrongdoing defendant has made all her good bargains using their value and all her bad bargains using her own, provided that these bargains involved drawing on the specific mixed fund created by the act of misappropriation. The lowest intermediate balance rule forbids claimants from asserting that the defendant still has the value of their asset if the mixed fund has been exhausted and no specific asset was acquired by drawing on it before its exhaustion. In order to reconcile either rule with the abstract fund conception of value, they would need to be explained as a set of deeply implausible psychological inferences. We would need to say that misappropriating others' assets always motivates a wrongdoer to make good bargains, which she would not otherwise have made, while leaving her propensity to make bad bargains unaffected—until the moment when she exhausts a particular mixed fund, when she ceases to make any bargains that are motivated by her access to the claimants' wealth. Both are obviously implausible as factual inferences from the evidence, and it is not clear why a court would draw such inferences in cases where plausible evidence of causation is, in fact, available. 2.117

2.2.3. Locating value without the aid of substitutions?

Thus, there is a clear lack of fit between the transactional focus of the tracing rules and the causal question about value that many scholars suggest that those rules are designed to answer. It is difficult to justify this lack of fit on the basis that the law of tracing is attempting to evade difficult factual problems by adopting a simpler and less forensically demanding approach to answering that question. However, it has been suggested that this problem of lack of fit does not arise because the value question is the wrong question—the rules are, indeed, intended to answer that very question—but because the rules are imperfect and in need of reform. Oesterle, for example, has argued that 'more accurate and yet equally practical rules are possible',[176] which aim to determine when, and by how much, a defendant has made himself better off as a result of a misappropriation. A swollen assets version of tracing,[177] notably the augmentation version proposed by Evans, might be proposed on this basis. 2.118

[176] Oesterle (n 157) 191.

[177] Discussed in Chapter 1 this volume, Section 1.1.3.

2.119 In line with the underlying model of value as an abstract description of a person's financial situation, rather than as a characteristic of particular assets, these approaches to tracing jettison the requirement of transactional links between specific assets. They focus, instead, on the causal consequences of the defendant's actions. Some focus on causation as it relates to particular assets, looking at whether the defendant has acquired or retained some specific asset as a result of his initial misappropriation. Such a model would capture scenarios like that of Oesterle's thief, who still has some gold coins because he has spent the claimant's money on meeting his necessary expenses instead. Others, like Evans' model, focus on the consequences of the defendant's misappropriation as it affects the abstract amount of value at his disposal. This approach would apply in situations where a defendant is causally better off by some abstract amount, but where no specific asset can be pointed to as embodying this increase in the value at his disposal. Evans' swollen assets model would allow the claimant to say that a fraction of the value of each and every asset held by such a defendant represents the value of the misappropriated asset, and thus to claim a charge over all the assets securing a duty to pay over this amount.

2.120 As a matter of authority, the problem with all such models is that the English courts have so firmly and frequently rejected them.[178] Based on these decisions, the requirement of substitutions seems to be so important to the basic concept of tracing that a model that jettisons the requirement seems to be less an interpretation of the existing law than a proposal for its wholesale replacement. However, it might be suggested that there is a contradiction between these decisions and the courts' embrace of value language in describing the aim of tracing. It could be argued that, for the sake of coherence, the judges must either accept the swollen assets model of tracing, or give up the idea that the aim of tracing is to locate value.

2.3. Value as a Legal Construct

2.121 Cutts proposes that the courts take the latter approach. She suggests that the focus on transactions is central to the current law, but that the language of value is both redundant and misleading;[179] the real aim of the law is simply to determine the legal consequences of the defendant's transactions, an issue that ultimately depends on his intentions, and that should be addressed through a straightforward exercise of interpreting intentional transactions. However, this approach to tracing is, in its way, as inconsistent with authority as the swollen assets approach.

2.3.1. Problems with jettisoning the value model

2.122 One reason to be cautious about simply abandoning the link between tracing and some conception of value is the ubiquity of the recent judicial acceptance of the language of value. Judicial reasoning about tracing is now so dominated by the

[178] See the survey of the authorities in Chapter 1 this volume, Section 1.1.3.
[179] Cutts (n 5) 404.

idea—or, at least, the vocabulary—of value that an account of their decisions that discards that idea entirely, as wholly meaningless, lacks interpretive credibility.

However, the authority of the value model does not merely depend on the string of twenty-first century cases, following *Foskett v McKeown*, that expressly invoke the concept in describing the operation of tracing. As has been discussed, that language was initially proposed to account for long-entrenched features of the law that are puzzling without it. The key idea is that, just as following is about the location of assets, tracing is about locating the *value* of assets. Without some such idea, describing both the analogy and the distinction between tracing and following, it is difficult to know what to make of the substantive similarity between the rules of tracing and the rules of following, in the light of the analytical difference between the two processes highlighted by Birks and Smith. The approach of Birks and Smith, while highlighting the fictional character of older descriptions of tracing as a sub-category of following, preserves the continuity between the two by emphasizing that both are processes of identification and that the challenges of identifying value are in some ways similar to those of identifying things. 2.123

This argument only works if we can understand what identifying value means, and—given the incompatibility between the transactional character of tracing and any project of identifying value in its factual sense—define it in terms that are not evidential in character. However, it is only if we cannot find any alternative conception of value that makes sense of the law that we should reject the language of value outright. This is because such a rejection would not mean only that the judges have been simply misguided in their explanations of tracing over the past decade. It would also mean that the substantive rules of tracing are difficult to justify; they depend on an inexplicable analogy between deciding what a defendant intended when he acquired some asset, and deciding whether a claimant's wheat or beaver skins can be identified despite a defendant's decision to mix or transform these physical things. The basis for this analogy, which is so deeply rooted in the case law, simply falls away on Cutts' analysis. So, as a result, do the positive rules of tracing as they have developed since the nineteenth century. 2.124

Like proponents of the swollen assets model, Cutts rejects as misguided the current law's focus on identifying the particular legal mechanism by which a defendant acquires an asset, as a result of his decision to misappropriate a claimant's asset. What matters, in her view, is whether the parties to the claimant's acquisition of an asset intended that acquisition to be linked to his disposal of the claimant's asset: that is, whether their 'overall design'[180] reflected an intention that the defendant acquire the new asset as a result of dealing with the claimant's asset. This may be evidenced by the fact of a direct exchange between the two, but such evidence is neither conclusive nor necessary. 2.125

Thus, for example, she notes[181] that the law currently allows tracing where A pays £1,000 into a bank account held by C, and C then instructs his bank to credit B's account with £1,000, debiting that very account. In this scenario, a claimant 2.126

[180] Cutts (n 5) 401–02. [181] Cutts (n 5) 402.

entitled to the £1,000 paid into the account can say that the £1,000 received by B represents the traceable proceeds of his money. By contrast, where A pays £1,000 into a bank account held by C, and C then instructs his bank to debit a different account and pay £1,000 to B, the orthodox view is that the money received by B does not represent the traceable proceeds of the money initially paid by A.

2.127 Cutts suggests that, once the misleading idea of value moving from asset to asset is abandoned, we can see that it is irrational to distinguish between these two scenarios and to say that tracing is always possible in the first and impossible in the second. If A, when he paid C, did not intend to bring about the payment to B, it is not accurate to say that the £1,000 received by B represents the proceeds of the first payment just because C happened to draw on that particular bank account into which the payment was made. The fact that the same account was used to execute each step in the series of events that led to B's acquisition of the £1,000 'might be evidence pointing towards such a conclusion, but it is not itself conclusive'.[182] Conversely, the fact that B received money from one account in C's name does not exclude a finding that the money represents the traceable proceeds of money paid into a different account.

2.128 This approach, as Cutts acknowledges,[183] contrasts sharply with the traditional approach of the courts to tracing. In *Federal Republic of Brazil v Durant International Corporation*,[184] the Privy Council did hold that the overall purpose and effect of the defendant's transactions could be relevant to tracing in a case where there was no strictly chronological series of transactional links. However, Lord Toulson JSC presented this 'overall purpose and effect'[185] test as one with a limited field of application. He said that 'if the court is satisfied the various steps are part of a co-ordinated scheme',[186] it should then ignore any 'camouflage of interconnected transactions'[187] and permit tracing even if, 'either as a deliberate part of the choreography or possibly because of the incidents of the banking system',[188] credits and debits did not appear in the respective bank accounts of the defendant, his intermediary, and a recipient in a strictly chronological order. In such a case, all these credits and debits were to be treated as part of a single transaction, by which the 'depletion of the trust fund'[189] had been coordinated to bring about the acquisition of the substitute asset. He added that this finding had no bearing on the correctness of the decision in *James Roscoe (Bolton) v Winder*[190] and the lowest intermediate balance rule, because there was no suggestion in that case that there had been 'an overall transaction embracing the co-ordinated outward and inward movement of assets'.[191]

2.129 Thus, the approach in *Brazil v Durant International Corporation*, if accepted in English law, represents a limited exception from law's default approach, which is to focus on the particular repository of value that the defendant is dealing with, and the chronological order of his transactions. If he has emptied his bank account before crediting it with more money, this will normally prevent a claimant whose money was paid into the account before it was emptied from tracing into the increased

[182] Cutts (n 5) 401. [183] Cutts (n 5) 403. [184] [2015] UKPC 35.
[185] *Federal Republic of Brazil* (n 184) [38]. [186] *Federal Republic of Brazil* (n 184) [37].
[187] *Federal Republic of Brazil* (n 185) [188] *Federal Republic of Brazil* (n 186)
[189] *Federal Republic of Brazil* (n 184) [40]. [190] [1915] 1 Ch 62.
[191] *Federal Republic of Brazil* (n 184) [41].

credit balance. If he has paid the claimant's money into one account, which he has emptied by transactions that do not involve the acquisition of any specific asset, the claimant cannot point to a different account held by him as the traceable proceeds of the money originally paid into the emptied account. The motives of the defendant and the party he is dealing with—the overall purpose and effect of their mutual dealings—can displace these principles, according to *Brazil v Durant International Corporation*, in situations where these parties have deliberately created a co-ordinated scheme to facilitate the defendant's acquisition of one asset by disposing of another. In the absence of any such scheme, the rules of tracing remain tightly focused on identifying the particular fund that the defendant has made use of in acquiring a new asset, and this process is not merely an inquiry into the defendant's intentions.

The recent case of *FHR European Ventures LLP v Mankarious*[192] provides a good illustration of this traditional focus and its objective character. In that case, the second defendant, a company controlled by the first defendant, had received €10m in bribes, in breach of fiduciary duties owed to the claimants. The Supreme Court had decided[193] that these bribes were held, from the moment they were received, on a constructive trust for the claimants. The claimants then brought an action in the High Court, seeking, inter alia, a declaration of the extent of the equitable charge they held over the first defendant's freehold title to a house. It was conceded that £695,715.44 of the £1.8m purchase price of the house was derived from the bribe money; the disagreement was about how much of the £180,000 deposit paid by the first defendant was also derived from that money. 2.130

The €10m bribe had been paid into the second defendant's euro account with a Jersey bank in January 2005; immediately before the payment, the credit balance of this account was nil. The second defendant had also held a dollar account and a sterling account with the same bank. On 25 January 2005, the credit balance of the sterling account was nil. On that day, the account was credited with £251,137.97 from another source, and the balance was subsequently reduced to £101,047.97. In April 2005, the second defendant transferred £78,982.03 from the euro account, into which the trust money had been paid, to the sterling account. It then paid £180,000 to the vendor of the house, as the deposit. The claimants argued, invoking *Re Oatway*,[194] that the entirety of the deposit represented trust money. They said that the second defendant's bank accounts with the Jersey bank all represented a single mixed fund, and that—following *Re Oatway*—they were entitled to say that any profitable investment made using that fund represented the traceable proceeds of the trust money. 2.131

Master Clark rejected this argument, holding that the three bank accounts could not be treated as a single fund; each bank account was a separate asset, and the sterling bank account had become a mixed fund only when the £78,982.03 of trust money had been paid into it. On this basis, he held that—following *Re Hallett's Estate*—the trust money could have been the source of only £78,982.03 of the deposit and the 2.132

[192] [2016] EWHC 359.
[193] *FHR European Ventures LLP and others (Respondents) v Cedar Capital Partners LLC* [2014] UKSC 45.
[194] *Re Oatway* (n 73).

rest of the money must have come from the £101,047.97 in that account that was held by the defendant free from the trust.

2.133 In deciding whether the funds were mixed, Master Clark resorted to the traditional *Pennell v Deffell*[195] approach, drawing an analogy with following. What if, he asked,[196] the defendant had simply received and retained the bribe money as cash, and had paid the £101,047.97 from another source into a new bank account? In this scenario, there would be no mixed fund; the cash would be one asset, and the credit balance of the bank would be another. If the defendant untraceably spent the cash, the claimants could not have asserted that its value had been mixed with the bank account so that they could trace into transactions drawing on the bank account. The fact that they could physically identify their cash in the hands of the defendant would have precluded tracing its value into some other asset held by the defendant at the same time. Master Clark then concluded that there was no basis for a principled distinction between this scenario and one which the money was not retained as cash but paid into a new bank account, whether at the same bank where defendant's other accounts were held, or at a different bank. He said there was 'no distinction in principle to be drawn between these cases—as a matter of fact, the funds are not mixed'.[197]

2.134 It is difficult to explain this as a decision about the intention of the defendant or the vendor in entering into their transaction. It could be argued that the defendant, in paying the deposit on the house, *meant* to dispose of the £101,047.97 balance of the sterling account and not to use the balance of the euro account, directly or indirectly, except for the £78,982.03 that had been transferred into the sterling account already. But there is no evidence that Master Clark paid any attention to this question in deciding that this was what he had done. It was not the intention of the defendant that mattered, but the objective fact that he had used the sterling account at a moment in time when only £78,982.03 of the trust money had ever been paid into it.

2.135 This approach implies that an inquiry into whether a mixed substitution has taken place, such that a mixed fund can be identified, is an objective inquiry. It does not depend solely on evidence of the defendants' intentions or motives in entering into a transaction. This does not mean that evidence of intention is irrelevant, however. If it could have been shown that the vendor and the defendants had agreed that the money to buy the house would be paid out of the sterling account, but that the euro account would immediately be used to replenish that account, it is possible that the 'co-ordinated scheme' threshold would have been met and the *Brazil v Durant International Corporation* test could have been invoked by the claimants to overcome the problem that no mixed fund was, in fact, created by the defendants. But the question whether a mixed fund was created is not, itself, a pure question of intention and can be answered without reference to any positive evidence of intention.

2.136 If we take tracing to be a process of locating the value of the bribe money, in some sense, the decision in *FHR* can be better explained. Master Clark's decision can be

[195] See para 2.24 this chapter (n 59).
[196] *Mankarious* (n 192) [40].
[197] *Mankarious* (n 196).

understood as a decision that the value of the bribe money was to be found in the euro account, not the sterling account, until the moment that an actual transfer from one account to the other was executed. The analogy with following supports his approach. Cash that has been put in a drawer can be identified as being in that drawer and not elsewhere—such as mixed in a box of other cash—until a factual mixture has actually taken place. A claimant who is following cash[198] cannot argue that it has been physically mixed with some other cash of the defendant, for the purpose of invoking the cherry-picking rule, in a situation where no such physical mixture has taken place. In the same way, a claimant who is tracing value cannot argue that it has been mixed with some other value, for the purpose of invoking the cherry-picking rule, in a situation where no such mixture has taken place. The idea that tracing is about locating value makes more sense of decisions of this kind than the idea that it has nothing to do with questions of identification and is merely an exercise in interpreting the intentions of a person who has entered into a transaction.

2.3.2. Value as a dimension of rights: tracing and the power to control assets

As has been shown, however, the explanatory power of the value account of tracing, despite its intuitive appeal in making sense of the analogy between tracing and following, is limited by the ambiguity of the core concept of 'value'. Standard factual conceptions of value—as a characteristic of an asset, or as a description of a person's situation—are inconsistent with the transactional approach of the current law of tracing, and the law would require a radical overhaul to render the two consistent. 2.137

Smith accounts for this inconsistency by denying that tracing has anything to do with value in any of these factual senses, which allow us to describe the value of some asset as a 'fixed monetary amount' reflecting its worth. Instead, he says, the term 'value' in this context 'simply reifies that which inheres in an asset and which can be seen as passing into another form when that asset is exchanged for another asset'.[199] The question is what, if anything, this means and how it can support the appeal of the value model as an explanation of the tracing/following analogy. What is this 'value' that 'inheres in an asset', and can pass into another form as a result of an exchange transaction? What is the basis of an analogy between identifying value in this sense and identifying, for example, oil in a mixture? 2.138

Smith explains that value, in this sense, describes an aspect of what it means to own something. When a £100 note is used to buy a painting, he notes, it is 'the value inherent in *ownership* of the banknote' that is traceable into '*ownership* of the painting'.[200] The monetary value of ownership of the painting may be more, less, or 2.139

[198] It has been argued that physically following cash into a mixture is impossible at common law because of the principle that 'money has no earmark': for an overview of the authorities that supposedly support this proposition, and the argument that the law is much more limited in its effects, see Chapter 3, Section 3.3.2.1 this volume. However, as dicta in *Re Hallett's Estate* and other cases suggest, no such obstacle to following cash into mixtures exists for a holder of equitable title to the cash: see Fox (n 49) 247–50.

[199] Smith (n 1) 16.

[200] Smith (n 1) 16–17 (emphasis added).

the same as the monetary value of the ownership of the bank account. Nevertheless, when one right is exchanged for the other in a clean substitution, the value of the new right is wholly attributable to the other. This definition suggests that tracing is possible where one's ownership of a new asset—such as a painting—is attributable to one's ownership of some other asset, such as a bank account. Value, in this context, does not describe the monetary worth of an asset to someone, or on the market, but a dimension of what it means to legally own that asset.

2.140 The idea that ownership of assets includes ownership of their value is usually taken to mean that an owner not only has the liberty to make use of the asset, and the right to exclude others from it, but also the power to dispose of it. Weinrib, for example, following Hegel, describes this dimension of ownership as the right to realize the value of the asset that one owns through 'a set of legal operations–exchange and liability'.[201] In other words, owning the value of an asset means that one has the legal power to exchange it for something else, and the right to be compensated if the asset is injured or lost. On this view, a defendant who uses his ownership of a banknote to buy ownership of a painting has realized the value of the banknote by making the decision that the ownership of the painting is an adequate substitute—to him—for his ownership of the banknote. A defendant who has not decided to make a swap but whose asset has been lost or damaged may recover the value he *could* have obtained by exchanging it,[202] but for the wrong. Where an actual exchange transaction has taken place, it can be said that the value of the defendant's ownership of the banknote is now reflected in his ownership of the painting in this sense. His decision to acquire the painting is only made possible, as a matter of law, because of his ownership of the banknote: to be precise, because he possesses the legal power to alienate the banknote. The assets he obtains as a result of that decision, therefore, represent the realization of the value of that ownership, or of that legal power.

2.141 On this interpretation of the value model, the aim of tracing is to answer the question whether the defendant's acquisition of an asset is attributable to his decision to exercise a particular legal power, which he possesses by virtue of his ownership of another asset. Intention is, of course, important to this question—we may need to know what the defendant meant to do in order to know if he has, in fact, exercised a power—but it does not exhaust its content. What matters is whether the very legal power exercised by the defendant, in entering into a transaction, belongs to him only in virtue of his legal ownership of the asset. Thus, for example, suppose a defendant has a legal title to a banknote worth £100 and also has a bank account with a £100 credit balance. When he transfers the legal title to the banknote to X, and obtains a title to a painting in exchange, we have seen that he may or may not be worse off—he may or may not still have £100 of value at his disposal, in the factual sense. Nevertheless, he has obtained the title to the painting by using the legal power he possesses as owner of the banknote, and *not* the legal power he possesses as holder of the bank account. In this sense, we can say he has realized the value of one asset and not the other.

[201] E Weinrib, 'Correctively Unjust Enrichment' in Chambers, Mitchell, and Penner (n 150) 31, 34.
[202] *Kuwait Airways Corp v Iraqi Airways Co (No 6)* [2002] UKHL 19, [67] (Lord Nicholls).

Similarly, if another defendant draws on one particular bank account to buy a title to some land, it is the powers of disposition that he has as holder of *that* account that he has used to acquire the title to land. The fact that he happens to have another account with the same bank, or that he happens to have some cash in a drawer elsewhere, are equally irrelevant to the question which asset he has actually used to acquire the new asset: that is, the question which legal power, held by him, was actually exercised in his acquisition of that asset. 2.142

An account of tracing in these terms is, however, complicated by the fact that it is not the defendant who is supposedly tracing his value through these transactions. The basic structure of a claim based on tracing is that a claimant asserts that a defendant's decisions—his exercises of legal power in respect of some asset—have had the effect of realizing the *claimant's* value. How can such an approach be squared with the idea that ownership of value, by definition, consists in the power to make these decisions in the first place? A person who holds a legal title to a banknote can say that he is entitled to its value because he is entitled to decide whether, when, and for what, his title to that note will be exchanged. What are we to make of the assertion, made by such a claimant, that someone *else's* decision[203] to deal with the banknote represents a realization of the value of her own title to that note? 2.143

In this context, it is helpful to return to Weinrib's explanation of the two sets of legal operations that reflect the right to value. One dimension of value is the power of exchange. The other, according to Weinrib, is liability: the right to be compensated when others have wrongfully rendered exchange of the asset more difficult or impossible. These two elements of ownership are formally distinct, and may often be vested in different persons in English law. Thus, for example, such a division is at the heart of the institution of the trust. The trustee genuinely has ownership of the trust asset, and this includes possessing the legal powers to deal with or dispose of that asset. These powers reflect a key dimension of the right to value: they mean that the trustee has the legal capacity to decide when, and in exchange for what, the trust asset will be transferred to others. The beneficiary under the trust possesses the power to alienate her own interest in the trust asset, but has no power to deal with the trust asset itself. However, the trustee may be liable to her for the consequences of any exercise of that power. He owes her duties governing his exercise of his legal powers to deal with the trust asset and will be liable to account for the value of that asset if he breaches these duties. Thus, the beneficiary and trustee both hold a right to value, in rather different senses. The trustee has the power to control whether or how the value of the asset is realized; the beneficiary has a right to have that power exercised for her benefit, if at all, and to obtain a remedy if it is wrongfully exercised. 2.144

From this perspective, then, we can say that a claimant who asserts that the defendant's transaction has had the effect of realizing the value of *her* asset is making two arguments. First, she is arguing that the defendant's decision does qualify as a realization of the value of that very asset. That is, she is contending that he had, and 2.145

[203] Cf J Penner, 'Value, Property, and Unjust Enrichment: Trusts of Traceable Proceeds' in Chambers, Mitchell, and Penner (n 150) 306, 309: 'the right regarding value which ownership gives us . . . is a right to *act* in a certain way, not a right *to something* that is somehow already there'.

has exercised, legal powers to exchange or otherwise deal with the asset, and that this is the mechanism by which he has obtained some other asset now in his hands. Secondly, she is arguing that this exercise of power was a wrong; the decision was a realization of *her* value because she was owed a duty in relation to that exercise of power that has been breached. She is, in other words, asserting that the defendant has validly exercised a legal power over her in order to acquire the asset that he now holds, in circumstances where that exercise of that power was a breach of duty.

2.3.3. Tracing value and following things

2.146 The idea that such a claimant is *tracing* the *value* of her original asset describes this complex double claim in metaphorical terms. As Smith notes, the metaphor of value is a reifying one; it imagines that the claimant has an entitlement to some underlying quality or thing that inheres in the asset held by the defendant, and survives his decision to dispose of it in a new form. The old cases simply said that the asset itself survives the change in its form brought about as a result of the substitution; the modern cases say that the *value* of the asset survives into its substitutes.

2.147 Neither description captures a literal truth. The value of an asset cannot be 'located' in the ordinary spatial sense of the word; it is not a physical object that can be put in a bank account as a car is parked in a garage. When we say that the value of some cash is now in a bank account we are using a metaphor that, translated into literal terms, means that the account holder acquired the bank account by exercising his legal power to deal with the cash. The language of value is an intelligible way of describing this event—the defendant realized the value of the cash by opening the bank account, and so the claimant can locate the value of the cash in the bank account—but it does depend on metaphor. This does not mean, however, that it is inferior to the literal description of the event. In one sense, the metaphorical account is better, as long as we take it seriously as a metaphor; it tells us more than the literal description about the justification for the law's response to events of this kind and its reasons for treating them as analogous to events like physical transformation and mixture.

2.148 The reifying metaphor implies that something that belonged to the claimant at the start of the story is still in the hands of the defendant, albeit in a new form. This suggests two things about the law's response to a substitution. First, it captures the very old idea that substitution is an event that *ought* to make no difference to the claimant's rights; her entitlement to her value persists, despite the fact that her entitlement to a specific asset has been altered as a result of the defendant's decision. In this way, the metaphor of surviving value clarifies the connection between substitution and physical transformation, which underpins the older metaphor of tracing as a response to a change in form; both are events that alter the claimant's legal position in relation to some asset, in circumstances where the law considers that no such change ought to have taken place. Secondly, however, the introduction of the language of value refines that metaphor by drawing attention to the distinction between tracing and following. A wrongful physical transformation may wrongfully alter rights, just as a wrongful substitution does, but the two events are importantly different.

2.149 On this view, the analogy between tracing and following depends on understanding both as concerned with the consequences of a wrongful but effective decision by a defendant to alter the rights of a claimant. For example, consider Smith's example of a situation where A has taken B's car and painted it. In this situation, B's title to her car remains vested in her, but her practical ability to separate her title to her car from A's title to his paint is gone. One or other party, in this situation, must, in fact, lose his pre-existing legal rights. Either A still has his undisturbed title to his paint, or B still has her undisturbed title to the car. When courts hold that B can assert her title to her car despite the fact that it has been painted, or that she still has her title to some beaver skins despite the fact that they have been turned into a coat,[204] they are not merely stating facts that B has proven by recourse to evidence. They are describing a conclusion of law, holding that B's title survives, and A's does not.

2.150 Similarly, when B complains that A has taken banknotes held on trust for her and given them to a bank, receiving a new bank account in exchange, she is complaining that it is no longer possible for her to assert her entitlement to the banknotes as she could have done before A's exercise of his power to dispose of the notes to the bank. It is true that, as Smith points out, nothing has happened to the notes themselves—they have gone into a drawer in the bank—but something has happened to the claimant's entitlement to those notes. Her trustee no longer has title to the banknotes, and she cannot instruct him, therefore, to hand them over to her or to apply them for the trust purposes. Meanwhile, her claims against the bank, which may or may not exist, are different in kind from her claims against her trustee.[205] When a court holds that the transaction has made no difference to her rights, and that she can trace the value of her notes into the bank account, it is not describing a factual situation but is instead expressing a conclusion of law. In response to her complaint that she has been deprived of the rights that she previously held in respect of the notes, it holds that A's title to the new bank account has become the new subject matter of those rights. In this respect, tracing is similar to following; both respond to situations where a holder of vested rights is wrongfully deprived of those rights, or of the ability to enjoy them, by declaring that she is to have equivalent or analogous rights in relation to some new or transformed asset.

2.151 However, the value metaphor also highlights an important difference between tracing and following. Following is concerned with the identification of physical things, in a situation where the thing has been transformed or mixed with other things. The reason why the defendant is able to alter the claimant's rights, in these situations, flows from the very nature of a property right in a physical thing.[206] The content of a property right to a thing is always shaped by the character of the thing itself;[207] a title to a car cannot be enforced if the car itself has been physically destroyed, and a claimant cannot sue a stranger for taking her car if she cannot

[204] *Jones v De Marchant* (1916) 28 DLR 561 (see para 2.156 this chapter).

[205] See Chapter 6 this volume.

[206] See JS Rogers, 'Negotiability, Property, and Identity' (1991) 12 Cardozo Law Review 471.

[207] B McFarlane and S Douglas, 'Defining Property Rights' in J Penner and H Smith (eds), *Philosophical Foundations of Property Rights* (OUP 2013) 219–43.

show that the very car taken is the one that she owns. Any natural person possesses the power to destroy or vary rights of this kind, therefore, simply by virtue of her physical ability to alter objects in the physical world.

2.152 By contrast, the power to alter another person's legal position by substitution—by realizing the value of an asset through an exchange transaction—is a legal power. It is the legal system that determines if A's decision to transfer possession of some banknotes to a bank, in exchange for a new account, has any impact whatsoever on B's legal rights to those notes. The idea that, in such cases, one traces the *value* of the notes—not the notes themselves—captures the double-edged character of the law's response to cases of unauthorized substitution. It acknowledges that the defendant does have some legal power to realize the value of the notes, while also describing the right of the claimant to recover the proceeds of an exercise of that power.

2.3.4. Rules of tracing and rules of following

2.153 This account of tracing and following also allows us to make sense of the overlap between rules that respond to physical mixture and rules that respond to mixed substitutions. In both contexts, the result of the mixture is to make it practically or legally impossible to distinguish the rights of the different contributors. When A mixes 100 barrels of his own oil with 100 barrels of B's oil, it is a fiction to say that B still has her title to the oil and can, for example, sell it without bothering about A's oil. She has a new practical and legal problem that renders the assertion of this title impossible—she must somehow disentangle 'her' oil from the mixture before she can enforce her rights—and the law responds by allowing her to invoke, inter alia, the principle of subordinating wrongdoers.

2.154 Similarly, where A pays £100 of her own cash and £100 of B's cash into a single bank account, it is not possible for B to assert that A's bank account was obtained purely as a result of his exercise of the power to dispose of her £100. Nor, however, is it open to A to argue that she obtained the bank account purely by exercise of powers she held for her own benefit. The law cannot, in this situation, distinguish the rights of the claimant from the rights of another person and responds, where that other is a wrongdoer, by subordinating the wrongdoer to the claimant in analysing the results of the mixture.

2.155 The 'evidential impossibility' that Smith identifies as the basis for the principle of subordination of wrongdoers, therefore, is only concerned with an *evidential* problem in a special sense. The problem is not that facts that the claimant needs to prove cannot be proved, because the evidence is unavailable. It is, instead, that the claimant cannot practically separate the subject matter of her rights from the subject matter of another person's rights, and that she therefore needs the assistance of the court to cut the Gordian knot.

2.156 The point can be illustrated by reference to the facts of *Jones v De Marchant*,[208] analysed by Lord Millett in *Foskett v McKeown*.[209] The claimant owned a certain

[208] (1916) 28 DLR 561. [209] *Foskett* (n 4) 132–33.

number of beaver skins. Her husband took eighteen of these skins, without her consent, and instructed a furrier to make a coat out of them. Since the eighteen skins were not enough to complete the coat, the husband bought a further four skins from the furrier, with his own money. He then gave the completed coat to the defendant. The court held that the claimant was entitled to keep the entire coat, as against the defendant. Richards JA said that it did not matter that it was 'impossible, now, in examining the coat, to say which parts of it constitute the 18 skins'.[210] As against a wrongdoer and a gratuitous recipient from a wrongdoer, she was entitled to say that the other four skins had acceded to her eighteen skins and, therefore, could claim the entire coat.

Richard JA's statement might imply that the problem in the case arose from an evidential difficulty: it happened to be impossible to distinguish the fur originating from one beaver skin from another. However, it is implausible that the case would have been decided differently if, for example, the skins of two different species of animal had been used to make the coat so that it was possible to visually distinguish the contributions of the wife and her wrongdoing husband. As Lord Millett said in *Foskett v McKeown*, it was impossible to distinguish the property of the two contributors to the coat because a pro rata division of the coat was impossible. The reason for the impossibility was that the two sets of skins could not be unmixed and returned to their owners individually, and it 'would hardly have been appropriate to require the two ladies to share the coat between them'.[211] As a result, 'it was an all or nothing case in which the ownership of the coat must be assigned to one or other of the parties'.[212] 2.157

This demonstrates the kind of 'impossibility' addressed by the rules of tracing and following into mixtures. In *Jones v De Marchant*, it was impossible, or 'inappropriate', for the owners of the beaver skins to enjoy similar separate rights to the coat as they had previously enjoyed in relation to the skins. It is the character of the rights at stake, not any factual difference, which distinguishes *Jones v De Marchant* from a case of mixed fungibles where, as Lord Millett said, pro rata division would have been possible.[213] The difference between owning ten separate barrels of oil and being entitled to receive a quantity of ten barrels out of a mixture of twenty barrels matters less, from the perspective of the owner whose rights have been altered, than the difference between owning eighteen beaver skins and being entitled to a proportionate share of a coat made out of those skins. 2.158

From this perspective, therefore, the cherry-picking rule and the lowest intermediate balance rule are substantive rules of law, delineating the scope of the principle of subordination of wrongdoers, and must be justified as such. Their effect is that a defendant who has wrongfully made it impossible for a claimant to separate her own rights from his rights will be treated as dealing with that mixture primarily for the benefit of the claimant. However, the boundaries of the mixture are fixed—if the defendant tops up the mixture by introducing more assets of his own, he will not be treated as having made this decision, as well, for the benefit of the claimant. 2.159

210 *Jones* (n 208) 562.
211 *Foskett* (n 4) 133.
212 *Foskett* (n 211).
213 *Foskett* (n 211).

2.4. Conclusions

2.160 It has been argued that we can understand tracing by reference to the idea of locating value, if this idea of locating value is understood as a metaphorical construct. A claimant who traces the proceeds of an asset is arguing that a particular transaction, entered into by someone else, represents a realization of her entitlement to the value of that asset. I have argued that this means that the transaction involved an exercise of a legal power to deal with that asset, in breach of a duty owed to the claimant.

2.161 This version of the value model gives us a formal definition of a substitution, which provides a starting point for making sense of the tracing rules. However, as I have suggested, the formal definition does not take us very far without some engagement with the value metaphor on its own terms, as a metaphor. Its reification of the defendant's transactions tells us something about the justification for claims to traceable proceeds, and the normative concerns that motivate the judges in deciding whether a given transaction is properly characterized as a substitution or not. Chapter 3 offers a more developed account of these normative concerns, which can allow us to make sense of hard cases like mixed substitutions and tracing through payments of debts and the transactions of intermediaries.

3

The Principles of Tracing

As explained in Chapters 1 and 2, one reason for the difficulty in understanding the law of tracing is that the case law is rich in metaphor, fiction, and analogy. The judges speak of money turning into land, and things retaining their substance while changing their form; they draw analogies between paying money into a bank account and putting it in a box full of money; they say that a defendant must be deemed to intend to spend her own money rather than the claimant's in some situations, and vice versa in others, and draw analogies between tracing through a transaction and ratifying that transaction. As the work of Peter Birks and Lionel Smith shows, these devices can be deeply misleading if we take them literally as characterizations of the facts to which the judges are responding in these cases. Bank accounts are not boxes of money, and substitution is not physical transformation; the language of intention cannot be used to explain a right when the intention in question is wholly fictional, and most of the transactions through which tracing is possible are not capable of being ratified in the usual sense used in the law of agency. Similarly, the language of locating value, which supposedly debunks these figurative accounts of tracing, is itself inadequate as a literal explanation of what is happening on the facts of the cases. 3.01

It does not follow, however, that this long tradition of figurative descriptions of tracing can tell us nothing important about the concept. Chapter 2 suggested that the value metaphor, translated into literal terms, leads us towards a formal definition of an unauthorized substitution: it is a transaction that involves an exercise of a power to deal with an asset, in circumstances where that exercise of power is a breach of a duty owed to the claimant. This takes us some way towards making sense of the peculiarities of tracing; it suggests that the goal of tracing is to determine whether or not the defendant has acquired a particular asset by exercising a particular legal power, which has the effect of wrongfully varying the rights of the claimant. If this is correct, it follows as a matter of logic that one cannot trace into an asset that was not acquired by such an exercise of power, even if its acquisition or retention is a causal consequence of a past decision to wrong the claimant. But this immediately raises the question why tracing has this rather narrow goal to begin with. Why focus on identifying the legal power exercised in entering into a particular transaction rather than, for example, the factual consequences of the transaction and, in particular, its effects on the overall wealth of the defendant? What are the principles that justify the law's focus on transactional tracing and that explain its current limits? 3.02

This chapter analyses the figurative language that the judges have traditionally employed to describe tracing, with the aim of answering these questions of 3.03

principle. It looks at the judicial language used at key transitional moments in the case law, when the core concerns of the law of tracing were crystallized, and seeks to identify the normative concerns that underpin that language. It argues that the language does reveal a consistent set of interlocking normative concerns,[1] and that these can be reduced to two core principles that explain the law's focus on transactional tracing.

3.04 First, there is what Lord Millett in *Foskett v McKeown*[2] called the principle of subordination of wrongdoers. This principle does not only explain the law's response to mixed substitutions involving the assets of a wrongdoer, but also captures a central theme of the law's response to unauthorized substitution in general. Where the defendant's decision to transact with a third party has the legal consequence of wrongfully altering the rights of the claimant, the courts have responded by treating the intentions of the parties to that transaction as irrelevant to determining its legal consequences; reifying descriptions of the transaction, as a transformation of the claimant's thing, emphasize this disregard for the defendant's intentions and motives in entering into it. Instead, the claimant is free to determine the outcome in the manner that is most advantageous to her. The judges have explained this principle of subordination on the basis that, in its absence, the claimant would suffer a loss of rights that ought not to be permitted. This suggests that the principle operates as a kind of compensation for the claimant's legally mandated vulnerability to the effects of the defendant's decision-making power, allowing her to decide what the effect of a wrongful exercise of that power should be so far as the defendant's rights are concerned.

3.05 The second principle is that, where the defendant's decision involves the exercise of a power that he holds free from any duty to the claimant, his autonomy is to be protected even where he is a wrongdoer in some sense. Tracing involves a radical subordination of the defendant, allowing the claimant to insist that his decisions be treated as entered into for her ends and not his own. The rules of tracing limit such subordination to situations where the defendant's decisions involve the exercise of powers that he was not previously free to exercise on his own account or for the benefit of some person other than the claimant, taking his actual intentions seriously outside this context. The dominant metaphor of reification takes on a different significance here; it is used to emphasize the idea that the defendant's subordination to the claimant must have some limits or boundaries, and cannot capture the whole set of rights belonging to the defendant.

[1] Contra the view of Craig Rotherham, who suggests that the judicial formulations are deliberately incoherent and question-begging, because their principal aim is to hide the disconnect between the actual function of tracing (judicial redistribution of property rights, to achieve policy objectives) and axiomatic understandings of property rights that deny judges the power to redistribute private property rights in this way without Parliamentary authorization: see C Rotherham, 'The Metaphysics of Tracing: Substituted Title and Property Rhetoric' (1996) Osgoode Hall Law Journal 321, and *Proprietary Remedies in Context: A Study in the Judicial Redistribution of Property Rights* (Hart Publishing, Oxford 2002) 106–27.

[2] [2001] 1 AC 102, 132.

3.1. The Invention of Tracing

Lionel Smith identifies *Bale v Marchall*,[3] decided in 1457, as the earliest recorded example of a successful claim to traceable proceeds in English law. In that case, a cestui que use and her husband, Agnes and Robert Bale, sought relief in Chancery against the executor of her uncle's will, Nicholas Marchall; they alleged that her uncle had been enfeoffed of two plots of land in Southwark to her use, and had sold one of the plots for 50 marks and received 144 marks in rents and profits from the other without accounting for them. In 2009, Smith argued that these facts raised a crucial question for the court: should it respond to the sale of trust[4] land for 50 marks by imposing 'a pure debt, an obligation to repay any 50 marks', or should it instead impose an obligation to 'hold the particular 50 marks for the benefit of the beneficiaries'?[5] He argues that, if the question is put in those terms, it is obvious that the Chancellor would choose the second option, and this is what happened in *Bale v Marchall*. 3.06

Neither this question nor Smith's proposed answer to it appear anywhere in the recorded pleadings and decree of the court in *Bale v Marchall* itself. According to the Selden Society record of the case, Agnes and Robert Bale alleged[6] that her uncle, Thomas Hansard, had been enfeoffed of two plots of land to her use and had sold one plot to one Herbert Brews, a smith, 'for the sake of which land the said Thomas received [50 marks][7] unto the use of the said Agnes';[8] in relation to the other plot, he had received 'of the issues of the lands and tenements ... [9] marks yearly during [16] years, which is [144] marks'.[9] They added that they had 'of great tenderness and special love and trust' left all the money due to them 'to be always with the said Thomas and in his keeping without specialty or writing',[10] because he had led them to believe he would leave them the amount due in his will 'and much more because 3.07

[3] (1457) 10 SS 143, identified as the earliest such case in 'Transfers' in P Birks and A Pretto (eds), *Breach of Trust* (Hart Publishing 2002) 112 and 'Philosophical Foundations of Proprietary Remedies' in R Chambers, C Mitchell, and J Penner (eds), *Philosophical Foundations of the Law of Unjust Enrichment* (OUP 2009) 281.

[4] For the use as the legal ancestor of the trust, and for the differences between the medieval use and the modern trust, see generally J Barton, 'The Medieval Use' (1965) 81 LQR 562 and NG Jones, 'Uses, Trusts and a Path to Privity' (1997) CLJ 175, 176–82.

[5] L Smith, 'Philosophical Foundations of Proprietary Remedies' in Chambers, Mitchell, and Penner (eds), *Philosophical Foundations of the Law of Unjust Enrichment* (n 3) 302.

[6] The Bales also made various other allegations, including that Thomas had held various chattels to Agnes' use that he should have given her on the occasion of her marriage and that Marchall had personally employed 'undue means' to estrange him from his relatives and to make 'a feigned and pretended Testament ... in his ... feebleness at such time as he understood not well what he said or did': *Bale* (n 3) 146. Since the court grants a remedy only in respect of the money received in respect of the land, these allegations appear not to have been accepted as a matter of fact.

[7] As Smith notes, the English pleadings refer to 'l marc' but 'the context, and the indorsement' (at 150), show 'that this is a lower case L, that is a Roman numeral 50': Smith, 'Philosophical Foundations of Proprietary Remedies' (n 5) 300. This is borne out by the comments of the editor of the Selden Society record of the case, who summarizes it as a case 'where feoffees to uses sold part of the land and received 50 marks for it': 10 SS xxviii.

[8] *Bale* (n 3). [9] *Bale* (n 3) 144. The record states these numbers in Roman numerals.

[10] *Bale* (n 3) 145.

he had no more kindred living.'[11] In invoking the aid of the court of Chancery, they argued that Marchall had failed to pay over the amounts due to them 'against all right faith and conscience and to right heavy example and great peril to the soul of said Thomas',[12] and that they could have no recovery against him 'by course of the common law'.[13] Marchall replied, inter alia, that he had not known of the land that had been sold or that the other land had been held to Agnes' use;[14] the Bales responded that this was 'no sufficient answer'[15] to their complaint.

3.08 The decree of the court, as translated by the editor of the Selden Society report, was brief. Having seen, read, and understood the matters contained in the bill, the court considered 'that the within-written Robert and Agnes should recover against the said Nicholas, 194 marks of the goods and chattels of the within-written Thomas Hansard, deceased; to wit, 50 marks for the within-written lands and tenements sold by the said Thomas Hansard ... and 144 marks received by the said Thomas Hansard of the issue of other lands and tenements ... also specified in the said bill'.[16] No reasons are recorded.

3.09 From the perspective of the modern law, the most distinctive feature of this decree and this set of pleadings is the absence of any interest in the tracing exercise, as we now understand it. No one—claimant, defendant, or court—comments on the fate of the particular 50 marks after they were received from Herbert Brews, or distinguishes them from the 144 marks received in rents and profits from the land. The Bales do not allege that Thomas Hansard kept those particular coins up to the moment of his death, and point to a particular bag of money in Marchall's possession as the very one received from Brews; nor do they point to some specific goods and chattels that were bought with that money. Marchall does not say, in his defence, that the coins are lost or spent and that there is no way to identify what was bought with them. Nor does the judicial order betray any interest in the question of identification: Marchall is simply ordered to pay 194 marks 'of the goods and chattels' of Thomas Hansard.

3.10 This does not contradict Smith's interpretation of the decision: the outcome is consistent with a finding that Hansard had held his title to the particular 50 marks to the use of Agnes and the pleadings do refer to him having received it 'to her use'. What it does demonstrate is that the distinctive tracing inquiry had to be invented; it was not important enough to warrant attention until the question of the third-party effect of a claim became important. For Agnes and Robert Bale, proving that Hansard had sold the land that he had held to her use was enough to make Marchall liable to pay the amount received as its price, without any need to show that Marchall still had the money or its proceeds in the modern sense. This is because the liability of an executor need not depend on showing that the duty owed by the deceased was capable of binding third parties: Marchall would have been

[11] *Bale* (n 10). [12] *Bale* (n 3) 146. [13] *Bale* (n 10).

[14] As quoted by the Bales in their response to his reply, *Bale* (n 3) 148. The editor of the Selden Society report notes that Marchall's first reply to the allegations made against him are not available, 'because a large piece of this document is torn off' but that the main points can be gathered from the Bales' subsequent reply: *Bale* (n 12).

[15] *Bale* (n 14). [16] *Bale* (n 3) 150.

liable to pay Hansard's debts out of his assets as a personal representative,[17] quite apart from any liability he might have in his own capacity as a recipient. It was not necessary to show that Thomas Hansard had acquired the 50 marks from Herbert Brews under conditions that imposed a duty to give up that cash to Agnes Bale not only on Thomas himself, but also on others who acquired his title to those particular coins from him; Marchall's liability need not have depended on showing that he had received that very title, but could have been justified by reference to his status as Thomas' personal representative.

In *Mears v St John*,[18] this distinction and its bearing on the third-party consequences of a claim to traceable proceeds comes into clearer focus. In that case, the trustee had not only received several years' worth[19] of rents and profits from the trust land, like the feoffee to use in *Bale v Marchall*, but he had also 'with parcel of the profits purchased land in fee'.[20] When he died, under the rules of succession that then applied,[21] only his personal estate came under the control of his administratrix; his real property, including the estate in fee purchased using the trust money, descended directly to his heir.[22] One of the questions in the case was whether 'the heir shall be contributory',[23] ie whether the beneficiary under the trust had a right enforceable against the heir as well as the administratrix. 3.11

This would have meant something new. Unlike an executor or administrator,[24] an heir was not a personal representative of the deceased and could only be liable for debts of the deceased that had been created by deed and that expressly stated that the heir was to be bound.[25] Thus, if the heir had been made to contribute in *Mears v St John*, it would have meant that the beneficiary under the trust was owed something 3.12

[17] For an overview of situations in which an executor was liable as a personal representative of the testator, as opposed to liable in his personal capacity, see WS Holdsworth, *A History of English Law: Volume 3* (3rd edn, 1923) 578–79.

[18] (1596) 4 Co Inst 86, 4 Viner's Abbr 391; DEC Yale (ed), *Lord Nottingham's 'Manual of Chancery Practice' and 'Prolegomena of Chancery and Equity'* (CUP 1965) 260–61. Lord Nottingham calls it *Meers v St John* but, as it is reported as *Mears v St John* both in Coke's Institutes and in its subsequent citations in *Kirk v Webb* and *Halcott v Markant*, this variant on the spelling has been adopted here for the sake of consistency.

[19] According to Coke (n 18), ten years' worth: 'from the 23rd year of Queen Elizabeth [I] to the 33rd year of her reign'.

[20] Coke (n 18). For 'parcel' as an archaic synonym for 'part', see A Stevenson (ed), *The Oxford English Dictionary* (3rd edn, OUP 2010).

[21] See, now, the Administration of Estates Act 1925, s 33(1), which provides that both the real and personal property of a person who dies intestate will vest in his personal representatives as trustees with powers and duties of distribution in accordance with the scheme laid out in that Act.

[22] See F Pollock and FW Maitland, *The History of English Law Before the Time of Edward I* (2nd edn, 1898, Cambridge University Press reissue 1968) 359–61.

[23] Yale (n 18); Coke (n 18) 87.

[24] An administrator was made a personal representative, who could be sued on the debts of the intestate, in 1357, under the statute 31 Edw 3 1 c 11.

[25] See Holdsworth (n 17) 572–75. It became possible to demand that lands that descended to an heir be sold to pay an intestate's debts in 1830, by the statute 1 Wm 4 c 47. Under the Administration of Estates Act 1925, both real and personal property of a deceased person are now available to personal representatives for the purposes of paying debts: see the Administration of Estates Act 1925, s 32(1).

other than a debt, a pure obligation on the part of the deceased trustee to account for the amount of rents and profits received. In Smith's terms, he would have been owed an obligation that the very title to land obtained using the trust money be held for his benefit; such an obligation would have been capable of binding the heir by virtue of the descent of the title to him, without needing to show that he was liable as a personal representative of the trustee.

3.13 This step was contemplated, but not taken in *Mears v St John*. Sir Thomas Egerton MR[26] is reported to have cited *Bale v Marchall* as a relevant authority on the liability of the administratrix, but to have taken a very narrow view of its ratio.[27] According to Coke's report, he said he had seen a case in Chancery[28] in which the judges had held that where feoffees 'took the profits of the land, and received the rents, and made their executors, leaving assets to satisfy all debts over and above the said rents and profits', the executors could be 'charged to satisfy cestui que use'.[29] On this analysis, *Bale v Marchall* stood for the limited proposition that a debt arising from the duty to account for the profits of trust land—including, but not limited to, money arising from the sale of trust land—would bind an executor if the deceased had left enough assets to satisfy all his other debts as well. The crucial question whether the heir was to be contributory was left unanswered as a doubtful question. It seems that it was unnecessary to resolve the doubt in *Mears v St John* itself because the personal estate was sufficient to pay the value of all the rents and profits taken.

3.14 In *Kirk v Webb*,[30] by contrast, the point was vigorously argued because it made a practical difference on the facts. It was in argument in this case that the possibility of a claim to traceable proceeds was first canvassed, in terms that linked it to the distinctive tracing inquiry as it later came to be understood. After *Kirk v Webb*, the idea of tracing as a distinctive project began to take shape in the courts. As claims to traceable proceeds were recognized, and distinguished from other types of claim, the maxim 'money has no earmark' came to the fore as a key principle that limited the availability of claims of that kind. This chapter looks at the judicial language that was used to justify the distinctiveness of these claims, and the limitations imposed by the maxim that 'money has no earmark', at two key moments of transition in the law: *Kirk v Webb* and the cases interpreting it in the eighteenth century, and *Taylor v Plumer* and the cases interpreting it in the nineteenth. It argues that later developments in the law can be made sense of in the light of the core normative concerns revealed in this early case law, where the basic commitment to transactional tracing was established.

26 Later Lord Ellesmere.

27 Yale (n 18); Coke (n 18).

28 For the identification of this case 'in Anno 34 Hen 6' with *Bale v Marchall*, see L Smith, 'Transfers' in Birks and Pretto (eds), *Breach of Trust* (n 3) 131 (fn 94).

29 Coke (n 18) 87.

30 (1698) Prec Ch 84, 24 ER 41; also reported (1698) 2 Freem Ch 229, 22 ER 1177.

3.2. *Kirk v Webb*: Tracing into Land and 'Money Has No Earmark'

The dispute in *Kirk v Webb* arose out of difficulties in interpreting the terms of a settlement of land made in anticipation of the marriage of the Duke of Southampton[31] to the daughter of one Sir Henry Wood. Under the terms of the marriage settlement, made by the bride's father, she was to become the life tenant if her husband predeceased her without issue; on her death, her uncle, the Bishop of Litchfield and Coventry, was to become the life tenant and, on his death, the life tenant was to be one Sir Caesar Cranmer. The Bishop was also one of the trustees of the settlement. The settlement made no provision for what would happen if the Duchess predeceased the Duke. 3.15

In fact, the Duchess did predecease the Duke, dying of smallpox at the age of seventeen. Her uncle, the Bishop, having been—wrongly—advised that his life interest vested on her death, took possession of the lands, and 'enjoyed the profits for several years'.[32] According to one of the two reports of the case, the total amount of the rents and profits received constituted £2,700;[33] both reports agree that some part of this money was spent on purchases of freehold land,[34] although it was unclear exactly how much had been so used.[35] The Bishop devised his freehold land to one Webb, who was also the executor of his will. After the Bishop's death, the Duke of Southampton and Sir Caesar Cranmer litigated to determine who was entitled to enjoy the trust land in the events that had happened. The House of Lords concluded that neither of them had any interest during the lifetime of the Duke, and nor had the Bishop: since the settlement had failed to say what should happen to the land during this slice of time, it was 'an undisposed interest' and belonged to the heirs of the settlor, Sir Henry Wood.[36] 3.16

The claimant, Kirk, was the widower of the settlor's niece, who had been the settlor's heir during the time when the Bishop was in possession. He brought a claim against Webb, as the Bishop's executor, seeking an account of the profits that had been received out of the trust land. In addition, on the basis that there was or might or have been[37] a shortfall in the personal estate left by the Bishop, he sought a declaration that the land devised to Webb 'being purchased with his wife's money 3.17

[31] One of the illegitimate sons of Charles II, the Duke was married at the age of nine to the seven-year-old Mary Wood. For the circumstances of the marriage, see JM Rigg, 'FitzRoy, Charles, second duke of Cleveland and first duke of Southampton (1662–1730)', rev Matthew Kilburn, *Oxford Dictionary of National Biography* (OUP 2004, online edn, Sept 2014) [http://www.oxforddnb.com/view/article/9629, last accessed 8 January 2018].

[32] *Kirk* (n 30) 85, 41.

[33] (1698) 2 Freem Ch 229, 22 ER 1177.

[34] (1698) 2 Freem Ch 229, 22 ER 1177; *Kirk* (n 30) 87, 42.

[35] See Chapter 2, paras 2.38–2.39 on this aspect of the case.

[36] Ie there was a resulting trust in favour of the settlor, whose beneficial interest had descended to his heirs on his death. For 'automatic resulting trusts' of this type, see *Re Vandervell (No 2)* [1974] 1 Ch 269.

[37] The shortfall is explicitly identified only in Richard Freeman's report, which says that the Bishop had died 'leaving no personal assets to answer [the claimant's] demand': *Kirk* (n 33). The report in Precedents in Chancery frames the issue in more hypothetical terms, suggesting that the issue was raised by the claimant 'in case he had not a full satisfaction out of the Bishop's estate': *Kirk* (n 34).

were a trust for her ... and ought to be decreed to him[.]'.[38] Counsel argued that it was but 'justice and reason that the lands purchased with the profits should go in the same manner as the profits themselves would have gone'.[39] According to Freeman's report, he also emphasized the 'great mischief' that would result if, when a guardian or trustee used the money of his ward or beneficiary to buy land and then died leaving little or no personal estate, the heir could 'run away with the estate, and this court shall not reach him.'[40]

3.18 Lord Somers LC is reported to have reacted favourably to this argument at the outset, saying that the Bishop was a 'trustee, although he did not take himself to be one',[41] and that 'when a trustee laid out the money of cestui que trust in lands, he thought the lands might be followed'.[42] However, after argument, he changed his mind. Counsel for Webb had argued that the Statute of Frauds 1677 precluded a finding that land was held on trust in the absence of a declaration in writing,[43] contending that the alternative would be to 'introduce an utter uncertainty into all men's titles, for the best title may be spoiled by proving the purchase-money to be another person's'.[44] Powell J, whose view ultimately persuaded Lord Somers LC, accepted this argument, describing the claimant's argument as one that was 'against the Statute of Frauds and would let in all the mischiefs that it intended to prevent'.[45] Sir John Trevor MR agreed that the claim should be rejected on the facts, but is reported to have expressed doubt about the underlying principle: 'if it had been expressly and plainly proved that these purchases had been made with the profits of the trust estate, he thought it might have been otherwise'.[46] The evidence of 'a man who received great part of the profits of the trust, and paid the money for several of the purchases'[47] had satisfied the Master in Chancery who had been asked to investigate the facts, but this parol evidence was rejected as inadequate. The House of Lords affirmed the decision.[48]

3.19 In *Halcott v Markant*,[49] an attempt was made to distinguish *Kirk v Webb* on the basis of declared intention. The trustee, Markant, had been authorized by the settlor to sell the trust property and invest in land, which was then to be settled on trust for the beneficiary under the trust, the settlor's son. He subsequently bought an estate in land, known as Gressing Hall, in his own name. The beneficiary's mother gave evidence that he had asked her consent before buying this estate, telling her that he was going to do so with the trust money, and that he had declared 'several times',[50] after purchasing it, that he meant to sell it for the benefit of the beneficiary. However, no trust was ever declared in writing, and Markant died intestate and insolvent. Sir John Trevor MR is reported to have been 'very inclinable to help the plaintiff as far as might be',[51] and said that he thought that *Kirk v Webb* might be distinguished,

[38] *Kirk* (n 34). [39] *Kirk* (n 34). [40] (1698) 2 Freem Ch 229, 22 ER 1177.
[41] *Kirk* (n 34). [42] *Kirk* (n 34).
[43] Section 7 of the Statute provided that 'all declarations or creations of trusts' of land had to be manifested and proved by writing 'signed by the party to who is by law enabled to declare such trust', or they would be 'utterly void and of none effect'. See, now, the Law of Property Act 1925, s 53(1)(b).
[44] *Kirk* (n 34). [45] *Kirk* (n 34). [46] *Kirk* (n 34). [47] *Kirk* (n 34).
[48] (1699) 2 Eq Cas Abr 744. [49] (1689–1722) Prec Ch 168, (1701) 24 ER 80.
[50] *Halcott* (n 49). [51] *Halcott* (n 49) 169, 80.

'for there the party did not know himself to be a trustee, and had disposed of the lands'.[52] After citing *Mears v St John* and Coke's report of that case, he described Markant's oral declaration, coupled with his powers of sale under the will, as 'a good foundation for a trust', and said that 'perhaps this may be a resulting trust'.[53] However, in the end he dismissed the claim in respect of the land, saying that 'it was too hard for him because there was no express proof of the application of the trust money'.[54]

This brief judgment captures the constellation of ways in which a substituting transaction could, in principle, be plausibly characterized. Suppose that all we know, in a particular case, is that A once held his title to some cash on an express trust for B and has since used that money to buy title to some land from X. A number of stories about the factual context of this transaction could explain why A now holds his title to the land, acquired from X, on trust for B. One possibility is that A, knowing himself to be a trustee, made the purchase for the benefit of B. On this view, his use of the trust money could be invoked as a piece of evidence lending plausibility to a factual allegation that he had declared that he meant to hold that title to land on the terms of the original trust. Apart from problems with the admissibility of such evidence, in the absence of writing,[55] this argument would justify a decision that the land is now held on trust for B, since a landowner can be bound by his own express declaration of trust. 3.20

Another and related possibility, as in *Halcott v Markant* itself, is that the trustee's purchase could be explained as an authorized use of trust money. If the terms of the trust on which A holds the money stipulate that he can use it to buy land for B's benefit, and A then uses the money for this purpose, we can treat his decision to buy the land as a fulfilment of his past agreement with the settlor. This would also be a consent-based explanation of why B should be entitled to the land, once the sale has taken place; English law recognizes a range of circumstances[56] in which a promise to grant a right over an asset to another person, as soon as one has acquired that asset, has immediate proprietary effect at the moment of acquisition, and an authorized substitution by a trustee can be seen as an instance of the same principle at work.[57] 3.21

A third possibility is that these facts raise a presumption of resulting trust, as Sir John Trevor MR's elliptical reference to the idea of a resulting trust might suggest. 3.22

[52] *Halcott* (n 51). [53] *Halcott* (n 51). [54] *Halcott* (n 51).

[55] Law of Property Act 1925, s 53(1)(b), re-enacting the requirement that a declaration of a trust of land be evidenced by some writing, previously found in section 7 of the Statute of Frauds 1677. English law recognizes various circumstances in which an oral declaration of trust may, in combination with other facts, give rise to an enforceable trust of land: see, for example, *Rochefoucauld v Boustead* [1897] 1 Ch 196. While there is a dispute about the proper classification of these trusts, and whether they respond to the principle that gives effect to express declarations or some other principle, it is generally accepted that the declared intention of the supposed trustee is necessary, even if not sufficient, to justify the trust: see WJ Swadling, 'The Nature of the Trust in *Rochefoucauld v Boustead*' in C Mitchell (ed), *Constructive and Resulting Trusts* (Hart Publishing 2010) 115; YK Liew, '*Rochefoucauld v Boustead*' in C Mitchell (ed), *Landmark Cases in Equity* (Hart Publishing 2012) 423; B McFarlane, 'Constructive Trusts Arising on Receipt of Property Sub Conditione' (2004) 120 LQR 667.

[56] Eg *Pullan v Koe* [1913] 1 Ch 9; *Holroyd v Marshall* (1862) 10 HL Cas 191, 11 ER 999; *Webb v Austin* (1844) 7 Man & G 701, 135 ER 282.

[57] For this explanation of a beneficiary's rights to the proceeds of an authorized substitution, see RC Nolan, 'Property in a Fund' (2004) 120 LQR 108, 115.

On one view of the nature of the resulting trust,[58] this might be an explanation in terms of the trustee's past agreement with the claimant beneficiary, as opposed to with the settlor. In *Halcott v Markant*, the infant beneficiary's mother alleged that she had consented, on behalf of the beneficiary, to the use of trust money to buy the land. On this analysis, we might say that B's agreement to the use of her money to buy land in A's name indicates that she meant that land to be held on trust for her unless she can be shown to have intended something different. The communication of this intention to the trustee, A, would, on this view, justify us in concluding that he was bound by his own agreement to hold the land purchased on trust for her.

3.23 All these analyses derive their plausibility from one of our basic intuitions concerning the likely sources of property rights affecting land: the intentional act of a current or former owner of the land in question. One of the defining characteristics of ownership, as conventionally understood,[59] is that owners possess the power to alter the legal rights and duties of the world in general in respect of the asset that they own.[60] When A grants a legal property right over his land to B, other subjects of the legal system come under a new duty to B that replaces[61] or supplements[62] the duty that they previously owed to A;[63] they will now owe B a duty to keep off the land, and will need to negotiate with B, as well as or instead of A, in order to get access to it. Where A grants B an equitable interest in the land, as where he declares that he holds the title on trust for B, the effect on third parties will be more complex[64]—others will usually come under new duties to B only if they acquire A's title to the land or any interest in the land that derives from that title—but we can still explain these effects by reference to the core idea that it is owners, qua owners, who possess the power to produce such effects.[65] It is a function of A's status as owner of the land in question that, when he makes promises to B about that land, his decisions do not alter only his own legal position vis-à-vis B, but also have the potential to affect strangers to the transaction, like his own heirs or successors in title. Thus, if the heir to the land in *Halcott v Markant* had asked why he should come under any duty to

[58] For rival views on the source of the trust in these cases, see R Chambers, 'Is There a Presumption of Resulting Trust?' in Mitchell (ed), *Constructive and Resulting Trusts* (n 55); WJ Swadling, 'Explaining Resulting Trusts' (2008) 124 LQR 72; J Mee, 'Presumed Resulting Trusts, Intention and Declaration' [2014] CLJ 86. The approach in the text builds on Mee's account of the resulting trust as based on a presumption of intention.

[59] AM Honoré, 'Ownership' in AG Guest (ed), *Oxford Essays in Jurisprudence: First Series* (Clarendon Press 1962) 107, 118.

[60] B McFarlane, 'The *Numerus Clausus* Principle and Covenants Relating to Land' in S Bright (ed), *Modern Studies in Property Law: Volume 6* (Hart Oxford 2011) 308, 311: 'The acquisition of a property right ... provides the most striking exception to the general rule that an agreement between A and B, or indeed any conduct of B alone, cannot impose a new duty or liability on X'.

[61] Where X conveys his own title to the land to A.

[62] Where X grants a derivative interest in the land, such as a lease or an easement, to A.

[63] For this characterization of the effect of a transfer, see W Hohfeld, *Fundamental Legal Conceptions* (Yale University Press 1923).

[64] For an analysis of this characteristic of equitable powers and its relevance to tracing, see Chapter 7 this volume.

[65] Cf B McFarlane, 'The Centrality of Constructive and Resulting Trusts' in Mitchell (ed), *Constructive and Resulting Trusts* (n 55).

the infant beneficiary on the facts of the case, one plausible answer might be to point to the power of his predecessor in title, Markant, to bind him in this way and the fact that he had done so.

The problem of proof in *Kirk v Webb*—the absence of signed writing, as required by section 7 of the Statute of Frauds—could then be understood as a problem of proving that this owner's power had actually been exercised, ie that a declaration had in fact been made. As Sir John Trevor MR pointed out in *Halcott v Markant*, the facts of *Kirk v Webb* were, in any case, inconsistent with any such argument. The court could not have told Webb that he was under a duty to Kirk because the previous owner of the land he had inherited—the Bishop—had had the power to impose such duties on him and had intentionally done so. Since the Bishop had believed himself to be beneficially entitled to the trust money he had received, and since it appears that no one was aware that the land was held on trust for Kirk's wife until the House of Lords decision settling the point, it is unlikely in the extreme that he would have meant to use those profits to buy land for her benefit, let alone have declared a trust in her favour. 3.24

However, *Halcott v Markant* was not decided on the basis of this interpretation of *Kirk v Webb*. Instead, in line with what later became the standard interpretation of that case, the claim in *Halcott v Markant* was dismissed because 'there was no express proof of the application of the trust money'. Subsequent authority entrenched the idea that the problem in *Kirk v Webb* was not absence of evidence of a declaration—and the inherent implausibility of an allegation that there had been a declaration, on the facts of that case—but, instead, absence of evidence of the application of the trust money. In this way, the focus shifted from the asset purchased—land—to the asset used to buy it, and *Kirk v Webb* became associated with the maxim that 'money has no earmark'. 3.25

3.2.1. Reframing the requirement of a deed

In *Kinder v Miller*,[66] one Thomas Chalkley—'a meal-man of Uxbridge'[67]—had died intestate, leaving some cash[68] in his house. He was survived by his widow, the administratrix of his estate, and two minor daughters. Under the Statute of Distributions 1670, which then governed the distribution of assets in intestacy, the widow was entitled to one-third of the personal property and the remaining two-thirds should have been distributed equally among his children. Several witnesses testified[69] that the widow had used the cash found in the intestate's house to buy an estate in land. The deed conveying this estate to the widow made no reference to the source of the funds used to buy it, or to her status as administratrix of her 3.26

[66] (1701) Prec Ch 171, 24 ER 83; also reported as *Kendar v Milward* (1702) 2 Vern 440, 23 ER 882.

[67] *Kendar* (n 66). A meal-man was a dealer in grain or flour: see 'mealman, *n.*' in *The Oxford English Dictionary* (3rd edn, OUP 2001).

[68] There is a discrepancy between the two reports as to exactly how much cash was left in the house, £400 or £500.

[69] *Kendar* (n 66) 441.

late husband's estate, and did not include any declaration of trust.[70] The widow later conveyed it to trustees on to hold on an express trust for herself for life, with remainders to her daughters in tail, and remainders to her own heirs in the event of the deaths of the daughters without issue. After the daughters had both died without issue, the defendant, the widow's heir, took possession of the land. The widower of one of the daughters became the administrator of both their estates and brought an action against the defendant, asking that the land be 'made personal estate and to have two thirds of it, as being purchased with the money which belonged to the daughters to whom he was administrator.'[71]

3.27 The matter again came before Sir John Trevor MR, who again demonstrated a strong inclination to help the claimants. Rejecting the defendant's argument that *Kirk v Webb* barred a claim in respect of the land, in the absence of written evidence of a declaration of trust, he said, without elaboration, that 'that case did not govern this but stood on its own bottom.'[72] He said that the Statute of Distributions had vested an interest in the money in the daughters, and that 'it would be very mischievous to infants, if their money might be invested in land, and that land not liable to make them satisfaction'.[73] On this basis, he ordered the defendant to pay two-thirds of the purchase money to the claimant, 'and if it were not paid the land to be sold'.[74] On appeal, Lord Keeper Wright reversed this decision, holding that the case was 'within the reason of the case of *Kirk* and *Webb* ... that money had no ear-mark and could not be followed when invested in a purchase'.[75]

3.28 This is an important shift, in two respects. First, the language of tracing makes its appearance. The claim is contingent on proof that the mother used the very coins that were found in her husband's house to buy the land. There is a difficulty in proving this fact that arises from the special status of money—'money has no earmark'[76]—and this scuppers the claim. Secondly, subject to this point, the case represents a judicial acknowledgment that a proprietary claim ought to be available in the circumstances, for reasons that have nothing to do with the avowed intentions of the owner of the land in question, but instead depend on the consequences of her actions. In explaining why the widow's heir should, in principle, be obliged to sell the land inherited from her and pay a proportion of the proceeds to the clamant, the judge does not point to any intentional act of the widow exercising her powers as a landowner. Instead, he points to the harm to claimants that would flow from allowing their money to be spent on buying land, if no claims of this kind were available.

3.29 It is clear that, in *Kinder v Miller*, the widow's plans for the land did not include allowing it to pass to the husband of one of her daughters. As her attempt to settle the land on different express trusts showed, she wished it to pass to her own heir—the defendant—in the event of their deaths without issue. Sir John Trevor MR's reasoning indicates that this intention on her part is to be disregarded, because allowing her to

70 *Kinder* (n 66) 172. 71 *Kinder* (n 70). 72 *Kinder* (n 70).
73 *Kinder* (n 70). 74 *Kinder* (n 70). 75 *Kendar* (n 69).
76 For other uses of this maxim, notably in barring claims in detinue and trover where cash was misappropriated and then passed on to a third party, see D Fox, 'Bona Fide Purchase and the Currency of Money' (1996) 55 CLJ 547. See Section 3.3.2.1 this chapter for a more detailed account of the various functions of the maxim in the context of tracing and following.

decide what was to happen to the land bought with her daughters' money would be 'very mischievous' to their interests. Although his decision was overruled, on the grounds that it could not be proved that the money used to buy the land was the very cash to which the daughters were entitled, this aspect of his reasoning provides the basic framework of the subsequent case law, with its disregard for the defendant's intentions and plans in respect of assets purchased using other people's money and its focus on the consequences of these transactions on those others.

In *Deg v Deg*,[77] for example, *Kirk v Webb* was distinguished because the purchaser of the land had disclosed his use of trust money to buy land in a deed. Simon Deg, the life tenant under a marriage settlement made in 1695, had obtained control of some of the trust money from the trustees and used it to buy land in Derby and Mapleton. In a deed of February 1705, he purported to settle this land on new trusts, declaring in the recitals to the deed that he had purchased it using the money settled on trusts of the 1695 settlement. Lord King LC held that the maxim 'money has no earmark' did not present an obstacle to the claim where the use of the money could be proved by a deed, and declared that the beneficiary under the original settlement, Simon Deg's eldest son—also known as Simon Deg—was entitled to a 'specific lien'[78] upon the land. It was irrelevant, he held, that, in the 1705 deed, the father had also declared his intention to settle the land on quite different trusts;[79] it was not within his power to revoke or limit the trusts of the original settlement in favour of his eldest son. Nor did it matter that, in his subsequent will, he settled all his land in Staffordshire and Derbyshire on trust for his creditors. While a jury had held that this will represented the exercise of a power of revocation that he had reserved in the 1705 settlement, Lord King LC rejected the view that he had any such power in relation to the land purchased using the trust money: 'as to the lands in Derby, the testator the father's devise was as much void, as if the father had devised any other part of the estate of . . . Simon Deg the son.'[80] 3.30

Thus, *Kirk v Webb* became authority that, where A used B's money to buy land, B could not claim the land *unless* the use of his money in this way was evidenced by deed; where the use of the money could be evidenced by deed, B could claim the land from A or his heirs and it did not matter if A had bought the land with different intentions. In *Ryall v Ryall*,[81] which was followed in *Lane v Dighton*,[82] the requirement of a deed was dropped, and it was held that legatees under a will could in principle trace into land purchased by an executor using the testator's personal property, relying on evidence other than a written declaration. 3.31

In *Ryall v Ryall*, Lord Hardwicke LC commented that, in the earlier cases, courts of equity had been cautious about following money into land 'because it has no ear mark'.[83] He characterized this as a problem of proof, arising out of the competing 3.32

[77] (1727) 2 P Wms 412, 24 ER 791. [78] *Deg* (n 77) 415; 792.

[79] *Deg* (n 77) 413; *Deg* (n 78): after reciting that the land was purchased using money that had been settled on the terms of a 1695 marriage settlement, he added that 'there was a defect in the said settlement . . . in that there was no provision made for younger sons of [the] marriage' and 'therefore . . . for supplying that defect' conveyed the land to trustees on new terms.

[80] *Deg* (n 77) 419; 794. [81] (1739) 1 Atk 59, 26 ER 39.

[82] (1762) Amb 409, 27 ER 274. [83] *Ryall* (n 81).

interests of the parties, which posed 'no small temptation to perjury'.[84] However, he rejected the view that a declaration in writing was the only way to overcome this problem of proof, despite the Statute of Frauds: 'the means of coming at this by way of resulting trust is excepted out of the statute of frauds . . . if the estate is purchased in the name of one, and the money paid by another, it is a trust notwithstanding there is no declaration in writing by the nominal purchaser'.[85] On this basis, he ordered an inquiry into the question whether the executor had, in fact, used the testator's assets to buy the land; 'if it should plainly appear that [the testator's assets] have been so laid out,' he held, 'they ought to be restored to the personal estate of the testator'.[86]

3.33 Lord Hardwicke LC's use of the language of resulting trusts in *Ryall v Ryall*, and his use of the passive voice in describing the situations in which they arise—'if an estate *is purchased* in the name of one, and the money paid by another'—obscures an important distinction between claims to traceable proceeds and resulting trusts as conventionally understood. If an estate is purchased in the name of A, and the money is paid by B, the available interpretations of the situation will depend on who is making these decisions to purchase and to pay using B's money. It could be the case that the purchase is made by B himself, who directs the vendor to convey the land into the name of A. It could be the case that the purchase is made by A using B's money, but with the full consent of B. Or—as in *Ryall v Ryall* itself—it could be the case that A uses B's money to make the purchase without informing B of either the use of the money or the fact of the purchase.

3.34 The difference between these scenarios can be seen in its developed form in later cases. In *Fowkes v Pascoe*,[87] for example, a Mrs Baker had made several purchases of annuities, using her own money, over a period of years. In some cases, she bought these annuities in her own name; in others, she bought them in the name of the defendant, John Pascoe. After her death, it was argued that he held these annuities on trust for her, since they had been bought with her money. The Court of Appeal rejected the argument on the basis that there was sufficient evidence, on the facts, that the testatrix had intended a gift to the defendant rather than intending to constitute him a trustee and this evidence rebutted the presumption of resulting trust.

3.35 In arriving at this conclusion, Jessel MR paid close attention to the individual transactions by which the annuities were acquired and conveyed into the name of the defendant; in this sense, his analysis of the facts of the case resembles the tracing inquiry. However, unlike the tracing inquiry, Jessel MR's investigation of the circumstances surrounding the purchases of annuities by Mrs Baker did not stop once he had identified whose money (her own) was used to buy it. He also wanted to know why she had done so. He was particularly impressed by the fact that she had bought annuities in the defendant's name at the same time as she bought annuities in her own, on several occasions, using small separate sums to make each purchase. He said he could not 'reconcile with mental sanity'[88] the theory that she had done

84 *Ryall* (n 81). 85 *Ryall* (n 81) 60; 39–40. 86 *Ryall* (n 81).
87 (1874–75) LR 10 Ch App 343. 88 *Fowkes* (n 87) 349.

this with the intention of making the defendant a trustee for her: 'what trust—what object is there conceivable in doing this?'[89]

3.36 Thus, where A uses her own money to buy assets in B's name, the *why* behind the transaction, the 'object' that A is pursuing by using her own money in this way, makes a difference. We might say that there will be a trust in favour of A if she had no intention of benefiting B,[90] or if she intended[91] or has declared[92] that she means B to hold on trust for her. On any of these analyses, the intention of the person actually transacting with the seller of the annuities is of crucial importance to the interpretation of the effect of the transaction. The crude fact that A has used her own money, not B's, is only a guide—and not a decisive guide—to answering the real question, which is to do with intention. If Mrs Baker had made an express declaration that she meant Pascoe to hold the annuities on some particular trusts in his own or someone else's favour, this would certainly have prevented the court from drawing the conclusion that they were nevertheless held on trust for her, because they were bought using her money.

3.37 Contrast what would have happened if, instead, Pascoe had been the one to buy annuities in his own name, using Mrs Baker's money and without her knowledge or consent. In this situation, his intentions in transacting with the seller of the annuities would be irrelevant. If the pattern of his purchases had exactly matched the pattern of Mrs Baker's—sometimes buying annuities in her name, and sometimes in his own, using small sums of her money on each occasion—the court would still have held that the annuities bought in his own name were held on trust for her, without bothering to formulate any theory of his motives in adopting this approach. If, like Simon Deg, he had plainly declared his object in doing this—say, to provide for himself and his family—the court would have disregarded the express declaration and treated him as a trustee anyway.

3.2.2. The requirement of proving a transactional link

3.38 However, this disregard for the intentions of the defendant has limits. In interpreting *Kirk v Webb*, as has been shown, the courts began to use the maxim 'money has no earmark' to emphasize the necessity of a transactional link between the asset misappropriated by the defendant and the asset claimed by the claimant. It was not enough to show that the defendant had taken the claimant's money and that, later, he had obtained some land that he might possibly have bought using that money. The burden was on the claimant to prove that the very asset used to buy the land—the cash used, or the bank account drawn upon—was the asset that had been misappropriated.

3.39 In *Perry v Phelips*,[93] for example, a trustee had taken possession of land held on trust for his nephew and had received rents and profits from that land. Under the terms of the trust, the trustee was obliged to use the profits to buy more land and

[89] *Fowkes* (n 88).
[90] R Chambers, *Resulting Trusts* (Clarendon Press 1997) 16.
[91] Mee (n 58).
[92] Swadling (n 58).
[93] (1798) 4 Ves Jun 108, 110; 31 ER 56, 57.

settle it on trust for his nephew, after the nephew attained the age of twenty-one, but he failed to do this. He did, however, buy several estates in land after the date when he should have bought land for his nephew. After his death, his personal estate fell short of the amount in rents and profits that he had actually received, and it was argued that the nephew had a lien upon any estates in land he had purchased after the nephew attained the age of twenty-one. Counsel emphasized the harm that the claimants—beneficiaries under the nephew's will—would suffer if there were no claim to the land: there was 'no fund without resorting to the personal estate',[94] and so, if they could not claim the land, 'the money will be lost'.[95]

3.40 A Master in Chancery was appointed to inquire 'in what manner [the trustee] paid, applied, and disposed of, the personal estate and the rents and profits of the real estate, . . . and whether he laid out or invested the same or any part thereof in the purchase of any and what estates'.[96] He reported that there was no evidence to show how much the trustee had paid to buy the estates in land claimed by the claimants, or to show what had been done with the rents and profits of the trust estate. However, he found as a fact that '[the trustee] was, in his life-time, in the habit of laying out to the most advantage the moneys, which came to his hands, in Government securities, or mortgages, or in the purchase of lands, as opportunity offered.'[97] It could not, therefore, be proved that the trustee had used the trust money to buy the estates in land that were vested in him at his death. Counsel argued that he should nevertheless be treated as if he had done so, on the basis of a very broad interpretation of the maxim that equity sees as done that which ought to be done: 'where a man is bound to do an act, and does what may enable him to do it, he shall be taken to do that in performance of what he is bound to do.'[98]

3.41 In defending the view that English law recognized such a principle, he cited *Lechmere v Earl of Carlisle*[99] and other cases concerned with the doctrine of conversion. Under this doctrine, money held subject to an obligation to use it to purchase real property was[100] treated as being real property for the purposes of inheritance[101] and certain other legal rules;[102] conversely, land held subject to an obligation to sell it was treated as if it was personal property for the purposes of the same rules. In *Lechmere v Earl of Carlisle*,[103] Sir Joseph Jekyll MR had justified this doctrine in very broad terms, by reference to the idea that trustees should not, by breaching their duties, be able to prejudice beneficiaries: 'since at that rate it would

[94] *Perry* (n 93) 114; 59. [95] *Perry* (n 94) [96] *Perry* (n 93) 112; 58.
[97] *Perry* (n 93) 112–13; 58. [98] *Perry* (n 93) 116; 60.
[99] (1733) 3 P Wms 211, 24 ER 1033.
[100] Under the Trusts of Land and Appointment of Trustees Act 1996, s 3, this effect no longer occurs where the duty to buy or sell land arises under a trust (unless the trust is a testamentary trust and the testator died before 1 January 1997).
[101] Following the Administration of Estates Act 1925, this doctrine has had no role to play in the context of intestacies occurring after 31 December 1925, since the distinction between real and personal property was rendered irrelevant in that context by the Act.
[102] For example, whether a charging order could be imposed on land held on trust where the beneficiary under the trust was a debtor. Until the Charging Order Act 1979, such an order could not be made because the beneficiary was not treated as having an interest in the land itself but only in the proceeds of sale: *Irani Finance Ltd v Singh* [1971] Ch 59.
[103] *Lechmere* (n 99).

be in power of trustees . . . by delaying to do their duty . . . to affect the right of other persons'.[104] Instead, he held, the rule was that 'what ought to have been done shall be taken as done': 'a rule so powerful it is as to alter the very nature of things, to make money land, and, on the contrary, to turn land into money'.[105]

This justification—that the law will not allow the legal position of the claimant to be affected by another's failure to comply with a duty—has an obvious bearing on the problem faced by claimants in cases like *Kirk v Webb* and *Deg v Deg*. A trustee ought not to invest trust money in land for his own benefit, or on different trusts from those applicable to the trust money; where he has done this, he will have prejudiced the position of his beneficiaries by his breach of duty. The law responds, therefore, with the converse of the conventional maxim: equity sees as *not* done that which ought not to have been done. The counter-factual language[106] in which the judges describe this response echoes Sir Joseph Jekyll's account of the maxim as a rule 'so powerful as to change the very nature of things'. 3.42

In *Perry v Phelips*, however, counsel's attempted extension of the maxim was firmly rejected. Lord Loughborough LC commented that he would have liked to adopt the suggested approach but that principle and authority would not permit him to do so. It would have been desirable in every case where a person owed a debt for him to charge his land for the payment of those debts—he was even under a 'moral obligation'[107] to do so—but the fact that something was desirable, or morally obligatory, was not a sufficient basis, in English law, for finding that it had actually been done. He said that, if he could have directed the conduct of the trustee in *Perry v Phelips* itself, he would have taken care 'that the rents and profits should have been laid out in land'.[108] However, he could not treat him as having actually done this, where he had not had any such intention in buying the land and there was no evidence that he had, in fact, used the rents and profits of the trust money to do so: 3.43

I can find no case, no authority, no principle that enables me . . . where in point of fact I must be satisfied, the party did not mean to execute the trust or conceive himself to be under a trust, to hold, that the estate he purchased is subject to the trust.[109]

This response to counsel's argument in *Perry v Phelips* provides us with a kind of negative explanation of why it matters to prove a transactional link. Since the transactions by which the trustee bought the land did not qualify as substitutions—since the claimants could not show that the defendant had used the trust money to buy the land—the judge is bound to interpret the effect of these transactions by reference to the actual intentions of the person entering into them, even though he considers those intentions deplorable. Where a trustee acquires an asset with his own money, after he has misappropriated the claimant's money, the court will refuse to interpret the later transaction as giving rise to a trust unless the two are linked by something more than chronology: there must be a declared intention to create a trust, *or* the transaction must qualify as a substitution. Where it can be shown that the

104 *Lechmere* (n 99) 215; 1035. 105 *Lechmere* (n 104).
106 See Chapter 2, paras 2.22–2.24 this volume. 107 *Perry* (n 93); 31 ER 56, 60–61.
108 *Perry* (n 107). 109 *Perry* (n 93) 117.

defendant has used the claimant's money to buy the land, his intentions are irrelevant; where it cannot be shown that there is any such transactional link to the claimant's assets, his intentions are determinative, even if he is in some sense behaving badly.

3.44 Similar language appears in Sir William Grant MR's decision, in the later case of *Denton v Davies*,[110] to reject an invitation to ignore the chronology of transactions and permit a claim in a case where the defendant trustee had used trust money to pay off a debt incurred[111] to buy the land in question. Having decided that this transaction could not 'be presented as a purchase made with the trust money',[112] he went on to conclude that *therefore* 'there is no ground, upon which the Court, however it may disapprove of part of the Defendant's conduct, can direct these purchased estates to be conveyed to the same uses as the settled estates that had been sold'.[113] Absent proof of a transactional link, it was enough that the defendant had 'positively [denied] that he purchased with any view to a settlement'.[114]

3.3. *Taylor v Plumer*: Intention, Authority, and 'Money Has No Earmark'

3.45 In this way, the maxim 'money has no earmark' came to play an important role in limiting the availability of claims to land bought, or allegedly bought, by trustees, executors, and administrators using the money of beneficiaries, testators, and the intestate. In that context, the maxim meant that the claimant had to prove a genuine transactional link between her asset and the land acquired by the defendant. She had to show that it was her money that was used to buy the land in question. If she could, she could claim the land even where the defendant had no intention of buying it for her; if she could not prove the transactional link, the defendant's intentions would, instead, determine the effect of the transaction.

3.46 In a parallel development, the maxim 'money has no earmark' also began to play an important—and rather different—role in limiting the availability of claims to assets acquired by agents using chattels belonging to their principals. In *Burdett v Willett*,[115] it had been held that a merchant who had employed an agent or 'factor'[116] to sell his cloth was entitled to receive the proceeds of the sale in the event of the agent's bankruptcy. In *Whitecomb v Jacob*,[117] a limitation on this rule was articulated. Where a factor sold a merchant's goods, received the proceeds of sale and invested them in other goods, the court held that 'those goods shall be taken as part of the merchant's estate and not the factor's';[118] but, if the factor sold the goods and received money, becoming insolvent before he had invested the money in some other goods, it held that the money 'shall be looked upon as the factor's estate ... for in regard that

[110] (1812) 18 Ves Jun 499, 34 ER 406.
[111] See Chapter 4, Section 4.2.2 this volume on the limits of such tracing through the payment of a debt.
[112] *Denton* (n 110) 503; 408. [113] *Denton* (n 112). [114] *Denton* (n 112).
[115] (1708) 1 Eq Ca Ab 370, pl 3, SC, 23 ER 1017. See Chapter 6, paras 6.05–6.08 this volume for a more detailed analysis of this case.
[116] For the meaning of the term 'factor' in this context, see Chapter 6, para 6.05 this volume.
[117] (1710) 1 Salk 160, 91 ER 149. [118] *Whitecomb* (n 117).

money has no ear-mark, equity cannot follow that in behalf of him that employed the factor'.[119] Here, unlike the cases involving the purchase of land, the maxim does not mean that the claimant cannot prove that an exchange transaction has taken place because the original asset cannot easily be identified when it takes the form of money. Instead, it means that, even though he *can* show that an exchange transaction has taken place, he cannot identify the specific proceeds of that transaction to the satisfaction of the court; the *substitute* asset cannot be identified, because it has taken the form of money.

In *Scott v Surman*,[120] Willes LCJ put both elements of this case law—the availability of the claim to the proceeds, and the failure of such claims where the proceeds took the form of money—on a principled footing. In that case, the claimant, an overseas trader, had employed his brother, Richard Scott, to sell tar on his behalf and that of his business partner. In March 1739, the tar was imported from what was then the British province of Carolina to London; Scott received the bill of lading and sold the tar to buyers, Cornelius and Jeremiah Owen, to whom he owed a debt of £31. It was agreed that part of the price of the tar would be paid by a discharge of Scott's debt to the Owens, and the rest would be paid in promissory notes, four months after delivery of the tar. 3.47

In April 1740, after receiving two of the promissory notes due from the Owens, Scott committed an act of bankruptcy. The defendants, his assignees in bankruptcy, took possession of the promissory notes and cashed them when due; they also received the balance of the purchase price from the Owens. Under an Act of Parliament,[121] bounty money was payable on all imports of naval stores, including tar,[122] and the defendants also received a payment of this bounty money in respect of the tar. The claimants brought an action for money had and received against the defendants, seeking a payment of £358, 10s; this figure included the agreed purchase price of the tar and the bounty money, less the freight duty and other charges on the tar, which the defendants had paid. The Court of King's Bench held that they could recover £327, 10s; they could not recover the £31 value of the discharged debt, except as ordinary creditors in the insolvency, since that amount stood 'on just the same foot as if the bankrupt had received it in money before his bankruptcy'.[123] 3.48

Willes LCJ invoked 'the reason of the thing'[124] to explain the result. He noted that, if Scott had been bankrupted while the claimants' tar was still in his possession and the defendants had taken it and sold it, the claimants would have had a claim in trover. On the other hand, if Scott had sold the tar, received money for it, and the money 'had not been laid out again by him in any specific thing to distinguish it from the rest of his estate',[125] the claimants would have no action against the assignees 3.49

[119] *Whitecomb* (n 117) 161. [120] (1742–3) Willes 400, 125 ER 1235.

[121] (1705) stat 3 & 4 Ann c 10.

[122] For an overview of the general practice of offering bounty payments on the import or export of particular goods, thought to be of particular social and economic importance, see J Hoppit, 'Bounties, the Economy, and State in Britain 1689-1800' in P Gauci (ed), *Regulating the British Economy 1660-1850* (Ashgate Publishing 2011) 139–160.

[123] *Scott* (n 120) 401; 1236. [124] *Scott* (n 120) 404; 1238.

[125] *Scott* (n 120); 1237.

if they took possession of the money; they would have to come in as ordinary creditors in the insolvency. The present case was a 'middle case'[126] between these two scenarios, but was covered by the same reasons. The claimants would have been able to recover their goods if they remained unsold in Scott's hands 'because they remain in specie, and so may be distinguished from the rest of the bankrupt's estate'.[127] If, on the other hand, they had been sold for money, this characteristic would be lost: 'as money has no earmark, it cannot be distinguished'.[128] In the present case, the goods had been sold in exchange for things that could be distinguished from the rest of the bankrupt's estate—the promissory notes—and 'to be sure in reason the thing produced ought to follow the nature of the thing out of which it is produced, if it can be distinguished'.[129]

3.50 There are two key points about this explanation of the claim and its limits. First, the claim to the substitute is explained as an incident of the ownership of the original asset: it is the original asset that has 'produced' the substitute, the substitute shares its 'nature' as long as it can be distinguished, and thus 'in reason' the person who owned the original goods ought also to have its proceeds. In this account of a substitution, the particular parties to the substituting transaction—Scott, who agreed to sell the tar, and the Owens, who agreed to supply promissory notes and discharge the debt in exchange for it—drop out of the picture entirely. Instead, it is the original thing that produces the substitute, as a cow might calve or a tree might fruit.[130] In *Taylor v Plumer*, this reifying image takes on considerable significance; it is used by Lord Ellenborough CJ to reject narrower explanations for the source of the claimant's right and to affirm that the claim to the product does not depend on the defendant's authority to make the substitution or on the intentions of his counterpart in the exchange transaction.

3.51 Secondly, the problem of tracing money is explained on the basis that money received under a sale cannot be distinguished from any other money that might be in the possession of the bankrupt factor. Willes LCJ's analogy between the impossibility of tracing into money and the impossibility into tracing into the value of a discharged debt clarifies why this problem of identification matters. Even if the defendant is undoubtedly better off as a result of his decision to dispose of the claimant's asset—even if the abstract fund of resources at his disposal has been increased, either by an unidentifiable injection of cash or by the reduction of his liabilities—tracing is impossible unless a specific asset can be identified as the product of that decision. Lord Ellenborough CJ also affirmed this element of the *Scott v Surman* reasoning in *Taylor v Plumer*,[131] and its implications were developed in the later case law concerning tracing into bank accounts and through mixed substitutions.

126 *Scott* (n 125). 127 *Scott* (n 120) 1237–38. 128 *Scott* (n 124).
129 *Scott* (n 124).
130 See para 3.80 this chapter on the limits of this analogy between claims to traceable proceeds and claims to fruits.
131 (1815) 3 M & S 562, 105 ER 721.

3.3.1. Unauthorized substitution as a change of form

In *Scott v Surman*, counsel for the defendants had argued that the claimants could not claim the traceable proceeds of Scott's sale of the tar because that sale had been unauthorized. He had sold the tar on credit and 'a factor by general authority cannot sell on credit'[132] unless his principal has given him special authority to sell on these terms; thus, counsel suggested, the claimants would not have been bound to accept the sale and, for that reason, were not entitled to claim its proceeds. Willes LCJ rejected this argument on two grounds. First, he denied that a sale on credit was unauthorized; 'constant and daily experience'[133] showed that factors routinely sold their principals' goods on credit without requiring a special authority to do so. Secondly, he said that it did not matter if the sale was unauthorized: the claimants had a right to decide whether or not to demand the proceeds from the factor, or to pursue the buyers for their tar, and they had chosen to take the proceeds. 3.52

In *Taylor v Plumer*,[134] the argument based on the agent's want of authority took centre stage. In that case, Sir Thomas Plumer had authorized one Walsh, a stockbroker, to sell some of his shares and to account to him for the proceeds of sale. Walsh duly negotiated and completed the sales on 29 November 1811, received the proceeds into his personal bank account on 4 December, and paid them into Sir Thomas Plumer's bank account at Gosling & Co by cheque. On 29 November 1811, he also placed an order on his own account with an American stockbroker, requesting £10,000 worth of American shares, 'of such sort as would be most useful to a person going to America',[135] and promising to pay for these shares 'on the 4th or 5th of December'.[136] On 2 December, he placed an order with a jeweller to buy gold bullion, also in his own name. He placed these orders because he was on the verge of bankruptcy and unable to support his family, and meant to abscond to America to begin a new life.[137] At the time of placing the orders, he meant to pay for the stock and the gold using money misappropriated from another client, Oldham, whom he expected to give him a large sum of money. In fact, however, Oldham gave him a much smaller sum than he expected—only £1,500—and so he abandoned this scheme and instead 'conceived the intention of absconding with [Sir Thomas Plumer's] money when it should come into his hands',[138] and using it to complete his purchases of the gold and American shares. 3.53

[132] *Scott* (n 120) 406; 1239. [133] *Scott* (n 120) 407; 1239.

[134] *Taylor* (n 131); see also *R v Walsh* (1812) 4 Taunt 258, 128 ER 328.

[135] *R v Walsh* (n 134) 260; 329. [136] *R v Walsh* (n 134).

[137] See L Smith, 'The Stockbroker and the Solicitor-General: The Story Behind *Taylor v Plumer*' (1994) 15 Journal of Legal History 1, 3–9.

[138] *Taylor* (n 131) 563; 722. For a richer account of Walsh's motives, see his letter to his brother, Joseph, quoted by Smith at (1994) 15 Journal of Legal History 1, 7: 'Oh! my God, pardon my heinous offence. – Sir Thomas Plumer employed me to sell a large sum of stock to pay for an estate, and I have withheld a part of the proceeds. I might have taken it all; but I thought it crime enough for my future life to answer for to take what I conceived would be sufficient to maintain my family in competence and pay those debts which hung heaviest on my mind'. It appears that he had been less reluctant to defraud Oldham, whose 'mercenary disposition' he disliked: see Smith at (1994) 15 Journal of Legal History 1, 3.

3.54 On 5 December, Sir Thomas Plumer's money did come into his hands. Sir Thomas, considering that 'he had more money at his bankers than he wished to keep unemployed',[139] decided to invest in Exchequer bills and gave Walsh a cheque for £22,200 on his personal bank account, directing him to use it to buy the bills and deliver them immediately to either Sir Thomas or to his bankers. Walsh took the cheque to the bankers, who accepted it, duly debited Sir Thomas' account, and gave Walsh twenty-two £1,000 notes and one £200 note. Walsh used £6,500 of this cash to buy Exchequer bills, which he duly delivered to Sir Thomas that evening, and misappropriated the rest. He used eleven of the £1,000 notes to pay for the American stock, paying them to his broker and receiving share certificates and a sum in cash representing the difference between the price of the stock and the £11,000 he had paid. He gave a twelfth note to his brother-in-law, who gave him two cheques for £500 and £100 in exchange, keeping the rest to discharge a debt that Walsh owed him. The £500 cheque was then paid to the jeweller for £300 worth of gold bullion; this time, Walsh received his change in the form of a cheque.

3.55 He then fled to Falmouth by the mail coach on the same day, with the intention of absconding to Lisbon and then to North America, taking the share certificates and gold bullion with him. This act of flight on 5 December 1811 was an act of bankruptcy; under the doctrine of relation back which then[140] applied to bankruptcy, title to his assets retrospectively vested in his assignees in bankruptcy from this date onward. Sir Thomas Plumer's agent caught up with Walsh at Falmouth on 9 December. The agent took possession of the American share certificates and the gold bullion, and persuaded Walsh to execute a deed by which he declared that he assigned them to Sir Thomas on trust to pay him the £15,500 difference between the money misappropriated and the Exchequer bills actually purchased and delivered. By the same deed, Walsh also promised that he would be personally liable to pay Sir Thomas £15,500, with 5 per cent interest, and agreed to pay a penalty of £31,000 if he defaulted on this debt.

3.56 Sir Thomas subsequently sold the American shares and the gold bullion and kept the proceeds. Walsh's assignees in bankruptcy, Taylor and another, brought an action against him in trover. They argued that, since Walsh had obtained legal title to the stock and the gold when he bought them, title to these things must be deemed to have vested in themselves as his assignees on 5 December, when he committed his act of bankruptcy; he could not, therefore, have validly declared a trust of them in Sir Thomas' favour on 9 December and Sir Thomas, in taking and selling them, had committed the tort of trover. Counsel for Sir Thomas replied that title to these things had never vested in the assignees in bankruptcy because they were held on trust for Sir Thomas even before the declaration of 9 December: 'nothing passed by the assignment but what was in equity, as well as law, the property of the bankrupt'.[141]

[139] *Taylor* (n 138)

[140] Under the Insolvency Act 1986, s 278, the doctrine of relation back no longer applies in the bankruptcy context and title to a bankrupt's assets vest in the trustees in bankruptcy only at the date of the bankruptcy order.

[141] *Taylor* (n 131) 570; 724. This account of the effect of bankruptcy, initially formulated by Willes LCJ in *Scott v Surman*, has now been put on a statutory footing: Insolvency Act 1986, s 283(3)(a).

Lane v Dighton,[142] *Scott v Surman*,[143] and *Whitecomb v Jacob*[144] were all cited as relevant precedents, and both sides formulated a principled explanation of these cases, the claimants in narrow terms and the defendant in broad terms.

Counsel for the claimant assignees in bankruptcy, Marryat, explained these earlier cases in the language of authority: 'where the land is purchased in the execution of the trust, the Court will hold it subject to the trust, but where the purchase is a breach of trust, cestui que trust stands merely as a simple contract creditor[.]'.[145] He cited *Perry v Phelips*[146] as authority for this limitation but, on being pressed by Lord Ellenborough, he conceded that there was very little clear authority either way, since it was not clear whether the transactions were unauthorized in any of the earlier cases.[147] Meanwhile, counsel for the defendant, Abbott, denied that the distinction between authorized and unauthorized was of central importance, but instead framed the issue in the language of identification of things: 'the true distinction is not whether the property in the hands of the factor ... has been acquired by him in pursuance of his trust, but whether it can be specifically distinguished and ascertained to belong to the principal and not to the bankrupt'.[148] 3.57

It was in the context of his response to this argument that Lord Ellenborough CJ invoked the idea that a claimant's rights to a thing persist through any change in the form of the thing and characterized an unauthorized substitution as a change in form.[149] He put his objection to Marryat's argument, which he described as 'mischievous in principle and supported by no authorities in law',[150] in two ways. First, looking at the matter from the claimant's perspective, he said that when property 'in its original state and form' was 'covered with a trust' in favour of the claimant, no 'change of that state or form'[151] could 'divest'[152] the claimant of his rights under the trust. Secondly, looking at the matter from the defendant's perspective, he said that an 'abuse of trust' could 'confer no rights on the party abusing it, nor on those who claim in privity with him.'[153] Like Sir John Trevor MR in *Kinder v Miller*, he focused on the legal consequences of the substituting transaction, if a claim to its proceeds were denied, as its most important feature. If Sir Thomas Plumer had no claim to the gold and the shares, Walsh's abuse of trust would have been effective in divesting Sir Thomas of his rights to the banknotes, and in conferring new rights on Walsh and those who claimed in privity with him, like his assignees in bankruptcy. The claim to traceable proceeds was justified by the need to avoid these objectionable consequences; it did not depend on showing that Sir Thomas had authorized Walsh's transactions. 3.58

Nor did it depend on showing that he had ratified those transactions, in the strict sense. In *Scott v Surman*, Willes LCJ had addressed the problem of the factor's supposed lack of authority to sell on credit in language that echoed the doctrine of 3.59

142 *Taylor* (n 141) (counsel for the defendant); *Taylor* (n 131) 573; 725 (counsel for the claimants).
143 *Taylor* (n 131) 569; 724 (counsel for the claimants); *Taylor* (n 141) (counsel for the defendant).
144 *Taylor* (n 143) (counsel for the claimants); *Taylor* (n 131) 572; 725 (counsel for the defendant).
145 *Taylor* (n 131) 568; 723. 146 *Taylor* (n 145). 147 *Taylor* (n 144).
148 *Taylor* (n 141). 149 See Chapter 2, para 2.10 this volume.
150 *Taylor* (n 131) 574–75; 725–26. 151 *Taylor* (n 131) 574; 725.
152 *Taylor* (n 151). 153 *Taylor* (n 151).

ratification. He described the claimants having the right, if they chose, 'to confirm the sale'[154] even if it were outside the scope of the factor's actual authority. In *Taylor v Plumer*, however, Lord Ellenborough CJ firmly rejected the idea that Sir Thomas' claim was based 'on any supposed adoption and ratification on his part'[155] of Walsh's transactions. He noted the existence of the deed that Sir Thomas' agent had compelled Walsh to execute, declaring that he owed Sir Thomas a personal debt in the amount of £15,500, and said that this deed would have been fatal to the claim if the outcome in the case had depended on ratification: by demanding that Walsh personally repay the money he had spent in buying the gold and shares, Sir Thomas had 'disapproved and disallowed that act [of sale] instead of adopting and confirming it'.[156] However, this did not matter. Sir Thomas' claim to the proceeds did not depend on showing that he could, and had, ratified the transaction, any more than it depended on showing that the transaction was authorized from the outset. Instead, it depended on its character as a change in the form of his original thing.

3.60 Thus, Lord Ellenborough CJ's characterization of the unauthorized substitution as a change in the form of the original thing, in *Taylor v Plumer*, is not a purely decorative rhetorical flourish. It is an important element in his reasoning, playing a key role in explaining the substantive outcome in the case. He uses the metaphor of transformation to distinguish cases of unauthorized substitution from two other situations where A's transaction with X might give rise to a right in favour of B in English law, neither of which cover the facts of *Taylor v Plumer*: an authorized disposition of B's assets by A, and an unauthorized transaction by A that could be ratified by B. To understand the point of the metaphor, and the normative work that it does, it is therefore useful to compare the facts and outcome in *Taylor v Plumer* with the operation of these other doctrines.

3.3.1.1. Tracing contrasted with claiming through an authorized disposition

3.61 An authorized disposition occurs where A holds a power to deal with or dispose of B's assets, which he is entitled to exercise in certain defined circumstances, and which he then exercises in those circumstances. Walsh, when he sold Sir Thomas Plumer's shares and received the proceeds of sale on 29 November 1811, was carrying out an authorized disposition: Sir Thomas had directed him to sell the shares, had allowed him to negotiate the terms of the sales, and had authorized him to receive the proceeds of sale in his own bank account before accounting to him for their value. Assuming that none of these transactions represented a breach of duty, their effect would have been to divest Sir Thomas of his rights in the shares and to give him a right[157] to the proceeds instead. As counsel noted in the case itself, Sir Thomas

[154] *Scott* (n 132). [155] *Taylor* (n 131); 727. [156] *Taylor* (n 131) 579–80; 727.

[157] The content of this right would have depended on the terms of his agreement with Walsh. Since he had apparently authorized Walsh to pay the money into his own bank account, and to account for the proceeds by cheque, it is likely that it was not meant to be proprietary in character and Walsh could have satisfied his obligation by paying him the abstract amount received from any source: see *Kirkham v Peel* (1880) 43 LT 171, discussed in Chapter 6 this volume at paras 6.12–6.15. For a discussion of

would not merely have been entitled to the proceeds of an authorized disposition of this kind; he would have been 'bound to take'[158] them. This was true in two senses.

First, as against Walsh, he could not have refused to take the amount realized by the actual sales and demand that Walsh pay him some other sum instead. Since these sales did not involve any breach of duty, the risk involved in them lay on his shoulders. If the shares had unexpectedly risen in value on the day after they had been sold, so that Sir Thomas suffered a net loss as a result, this would not have been Walsh's concern, assuming that he was not in breach of any duty of care in failing to predict the rise in value.[159] Walsh would have discharged his duty to Sir Thomas by accounting to him for the proceeds actually realized, even if these were less than the ultimate market value of the shares sold. In Hohfeldian terms, this dimension of the authorized disposition describes a privilege[160] held by Walsh: he was under no duty not to sell the shares in the circumstances, Sir Thomas had no right to require him not to sell them in those circumstances, and thus could not be owed any secondary duties to be compensated in the event of any loss flowing from the sale. 3.62

Secondly, as against the rest of the world, Sir Thomas could not have disavowed the legal consequences of the sale of the shares. The intentional act of his agent, acting within the scope of the powers conferred on him, would have had the same effect as Sir Thomas' own act.[161] Thus, after the sale, he could not have demanded the dividends due on the shares be paid to him, instead of the buyers, and he could not have sued the buyers to demand possession of the share certificates. Walsh's act would have been effective in changing the legal relations between Sir Thomas and the relevant companies, and the companies and the buyers of the shares. In Hohfeldian terms, this dimension of the authorized disposition describes the exercise of a power[162] held by Walsh, correlative to a liability in Sir Thomas. Before the sale, Sir Thomas had the right to receive dividends on the shares, as well as having the other rights of a shareholder. After Walsh's decision to sell, he no longer had these rights and the buyers had them instead. 3.63

These effects of an authorized substitution cannot be explained simply as a response to the claimant's own consent to the loss of his rights, since they arise in response to the conferral of authority by any relevant person, usually a past or present owner of the asset in question. On the facts of *Taylor v Plumer*, Walsh's authority derived from Sir Thomas Plumer's actual consent; he could not object to Walsh's dealings with his shares as a wrong because he had consented to those dealings, 3.64

the circumstances in which a principal may gain a proprietary right to the proceeds of an authorized disposition in the hands of his agent, see B Geva, 'Authority of Sale and Privity of Contract: The Proprietary Basis of the Right to the Proceeds of Sale at Common Law' (1980) 25 McGill Law Journal 32.

[158] *Taylor* (n 131) 569; 723.

[159] Eg *Gokal Chand-Jagan Nath v Nand Ram das-Atma Ram* [1939] AC 106. If Sir Thomas had directed him to sell on that specific day, then he would not have been liable even if, in fact, a prudent seller would not have sold then: see *The Overend & Gurney Company v Gibb* (1871–72) LR 5 HL 480.

[160] D Campbell and P Thomas (eds), *Fundamental Legal Conceptions As Applied in Judicial Reasoning by Wesley Newcomb Hohfeld* (Ashgate 2001) 21–27.

[161] *Pickering v Busk* (1812) 15 East 38, 104 ER 758.

[162] Campbell and Thomas (n 160) 14–21.

and those dealings could vary his existing rights for the same reason. However, the effect would have been similar if Walsh's authority had derived from the decision of someone else, such as a previous owner of the shares. For example, suppose that A receives shares from C to hold on trust for B, on terms that authorize him to deal with or dispose of the shares for B's benefit; in this scenario, his authorized dealings with the shares will bind B, even if B has never consented to them.[163] This does not mean only that B cannot complain of these authorized dealings as a wrong, but also that he must accept that A's intentional act represents a good reason why his own legal position should be changed.[164]

3.65 This respect for the decision of a person on whom authority has been conferred explains a number of features of the law's response to authorized dispositions. For example, the courts will not interfere with the exercise of any discretion possessed by the bearer of such authority, unless he is in breach of his duties.[165] Similarly, where the authorized disposition is an authorized substitution, the content of any claims to the substitute will be shaped by the intentions of the person who made the disposition. For example, a trustee may have a power of appropriation[166] that entitles him to decide which beneficiary shall have the benefit of a particular investment. If he acts within the scope of this power when making that investment and allocating it to one beneficiary, a different beneficiary cannot argue that his intentions should be disregarded in her favour merely because the purchase of the investment involved the use of trust assets,[167] and the particular investment has happened to appreciate in value.[168]

3.66 In this way, the law's response to an authorized disposition involves taking the intentions of the authority holder seriously. As between claimant and defendant, the claimant's inability to reject the adequacy of the proceeds of an authorized substitution, and to bring other claims against the defendant, is explained by the defendant's liberty or privilege to exchange the claimant's assets for those proceeds. As between claimant and the rest of the world, the claimant's inability to reject the proceeds of an authorized substitution, and assert his rights in respect of the original asset, is explained by the defendant's power to alter his legal position in this way.

[163] *State Bank of India v Sood* [1997] Ch 276. For a discussion of the complex interaction between this doctrine, arising from the express conferral of powers of disposition on trustees, and the modern statutory framework governing trusts of land, see C Harpum, 'Overreaching, Trustees' Powers, and the Reform of the 1925 Legislation' (1990) 49 CLJ 277; G Ferris and G Battersby, 'The General Principles of Overreaching and the Modern Legislative Reforms 1996-2002' (2003) 119 LQR 94; and N Jackson, 'Overreaching in Registered Land Law' (2006) 69 MLR 214.

[164] J Raz, 'Voluntary Obligations and Normative Powers' (1972) 42 Proceedings of the Aristotelian Society 79.

[165] See, in relation to discretionary powers conferred on trustees, *Pilkington v IRC* [1964] AC 612 and *Pitt v Holt* [2013] UKSC 26. In relation to discretionary powers conferred on agents, see *Elidor Investments SA v Christie's, Mansons Woods Ltd* [2009] EWHC 3600 and *Torres Asset Funding Ltd v Royal Bank of Scotland* [2013] EWHC 270, per Sales J at [35]. Cf M Ashdown, *Trustee Decision Making: The Rule in Re Hastings-Bass* (OUP 2015).

[166] See, generally, L Tucker and others, *Lewin on Trusts* (19th edn, Sweet & Maxwell 2015) 36-075 to 36-090.

[167] Eg *In re Richardson* [1896] 1 Ch 512; *Rich v Whitfield* (1866) LR 2 Eq 583.

[168] Cf *In re Marquess of Abergavenny's Estate Act Trusts* [1981] 1 WLR 843.

Both power and privilege appear to be explained by the same principle: the law's acknowledgement of the authority conferred on the defendant by an owner of the original asset, whether this is the claimant or someone else.

3.67 Where a disposition of that asset is unauthorized, by contrast, the explanatory force of an owner's decision to confer authority on the defendant seems to run out. The law does not have the same reason to treat that transaction as binding on the claimant, the person whose assets have been dealt with, in either of the two senses sketched earlier. When Walsh used Sir Thomas Plumer's banknotes[169] to buy gold and American shares, it could not be said that Sir Thomas was 'bound' to accept that decision in the sense that Walsh held any privilege to make it; clearly, the transaction was a breach of duty, and Sir Thomas was entitled to complain of it and, for example, to demand that Walsh pay him the value of the cash spent in this unauthorized fashion. It would not have made sense for Walsh to point to the authority that Sir Thomas had conferred on him to buy Exchequer bills as a reason why he should be satisfied to take the gold and shares that had been bought instead and to make no further claims.

3.68 Counsel suggested that this fact made all the difference. Since Walsh had no authority to use the banknotes in that way, Sir Thomas was not obliged to accept the consequences of his decision to do so. Since he was not obliged to accept the proceeds of Walsh's transactions, then, there was no reason to treat him as entitled to them: 'it is only so long as he would be bound to accept [the property] that he can reasonably call it his own'.[170] As we have seen, Lord Ellenborough CJ rejected this argument on the grounds that, if accepted, it would mean that Sir Thomas would have been divested of his rights by a wrongful change in the form of his property. The question is why this is so, given counsel's argument that Sir Thomas was not *bound* to take the proceeds, in the sense that he would have been bound to take them if the transaction had been authorized. If the transaction represented a nullity from Sir Thomas Plumer's perspective—if he was free to disavow the transaction, reject the proceeds, and demand his original banknotes back—in what sense can it still be described as involving any loss of rights on his part?

3.69 The answer seems to be that, although Walsh did not have a privilege to dispose of the cash as against Sir Thomas—in that it was a breach of duty for him to do so—he nevertheless had some power to do so, vis-à-vis the stockbroker and the jeweller who received the cash from him. On the facts of the case, it is not obvious that Sir Thomas could have recovered the banknotes in the hands of these third parties. If, as Lord Ellenborough CJ's phrasing seems to suggest,[171] Walsh had obtained a legal title to the notes from the bank, which he held on trust for Sir Thomas, the transaction would have been effective in conveying that title to these strangers; the question whether they then came under any duty to Sir Thomas would depend on whether they had given value and had notice of his title.[172] If, on the other hand, Sir Thomas

[169] It is a disputed question whether Sir Thomas had a legal or equitable title to those notes: see Chapter 3, para 3.68 this volume.
[170] *Taylor* (n 131) 569; 723–24.
[171] 'If the property in its original state and form was covered with a trust': *Taylor* (n 131) 574; 725.
[172] *Pilcher v Rawlins* (1871–72) LR 7 Ch App 259.

had a common law title to the notes, the currency of money means that this title was unlikely to have survived Walsh's transactions with them;[173] again, his claims would depend on whether they had given value and had notice of his title to them.

3.70 Thus, although Sir Thomas was not 'bound to accept' Walsh's transactions in the first sense, being entitled to treat them as breaches of duty, it was nevertheless not open to him to treat them as simply irrelevant legal nullities in the second sense. If he was a beneficiary under a trust, the effect of each transaction was to transfer his trustee's title to the trust asset to a stranger and thus—at best—to significantly alter the rights he had prior to that transaction. If he was an owner at common law, the effect of the sale was to potentially destroy the duties of non-interference with the cash previously owed to him by all subjects of the legal system, including the jeweller and the stockbroker. It is true, therefore, that Walsh's 'abuse of trust'—his decision to use the banknotes to buy gold and shares—had the effect of divesting Sir Thomas of his existing rights in some sense.[174] It is this vulnerability to a loss of rights on his part that explains Lord Ellenborough CJ's characterization of the facts. If the claim to traceable proceeds had been denied, Walsh and his successors in title would indeed have obtained new rights by that very act of abuse of trust. Title to the gold and the shares would have been vested in Walsh by their owners precisely in consideration for his decision to convey title to the banknotes to them, despite the legal consequences of that decision for Sir Thomas' previously vested rights, and despite Walsh's obligation not to make such a decision.

3.71 The metaphor of reification captures the key difference between a claim to the proceeds of an authorized disposition and this account of a claim to traceable proceeds. In the case of the authorized disposition, the law's response can be explained by its respect for the decision-making authority of the defendant, itself derived from the decision of a former or current owner to confer that authority on him. That respect for his authority shapes the availability of the claim, and its content, and thus it is best explained by characterizing the substitution as an intentional act. By contrast, claims to traceable proceeds respond to decisions that the law considers should not have been made at all, but that nevertheless have prejudicial legal consequences for the rights of the claimant. The metaphor of reification captures this idea by completely dropping the language of intentional action from the account of what the defendant has done in transacting with a third party. Later reifying descriptions of tracing[175]—presenting it as a matter of things becoming other things, or of value moving from one repository to another—highlight the irrelevance of the intentional character of the particular series of contracts or bargains entered into by a particular defendant and instead focus our attention on the consequences of those bargains for the rights of the claimant.

[173] *Miller v Race* (1758) 1 Burrow 452, 97 ER 398. It is more likely that the banknote given by Walsh to his brother-in-law in discharge of his debt to him might have been recoverable, since it is arguable that the brother-in-law would have had notice of Sir Thomas Plumer's title.

[174] For an analysis of the forms that such vulnerability can take at common law, see Chapter 8 this volume.

[175] See Chapter 2 this volume.

3.3.1.2. *Tracing contrasted with ratification*

This disregard for the intentional character of the substituting transaction also explains the difference between tracing through a transaction and ratifying it. The conventional understanding of ratification,[176] in English law, is that it is an option available to a principal where his agent, or someone claiming to be his agent,[177] purports to deal with a third party on his behalf even though she lacks the authority to do. For example, suppose that A is B's employee but does not have any authority to enter into contracts or make purchases on B's behalf. Nevertheless, she buys a car from X and alleges, to X, that she is doing so as B's agent; she promises X that B will pay him £1,000 as the price of the car and then takes possession of the car, purportedly on B's behalf. On these facts, assuming that A had neither actual nor apparent[178] authority to enter into any such transaction on B's behalf, X will not have any claim against B. He cannot sue B for the agreed price of the car, and his only remedies will be against A and, perhaps, recipients of the car from A.[179] However, it is open to B to change this by ratifying the transaction, treating it as if it was entered into with his authority. For example, on learning what A has done, he might take possession of the car and began to use it for his own purposes.[180] If he does this, the effect is that the transaction is treated as if it had been authorized.[181] Title to the car vests in B from the moment of ratification,[182] provided that no third-party rights have intervened,[183] and X can sue him for the agreed price.[184] 3.72

This doctrine, in its strict sense, cannot explain the outcome in *Taylor v Plumer*. Walsh, when he purchased the gold and the shares, did not represent himself[185] to the jeweller and the stockbroker as Sir Thomas Plumer's agent and they clearly meant to deal with Walsh as a principal and not as Sir Thomas' agent. This is fatal to an analysis based on ratification in English law. A principal cannot take the benefit 3.73

[176] See, generally, P Watts (ed), *Bowstead & Reynolds on Agency* (20th edn, Sweet & Maxwell 2016) paras 2-047–2-098.

[177] As in *Lyell v Kennedy* (1889) 14 App Cas 437.

[178] That is, assuming that B was not estopped from denying A's authority to make the purchase by his own direct or indirect representations to X: see *Acute Property Developments Ltd v Apostolu* [2013] EWHC 200 (Ch), per Nicholas Strauss QC at [23]–[25].

[179] Since A fraudulently misrepresented to X that he was contracting with B, not with A herself, it is arguable that the contract for sale of the car is void, so that title to the car never passed to A: see *Hardman v Booth* (1863) 1 H & C 803, as explained in *Shogun Finance Ltd v Hudson* [2004] 1 AC 919, per Lord Phillips at [128]. For criticisms of this analysis, see WJ Swadling, 'Unjust Delivery' in A Burrows and A Rodgers (eds), *Mapping the Law: Essays in Memory of Peter Birks* (OUP 2006) 277.

[180] For examples of such ratification by conduct, see *Allard v Bourne* (1863) 15 CB (NS) 468, 143 ER 868 and *Smith v The Hull Glass Company* (1852) 11 CB 897, 138 ER 729.

[181] Cf *United Australia Ltd v Barclays Bank Ltd* [1941] AC 1, per Lord Atkin at 28: 'the lack of authority disappears'.

[182] *Lawson (Inspector of Taxes) v Hosemaster Machine Co* [1966] 1 WLR 1300; cf M Bridge, (ed), *Benjamin's Sale of Goods* (9th edn, Sweet & Maxwell 2016) para 1-0174 and authorities cited there.

[183] *Bird v Brown* (1850) 4 Ex 786, 154 ER 1433; *Presentaciones Musicales SA v Secunda* [1994] Ch 271; *Borkan General Trading Ltd v Monsoon Shipping Ltd* [2003] EWCA Civ 935, per Clarke LJ at [66] to [79].

[184] *Cornwal v Wilson* (1750) 1 Ves Sen 509, 27 ER 1173.

[185] If he had done so, ratification may have been possible even if he had privately intended to take the gold and shares for his own benefit: *Re Tiedemann and Ledermann Freres Arbitration* [1899] 2 QB 66.

of an unauthorized transaction by his agent where the other party to that transaction had no idea of his existence at the time of the transaction. This is so even where—unlike in *Taylor v Plumer* itself—the agent intends to act as an agent and expects his undisclosed principal to ratify the unauthorized transaction.[186] Although the logic of this rule has been criticized,[187] given that an undisclosed principal can take the benefit of an authorized disposition,[188] even its reversal would not capture a case like *Taylor v Plumer*, where *neither* party to the relevant transaction—neither the putative agent, nor the third party he is dealing with—intended the supposed principal to acquire any rights under that transaction. At the time of the transactions, Walsh had no intention, subjective or objective,[189] to acquire these assets as an agent for Sir Thomas Plumer and so it would be inapposite to describe Sir Thomas as an undisclosed principal at all. The doctrine of ratification 'would not be appropriately invoked to allow intervention by a person, uncontemplated by the purported agent, who simply found it convenient to ratify the transaction'.[190] Tracing, by contrast, can be invoked to allow precisely such an intervention, by a person who is not within the contemplation of either the supposed agent or his counterpart in the exchange transaction.

3.74 In this way, the contrast between tracing and ratification again draws our attention to how tracing disregards the intentions of the parties to a transaction in interpreting its consequences. From the perspective of justification, ratification might be thought to make sense because the third party who is bound by the unauthorized transaction, as a result of the decision of the principal to ratify it, is getting what she bargained for;[191] on this view, her own intentions supply a reason why it should be open to the principal to bring about a transfer of her rights to him, if he so chooses, in accordance with the terms of the bargain agreed with the agent. This explanation cannot hold in a case like *Taylor v Plumer*, where the jeweller and the stockbroker had no intention of transferring their rights to anyone but Walsh.

3.75 However, Lord Ellenborough CJ's rejection of accounts of tracing in terms of ratification has had somewhat chequered subsequent history. Although the possibility of tracing cannot be explained on the basis of ratification in the strict sense, analogies to ratification occasionally recur in the subsequent case law,[192] and

186 *Keighley, Maxted & Co v Durant* [1901] AC 240.

187 Watts (n 176) para 2-061.

188 See generally Watts (n 176) paras 8-069–8-081.

189 In that his subjective intent was to acquire the assets for his own use, and he had not made any communication to Sir Thomas about his decision to buy the assets, from which Sir Thomas might have objectively deduced an intention to acquire them as his agent. For the view that a transaction for the benefit of an undisclosed principal will be binding only where an agent's intention to act for that undisclosed principal is objectively discernable to the principal, and not merely an uncommunicated subjective intent on the part of the agent, see *Magellan Spirit ApS v Vitol SA* [2016] EWHC 454 (Comm), per Legatt LJ at [16]–[20].

190 See (n 189).

191 Watts (n 176) para 2-068.

192 Eg *Twiss v White* (1826) 1 Bing 487, 130 ER 601, per Best CJ at 130 ER 601, 602: 'the Plaintiff by demanding the proceeds in the hands of the Defendant ratified the bargain ... and, according to the principles established in the case of *Taylor v Sir Thomas Plumer* ... was entitled to follow the proceeds in the hands of the defendant'. See, in a similar vein, *Dudley v Champion* [1893] 1 Ch 101, per North J at 113 and *Buhr v Barclays Bank* [2001] EWCA Civ 1223, per Arden LJ at [49].

have been used to explain the supposed limits of common law tracing.[193] The core appeal of the analogy can be explained on the basis of the structural similarity in the content of the right obtained by the claimant in the two situations. Like a principal who has a right to ratify an unauthorized transaction, a claimant who can identify the traceable proceeds of his assets has a choice as to whether to take those proceeds or, instead, to pursue other remedies;[194] when the choice is made, certain other claims that might otherwise have been available to him on the facts become unavailable. As the House of Lords explained in *United Australia v Barclays Bank Ltd*,[195] courts have sometimes used the fictitious[196] language of ratification to describe a claimant's exercise of a freedom to elect between inconsistent rights, or between alternative remedies, in a number of situations where an analysis based on actual ratification is impossible or irrelevant.

In *Marsh v Keating*,[197] for example, the language of ratification played a complex role both in counsel's argument that no claim was available and in the judicial rejection of that argument. In that case, one Henry Fauntleroy had used a forged power of attorney to sell[198] stock in the Bank of England belonging to the claimant, Mrs Ann Keating, to a third party, Tarbutt. The proceeds of sale were paid into a bank account that Fauntleroy jointly held with the other partners in his firm, Marsh & Co, and Mrs Keating brought an action for money had and received against the surviving[199] partners, seeking to recover the amount of the proceeds that had been paid into their bank account. The action was resisted by the assignees in bankruptcy of the partners, denying that their receipt of the proceeds had given rise to any obligation to pay her the money.[200] The matter was brought before the House of Lords on a writ of error, and argued before twelve judges who were asked to advise the House.[201] 3.76

Counsel for the assignees in bankruptcy, Sir Edward Sugden, argued that Mrs Keating could not show that she had been entitled to the proceeds of sale of the stock at the time that they were received by Marsh & Co, because she had not ratified their sale and did not have the right to do so. She had not done anything to affirm the sale of the stock to Tarbutt and had, in fact, written to the Bank of England to complain of the sale and to ask for her stock to be replaced; since she could not 'at once affirm 3.77

[193] See Section 3.3.2.3 this chapter.

[194] *Lipkin Gorman v Karpnale Ltd* [1991] 2 AC 548, per Lord Goff at 573: ' "tracing" ... property into its product involves a decision by the owner of the original property to assert his title to the product in place of his original property. This is sometimes referred to as ratification. I myself would not so describe it[.]'

[195] [1941] AC 1. [196] *United Australia* (n 195) per Lord Atkin at 27.

[197] (1834) 1 Bing (NC) 198, 131 ER 1094. Also reported at (1834) 2 Cl & Fin 250, 6 ER 1149.

[198] See Chapter 8 this volume for a more detailed analysis of the case.

[199] By the date of the litigation, Fauntleroy himself was dead. He was the last person in England to be executed for forgery, having been hanged outside Newgate prison on 30 November 1824: see R Davenport-Hines, 'Fauntleroy, Henry (1784–1824)', *Oxford Dictionary of National Biography* (OUP 2004).

[200] Like other victims of Fauntleroy's forgeries, Mrs Keating ultimately assigned her claims against the partners to the Bank of England, who reached a settlement with the assignees in bankruptcy that was subsequently approved by the court: for the details of the settlement, see *Marsh* (n 197) 291; 1164.

[201] For the history of the proceedings, see J Edelman, 'Marsh v Keating' in C Mitchell and P Mitchell (eds), *Landmark Cases in the Law of Restitution* (Hart Publishing 2006) 97, 106.

and disaffirm the same act',[202] he argued, this complaint about the sale closed off the possibility of claiming its proceeds by way of ratification, even if ratification had been an option on the facts. He also argued that it had never been an option, for two reasons. First, doing so would involve ratifying a forgery—Fauntleroy having relied on a forged power of attorney to bring about the sale—and ratification of a forgery was impossible.[203] Secondly, ratification could not be used to prejudice third parties to the transaction ratified, like Marsh & Co: while Mrs Keating might possibly have 'affirmed the transfer as against Fauntleroy, and treated the produce as money had and received to her use in his hands, she has no such election against Marsh and Co, between whom and herself there was no privity'.[204]

3.78 In reply to this argument, counsel for Mrs Keating cited *Taylor v Plumer*, and drew on the property logic invoked by Lord Ellenborough CJ in that case. In *Taylor v Plumer*, he said, 'Sir Thomas Plumer did not claim through the fraud or felony of Walsh the broker, but in defiance of them'.[205] The argument in *Taylor v Plumer* had not been that Walsh's fraudulent transactions were meant to benefit Sir Thomas, so that Sir Thomas could take advantage of them, but instead that Walsh could not have obtained a good title to the assets obtained under those transactions: '[o]ne cannot be allowed to make title through fraud and felony'.[206] Similarly, Mrs Keating was not affirming Fauntleroy's fraudulent transaction but was instead denying his title to the proceeds of sale and, thus, denying Marsh & Co's title to those proceeds as well. She was, he went on to say, entitled to the proceeds of sale because they represented the 'fruits'[207] of her stock; her right to recover their value from the partners was analogous to the right she would have had to recover the value of her plate, if a wrongdoer had stolen it and it could be traced to his partners.[208]

3.79 Thus, the arguments in *Marsh v Keating* pitted an analysis based on ratification against the reifying logic embraced by Lord Ellenborough CJ in *Taylor v Plumer*. The argument based on ratification focused on whether the transaction of sale could be and had been affirmed by the claimant as a valid expression of her own will, linking that issue to the question of unfair prejudice to third parties who may have acquired rights subsequent to the transaction and prior to the supposed decision to affirm the transaction. The rival argument characterized the proceeds of sale as the 'fruit' of the original asset, and suggested that the claim to recover the proceeds was simply a matter of asserting one's vested property rights against the world in general.

3.80 In delivering the advice of the judges to the House of Lords, however, Park J neither applied the normal limits of ratification to the claim nor adopted counsel's full-blown property logic. He held that Mrs Keating was not, in claiming the proceeds of sale of the transaction, actually affirming the validity of the sale in any sense: she was not seeking 'to confirm the title of the transferee of the stock',[209] but instead was 'looking only to the right of recovering the purchase money',[210] which was independent of such confirmation. However, he also said that *by* the act of claiming the purchase money, she had in fact strengthened the title of the transferee

[202] *Marsh* (n 197) 269; 1156. [203] *Marsh* (n 197) 271; 1157. [204] *Marsh* (n 202).
[205] *Marsh* (n 197) 278; 1160. [206] *Marsh* (n 205). [207] *Marsh* (n 205).
[208] *Marsh* (n 205). [209] *Marsh* (n 197) 286; 1162. [210] *Marsh* (n 209).

of the stock. The effect of claiming the proceeds would be to effectively bar any claim she would otherwise have had against Tarbutt, and stop her from 'seeking any remedy against, or questioning in any manner, [his] title'.[211] Like ratification of a transaction, the decision to claim a substitute asset cut off one possible claim that might otherwise have arisen on the same facts: a claim to the original asset sold. The claimant had a choice: she could adopt the 'circuitous process'[212] of somehow recovering her stock, either from Tarbutt or the Bank of England, or instead she could 'abandon all further concern with her stock, and ... consider the price which was paid by the purchaser for that which was her stock, to be her money'.[213] It is implicit in this analysis that she could not do both: in order to claim the traceable proceeds of the stock as her money, she was obliged to give up all claim to the stock itself.

This approach pushes against the logic of characterizing the proceeds of a sale of an asset as a fruit of that asset. If the law treated the proceeds of sale of a thing in exactly the same way as it treated fruits—if the money obtained by selling a ewe was the same kind of thing as a lamb born to the same ewe—no question of election between the original and the product would arise, as Lionel Smith has noted.[214] The owner would be perfectly entitled to recover both her ewe and its product, the lamb. In *Marsh v Keating*, by contrast, Mrs Keating could only recover the proceeds of the transaction by accepting that it had been effective in stripping her of her vested rights. In this way, the analogy between tracing and ratification reveals the limits of the reifying metaphors that have otherwise dominated judicial accounts of tracing. The characterization of an exchange transaction as a change in the form of the claimant's thing depends on how she herself chooses to characterize it, and one consequence of characterizing it in this way is that she must accept that it has been effective *as* a substitution: that is, in wholly depriving her of her vested rights in the original asset,[215] and stripping her of the claims she might otherwise have against the recipient of that asset. 3.81

3.3.2. Tracing into money at law and in equity

The language of ratification has also been used to explain the supposed problem with tracing into mixed substitutions at common law, which is conventionally attributed to Lord Ellenborough CJ's well-known and much-analysed dicta on the subject of tracing into money in *Taylor v Plumer*. Having held that a right to a substitute asset could not be defeated simply because the substitution was unauthorized, he went on to comment, obiter, on when such a right would be defeated: it would be defeated where the product of the substituting transaction could not be ascertained, 3.82

[211] *Marsh* (n 209). [212] *Marsh* (n 197) 284; 1162. [213] *Marsh* (n 212).

[214] L Smith, *The Law of Tracing* (Clarendon Press 1997) 21–24.

[215] Cf J Penner, 'Value, Property, and Unjust Enrichment: Trusts of Traceable Proceeds' in Chambers, Mitchell, and Penner (eds), *Philosophical Foundations of the Law of Unjust Enrichment* (n 3) 309: 'When one realizes the exchange value [of one's property], what one must *relinquish* is one's property. One never has the two of them at the same time, as anyone who has ever bought high and was forced to sell low will tell you'.

and this would be the case 'when the subject is turned into money and mixed and confounded in a general mass of the same description'.[216] Echoing the analysis of Willes LCJ in *Scott v Surman*, he described the problem in such cases as one of fact rather than law,[217] and added that it did not apply where money was 'in a bag, or otherwise kept apart from other money, guineas, or other coin marked (if the fact were so) for the purpose of being distinguished'.[218]

3.83 These dicta have been variously interpreted and re-interpreted in the subsequent case law. Judges have disagreed both about when they apply, what they mean, and whether they are justified. Thus, it has been suggested at different times that these dicta bar tracing into bank accounts,[219] as well as into and out of mixed substitutions;[220] they have been treated as applying such restrictions to anyone except a beneficiary under a trust,[221] or a principal in a fiduciary relationship.[222] Understood as imposing a bar on tracing into and out of mixed substitutions, these dicta have been rejected as an indefensibly limited or simple-minded understanding of the possibilities of tracing;[223] defended on the basis that the kind of tracing at issue in *Taylor v Plumer* operates by a kind of ratification and ratification becomes impossible once a mixed substitution has taken place;[224] and again criticized on the grounds that this supposed distinction between common law and equitable tracing is itself unprincipled.[225]

3.84 In order to understand these divergent views, it is important to distinguish between Lord Ellenborough CJ's account of the problem with tracing into money and later judicial explanations of the problem with tracing into money *at common law*. The latter problem can only be understood in the context of a historic misunderstanding of the outcome of *Taylor v Plumer*,[226] in which courts[227] and commentators[228]

[216] *Taylor* (n 131) 575; 726. [217] *Taylor* (n 216). [218] *Taylor* (n 216).

[219] Eg *Re Strachan* (1876) 4 Ch D 123, per Bramwell JA at 128; *Sinclair v Brougham* [1914] AC 398, per Lord Haldane LC at 420–21; *Banque Belge pour l'Etranger v Hambrouck* [1921] 1 KB 321, per Scrutton LJ at 330.

[220] *Ex parte Dale* (1879) LR 11 Ch D 772; *Re Hallett's Estate* (1880) 13 Ch D 696; *Re Diplock* [1948] 1 Ch 465; *Agip (Africa) Ltd v Jackson* [1990] Ch 265 (HC) and [1991] Ch 547 (CA).

[221] *Re Strachan* (n 219); *Ex parte Dale* (1879) LR 11 Ch D 772.

[222] Eg *Re Diplock* [1948] 1 Ch 465; *Agip (Africa) Ltd v Jackson* (n 220); *Trustee of FC Jones v Jones* [1997] Ch 159.

[223] Eg *Re Hallett's Estate* (n 220). Cf M Scott, 'The Right to "Trace" at Common Law' (1966) 7 University of Western Australia Law Review 463, 470, criticizing 'the picture so often drawn in this context of that poor mutt, the common lawyer, able to grasp the identity of specific coins, but retiring mouth agape in baffled amazement once they are mixed with other coins'.

[224] In *Re Diplock* [1948] Ch 465, 519.

[225] Eg *Agip (Africa) Ltd v Jackson* [1990] Ch 265 (HC), per Millett J at 289; *Foskett* (n 2), 128 (Lord Millett) and 113 (Lord Steyn).

[226] The character and implications of this misunderstanding of *Taylor v Plumer* were first explored by R Goode, 'The Right to Trace and Its Impact in Commercial Transactions' (1976) 92 LQR 360 and by S Khurshid and P Matthews, 'Tracing Confusion' (1976) 95 LQR 78. Lionel Smith has since demonstrated the historical accuracy of Khurshid and Matthew's interpretation of *Taylor v Plumer*: see L Smith, 'Tracing in *Taylor v Plumer*: Equity in the Court of King's Bench' [1995] LMCLQ 240, and Millett LJ's endorsement of Smith's account of the history in *Trustee of FC Jones v Jones* (n 222) 169.

[227] Eg *Sinclair v Brougham* (n 219) per Lord Haldane at 419; *Re Diplock* (n 224).

[228] See Khurshid and Matthews (n 226) 79 and sources criticized there.

took the decision to be authority that Sir Thomas Plumer had acquired a possessory common law title to the substitute assets, of a kind that would have enabled him not only to resist an action in trover but to bring one[229] if the gold and share certificates had been taken from him.[230] Once this is understood, the essential continuity between Lord Ellenborough CJ's dicta in *Taylor v Plumer* and the later case law setting the limits of tracing in equity becomes clear. In both contexts, judges use the metaphor of the box or bag of money to express their aim of protecting other assets of the defendant—which he might hold in his own right or for the benefit of someone other than the claimant—from the subordinating effects of tracing. The supposed distinction between law and equity, in this context, does not arise from any special blindness of the common law to facts like the payment of money into a mixed bank account, but rather responds to the different confiscatory consequences of common law rights and equitable constructs like the trust and the charge.

3.3.2.1. 'Money has no earmark': tracing and following physical money

The maxim that 'money has no earmark', and the associated distinction between money in and out of a bag, has served a number of functions in English law. As we have seen, it was used to rationalize the supposed problem with tracing into purchases of land arising from *Kirk v Webb*. It was also used to limit the reach of common law titles to money, restricting the liability of remote recipients of cash in detinue and trover.[231] In this context, it defined the liability of agents and bailees who had been entrusted with cash that they had misappropriated or failed to return, limiting the availability of claims in detinue and trover against such parties and requiring the owner to sue, instead, in account or debt.[232] Finally, as in *Whitecomb v Jacob*,[233] it was used to limit the reach of claims to traceable proceeds where goods were exchanged for money. In order to understand Lord Ellenborough CJ's account of the problem of tracing into money in *Taylor v Plumer*, it is necessary to distinguish between these different functions of the maxim, and the different characteristics—and definitions—of 'money' to which it responded. 3.85

In *Miller v Race*,[234] Lord Mansfield dismissed the relevance of the language of earmarking to claims against remote recipients of misappropriated or stolen cash. He said that, although it had been 'quaintly said'[235] that money could not be followed because it had no earmark, this was not true. The real reason why an owner of stolen money could not recover it—earmarked or not—from certain recipients 3.86

229 This view of *Taylor v Plumer*, as giving rise to a common law title capable of supporting actions in conversion against all subsequent recipients of the substitute asset, was rejected by the House of Lords in *Lipkin Gorman* (n 194).

230 See, for example, D Cuthbertson, 'Tracing at Common Law—Myth or Reality?' (1967) 8 University of Western Australia Law Review 402, at 406: 'it seems clear that had Sir Thomas been the plaintiff, he would have succeeded in trover'.

231 See Fox, 'Bona Fide Purchase' (n 76).

232 *Core's Case* (1536) 1 Dy 20a, 73 ER 42; *Higgs v Holiday* (1598) Cro Eliz 746, 78 ER 978.

233 *Whitecomb* (n 117).

234 *Miller v Race* (n 173).

235 *Miller v Race* (n 173) 457; 401.

from the thief was because of the currency of money, which prevented its recovery 'after it [had] been paid away fairly and honestly upon a valuable and bona fide consideration'.[236] The policy reasons that support this rule are obvious; money would not be able to perform one of its vital social and economic functions, as a universal medium of exchange,[237] if each transaction involving money required the payee to investigate the title of the payer or risk liability to an unknown former owner who has wrongly been deprived of possession.[238]

3.87 However, Lord Mansfield's account of the maxim does not capture the full range of its historic uses, both in the context of following money and in the context of tracing into money. His explanation provides a reason for limiting the availability of claims against remote recipients of stolen or misappropriated money, on the grounds that there are distinctive policy reasons for protecting bona fide purchasers for value of assets that perform the functions of 'money'.[239] This rationale applies only to money and other assets that serve some of the functions of money, like negotiable instruments.[240] It does not apply to chattels that do not serve these functions; nor does it apply to money when it is not being used as currency but is instead being treated as a unique chattel.[241] For the same reason, the defence is not available where the dispute is between the original owner of the money and a person who is under a direct obligation to give it back, such as a bailee or a thief; nor does it apply in favour of a recipient who has not given value, or who is not in good faith,[242] or to the trustees in bankruptcy of such a recipient or the thief himself. Conversely, it is available whether or not the money in question is in a bag, earmarked, or otherwise factually distinguishable from other money in the hands of the defendant.[243]

3.88 By contrast, the early case law that made it difficult to follow money did not track these concerns.[244] Thus, in the context of following, the law treated coins in the same way as other fungible chattels[245] like barley, corn, and hay. Where the claimant

[236] *Miller v Race* (n 235).

[237] For the various functions of money, including as a universal medium of exchange, see D Fox, *Property Rights in Money* (OUP 2008) 6–10.

[238] *Miller v Race* (n 173) per Lord Mansfield 459; 402: 'A bank-note is constantly and universally, both at home and abroad, treated as money, as cash; and paid and received, as cash; and it is necessary, for the purposes of commerce, that their currency should be established and secured'.

[239] For the various assets that are seen as performing that function in English law, see Fox, *Property Rights in Money* (n 237) 10–17.

[240] Such as cheques, bills of exchange, and promissory notes, which are now regulated by the Bills of Exchange Act 1882.

[241] Eg *Moss v Hancock* [1899] 2 QB 111.

[242] Eg *Clarke v Shee & Johnson* (1774) 1 Cowp 197, 98 ER 1041.

[243] Thus, in *Miller v Race* itself, the stolen banknote was a handwritten note that named one William Finney on its face as the payee. See also *Wookey v Pole* (1820) 4 B & Ald 1, 102 ER 839, per Best CJ at (1820) 4 B & Ald 1, 7 and 102 ER 839, 841: 'It is not because the loser cannot know his money again that he cannot recover it from a person who has fairly obtained the possession of it; for if his guineas or shillings had some private marks on them by which he could prove they had been his, he could not get them back from a bona fide holder'.

[244] Although, as Fox has noted, the case law that made it difficult to follow money did crudely serve the core policy function of the defence of bona fide purchase until new forms of money, which did not possess the characteristic of physical fungibility, became prevalent: see Fox, 'Bona Fide Purchase' (n 76) 554–63.

[245] For this case law, see D Fox, '*Banks v Whetston* (1596)' in S Douglas, R Hickey, and E Waring (eds), *Landmark Cases in the Law of Property* (Hart Publishing 2015) 3, 13–23, and authorities cited there.

was invoking an immediate right to possession of chattels of this kind, the law asked whether the claimant's chattels were factually distinguishable from other chattels of the same kind that might belong to someone else: was the money in a bag? Was the wheat in a separate cart?[246] Detinue would lie for money in a bag;[247] it would not lie for money that was not in a bag.[248]

This case law, with its sharp distinction between money in or out of a bag, and its lack of attentiveness to the difference between money and other fungible chattels, suggests that there are two parallel concerns that might affect the assertion of proprietary rights over money. The distinctive economic functions of money justify the law in protecting recipients in good faith who have acquired money as currency and for value. Meanwhile, the physical fungibility of some kinds of money—notably coins—can create evidential problems with asserting title to that money in the hands of others, because the claimant's coins cannot readily be distinguished from other coins in the possession of the defendant. 3.89

In *Ford v Hopkins*,[249] the lack of perfect overlap between the two rationales became clear. In that case, the claimant had entrusted a goldsmith[250] with certain lottery tickets, authorizing him to receive the money due on them but not to deal with them in any other respect. In breach of these instructions, the goldsmith had delivered them to the defendant. It was argued that the defendant had given good consideration for the lottery tickets,[251] but Holt CJ rejected the view that this had any effect on the claimant's claim against him in trover. He distinguished between money and 'bank-notes, Exchequer-notes, and million-tickets' on the basis that 'money or cash is not to be distinguished, but these notes or bills are distinguishable, and cannot be reckoned as cash, and they have distinct marks and numbers on them'.[252] There are two reasons given here why trover will lie for the lottery tickets and other similar notes, including banknotes. First, such notes 'cannot be reckoned as cash': that is, in his view, they do not perform the economic functions of money.[253] Secondly, 'they have distinct marks and numbers on them'; unlike coins, banknotes and lottery tickets can be physically distinguished from each other and so it can be proved that a particular note in the hands of the defendant is the very note that was once taken from the claimant. 3.90

In *Miller v Race*, Lord Mansfield sharply criticized this passage in the report of *Ford v Hopkins*, doubting that Holt CJ's reference to banknotes could have been accurately reported.[254] Denying the supposed similarity between lottery tickets and banknotes, he noted that lottery tickets are capable of varying wildly in value so that the difference between one lottery ticket and another may be very important: 'land is 3.91

246 (1483) YB Hil 22 Edw IV, pl 17, fol 50, cited by Fox (n 245) at 18.

247 *Isaack v Clark* (1615) 2 Bulst 303, 80 ER 1149.

248 *Core's Case* (n 232).

249 (1700) 1 Salk 283, 91 ER 250.

250 For the banking functions performed by goldsmiths at this period, see Fox, 'Bona Fide Purchase' (n 76) at 554–57.

251 *Ford* (n 249) 284; 251.

252 *Ford* (n 251).

253 For the plausibility of this view of promissory notes in 1700, and the later evolution of the law on this point, see Fox, 'Bona Fide Purchase' (n 76) at 561–62.

254 *Miller v Race* (n 238).

not more specific than lottery tickets are'.[255] Banknotes, by contrast, were currency, being universally treated as cash, and it was important that they continue to be so treated; this requires that they be considered interchangeable with each other in terms of value, with the face value of a note representing its value to each recipient within the relevant monetary system. Even though such notes might not be fungible in the physical sense—in that each note possesses distinguishing marks that allow it be identifiable in a mixture, or as it passes from hand to hand—there are good reasons for insisting that they be treated as fungible by the law. They could not otherwise serve the role of currency. The two rationales for 'money has no earmark'—physical fungibility and the economic necessity for legal fungibility—thus come apart in the case of banknotes. While a claimant may easily be able to identify his very note in the hands of a defendant, there may nevertheless be good reasons for preventing him from bringing any claims against that particular defendant. In Smith's terminology, this is a rule of claiming, not a rule that solves a problem of following.[256] Problems that arise when money actually loses its physical identity, as in *Ward v Aeyre*,[257] are handled differently.[258]

3.92 If we turn to the work done by the maxim 'money has no earmark' in the context of tracing, we find that this case law tracks the problem of identification, rather than the concerns addressed by the currency of money. Thus, the maxim was never treated as a bar to tracing into promissory notes or banknotes, even after these were acknowledged as serving the economic functions of money. In *Ryall v Rolle*,[259] the scenario where a factor sold goods for 'ready money'[260] was distinguished from one where he sold them either for a promise of future payment[261] *or* for a promissory note.[262] In the first scenario, where goods were sold for cash, the factor's principal was obliged to come in as an ordinary creditor in the insolvency of the factor and had no personal claims against the assignees in bankruptcy. In the two other scenarios—where the factor sold the goods for a promise of future payment, or for a promissory note—the debt or the note would be held to the principal's use. If the money due on them were paid to the assignees in bankruptcy of the factor, the principal would then have an action for money had and received against the assignees personally.[263]

3.93 Similarly, in *Gladstone v Hadwen*,[264] decided by Lord Ellenborough CJ a year before *Taylor v Plumer*, there was no suggestion that it was specially problematic to trace into banknotes. In that case, one Sill had received bills of exchange from Hadwen under a contract that he had induced Hadwen to enter into under the influence of a fraudulent misrepresentation.[265] After receiving the bills, he gave

[255] *Miller v Race* (n 238). [256] See Chapter 2 this volume.
[257] (1615) 2 Bulst 323.
[258] See paras 2.40–2.46, and 2.50–2.52 in Chapter 2 this volume.
[259] (1749) 1 Atk 165, 26 ER 107. [260] *Ryall* (n 259) 172; 112.
[261] As in *Burdett* (n 115). [262] As in *Scott* (n 120).
[263] *Ryall* (n 259) 172; 112. See also *Ex parte Dumas* (1754) 1 Atk 232, 26 ER 149, per Lord Hardwick LC at 1 Atk 234, 26 ER 150: 'The court of Common Pleas in a case the name of which I do not remember determined that notwithstanding goods so consigned were sold, yet as the factor took *notes instead of money* for them, that the principal was intitled to the notes, and not the creditors at large' (emphasis added).
[264] (1813) 1 M & S 517, 105 ER 193.
[265] He had purported to grant Sill security for the loan of the bills of exchange by assigning him rights over some coffee due to arrive from Jamaica. In fact, he had no rights in respect of the coffee to assign.

them to his trading partner in London, who discounted some of them and received banknotes in exchange. Sill later 'felt uncomfortable'[266] about this transaction and, having disclosed the facts to Hadwen, promised him that he would have the bills and money brought back from London and would return them. After he had made this promise, he committed an act of bankruptcy; sometime after the act of bankruptcy, he regained possession of the bills and banknotes and returned them to Hadwen. The assignees in bankruptcy, like the assignees in *Taylor v Plumer*, brought an action in trover against Hadwen, seeking to recover both the original bills and the banknotes for which some of them had been discounted.

Lord Ellenborough CJ dismissed the action on the grounds that the contract had been rescinded before the act of bankruptcy, so that title to the bills of exchange had never vested in the assignees in bankruptcy.[267] He held that this meant that the assignees could not recover the banknotes either: since they 'were not mixed with the rest of the bankrupt's property, and [were] capable of being distinctly traced', the notes stood 'in the same position as the bills themselves'[268] and Hadwen was entitled to keep them. This can be contrasted with the accounts of the law given in cases like *Whitecomb v Jacob* and *Ryall v Rolle*, where we are told that the mere exchange of the claimant's asset for money, which has no earmark, extinguishes the claims he would otherwise have to the traceable proceeds of his assets. Like his dicta in *Taylor v Plumer*, Lord Ellenborough CJ's decision in *Gladstone v Hadwen* implies that there is a problem with tracing into money only when there has been some sort of physical mixture with the rest of the bankrupt's property, such that the individual notes or coins can no longer be distinguished from other notes or coins in his possession. On this view, there is no objection to tracing into banknotes, despite their status as currency, where the claimant can surmount the evidential obstacle and identify his notes by pointing to their individual characteristics, such as the appearance of his own name on the face of the note as payee, or the serial numbers on a modern Bank of England note. 3.94

This focus on physical identification also aligns with the dicta in *Taylor v Plumer* and other cases that suggest that the problem can be overcome when money, in any form, is received in a bag or other repository that allows it to be distinguished from other money in the hands of the defendant. Thus, for example, in *Tooke v Hollingworth*,[269] Lord Kenyon CJ said that a merchant who had entrusted his goods to a factor who became a bankrupt could specifically recover his goods, provided that 'the goods remain distinguishable from the general mass of [the bankrupt's] property';[270] 'nay,' he went on to say, 'if the goods be sold and reduced to money, *provided that money be in separate bags and distinguishable from the factor's other property*, the law is the same'.[271] This echoes Lord Ellenborough CJ's distinction, in *Taylor v Plumer*, between an 'undivided and indistinguishable mass of current money'[272] and money in a bag. 3.95

266 *Gladstone* (n 264) 519; 194.
267 See Chapter 6, paras 6.22–6.23 this volume on this aspect of the case.
268 *Gladstone* (n 264) 527; 197.
269 (1793) 5 TR 215, 101 ER 121.
270 *Tooke* (n 269) 227; 127.
271 *Tooke* (n 270) (emphasis added).
272 *Taylor* (n 218).

3.96 At first sight, therefore, the problem addressed by the maxim in the context of tracing thus looks like the evidential problem of dealing with physical mixtures that we have already examined in the context of following,[273] rather than the problem of the currency of money addressed in *Miller v Race*. The first question that arises is why it cannot then be solved in the same way. We have seen that the law responds to a physical mixture of indistinguishable chattels belonging to different people by imposing a kind of[274] tenancy in common of the mixture, giving each owner a share proportionate to her contributions to the bulk. In *Ward v Aeyre*,[275] the court responded to a physical mixture of money by confiscating the contribution of the party at fault and treating the innocent party as the owner of the whole. There is no suggestion in the report of the case that this rule was peculiar to money, and did not apply to other fungible chattels, and the analogy to corn invoked by Coke CJ suggests the reverse.[276] In *Indian Oil Corporation Ltd v Greenstone Shipping SA (Panama)*,[277] the decision in *Ward v Aeyre* was rationalized as an application of the evidential rule in *Armory v Delamirie* on the basis that 'it seems likely that the proportion which each part had contributed to the mixture could no longer be determined'.[278] The implication is that, if the proportions had been known in *Ward v Aeyre*, the evidential presumption against the wrongdoer would have been displaced and some kind of tenancy in common[279] of the mixed heap of money would have been imposed. Neither case provides any authority for a rule paralleling the approach in *Whitecomb v Jacob*, under which A's mixture of B's money with her own has the effect of extinguishing all B's proprietary claims, regardless of fault, and there is direct authority contradicting such a result.

3.97 In *Jackson v Anderson*,[280] the claimants had authorized one Fielding, who was based in Buenos Aires, to sell linen goods on their behalf. Fielding promised to account to them for the proceeds of sale by shipping 1,969 Spanish dollars to England in four trunks. In fact, the dollars that he set aside for the claimants were shipped in a barrel that included a total of 4,718 dollars, so that it could not be known which of these were the 1,969 dollars that belonged to the claimants. It was held that this 'intermixture of property'[281] did not prevent the claimants from bringing an action in trover against the defendant, to whom Fielding's agents had transferred the bill of lading, and who had pledged the whole barrel to the Bank of England. Since the claimants' dollars must have been somewhere in the barrel, the defendant's act of pledging the entire

[273] See Chapter 2 this volume. [274] See (n 279). [275] *Ward* (n 257).

[276] *Ward* (n 257): 'for that his own proper money, *or corn* cannot now be known, and therefore by this his intermingling, being his own act, and of his own wrong, by the law he shall lose all' (emphasis added).

[277] [1987] 1 QB 345. [278] *Indian Oil Corporation Ltd* (n 277) 361.

[279] It has been argued that the law's response to all mixtures of this kind does not give rise to a genuine tenancy in common, but only continuing individual ownership of the individual units within the mixture: see Smith, *The Law of Tracing* (n 214) 75. Others have argued that mixtures of money differ from other mixtures, and that continuing ownership of individual units within the mixture is the norm for money alone: for this view, see P Birks, 'Mixtures' in N Palmer and E McKendrick (eds), *Interests in Goods* (2nd edn, LLP 1998) 227, 240; R Hickey, 'Dazed and Confused: Accidental Mixtures of Goods and the Theory of Acquisition of Title' (2003) 66 MLR 368, 378–79. On either of these views, the law's response to physical mixtures of money differs from the response to the receipt of money described in cases like *Whitecomb v Jacob*.

[280] (1811) 4 Taunt 24, 128 ER 235. [281] *Jackson* (n 280) 29; 237.

barrel must have including a purported disposition of their dollars as well and this was enough to found the claim. The dicta in *Whitecomb v Jacob* and *Ryall v Rolle*, by contrast, insist on separate identification of the money up to the moment of receipt by the assignees in bankruptcy. These cases do not countenance the possibility that, where assignees in bankruptcy have received all the money of a bankrupt factor, the action in money had and received will lie on the same grounds that trover lay in *Jackson v Anderson*: because the claimant's money must[282] exist somewhere in the mixed mass of money belonging to the bankrupt, received by the assignees.

However, there is an important difference between the facts of cases like *Ward v Aeyre* and *Jackson v Anderson*—mixtures of money within an identified 'heap' or barrel—and the scenario addressed in *Whitecomb v Jacob* and *Ryall v Rolle*. These cases do not describe situations where the bankrupt agent has mixed his principal's coins with her own in some specific and identifiable repository, like a barrel or a purse. Instead, they describe the receipt of loose currency that cannot, factually, be distinguished from all the other currency in the possession of the defendant. In such a scenario, the only way to overcome the following problem would be to treat all the currency in the hands of the defendant as a single bulk,[283] whatever its source, and to impose the equivalent of a tenancy in common over all her cash. Although such a solution is formally possible, the courts have chosen not to do this. Instead, as the recurrent image of money in a bag suggests, the rule is that the claimant's assets must be somehow segregated from the general assets of the defendant. They may be segregated within the bounds of a particular mixture or bulk, that includes some of her assets, but this bulk must itself distinguishable from the remainder of her assets. It is this requirement of segregation that is expressed by the maxim that money has no earmark in cases like *Whitecomb v Jacob* and *Ryall v Rolle*. 3.98

This requirement can be rationalized on the basis of a principle of protecting the defendant's own pre-existing rights. The law is prepared to countenance a limited infringement of these pre-existing rights, forcing her into a kind of co-ownership in cases where there has been a mixture between her assets and the claimant's that takes the form of an identified bulk that can be segregated from her other assets. It is not, however, prepared to stretch this principle so far that all the currency in her possession is to be treated as such a bulk without her consent.[284] 3.99

This account of the maxim also explains how the courts used it to rationalize *Kirk v Webb*, interpreting that case as authority that a claimant must discharge the burden of proving a transactional link between his money and land purchased by a 3.100

[282] In line with the usual approach of the law to wrongful mixtures, a mere possibility that the claimant's money has not been untraceably spent by the bankrupt might be enough to justify such an argument: where the bankrupt was a wrongdoer, who was under a duty to keep the claimant's money separated from his own, the principle in *Armory v Delamirie* might have been invoked to shift the burden of proof. See Chapter 2, Section 2.1.2.1 this volume.

[283] For the analogous idea that property rights can arise on a sale of a particular quantity of unascertained goods, provided that the goods in questions form part of an identified bulk, see the Sale of Goods Act 1979, s 20A. A bulk is defined by section 61(1) of the Sale of Goods Act 1979 as '... a mass or collection of goods of the same kind which (a) is contained in a defined space or area; and (b) is such that any goods in the bulk are interchangeable with any other goods therein of the same number or quantity'.

[284] Cf *Re Goldcorp Exchange Ltd* [1994] 1 AC 74.

defendant before he can claim that the defendant's title to the land is held for him, in the face of positive evidence of the defendant's contrary intentions. If a defendant has taken the claimant's cash, and has later used some cash to buy land, we need to know whether the cash used to buy the land was the very cash that was taken from the claimant. This is because, if it was not that very cash, it must have been money that the defendant held either for her own benefit or subject to duties owed to some person other than the claimant. If she holds money in either capacity, the law has a reason[285] for respecting her intentions in entering into transactions using that money, and thus for refusing to permit the subordinating consequences of tracing to operate. Similarly, if she sells the claimant's land in exchange for cash, and we later find her in possession of that amount of money in cash, we need to know whether the cash she now possesses is the very cash obtained in exchange for the claimant's land. If it is not, it must be money that she obtained by some other means, either for her own exclusive benefit or subject to duties owed to some other person; in these situations, the law again has a reason to respect her decision to retain that money or use it for some other purpose, such as the satisfaction of a debt owed to some person other than the claimant. In this way, we can see how the two uses of the maxim 'money has no earmark' are underpinned by a single principle: that of respect for the defendant's decision-making authority, as it pertains to assets held by him for his own benefit or for the benefit of persons other than the claimant.

3.3.2.2. Bank accounts as bags: the rejection of swollen assets tracing

3.101 There is a clear continuity between this principle and the later case law governing tracing into mixed substitutions, such as a mixed bank account. The image of money in a box or a bag dominates the leading cases in which the possibility of such tracing was first recognized[286] and extended beyond the context of trustees and beneficiaries.[287] In *Pennell v Deffell*,[288] Knight-Bruce LJ responded to the payment of money from various sources into mixed bank accounts by invoking the analogy of a physical mixture of currency in a box, asking what would have happened if the trustee had placed the 'very coins and the very notes received by him ... in a particular repository—such as a chest—mixed confusedly together as among themselves; but in a state of clear and distinct separation from everything else'.[289] In *Re Hallett's Estate*,[290] Jessel MR said that *Whitecomb v Jacob* and *Ryall v Rolle* were

[285] On particular facts, these default reasons for respecting the defendant's decisions, when these involve the use of his own assets or the authorized use of assets belonging to someone else, may be cancelled out by other normatively relevant considerations. For example, he may have promised to acquire the property in question for the benefit of a claimant, who has detrimentally relied on the promise: see *Matchmove Ltd v Dowding* [2016] EWCA Civ 1233. These reasons are independent of the particular normative concerns that motivate transactional tracing, explained in the text. For this account of how the law shapes practical reasoning, see J Raz, *Practical Reason and Norms* (3rd edn, OUP 1999).

[286] *Pennell v Deffell* (n 20).

[287] *Re Hallett's Estate* (n 220).

[288] *Pennell* (n 20). For a detailed account of the facts of this case, see Chapter 2, para 2.11 this volume.

[289] *Pennell* (n 20) 381; 555.

[290] *Re Hallett's Estate* (n 220).

no longer good law,[291] and that Lord Ellenborough CJ's dicta in *Taylor v Plumer* on the subject of earmarking money could be explained because his 'knowledge of the rules of Equity was not quite commensurate with his knowledge of the rules of Common Law'.[292] Nevertheless, in addressing the problem of mixed bank accounts and dismissing the supposed objection to tracing into such accounts on the authority of the maxim that 'money has no earmark',[293] he retained the central image of money in a bag.

He began his analysis by postulating a case where a trustee had taken 1,000 sovereigns of trust money, put them in a bag, and then added a sovereign of his own. In such a case, he asked, could it be supposed that equity would prevent the beneficiary from taking 1,000 of the sovereigns in the bag?[294] Rather than invoking the idea of the tenancy in common, which appears in the modern case law on following into physical mixtures, he invoked the idea of the equitable charge: 'I do not like to call it a charge of 1,000 sovereigns on the 1,001 sovereigns, but that is the effect of it'.[295] He then argued that the same principle applied where the trustee substituted a single intangible asset—a bank account—for the mixed bag of money. As in the case of the mixed mass of money found in a single bag, the beneficiary could have a charge over the single debt constituted by the bank account that reflected the amount of her contribution to the credit balance of the account. When Lord Ellenborough CJ denied that tracing was possible when money was mixed with an indistinguishable mass of other money, this was because—according to Jessel MR—he simply did not know that an equitable charge existed as an option for sorting out competing claims when money was 'put into a bag or into an undistinguishable mass'.[296] Contrary to his dicta in *Taylor v Plumer*, and the other authorities in favour of the maxim that 'money has no earmark', tracing would not fail where money was mixed in a bag, or in a bank account, because the mechanism of the equitable charge could be invoked to address the problems of identification that arose on such facts. 3.102

As has been argued, however, a mixture of money in a bag was not the central case addressed by the maxim in these earlier cases. Rather, the problem was the receipt of loose currency. For Jessel MR's solution to capture such a case, and to genuinely reverse the older approach, it would be necessary for the notional[297] charge that he invoked in *Re Hallett's Estate* to be imposed over all the currency in the possession of the defendant, whether or not in a bag. In the modern context, claimants are far more likely to be tracing into intangible assets than into physical coins that must then be followed. In the context of such following, the question addressed by the maxim was whether the claimant's money must be in a bag, physically segregated from the remainder of the defendant's money. In the context of tracing, that question may be translated as asking whether the claimant's value must be held in the form 3.103

[291] *Re Hallett's Estate* (n 220) 714. [292] *Re Hallett's Estate* (n 220) 717.

[293] The view that the maxim barred tracing into mixed bank accounts, except where the dispute was between a trustee and a beneficiary, was put forward by Fry J in *Ex parte Dale* (1879) LR 11 Ch D 772.

[294] *Re Hallett's Estate* (n 220) 711. [295] *Re Hallett's Estate* (n 294).

[296] *Re Hallett's Estate* (n 220).

[297] So described by Millett J in *El Ajou v Dollar Land Holdings plc (No 1)* [1993] 3 All ER 717, 737.

of a single bank account or asset, distinct from the rest of the defendant's wealth. In other words, it becomes a question about swollen assets. What if the defendant has made use of the claimant's assets in a way that has increased the abstract amount of wealth at his disposal, but this increased wealth cannot be identified in the form of some distinct asset in his hands?

3.104 The discharge of a debt is a paradigm example of such a situation. In *Scott v Surman*,[298] Willes LCJ treated the problem of tracing into the value of a discharged debt as precisely analogous to the problem of following into the receipt of loose currency. The £31 of the claimants' money used to discharge a debt owed to the bankrupt could not be treated as money had and received by the assignees, because it stood 'on the same foot as if the bankrupt had received it in money before his bankruptcy'.[299] The discharged debt could no more be distinguished from the general assets of the bankrupt than one piece of loose currency could have been distinguished from other currency in his hands. One possibility raised by *Re Hallett's Estate* is that equity's mechanism of a charge could be as easily invoked to solve this problem as the problem of tracing into a mixture of money in or out of a bag; all the defendant's assets could be subjected to a charge in favour of the claimant, securing an obligation to pay over the amount of the discharged debt. The principled objection to doing this, which underpins the original uses of the maxim that money has no earmark, also explains why the courts have rejected this possibility and the language in which they have done so. In *Re Hallett & Co*,[300] decided fourteen years after *Re Hallett's Estate*, the Court of Appeal addressed and rejected the idea that *Re Hallett's Estate* had made so fundamental an alteration in the law's priorities.

3.105 In that case, one Hallett and his co-trustee, Colonel Blane, had held certain debentures in a company called Hewitt & Co on trust for a widow. Hallett was a partner in a firm of bankers, Hallett & Co, with whom the trust bank account was held. The partners in this firm had been authorized to receive the £1,600 due from Hewitt & Co when the debentures held on trust matured, and to pay it into the trust bank account. Hallett & Co had a number of other clients who also held debentures in Hewitt & Co, on whose behalf they both received money and made payments to renew clients' investments with that company. On 31 January 1893, when the £1,600 due under the trust debentures became payable, Hallett & Co owed Hewitt & Co a total debt of £1,900 on behalf of their various other clients. On 3 February that year, they set off these debts, paying £300 to Hewitt & Co by a cheque drawn on themselves, crediting the trustees' account with themselves in the amount of £1,600, and debiting the accounts of their other clients by £1,900. At the end of each day's trading, Hallett & Co paid their total receipts into their own account with a different bank, Cocks, Biddulph & Co.

3.106 In May 1893, the partners in Hallett & Co were bankrupted. On this date, their bank account with Cocks, Biddulph & Co was in credit to the amount of £4,171. Colonel Blane argued that he could trace the £1,600 of trust money into this bank account, and so ought to be paid this amount out of that account in preference to

[298] *Scott* (n 120). See paras 3.47–3.50 this chapter.

[299] *Scott* (n 124).

[300] [1894] 2 QB 237.

other creditors. At first instance, Vaughan Williams J upheld the claim, applying what he took to be the principle in *Re Hallett's Estate*. Having found as a fact that the bank account was 'in credit to the extent of £1,600 more than it would have been but for the payment off of these debentures',[301] he held that '£1600 of the £4000 odd standing to the credit at the date of the failure must be deemed to be £1600 of trust money'.[302]

3.107 The Court of Appeal overruled the decision, holding that tracing was impossible because the transaction of setting off the debts was not equivalent to the payment of £1,600 by Hewitt & Co in a form that could be traced. Counsel argued that, 'having regard to the modern forms of business',[303] the two were functionally equivalent: it was as if Hallett & Co had received a cheque for £1,600 from Hewitt & Co, and paid a separate cheque in the amount of £1,900 to them. However, the Court of Appeal rejected the idea that the two fact situations were equivalent for the purposes of tracing. On the facts of the case, Hallett & Co had not in fact received 'any money or tender of money or anything tangible which it would be possible to follow or to lay hands upon';[304] 'nothing was received by them in specie, notes, cheques, or coin'.[305] Colonel Blane, the co-trustee, could not show that 'there was anything in existence representing that which the bankers we authorized to collect';[306] he could only show 'a transaction between Hallett & Co and other persons',[307] and this was not enough. Nor could he show that any specific payment into the Cocks, Biddulph & Co account represented the £1,600 notionally received from Hewitt & Co: 'the money was not ear-marked, and cannot be identified'.[308] The argument that *Re Hallett's Estate* had any application was firmly rejected; that decision, Davey LJ said, 'in no way qualifies the rule that there must be a specific thing capable of being followed'.[309]

3.108 The view that tracing is impossible where the defendant does not receive any specific tangible thing, but only enters into a transaction with another person, is untenable as a literal description of the law. It is well-established that an increase in the credit balance of a bank account does not mean that any tangible cash in the possession of the bank is allocated to the account-holder,[310] but only that the bank comes under an obligation to pay her the increased amount on demand.[311] Every payment into or out of a bank account is thus only a transaction between persons: it involves an adjustment of debts between the account-holder and his bank

301 *Re Hallett & Co* (n 300) 240.
302 *Re Hallett & Co* (n 300) 241.
303 *Re Hallett & Co* (n 300) 242.
304 *Re Hallett & Co* (n 300) 244 (per Lord Esher MR).
305 *Re Hallett & Co* (n 304) (per Davey LJ).
306 *Re Hallett & Co* (n 304) (per Lord Esher MR).
307 *Re Hallett & Co* (n 304) (per Lord Esher MR).
308 *Re Hallett & Co* (n 304) (per Lopes LJ).
309 *Re Hallett & Co* (n 300) 245.
310 *Foley v Hill* (1848) 2 HL Cas 28, 9 ER 1002.
311 Cf *R v Preddy* [1996] 1 AC 816, per Lord Jauncey at 841: 'I start with the proposition that the money in a bank account standing at credit does not belong to the account holder. He has merely a chose in action which is the right to demand payment of the relevant sum from the bank.'

and, sometimes, between the account-holder's bank and other banks via the relevant clearing system.[312]

3.109 We cannot, therefore, take the supposed requirement of an identifiable tangible thing, articulated in *Re Hallett & Co*, literally. The Court of Appeal made it clear that the claim would have succeeded if Hewitt & Co had handed a cheque for £1,600 over to Hallett & Co, and this cheque had then been used to increase the credit balance of the account with Cocks, Biddulph & Co.[313] That version of the facts would have begun with the receipt of a tangible thing, the cheque. However, in tracing into the bank account, Colonel Blane would not have been following that particular thing into the hands of the bank that took it. He would, instead, have been tracing through a transaction between persons: Hallett & Co's decision to hand the cheque over to the bank, and the bank's decision to accept it and so increase its debt to them by £1,600. Tracing would also have been possible if there had been no tangible thing at the outset. Thus, if Hewitt & Co had instructed its own bank to debit its account by £1,600 and to have that amount credited to Hallett & Co's account with Cocks, Biddulph & Co, the trustees would have been able to trace into that account.[314]

3.110 The idea that tracing requires a 'specific thing', the receipt of money that is 'earmarked' in some way, cannot therefore mean that it requires an identifiable physical object that can be followed as it passes from hand to hand. Rather, the metaphor of earmarking tangible assets, in this context, does the same work as it always did: it describes the twin requirements of segregation of assets and proof of transactional links, which bar both causal tracing and swollen assets tracing. On the facts of *Re Hallett & Co*, it was impossible to trace through bankrupt partners' decision to set off the two debts against each other because the gain obtained by that transaction—the discharge of £1,600 of a £1,900 debt—could not be located in any asset held by the bankrupts, capable of being distinguished from the rest of their partnership assets. Nor was it possible to get around this problem by tracing from the set-off to the ultimate credit balance of their account with Cocks, Biddulph & Co, because there was no transactional link between the two. The partners' decision to increase the credit balance of the latter account at the end of each trading day, by paying all their receipts into it, could not be shown to involve any alteration in the trust beneficiary's rights, even though their earlier decision to alter her rights may have[315] increased the overall pool of assets at their disposal. If the court had allowed tracing into the unrelated bank account, it would have disregarded the partners' ownership of all money actually paid into that account and their freedom to decide

[312] See, generally, B Geva, 'The Clearing House Arrangement' (1991) 19 Canadian BLJ 138. On the history and current operation of the various inter-bank funds transfer systems that exist in the UK, see EP Ellinger, E Lomnicka, and CVM Hare, *Ellinger's Modern Banking Law* (OUP 2011) 557–69.

[313] *Re Hallett & Co* (n 300) per Lord Esher MR at 244 and Davey LJ at 245.

[314] For an early example of such tracing through payment instructions alone, see *Marsh* (n 197).

[315] Davey LJ doubted Vaughan Williams J's factual conclusion that there had in fact been any such increase, since the effect of reducing their indebtedness to the other clients was to incur a fresh debt to the trustees: see *Re Hallett & Co* (n 304). However, he also joined with the other judges in holding that the requirement of specific property that could be followed was a distinct requirement, which would have precluded tracing even if the causal test had been met: *Re Hallett & Co* (n 304).

what to do with that money. If it had allowed tracing based on the transaction of set-off, in the form of a charge over all the assets of the bankrupt partners, it would have disregarded the partners' ownership of those assets and their freedom to decide how to use or retain those assets.

3.3.2.3. *The problem of 'common law tracing'*

In the nineteenth century, the question whether it was possible to trace into a bank account was answered in the affirmative in *Small v Attwood*.[316] The question whether it was possible to trace into, and out of, a mixed bank account was answered in the affirmative in *Pennell v Deffell*.[317] Yet, there has been a parallel stream of authority suggesting that—in the light of Lord Ellenborough CJ's dicta in *Taylor v Plumer*—these forms of tracing are in some sense peculiar to equity. There are a few dicta suggesting that tracing into bank accounts is impossible at common law.[318] While this view has since been rejected,[319] the view that tracing into a *mixed* bank account is impossible at common law remains a theme in the modern case law.[320] 3.111

In *Re Diplock*,[321] adopting an obiter view expressed by Lord Parker of Waddington in *Sinclair v Brougham*,[322] the Court of Appeal offered a justification of the supposed divergence between law and equity on this point on the basis that common law tracing depends on ratification. The common law claim 'proceeded on the basis that the unauthorized act of purchasing was one capable of ratification by the owner of money'.[323] Ratification of a purchase, however, was only possible where the thing purchased could be physically identified and this ceased to be possible when a mixture had taken place: 'Once the money of B became mixed with the money of A its identification in a physical sense became impossible, owing to the fact of mixture there could be no question of ratification of an unauthorized act'.[324] The argument, then, is that common law tracing works by treating an unauthorized substitution as if[325] it is a transaction that can be ratified by the claimant; this possibility is closed off if there has been a physical mixture, or a mixed substitution, because 'the materialistic approach of the common law coupled with and encouraged by the limited range of remedies available to it ... prevented the common law from identifying money in a mixed fund'.[326] 3.112

[316] (1831–1832) You 407, 507, 159 ER 1051, 1092, reversed by the House of Lords on a different point in (1838) 7 ER 684.

[317] *Pennell* (n 20).

[318] *Sinclair v Brougham* (n 219) per Lord Haldane LC at 420–21; *Banque Belge pour l'Etranger v Hambrouck* (n 219).

[319] *Re Diplock* (n 224) followed in *Trustee of FC Jones v Jones* (n 222).

[320] *Shalson v Russo* [2003] EWHC 1637 (Ch), [2005] Ch 281, per Rimer J at [103]–[104]; *LAH v Lee* [2007] EWHC 2061 (Ch), per Etherton J at [256]–[257].

[321] *Re Diplock* (n 224). [322] [1914] AC 389, 441. [323] *Re Diplock* (n 224) 519.

[324] *Re Diplock* (n 323).

[325] As has been explained, conventional understandings of ratification will not capture most cases of unauthorized substitution, where the other party to the exchange is unaware of the claimant's rights over the asset exchanged: see para 3.72 this chapter.

[326] *Re Diplock* (n 224) 520.

3.113 The key to this explanation of the supposed problem of common law tracing is to be found in the reference to the limited range of remedies available at law. In *Re Diplock*, the Court of Appeal suggested that the common law was incapable of recognizing the existence of a trust, or any other mechanism whereby it could be said that an asset was vested in A but B nevertheless had rights in respect of that asset.[327] This makes a significant difference to how law and equity respond to authorized transactions involving other people's assets. Suppose that A is a trustee, holding banknotes on trust for B. B then authorizes A to use the banknotes to buy gold bullion from X, and A does so. The effect of the transaction between A and X is that X's title to the gold passes to A, who will then hold it on trust for B. Suppose, by contrast, that A is an agent, who is in possession of banknotes belonging to B, his principal. B then authorizes him to use these banknotes to buy gold bullion from X. When A does so, title does not pass to A at all; it passes *through* A, directly to B.[328]

3.114 The argument in *Re Diplock* depends on defining the remedial consequences of an unauthorized substitution as identical to those of an authorized—or ratified—exchange. In that case, *Taylor v Plumer* was treated as authority for what Khurshid and Matthews have called the 'exchange product theory'[329] of common law tracing: that is, as authority for the view that a common law owner of a chattel gets a common law title to any exchange product of that chattel, which she is entitled to enforce against all third parties in the same way that she could enforce her title to the original asset. On this understanding of *Taylor v Plumer*, Sir Thomas Plumer held a legal title to the banknotes in the possession of his agent, Walsh. When Walsh exchanged these banknotes for gold bullion and stock certificates, the *legal* titles to the gold and stock passed from their previous owners—through Walsh—directly[330] to Sir Thomas. He thus gained an immediate right to possession of these things, which he could have enforced against the entire world, including Walsh's assignees in bankruptcy.

3.115 As Lionel Smith has demonstrated,[331] this analysis represents a misunderstanding of the actual decision in *Taylor v Plumer*, which was consistent with a finding that Walsh held the gold and stock on trust for Sir Thomas Plumer. The broader implications of this historic and longstanding misreading of *Taylor v Plumer* are discussed in Chapter 8. For the purposes of understanding the principles of tracing, what matters is that the supposed limits of common law tracing, as articulated in the later case law, can be shown to arise from that misunderstanding. Suppose, for example, that an agent pays her principal's money into a new bank account, which she has opened for the purpose. If she has been authorized to open the account in the principal's name, the effect of the transaction will be to create a direct legal relationship between the principal and the bank; the bank will owe a duty to pay

[327] *Re Diplock* (n 323). [328] See Chapter 6, paras 6.81–6.83 this volume.
[329] S Khurshid and P Matthews, 'Tracing Confusion' (1979) 95 LQR 78, 79.
[330] Or did so from the moment that Sir Thomas chose to 'ratify' the transaction, in accordance with the explanation given in *Re Diplock*.
[331] Smith, 'Tracing in *Taylor v Plumer*' (n 226).

the credit balance to the principal, not the agent,[332] and will not be able to satisfy its indebtedness by paying the agent rather than the principal.[333]

In *Trustee of FC Jones v Jones*,[334] the Court of Appeal seems to have held that this is also the remedial consequence of tracing, at common law, into an unmixed bank account. It will be recalled[335] that, in that case, Mrs Jones had received cheques from her bankrupt husband, which she had then used to open an account with a firm of commodity brokers. She then instructed the brokers to pay the money due to her on this account—arising from her successful speculations in the potato futures market—into a bank account that she opened for the purpose with Raphaels & Co. On receiving competing demands for payment from the husband's trustee in bankruptcy and Mrs Jones, the bank interpleaded and paid the amount of the credit balance of the account into court. At first instance, the judge held that Mrs Jones had received the cheques from her husband on constructive trust for the trustee in bankruptcy and that, therefore, she also held her bank account on trust for him. On this basis, he ordered that the money in court be paid to the trustee in bankruptcy. The Court of Appeal affirmed the order, but rejected the judge's view that either the cheque or the bank account were held on trust; rather, Millett LJ said, Mrs Jones had never had 'any interest, legal or equitable in these moneys'[336] in any of the forms that it had taken. She had not had a legal title to the cheque;[337] the debt apparently owed to her by the commodity brokers 'in reality belonged to the trustee';[338] and the bank account, too, represented 'a debt owed by Raphaels apparently to [Mrs Jones] but in reality to the trustee'.[339] This meant, he said, that the claimant was 'entitled to bring an action for debt against Raphaels and obtain an order for payment',[340] and that it was the claimant—not Mrs Jones, the named account-holder, with whom the bank had intended to contract—who could 'give a good receipt to Raphaels'.[341] 3.116

As David Fox points out,[342] such a response to an unauthorized substitution has a number of problematic aspects, which could be avoided if the law responded by imposing a trust of the bank account instead. The common law response, as described by Millett LJ in *Trustee of FC Jones v Jones*, implies that a bank can involuntarily find itself in a direct contractual relationship with one person as a result of its decision to contract with another, even though neither party to the contract intended any such result. If the account-holder is not 'in reality' owed the debt represented by the bank account, this must mean that a bank cannot discharge its indebtedness under such an account by paying the named account-holder. This suggests that, where the account-holder purportedly draws on the account, before the bank discovers 3.117

332 Cf *Montgomerie v United Kingdom Mutual Steamship Association* [1891] 1 QB 370, per Wright J at 371: 'where a person contracts as agent for a principal the contract is the contract of the principal, and not that of the agent; and, prima facie, at common law the only person who may sue is the principal, and the only person who can be sued is the principal.'

333 Unless the agent has actual or apparent authority to accept the payment on behalf of the principal: see, for example, *NIML Ltd v Man Financial Australia Ltd* (2006) 15 VR 156.

334 [1997] Ch 159. 335 See Chapter 2, para 2.101 this volume for the facts of this case.

336 *Jones* (n 334) 171. 337 *Jones* (n 334) 170. 338 *Jones* (n 334) 167.

339 *Jones* (n 334) 167. 340 *Jones* (n 336). 341 *Jones* (n 336).

342 D Fox, *Property Rights in Money* (n 237) 194. See also P Birks, 'On Taking Seriously the Difference between Tracing and Claiming' (1997) 11 TLI 2, 7.

the existence of the unknown claimant, the actual amount of the debt remains the same; if the claimant subsequently demanded payment, the bank would be obliged to pay again and seek redress against the account holder. Such an understanding of the effect of common law tracing seems to fly in the face of Lord Goff's comment, in *Lipkin Gorman v Karpnale Ltd*,[343] that, although common law tracing does not depend on ratification, it has 'one feature in common with ratification, that it cannot be relied upon so as to render an innocent recipient a wrongdoer'.[344] The idea that the common law can trace into a bank account is, therefore, genuinely problematic if it means that that claimant gets a common law title to such an account—that is, if it means that the effect of a substitution is to bring about an involuntary assignment of the chose in action at law in favour of the claimant, without notification of the debtor.

3.118 The idea that it is possible to trace into a *mixed* bank account is even more difficult to square with this exchange-product account of common law tracing. The common law does not recognise the possibility of a tenancy in common over a chose in action.[345] Thus, if it were possible to identify the balance of a mixed bank account as the traceable product of one's common law title to an asset—and so to assert a common law title to that bank account—the only possible remedial response would be confiscatory. We would be obliged to treat the claimant either as a joint account-holder with the defendant or, as in *Trustee of FC Jones v Jones*, as the sole 'real' account holder. Both responses prejudice the position of a third party: the bank. Both these problems can be avoided by invoking equity's constructs of the charge or the trust; these make proportionate sharing possible, and distinguish between the content of the right held on trust or subject to a charge—the right of the account-holder against the bank—and the rights that may affect the exercise of that right by the account-holder.

3.119 Thus, in the absence of equitable constructs like the charge or the trust, common law mechanisms for tracing into choses in action or into mixed funds would have a confiscatory effect on the rights of the defendant, as well as prejudicial consequences for third parties. The basic principle of preserving the defendant's vested rights can explain why, if substitution does give rise to *common law* rights to the substitute asset, the possibilities of such tracing must be limited to avoid these consequences. The most obvious solution to this problem is to reject the view that a common law claimant gets such rights over the substitute asset,[346] and to instead make use of the equitable constructs of the charge and the trust in all cases.[347] These constructs, unlike common law property rights, can enable multiple parties to assert proprietary claims in relation to the same intangible asset or chose in action, without confiscation or prejudice to the rights of third parties.

[343] *Lipkin Gorman* (n 194). [344] *Lipkin Gorman* (n 194) 574.

[345] Co Litt s 315; *Re McKerrell* [1912] 2 Ch 648.

[346] This does not mean that common law owners of assets cannot bring claims for the traceable proceeds of those assets, only that the rights to the proceeds that they assert must be equitable in content if they are to capture, for example, mixed funds.

[347] See L Smith, 'Simplifying Claims to Traceable Proceeds' (2009) 125 LQR 338.

3.4. Justifying the Principles of Tracing

It has been argued that the courts have traditionally justified the existence of claims to traceable proceeds on the grounds that, if such claims were denied, the defendant would be permitted to acquire rights by depriving the claimant of her own rights. Conversely, they have justified the requirements of transactional tracing on the basis of protecting the pre-existing rights of the defendant, preserving her freedom to deal with assets as she sees fit where these dispositions do not involve exploiting the claimant's vulnerability to a loss of rights. What is the justification for these principles? 3.120

3.4.1. Protecting the vulnerable claimant: subordination of wrongdoers

In *Foskett v McKeown*,[348] Lord Millett explained his rejection of causal tracing in terms that helpfully illuminate the basis for transactional tracing. One of the arguments against transactional tracing that he dismissed, in that case, was the argument that the outcome represented a windfall for the beneficiaries under the trust. It will be recalled that the trustee had misappropriated £20,440 of trust money to pay the premiums on his life insurance policy. Although this was the amount of the beneficiaries' loss arising from that particular breach of trust, they were entitled to recover much more: 40 per cent of the proceeds of the policy, which amounted to £400,000. Lord Millett said that this apparently undeserved windfall was not unjust, because the case was analogous to a one where A used B's money to buy a lottery ticket that then turned out to be a winning ticket. In such a case: 3.121

> Had B discovered the fraud before the draw, he could have decided whether to keep the ticket or demand his money back. *He alone has the right to decide whether to gamble with his own money.* If A keeps him in ignorance until after the draw, he suffers the consequence. *He cannot deprive B of his right to choose what to do with his own money; but he can give him an informed choice.*[349]

As so often in the tracing case law, this statement seems somewhat counterfactual. If A has actually spent B's money on a lottery ticket, the one thing that B is unlikely to be able to do is to get his money—the very notes and coins spent by A—back. He can demand that A pay him an equivalent amount of money, or he can take his chance with the lottery, or he can try his doubtful remedies against the third party who has received his cash in consideration for selling the lottery ticket to A. It is not open to him to simply undo A's decision to deprive him of his right to choose what to do with his own money. As the reference to gambling suggests, the key feature of the situation is B's vulnerability to the risks arising from A's wrongful decisions to deal with his money. As a result of those decisions, B's freedom to decide whether or not to gamble with that particular money—or his right to have such decisions made 3.122

[348] *Foskett* (n 2). [349] *Foskett* (n 2) 134 (emphasis added).

in his interests, in accordance with the terms on which the power to make them was held—is lost. The law responds by stripping A, too, of his freedom to determine the consequences of that particular transaction for himself, even though he is the person who has brought it about. He is, instead, obliged to concede the interpretation of the transaction that best suits B.

3.123 Thus, in *Foskett v McKeown* itself, Mr Murphy clearly intended to benefit his family by taking out the life insurance policy and paying the premiums under it; like his predecessors, Simon Deg and the widow in *Halcott v Markant*, he expressed these intentions in the form of an elaborately detailed express trust.[350] However, he was not at liberty to use the trust bank accounts to pursue this end, and his decisions to draw on it to pay some of the premiums on his life insurance policy had the effect of depriving the claimants of their right to have the bank account used for their exclusive benefit. These were not, therefore, decisions that he was free to make for the sake of the ends that he himself wished to pursue, ie to benefit his own family. Once he had used the trust money to pay the premiums under the insurance policy, his contract with the life insurance company became, in part, a gamble with the claimant's money; as a result, his decisions as to who ought to have the benefits paid out under that contract, in the event of his death, were no longer wholly to be respected.

3.4.2. Protecting defendant autonomy: the requirement of a defined fund

3.124 This reasoning will not, however, cover a case where A's particular decision does not exploit B's vulnerability in this way. Thus, if we return to Oesterle's examples of what causal tracing would look like,[351] we can see that this justification of tracing will not stretch to produce the outcomes that he considers to be the most rational. Oesterle imagines the case of a thief who has $100 of his own in gold coins and who has stolen bearer bonds worth $100 from the claimant. The thief keeps the gold coins under his bed and spends the stolen bearer bonds on food, which he consumes. In Oesterle's view, the gold coins are the product of the bearer bonds if the claimant can show that the thief would have spent them on food, instead of the bearer bonds, if he had not committed the theft. In the light of the subordinating principle that underpins the whole concept of tracing, we can translate this to mean that the claimant, because he was the owner of the bearer bonds, should be entitled to treat the thief's decision to keep the gold coins as if it was entered into for her benefit.

3.125 The objection to this argument is that, although the thief is a wrongdoer and his wrong justifies making him personally liable to pay the claimant $100, it is not clear why his theft of the bearer bonds should deprive him of his pre-existent freedom to decide what to do with the gold coins, which he has derived from some source other than the theft. If he has an absolute legal title to the coins, obtained under a legally valid transaction, he is entitled to make use of them, or not, as he pleases. If he acquired them on trust for another person, or indeed has misappropriated them

[350] *Foskett* (n 2) 108. [351] See Chapter 1, para 1.27 this volume.

from someone else, his decisions must be treated as entered into for that other's benefit. In either case, there is no justification for treating his decisions to keep or use the gold coins as entered into for the benefit of the claimant. Either the thief acquired the coins in circumstances that left him at liberty to decide what to do with them, or in circumstances that imposed duties on him in favour of persons other than the victim of the theft of the bearer bonds. The use of the bearer bonds to buy food does not give us any compelling reason why either this liberty or this duty, in relation to the gold coins, should be abrogated. The claimant's ownership of the bearer bonds entitles him to complain that the defendant should not have deprived him of the right to decide whether or not to use those bearer bonds for the purpose of feeding a thief. This does not, in itself, entitle him to deprive the defendant of his own freedom to decide what to do with assets obtained under a completely unrelated transaction. Lord Millett's explanation in *Foskett v McKeown* only captures a situation where the very power exercised by the defendant, in acquiring an asset, is one that the claimant has a right to control or to have exercised for her benefit.

3.5. Conclusion: Defining an Unauthorized Substitution

We are now in a position to address the problem that underpins the whole puzzle of tracing: that of defining the concept of an unauthorized substitution in terms that unify the variety of fact situations covered by the law of tracing. The core case of an unauthorized substitution is, as we have seen, exchange. Where a trustee makes an unauthorized sale of a trust asset, and receives cash in exchange, the cash is the traceable product of the trust asset and the beneficiary under the trust has claims in respect of it. Modern accounts of the law say that this is because the cash represents the value of the trust asset, which has been wrongfully realized by the trustee. What this means is that the trustee's decision to transfer the trustee's title to the trust asset to a stranger was one that exploited the claimant's vulnerability to a loss of rights arising from the trustee's legal power to make decisions of this kind. 3.126

The normatively important dimension of an unauthorized substitution, therefore, is that it represents a situation where A has been enabled to acquire an asset by his decision to exploit B's vulnerability in this way. This does not describe a merely causal relationship between the decision and the acquisition but a transactional one. We have seen that tracing is not possible where A has decided to spend B's money on food and this enables him, in a causal sense, to use some other cash in his possession to acquire a title to some gold from a stranger, X. His misappropriation of B's money does not have any impact on his freedom to deal with other cash that he owns; thus, his decision to acquire X's gold by transferring that cash to X cannot be subordinated to B's interests in the way that tracing requires. By contrast, when he acquires title to the gold from X in consideration for a transfer of B's cash, we can attribute A's ability to complete the transaction—to comply with the condition necessary for X to transfer her title to the gold to him—to his exploitation of B's vulnerability. In other words, tracing is possible whenever A's acquisition of an asset depends on a decision, by A, to exploit his power to deal with B's assets. It is not possible where the 3.127

terms on which A acquires an asset from X are wholly independent of his power to exploit B's assets, even though there is some causal or other factual link between the two events of acquisition and exploitation.

3.128 At the level of detail, this account of tracing raises questions about the kind of transaction that qualifies as an exploitation of the claimant's vulnerability in this way, and about the circumstances in which the principle of preserving the defendant's autonomy will preclude tracing through certain transactions or into certain assets. The next two chapters look at how the law has answered these questions. Chapter 4 discusses a range of situations that arise where a claimant is tracing through the transactions of a defendant who is a wrongdoer. Chapter 5 considers the rules that govern the special case where the claimant is tracing through the transactions of a wrongdoer who is also dealing with the assets of another innocent co-contributor to the same fund.

4

Rules of Tracing I

Against a Wrongdoer

The status of a defendant as a 'wrongdoer' can play an important role in determining when and how a claimant can successfully trace through her transactions. It is sometimes suggested that all the work in this context is done by the evidential principle in *Armory v Delamirie*, which enables a court to draw negative inferences of fact against a wrongdoer who is responsible for a lack of relevant evidence. As we have seen, that principle does play a role in the context of tracing, but its function is relatively limited. Tracing is not a purely evidential process, and some of normative functions performed by the rules that subordinate wrongdoers cannot be explained simply as applications of the evidential rule in *Armory v Delamirie*. This chapter argues that the law employs a principle of subordination of wrongdoers in three distinct contexts. These differ in their definitions of who is a wrongdoer, as well as in their substantive consequences, and it is therefore practically important to discuss them separately. 4.01

First, as discussed in Chapter 2, the evidential principle in *Armory v Delamirie* does indeed play some role in the context of tracing: it will sometimes assist a claimant in situations where there are evidential gaps in the transactional history of an asset. This principle applies where the act of failing to keep an accurate record, or concealing or destroying relevant evidence, is itself a wrong on the part of the defendant. Its effect is to allow the court to draw negative inferences against such a wrongdoer, unless he can discharge the burden of disproving these inferences. 4.02

Secondly, as was argued in Chapter 3, the rules of tracing are underpinned by a general principle that subordinates the interests, and intentions, of a wrongdoer when entering into transactions that exploit the claimant's legal vulnerability to his decision-making power. This is a substantive principle of law, not a rule of evidence, and is limited only by a principle of preserving the autonomy of the wrongdoer when she is making use of her own assets or assets belonging to someone other than the claimant. In this context, a wrongdoer is anyone who—knowingly or unknowingly—deals with the assets of another, in circumstances where she is not at liberty to do so. The question whether a given defendant *has* a power of this kind, which justifies the subordinating consequence of tracing, is a question about the types of legal relationships that generate claims to traceable proceeds. Its exact parameters are addressed in Chapters 6–8. This chapter looks at the kinds of exploitation that are captured by the rules of tracing in cases where such a power-duty nexus undoubtedly 4.03

exists, as where the defendant is an agent, trustee, or company director. It explains how the twin principles of protecting the vulnerable claimant from exploitation and preserving the autonomy of the defendant can justify the rules that delineate which transactions qualify as clean substitutions.

4.04 Finally, there is a special application of the principle of subordination that applies in the context of mixed substitutions: the cherry-picking rule, which allows a claimant to allocate transactions drawing on a mixed fund in a manner that suits her own best interests. In this context, it is unclear, as a matter of authority, whether the status of a wrongdoer belongs only to a person who has breached a fiduciary duty by the act of mixing her own assets with the claimant's. I argue that the principle of subordination justifies cherry-picking only where the very act of creating a mixed fund is a wrong, but that, contrary to dicta in some cases, the wrong in question need not be a breach of fiduciary duty in the strict sense of a duty to avoid making an unauthorized profit from one's position.

4.1. Lack of Evidence of Transactional History

4.05 Tracing usually requires a claimant to affirmatively prove the transactional links between his original asset and the asset that he wishes to identify as its traceable product. It is not usually enough for him to show that the defendant has, in the past, misappropriated his assets and that she cannot, or refuses to, identify the source of every asset that she now holds: it is up to the claimant 'to adduce evidence to prove the necessary nexus'[1] between the original misappropriation and the other asset or assets that he now wishes to claim.

4.06 This does not, however, mean that the claimant must be able to positively, and with total certainty, identify each and every transaction that leads from her asset to the substitute asset. The ordinary civil standard of proof applies, so that courts may infer the existence of transactional links based on various factors that suggest the likelihood of such links, on the balance of probabilities. Absence of alternative funds to make a purchase,[2] the intentions motivating the original misappropriation,[3] and the timing, amounts,[4] and context of payments have all been used as evidence justifying the relevant inference.

4.07 In *Lane v Dighton*,[5] for example, Dighton had contracted to purchase an estate in land at a price of £6,600. He paid £660 as a deposit, and agreed to pay the remaining £5,940 of the purchase price by buying bank annuities of this value and settling it

[1] *Serious Fraud Office v Lexi Holdings plc* [2008] EWCA Crim 1443, [53] (Keene LJ). See also *Islamic Republic of Pakistan v Zardari* [2006] EWHC 2411, [61]–[63] (Lawrence Collins J). Contrast the view taken by Hobhouse J in *Westdeutsche Landesbank Girozentrale v Islington LBC* [1994] 4 All ER 890, reversed by the House of Lords on another point [1996] AC 669.

[2] Eg *Lane v Dighton* (1762) Amb 409, 27 ER 274; *Willis v Willis* (1740) 2 Atk 71, 26 ER 443; *Harford v Lloyd* (1855) 20 Beav 310, 52 ER 622; *Wilkins v Stevens* (1842) 1 Y & CCC 431, 62 ER 957; *Black v Freedman & Co* (1910) 12 CLR 105; *El Ajou v Dollar Land Holdings plc (No 1)* [1993] 3 All ER 717 (HC).

[3] Eg *Lane* (n 2); *Harford* (n 2); *Relfo Ltd (In Liquidation) v Varsani* [2014] EWCA Civ 360.

[4] Eg *El Ajou* (n 2); *Relfo Ltd (In Liquidation)* (n 3).

[5] *Lane* (n 2).

on trust for persons nominated by the vendors. He subsequently prevailed upon the trustees under his marriage settlement to let him sell some of the trust assets, receiving over £4,000 as their price.[6] On the same day that he received the proceeds of sale of the trust stock, he bought annuities and settled them on trust as promised, in consideration for which the estate was conveyed to him. Master Bonner found as a fact that he did not have 'money sufficient to purchase the [stock] without employing in such purchase the [proceeds of sale of] the ... trust stock, or some part thereof'.[7] Coupled with the timing of the transactions, and Dighton's known intentions[8] in selling the trust stock, the court concluded that this was adequate evidence that the trust money had been used to buy the stock that was used to acquire the land.[9]

Similarly, in *Relfo Ltd (In Liquidation) v Varsani*,[10] the Court of Appeal inferred that there must have been transactional links between two payments based on the available evidence about the surrounding context of those payments, and even though the exact character of the relevant links was unknown. In that case, one Mr Gorecia, a director of Relfo Ltd, misappropriated £500,000 from the company bank account and, having converted it to a US dollar amount of $890,050, paid it into a Latvian bank account held in the name of a company called Mirren Ltd. On the following day, a payment of $878,479.35 was made to Mr Varsani from the Ukrainian bank account of a company called Intertrade Group LLC. At the then exchange rate, this was the dollar equivalent of £500,000 less 1.3 per cent. Mr Varsani was well known to Mr Gorecia, and had previously had a stake in Relfo Ltd. At first instance, Sales J found as a fact that Mr Gorecia's intention, in making the payment to Mirren Ltd, was to bring about the Intertrade payment to Mr Varsani. However, the liquidator of Relfo Ltd could not, on the bank records available to him, show how this had actually been done: he could not identify 'specific transactions passing between the Mirren and Intertrade accounts to show how the Relfo/Mirren payment was translated into the Intertrade payment.'[11] 4.08

The Court of Appeal concluded that, on these primary findings of fact, it could infer that Mirren had agreed with Intertrade that it would transfer the £500,000 received from Relfo Ltd to some unknown person, in consideration for Intertrade agreeing to pay the dollar amount to Mr Varsani.[12] The facts that justified this inference included the similarity in the amount and the timing of the two payments, the absence of any consideration given by Mr Varsani for the payment to him, Mr Gorecia's intentions in misappropriating the funds, the prior dealings between Mr Gorecia and Mr Varsani, and the fact that both Mr Varsani and Mr Gorecia had a 4.09

[6] The exact figures are not clear from the report, where two inconsistent figures are given (£4,010, 10s and £4,100, 10s): *Lane* (n 2) 412; 275.

[7] *Lane* (n 6).

[8] The claimants had introduced into evidence 'a paper, all of the hand-writing of Dighton ... in which he takes note that the trust stocks had been sold and *the money laid out, from time to time, in the purchase of land*': *Lane* (n 2) 410; 274 (emphasis in the original).

[9] *Lane* (n 6). [10] *Relfo Ltd (In Liquidation)* (n 3).

[11] *Relfo Ltd (In Liquidation)* (n 3) [13] (Arden LJ).

[12] *Relfo Ltd (In Liquidation)* (n 3) [61] (Arden LJ).

history of dealing with Ukrainian businessmen with access to money-laundering vehicles and who were used to preparing false records.[13]

4.10 In both *Lane v Dighton* and *Relfo Ltd v Varsani*, evidence of the intention motivating the original misappropriation was a factor justifying the inference of a subsequent transactional link. However, as Arden LJ stressed in *Relfo v Varsani*, evidence of such an intention is only one of the 'basket of factors'[14] that may justify such an inference. As has been argued, tracing is an objective inquiry that seeks to identify the legal powers exercised by a person in actually acquiring, and transferring, an asset.[15] Evidence of the intentions behind an initial misappropriation is not sufficient,[16] in the absence of other evidence, to justify a finding that a person has in fact acquired an asset under a transaction that involved the exercise of such a power. Nor is evidence of intention necessary, if other evidence indicating the existence of an objective transactional link is available. For example, in *El Ajou v Dollar Land Holdings plc (No 1)*,[17] Millett J inferred that there was a transactional link between a payment into one bank account and a payment into another account, a few weeks later, even though he found that the available evidence about the intention behind these transactions was 'too speculative to form the basis of any inference'.[18] Nevertheless, the existence of an objective transactional link could be inferred from the similarity in the amounts of the two payments,[19] the fact that the same bank had received the first payment and originated the second payment,[20] and—as in *Lane v Dighton*—the fact that the fraudsters whose transactions were at issue did not have any substantial funds available to them that were not the proceeds of the fraud.[21]

4.1.1. Presumption against a wrongdoer

4.11 There is no question of a formal reversal of the burden of proof in these cases. In *El Ajou v Dollar Land Holdings plc (No 1)*,[22] the dispute was between the victims of the original fraudulent misappropriations and a company that, they alleged, had received the traceable proceeds of the misappropriated assets. Neither the claimants nor the recipient had any control over the bank accounts in question, and so the recipients were not responsible for the lack of evidence about what had been done with the claimants' money. The burden of proof, therefore, lay with the claimants, and they succeeded in discharging that burden on the balance of probabilities standard. As Millett J explained, the position would have been different if the dispute had been between the victims of the fraud and the fraudsters themselves: in such a case, the

[13] *Relfo Ltd (In Liquidation)* (n 3) [58] (Arden LJ).

[14] *Relfo Ltd (In Liquidation)* (n 3) [57] (Arden LJ).

[15] See paras 4.34–4.35 this chapter for a discussion of the facts of *Relfo Ltd v Varsani* from this perspective.

[16] *Relfo Ltd (In Liquidation)* (n 14).

[17] *El Ajou* (n 2), reversed by the Court of Appeal on a different point at [1994] 2 All ER 685.

[18] *El Ajou* (n 2) 735. [19] *El Ajou* (n 18). [20] *El Ajou* (n 18).

[21] *El Ajou* (n 18). For other examples of the court drawing such an inference from the absence of any alternative sources of funding, see *Harford* (n 2) and *Dyson v Curtis* [2010] EWHC 3289 (Ch), [137]–[142] (HHJ Grant).

[22] *El Ajou* (n 2).

court would have been prepared to infer the existence of a transactional link between the two payments unless the fraudsters could provide evidence to the contrary.[23]

As has been shown,[24] this is an application of the broad evidential principle in *Armory v Delamirie*, which may be invoked when the answer to a question of fact cannot be ascertained as a result of the wrongdoing of one of the parties. Its effect, in these situations, is that the court will draw negative inferences against the party who is responsible for the absence of the relevant evidence, unless she can positively disprove the truth of those inferences. 4.12

4.1.1.1. Defendant's legal responsibility for gap in evidence

In the context of tracing, the principle applies where a defendant had a duty to keep an accurate account of his transactions involving the claimant's money, has failed to do so, and this failure is the cause of the evidential problems faced by the claimant in proving the existence of transactional links.[25] 4.13

In *Lupton v White*,[26] for example, the defendant's agents had not only physically mixed his lead ore with that of the claimant, but had also failed to keep a proper account of the ore sold, so that the proceeds of sale of the claimant's ore could not be distinguished from the proceeds of sale of the defendant's.[27] Lord Eldon LC, in drawing the inference that all the ore sold was the claimant's unless the defendant could prove otherwise, emphasized the fact that the defendant and his agents had been authorized by the court to mine the claimant's mine, and to sell the ore obtained from it, but only on the condition that distinct accounts would be kept. The parties, he said, were therefore 'to be considered, not as man acting towards man, but with reference to an undertaking by one man to leave the other as safe, as if the protecting hand of this Court had been over him'.[28] He distinguished the situation from one where one party had dealt with property belonging to another, not knowing of that other's claims, and had failed to keep any account. In such a case, where the defendant was under 'no obligation to keep accounts',[29] 'the account would be directed, not according to the strict course, but in such a manner as under all the circumstances would be fit'.[30] The reversal of the burden of proof, which justified the outcome in *Lupton v White*, would not operate. 4.14

The principle was more recently applied in *Sinclair Investments (UK) Ltd v Versailles Trade Finance Ltd*.[31] In that case, Versailles Trade Finance Ltd ('VTFL') had received money from another company, Trading Partners Ltd ('TPL'), on trust[32] for 4.15

[23] *El Ajou* (n 2) 734. [24] See Chapter 2, Section 2.1.2.1 this volume.

[25] *Lord Chedworth v Edwards* (1802) 8 Ves Jun 47, 32 ER 268; *Lupton v White* (1808) 15 Ves Jun 432, 33 ER 817; *Harford* (n 2); *Sinclair Investments (UK) Ltd v Versailles Trade Finance Ltd* [2011] EWCA Civ 347.

[26] *Lupton* (n 25). For a detailed account of the facts, see Chapter 2, paras 2.42–2.44 this volume.

[27] *Lupton* (n 25) 434; 818: 'the account of sales of lead in the book, entitled "The Accounts of Little Ing," and several other books produced, have been so kept or contrived as to prevent a true discovery'.

[28] *Lupton* (n 25) 438; 820. [29] *Lupton* (n 25) 443; 821. [30] *Lupton* (n 29).

[31] *Sinclair Investments (UK) Ltd* (n 25) overruled by the Supreme Court on a different point in *FHR European Ventures LLP v Cedar Capital Partners LLC* [2014] UKSC 45 (see Lord Neuberger at [50]).

[32] As conceded by counsel for VTFL: *Sinclair Investments (UK) Ltd* (n 25) [132] (Lord Neuberger MR).

the purpose of buying goods and entering into factoring transactions for the benefit of TPL's clients.[33] Under the terms of the agreement, VTFL promised to keep any bank accounts used for the purpose of TPL's business separate, opening them in the name of TPL. In fact, however, the director of both companies, Mr Cushnie, was engaged in a fraudulent scheme, and the money passed to VTFL was not used in accordance with the terms of the agreement. Part of it was used, in 'a classic Ponzi scheme',[34] to pay 'profits' on the supposed transactions using their money to TPL's clients. Mr Cushnie's associate and co-director, Mr Clough, stole part of it. The rest was circulated around a number of other companies controlled by Mr Cushnie, with the aim of inflating VTFL's apparent turnover and raising its share price, in a series of complex 'cross-firing' transactions. VTFL's accounts were falsified, with the various transactions between the companies controlled by Mr Cushnie disguised as sales to customers, and so the company accounts were an evidential 'black hole' or 'maelstrom',[35] within which no specific transactions involving the money held on trust for TPL could be accurately identified. On these facts, the burden of proof was reversed, so that VTFL's administrative receivers bore the burden of showing that the money they had recovered by realizing VTFL's book debts were not the proceeds of trust money.

4.16 As Sales J explained in *Relfo Ltd v Varsani* at first instance,[36] this reversal of the burden of proof in *Sinclair Investments (UK) Ltd v Versailles Trade Finance Ltd* depended on the responsibility of the actual defendant to the litigation, VTFL, for the absence of the relevant evidence. VTFL was a fiduciary that had owed duties to TFL to keep accurate accounts, which it had breached, and the evidential difficulties in the case were directly attributable to this breach. It is the combination of these three factors—the existence of a duty owed by the actual defendant to the litigation, the breach of that duty by the defendant, and the direct connection between that breach of duty and the absence of relevant evidence—that triggers the application of the principle in *Armory v Delamire*, in the context of tracing, as in other contexts.[37] Thus, it was not applied in *Relfo Ltd v Varsani*, as Sales J found that all three elements were absent.[38]

4.17 First, the defendant to the litigation, Mr Varsani, was not the wrongdoing fiduciary himself, but a recipient. As in *El Ajou v Dollar Land Holdings plc (No 1)*, this precluded the invocation of the evidential presumption in *Armory v Delamirie* against him.[39] A claimant who is unable to prove transactional links, because of a wrongful failure to keep proper records of transactions, can only place the burden of disproving such links on the wrongdoer herself or on her representatives.[40]

[33] The claimant, Sinclair Investments (UK) Ltd, was one of TPL's clients and had taken an assignment of that company's claims against VTFL.

[34] *Sinclair Investments (UK) Ltd* (n 25) [159] (Lord Neuberger MR).

[35] *Sinclair Investments (UK) Ltd* (n 25) [135] (Lord Neuberger MR).

[36] [2012] EWHC 2168 (Ch).

[37] *Keefe v The Isle of Man Steam Packet Co* [2010] EWCA Civ 683.

[38] *Relfo Ltd* (n 36) [73]–[76].

[39] *Relfo Ltd* (n 36) [75].

[40] Such as the administrative receiver in *Sinclair Investments (UK) Ltd v Versailles Trade Finance Ltd* itself.

The burden of affirmatively proving transactional links, however, remains on the claimant when the defendant to the litigation is, instead, a recipient of assets from the wrongdoer. This is an important point of difference between the evidential principle in *Armory v Delamirie* and the substantive cherry-picking rule, with which it is sometimes conflated.[41] The former can be invoked only in litigation against the person whose breach of duty has caused the evidential difficulty in question, or against her representatives. The latter can be invoked to prove that assets obtained by a wrongdoer are the traceable proceeds of the claimant's assets, even where the actual litigation—based on the assertion of proprietary claims over the proceeds—is against a subsequent recipient who has not given value.[42]

Secondly, the wrongdoing fiduciary on the facts of *Relfo Ltd v Varsani*—Mr Gorecia—was not directly responsible for the evidential obstacles faced by the claimant company. Although he had breached his duty to the company by transferring money from its bank account to Mirren Ltd, the money was still traceable at that point. The later decisions that rendered tracing evidentially difficult—Mirren's failure to keep records of its dealings with Intertrade and others—were not made by him, and he was not in a position to exercise control[43] over those decisions. Thus, the mere fact that there was a breach of fiduciary duty on the facts, which was in some way causally linked to the evidential problems later faced by the claimant, was not enough to justify a reversal of the burden of proof. The breach in question had to involve the failure, on the part of the wrongdoer himself, to preserve the relevant evidence. 4.18

Thirdly, the persons who were directly responsible for the evidential difficulties on the facts of *Relfo Ltd v Varsani*—Mirren, Intertrade, and perhaps any others with whom they had dealt—did not 'owe Relfo duties in equity to maintain those payments as separate, unmixed funds'.[44] This cannot mean that these intermediate recipients were under no liability whatsoever to Relfo Ltd. If Relfo Ltd had litigated against Mirren Ltd when the money was still held in that company's bank account, it seems likely that it would have succeeded in the claim;[45] it could also have claimed any traceable proceeds of the money obtained by Mirren Ltd itself.[46] Rather, the issue was the absence of any duty to keep accurate records, distinguishing transactions involving Relfo Ltd's money from its own. 4.19

In *Relfo Ltd v Varsani* itself, Sales J described the duty that justified the reversal of the burden of proof as a fiduciary duty.[47] It is true that, in many situations where a defendant is empowered to deal with the claimant's assets and has a duty to keep a record of his transactions involving those assets, he is likely to be a fiduciary in 4.20

[41] See Chapter 2, Section 2.1.2.2 this volume.

[42] *Foskett v McKeown* [2001] 1 AC 102, 131 (Lord Millett): 'It is ... impossible to distinguish between the case where the investment is retained by the trustee and the case where it is given away to a gratuitous donee.' On cherry-picking in general, see Section 4.3.2 this chapter.

[43] *Relfo Ltd* (n 39). [44] *Relfo Ltd* (n 39). [45] *Re Montagu's ST* [1987] Ch 264.

[46] Since it appears that Mirren Ltd gave no consideration for the receipt of the £500,000 and could not therefore have had the defence of bona fide purchase for value without notice: *Re Montagu's ST* (n 45).

[47] *Relfo Ltd* (n 39).

the strict sense: that is, in the sense that he owes the claimant the conventional fiduciary duties not to profit from his position and to avoid conflicts.[48] However, this is not always the case. In *El Ajou v Dollar Land Holdings plc (No 1)*, as has been mentioned, Millett J would have been prepared to invoke the presumption against the fraudsters whose transactions were at issue, even though he held that they did not owe any fiduciary duties to the claimants.[49] Similarly, in *Harford v Lloyd*,[50] the presumption was invoked against a recipient of misdirected assets, who was found to have colluded in the misappropriation of those assets but who could not be characterized as a fiduciary in the conventional sense.

4.21 In that case, the testator had bequeathed certain consols to the trustees of the Bristol Royal Infirmary, to hold on trust for the purposes of the infirmary; he had appointed the claimant, the treasurer of the infirmary, as the executor of his will. One Rees, in whose house the testator had died, managed to convince the trustees of the infirmary to renounce probate by misrepresenting the value of the assets. With the assistance of the first defendant, Lloyd, who stood surety for him to the court, Rees then got himself appointed as administrator of the estate and sold the consols, exchanging them for a cheque in the amount of £1,342, which he kept, and £4,500 in banknotes, which he gave to Lloyd. Both he and Lloyd opened new bank accounts, and Rees paid the cheque into his account and Lloyd paid the £4,500 in banknotes into his.

4.22 After this, there was 'a great deal of intermixture, backwards and forwards, of cheques which renders the tracing of them extremely difficult'.[51] Lloyd later spent £2,908 to acquire certain securities, some of which he transferred to the second defendant, his wife. The claimant argued that these securities were held subject to a charge in his favour, on the basis that they represented the traceable proceeds of the consols. There was no direct evidence of a transactional link between this £2,908 and the two bank accounts into which the proceeds of sale of the consols had been paid. However, Sir John Romilly held that the burden of proof lay on Lloyd to show that 'these moneys did not come from [the testator's estate], *for* it is, in my opinion, proved that Lloyd knew that everything that he received ... was derived from [that] estate'.[52] Mrs Lloyd was in no better position since she also knew of the fraud.[53] It appears, therefore, that the defendant need not be a fiduciary in order to be under a duty to keep accurate records of his transactions, such that the principle in *Armory v Delamirie* will justify the drawing of negative inferences against him if he does not do so. Knowledge that one is dealing with assets of another person seems to be enough. If this is right, the view that the presumption would not have been available even if Mirren Ltd had been the defendant in *Relfo Ltd v Varsani* depends on an assumption that Mirren Ltd was an innocent recipient on the facts, unaware of Relfo Ltd's probable claims over the money. Where the defendant knows

48 See Chapter 6, Section 6.2 this volume.

49 *El Ajou* (n 2) 734 (Millett J): 'They were simply swindled. No breach of any fiduciary obligation was involved.'

50 *Harford* (n 2).

51 *Harford* (n 2) 318; 625.

52 *Harford* (n 51) (emphasis added).

53 *Harford* (n 2) 320; 626.

of the claimant's probable claims over the assets under her control, *Harford v Lloyd* suggests that a failure by such a defendant to keep accurate records of her own transactions[54] involving those assets will justify the invocation of the principle in *Armory v Delamirie* against her.

4.1.1.2. Effect of the presumption

As has been noted, the effect of the principle in *Armory v Delamirie* is that the court is prepared to draw negative inferences against the defendant who is responsible for a lack of relevant evidence, and to place the burden of disproving those inferences on him. The extent of the burden on the defendant, in such a case, is the same as that which would otherwise be placed on the claimant: ie he must prove that, on the balance of probabilities,[55] the asset claimed by the claimant is unlikely to be transactionally linked to the misappropriated assets. 4.23

In this context, a defendant may appeal to what is realistic[56] and consistent with the evidence that is, in fact, available. Thus, for example, in *Lord Chedworth v Edwards*,[57] Lord Eldon was prepared to infer that the defendant steward, who had failed to keep any records of what he had done with his employer's money for nineteen years,[58] had purchased the stock standing in his name using his employer's money. However, he refused to draw the same inference in relation to the credit balance of the steward's bank account. As two years had elapsed since the last misappropriation by the steward, he said, 'it was too much to infer that it was the same money unconverted';[59] while it was probable that stock purchased using the employer's money had simply been retained, it was improbable that money paid into a bank account had not subsequently been drawn out and replaced by money from other sources. On similar grounds, in *Serious Fraud Office v Lexi Holdings plc*,[60] the Court of Appeal rejected the argument that the presumption against a wrongdoer could be invoked to justify a decision that *all* the assets of the wrongdoing defendant represented the traceable proceeds of the misappropriated assets: neither 'presumption nor reasonable inference'[61] could justify such a conclusion. 4.24

4.2. Tracing Through Clean Substitutions

In this way, therefore, the requirement of proving that a substitution or chain of substitutions has taken place is less onerous than might be supposed; the claimant 4.25

[54] Contrast *El Ajou* (n 2), where the defendants were eventually held to be knowing recipients by the Court of Appeal (see [1994] 2 All ER 685) but where the transactions in question were not under their own control.

[55] *Sinclair Investments (UK) Ltd v Versailles Trade Finance Ltd* [2011] EWCA Civ 347, [141] (Lord Neuberger).

[56] *Gulati v MGN Ltd* [2015] EWHC 1482 (Ch), [88] (Mann J).

[57] *Lord Chedworth* (n 25).

[58] See Chapter 2, para 2.44 this volume for the facts.

[59] *Lord Chedworth* (n 25) 40; 269.

[60] *Serious Fraud Office* (n 1).

[61] *Serious Fraud Office* (n 1) [55] (Keene LJ).

may appeal to the probabilities of the case, given the surrounding context of those transactions that she can identify, and may sometimes be able to invoke the presumption against wrongdoers where she is litigating against certain defendants. However, as we have seen, the primary work done by the rules of tracing is not really evidential but normative. The claimant does not only need to prove—by whatever evidence, and relying on any evidential presumptions applicable on the facts—that there has been some kind of transaction that somehow connects the asset acquired by the defendant and the asset misappropriated from her. She also needs to show that this link is of the right kind and, unless she is lucky enough to be able to prove a straight chain of direct swaps taking place in perfect chronological order, this will involve some engagement with the complexities of the rules of tracing as they apply to particular fact situations.

4.26 We have seen that tracing captures cases where A's very act of transacting with a third party, from whom he acquires an asset, involves an exploitation of his power to deal with the assets of B. The core case of such a transaction—exchange—takes the form of a direct swap of assets, taking place in chronological order. *Taylor v Plumer*[62] is a prototypical example. The agent, Walsh, went to his principal's bank on the morning of 5 December 1811, received banknotes belonging to his principal, and then took them to a stockbroker on the afternoon of the same day; he physically handed over eleven of the very notes he received from the bank, and the stockbroker gave him his change and the share certificates he wished to buy.[63] We can readily see how, in such a case, Walsh acquired the shares in question by the very act of abusing his power to deal with his principal's banknotes. The stockbroker transferred the share certificates to Walsh only in consideration for receipt of title to the banknotes, and the decision to confer title to the banknotes on the stockbroker was one that Walsh was not at liberty to make for his own benefit.

4.27 However, this analysis becomes less straightforward if we only slightly complicate the story. In *Taylor v Plumer*, Walsh had ordered the stockbroker to buy the shares for him on 29 November 1811, promising to pay with money he did not actually have at that point. As we have seen,[64] his intentions at the time that he made this promise had been to misappropriate the money from another client—not Sir Thomas Plumer, his ultimate victim—and his power of making legally binding promises was, of course, not one that he held subject to any duties to Sir Thomas. What if he had purchased and taken possession of the stock on 29 November itself, with the stockbroker accepting a promise of payment as consideration for the transfer? Would his subsequent satisfaction of the debt, using Sir Thomas Plumer's money, have brought his initial decision to acquire it within the scope of the principle of subordinating wrongdoers?

[62] (1815) 3 M & S 562, 105 ER 721. See Chapter 3, Section 3.3 this volume for a more detailed analysis of the facts.

[63] For a detailed hour-by-hour description of Walsh's 'busy day' on 5 December 1811, when he completed all these transactions and began preparations for his attempted flight to America, see L Smith, 'The Stockbroker and the Solicitor-General: the Story Behind *Taylor v Plumer*' (1994) 15 Journal of Legal History 1, 5–7.

[64] See Chapter 3, para 3.52 this volume.

There might be two objections to tracing on such facts, one based on the chronological sequence of events and another based on the related but distinct problem of tracing through the payment of a debt. On one hand, it might be argued that tracing only makes sense when the defendant's transfer or other disposition of the claimant's asset is earlier in time than his own acquisition of an asset from a third party. On this view, if Walsh had acquired the stock from the stockbroker at 11am, and had then handed Sir Thomas Plumer's banknotes to him at noon, tracing would be impossible; the exact terms of the bargain between Walsh and the stockbroker would make no difference if this had been the order in which the relevant payments were made. On the other hand, it might be argued that—while the chronological sequence of payments need not, in itself, determine whether or not tracing is possible—any acquisition of an asset on credit does preclude tracing. In such a case the defendant has acquired an asset by his promise to pay, and not by his actual decision to transfer the claimant's money;[65] the principle of protection of defendant autonomy would be violated if the law collapsed the decision to incur a debt into the later decision to repay the debt using the claimant's money. 4.28

If the problem of so-called backwards tracing is framed in this way, we can see the strength of the objections to such tracing as well as the limited scope of those objections. The chronological sequence of transactions must matter to tracing, at least to some extent, because a defendant cannot be described as having exploited a power that he does not have. A defendant cannot acquire an asset by exploiting his control over the claimant's assets if, at the date of the relevant acquisition, he did not have any such control over the claimant's assets in the first place. If Walsh had purchased the shares outright on 29 November, and misappropriated Sir Thomas Plumer's money only on 5 December 1811, how could his decision on 29 November be said to have involved any exploitation of his control over Sir Thomas Plumer's banknotes? He had not stolen them yet. For tracing to be possible, therefore, the misappropriation of the claimant's assets must normally chronologically precede the transaction under which the defendant has acquired a substitute asset. 4.29

Similarly, a defendant's power to incur debts, and thereby acquire assets, is one that he possesses in his capacity as a legal person rather than in his capacity as the person in control of any particular fund of assets. The fact that he later performs his promise by using his control of another person's assets may justify that other in claiming the benefit of the decision to discharge the debt, an effect that English law allows via the remedy of subrogation to the rights of the creditor.[66] However, this is normatively wholly different from allowing the claimant to take the benefit of the earlier decision to acquire an asset by incurring a debt in the first place. The principle of protecting the defendant's autonomy justifies the law's refusal to collapse these 4.30

[65] Cf M Conaglen, 'Difficulties with Tracing Backwards' (2011) 127 LQR 432, 450: 'The asset that the vendor accepted in return for agreeing to pass title in the goods to the purchaser was the benefit of the debt, not cash.'

[66] As in *Boscawen v Bajwa* [1996] 1 WLR 328; see also *Law Society v Haider* [2003] EWHC 2486 (Ch).

two decisions by treating the defendant's freedom to bind himself to pay a debt as one that must be subordinated to the claimant's ends.

4.31 The force of these arguments depends, however, on showing that the defendant's decisions are genuinely independent of each other. A defendant who acquires an asset by incurring a debt that he intends to repay using a particular fund is, in reality, making a decision that relies on his—actual or anticipated—control of that fund. The difference between such a case and a case where the defendant directly exchanges the claimant's asset for a substitute is formal, rather than substantive, and the principle of respect for a defendant's autonomy in dealing with his own assets could not justify distinguishing the two scenarios. If the chronological sequence of payments, or the legal structure of the transaction, could preclude tracing in situations of this kind, defendants could easily evade the reach of the law of tracing by simply structuring their transactions appropriately. For example, suppose Walsh had received the share certificates at 11am on 5 December 1811, with Sir Thomas Plumer's banknotes in his pocket, intending to come back and pay for them at noon using those very notes. This would clearly have been a decision that presupposed his control over Sir Thomas Plumer's money, and it would be unprincipled to allow him to escape the reach of the law of tracing merely because of the chronological sequence of payments that enabled completion of the transaction. Nor would it matter if the stockbroker transferred the stock to him in reliance on a promise to pay, rather than in reliance on an outright transfer of the banknotes—if Walsh himself had made the promise in the belief that he could perform it only using Sir Thomas Plumer's money, the principle of protecting Sir Thomas Plumer from Walsh's exploitation of his control over that money would capture this case.

4.2.1. Chronology of transactions and chronology of payments

4.32 This explains why the chronological sequence of transactions makes a significant difference to tracing, while the chronological sequence of payments need not do so. In *Serious Fraud Office v Lexi Holdings plc*,[67] for example, the court gave considerable weight to the fact that the defendant had acquired his matrimonial home in 1998 and had, according to the claimants, obtained misappropriated funds from them in 2006. A purchase made in 1998, Keene LJ said, 'could not possibly have derived in any way from, or been mixed with, the misappropriations . . . in 2006'.[68] When M bought his matrimonial home in 1998, he must have acquired it from the vendor in reliance on funds derived from other sources, since he had not, at that stage, misappropriated the assets belonging to Lexi Holdings plc and there was no evidence he had relied on his anticipated control over those assets when entering into that transaction. If the chronology had been reversed, so that M had received the misappropriated company assets in 1998 and bought his house in 2006, it would at least have been arguable that he could have exploited his control over

[67] See Chapter 1, para 1.37 this volume for the facts of the case.
[68] *Serious Fraud Office* (n 1) at [51].

the company's assets to acquire the house.[69] A transaction entered into on a date when the defendant did not have control over the claimant's assets at all could not have involved any exploitation of that control on his part. For tracing to be possible, the chronological sequence of transactions—that is, of decisions by the defendant to acquire or transfer assets—must be such that the defendant had the power, at the time of making his decision, to deal with the assets of the claimant.

This does not mean, however, as *Relfo Ltd v Varsani* demonstrates,[70] that tracing requires a purely chronological sequence of *payments*. As has been explained, in *Relfo Ltd v Varsani*, the Court of Appeal inferred that Mirren Ltd had promised to make a payment out of a particular bank account to some person or persons if Intertrade would make a payment to Mr Varsani. It is clear that they could not have fulfilled this promise before the payment to Mr Varsani was, in fact, made, since the Mirren Ltd bank account remained in credit until after the date of the Intertrade payments. Arden LJ held that this did not preclude tracing on the facts: tracing did not require that 'payments should occur in any particular order, let alone chronological order'.[71] What mattered was that the fact that Mirren had made an arrangement to reimburse Intertrade for its payment to Mr Varsani, and that this arrangement 'exploited and used the value inherent in Relfo's money that had been paid into Mirren's account'.[72] It constituted such an exploitation and use of that value because, as Arden LJ had already found,[73] Mirren had not merely agreed to reimburse Intertrade, but had agreed to do so by drawing on the very bank account that was transactionally linked to Mirren's money. 4.33

This illustrates the distinction between the chronological sequence of transactions, on the one hand, and the chronological sequence of payments on the other. It was important that, at the date of its arrangement with Intertrade, Mirren already had acquired the power to 'exploit and use' Relfo Ltd's money, in the form of the bank account that it held for Relfo Ltd's benefit. The exact mechanism by which Mirren exploited its control over the bank account that it held for the benefit of Relfo—whether by directly drawing on that account, or by binding itself by a promise to do so—did not matter, provided that it did have such control at the date of the transaction. 4.34

4.2.2. Tracing through the repayment of a debt

Similarly, where a defendant has incurred a debt to acquire an asset and has then repaid the debt using the claimant's money, what matters is not the precise mechanism of acquisition, but rather the power that the defendant has exercised—or relied upon his future right to exercise—in making the decision to acquire that asset. In *Federal Republic of Brazil v Durant International Corp*,[74] the Privy Council rejected 4.35

[69] Although the long chronological gap might have persuaded a court, in the absence of clear evidence to the contrary, that it was inherently implausible to suppose that he had kept the money 'unconverted' until he could use it for the purpose of this acquisition: see *Lord Chedworth* (n 25) 432.

[70] *Relfo Ltd (In Liquidation)* (n 3). [71] *Relfo Ltd (In Liquidation)* (n 3) [63].

[72] *Relfo Ltd (In Liquidation)* (n 3) [62]. [73] *Relfo Ltd (In Liquidation)* (n 12).

[74] [2016] UKPC 35.

the broad proposition that 'money used to pay a debt can in principle be traced into whatever was acquired in return for the debt';[75] however, they held that such tracing would be possible where 'there is a close causal and transactional link between the incurring of a debt and the use of trust funds to discharge it'.[76]

4.36 Lord Toulson's analysis in *Durant* suggests that the existence of such a close causal and transactional link depends on the intentions of the defendant. Thus, he approved the decision in the Canadian case of *Agricultural Credit Corpn of Saskatchewan v Pettyjohn*[77] on the basis that the defendants in that case had always intended to use the claimant's money to repay the relevant debt.[78] *Foskett v McKeown* may also be analysed as a case of this kind. In *Foskett*,[79] the trustee entered into a life insurance contract with Barclays Bank in November 1986, had paid two premiums with his own funds in 1986 and 1987, and had drawn on the trust bank account to pay the premiums due in 1989 and 1990. The 1988 premium was paid by drawing on the trust bank account at a date when it was only in credit by £596.74, with the remaining £10,220 of the premium being supplied by drawing on the overdraft facilities associated with the account. The overdraft was subsequently paid off using trust money. In the Court of Appeal, Richard Scott V-C had held that it ought to be possible to trace through this repayment of the overdraft into the premium, since the deceased trustee in the case had the 'intention throughout to use [the] purchasers' money to pay the ... premium'.[80]

4.37 This account of the principled limits of backwards tracing is mirrored by the case law in which such tracing has been recognized[81] and rejected.[82] The courts have refused to accept the possibility of such tracing in situations where the defendant could not have contemplated, at the time of incurring the debt and acquiring the asset, that he would use the claimant's money to repay that particular debt. Where they have contemplated the possibility of backwards tracing, it is in cases where it is plausible that the defendant incurred the original debt with the intention of using the claimant's money to repay it.[83] In *Denton v Davies*,[84] for example, the trustee had incurred debts in order to buy land several years before he sold the trust assets, and had asserted that he had no intention—either at the time of the purchase of the land, or at the time that he sold the trust assets—of using the trust money to repay

75 *Federal Republic of Brazil* (n 74) [33] (Lord Toulson).
76 *Federal Republic of Brazil* (n 74) [34] (Lord Toulson).
77 *Agricultural Credit Corpn of Saskatchewan v Pettyjohn* (1991) 79 DLR (4th) 22.
78 *Federal Republic of Brazil* (n 74) [34]–[37].
79 For a more detailed account of the facts, see Chapter 1, paras 1.28–1.33 this volume.
80 [1998] Ch 265 (CA), 283, quoted by Lord Toulson in *Federal Republic of Brazil* (n 74) [24].
81 Eg *Hopper v Conyers* (1866) LR 2 Eq 549; *Patten v Bond* (1889) 60 LT 583; *Re Bendy* [1895] 1 Ch 109; *Bishopsgate Investment Management Ltd v Homan* [1995] Ch 211, 216–17 (Dillon LJ); *Jyske Bank (Gibraltar) Ltd v Spjeldnaes* (HC, 23 July 1997).
82 Eg *Denton v Davies* (1812) 18 Ves Jun 499, 34 ER 406; *Ashmall v Wood* (1857) 3 Jur NS 232; *Bishopsgate Investment Management Ltd v Homan* (n 81) 222 (Legatt LJ); *Moriarty v Atkinson* [2008] EWCA Civ 1604.
83 As in *Bishopsgate Investment Management Ltd v Homan* (n 81): 'there was an inference that when the borrowing was incurred it was the intention that it should be repaid by misappropriations of [the claimants'] moneys'.
84 (1812) 18 Ves Jun 499, 34 ER 406.

those debts. Sir William Grant MR held, briefly, that this use of trust money to repay a debt could not 'be represented as a purchase made with the trust money'.[85]

4.38 Contrast *Hopper v Conyers*,[86] where Kindersley V-C was willing to permit tracing through the repayment of a debt. In that case, the claimants were mortgagees who had deposited the title deeds of the mortgaged estate with a solicitor, Conyers. The £3,100 mortgage debt was due on 6 April 1856. Conyers entered into a contract to purchase an estate in land in his own name from one Jennings, and had agreed a completion date of 6 April 1856, instructing his clerk that the £3,100 mortgage money should be paid to Jennings as soon as it was received. However, the mortgagors contacted Conyers a few days before 6 April to tell him they would not be able to pay on time. In order to complete his purchase, therefore, Conyers used the title deeds of the mortgaged property as security to borrow £3,000 from his own bank. On 10 May 1856, when he received the £3,100 due from the mortgagors, he immediately used it to pay off his debt to the bank and to recover possession of the title deeds from them. The claimants argued that they could claim the estate in land purchased by Conyers in one of two ways. They could trace through his use of their mortgage deeds as security to raise the amount actually used to complete the purchase. Alternatively, they could trace through his use of their £3,100 to repay that debt. Kindersley V-C held that both options were available to them. In relation to the use of the £3,100 of client money to pay off the debt, he said the situation was the same as if Conyers had 'applied that money directly in paying for [the estate]'; 'the intermediate transaction of borrowing the money ... on the security of his clients' deeds, and then repaying it with his clients' money received from the mortgagors'[87] made no difference whatsoever.

4.39 On the facts, the arguments in favour of this characterization are compelling. Conyers' decisions certainly look like what Lord Toulson, in *Federal Republic of Brazil v Durant*, described as a single 'scheme',[88] 'embracing the co-ordinated outward and inward movement of assets'.[89] His anticipation that he would receive the mortgage money on 6 April, and his hasty decision to borrow the money instead when it was unexpectedly not forthcoming, suggest a clear intention to make use of the claimant's money to acquire the relevant land as soon as that money came within his control. Even if he had not used the claimants' mortgage deeds as security, but had induced the bank to lend to him on the strength of his own power to bind himself to repay the money, his actual intention to fulfil that promise by using his clients' money significantly weakens the autonomy-based argument for distinguishing the decision to borrow from the decision to take the client money.

4.2.3. Tracing through intermediaries and inter-bank payment systems

4.40 This focus on defining the decision of the defendant that is at stake, and assessing to what extent it involves the actual or anticipated exploitation of a power to deal with

[85] *Denton* (n 84) 503; 408. [86] *Hopper* (n 81). [87] *Hopper* (n 81) 553.
[88] *Federal Republic of Brazil* (n 74) [38]. [89] *Federal Republic of Brazil* (n 74) [41].

the claimant's assets, also simplifies the problems that have been thought to arise when tracing through a transaction involving intermediaries. These are situations where—rather than transferring B's asset to X, in consideration for a transfer of assets from X to himself—A transfers B's asset to X in consideration for a transfer to someone else, C.

4.41 For example, A may wish to procure a title to a cow for C and to use his control over B's title to a llama to achieve that result.[90] One option is for A to approach X and to agree a direct swap of title to B's llama for title to X's cow; having obtained title to X's cow, A may then convey it to C. This is a straightforward exchange transaction, and B can plainly trace the value of his title to the llama into A's title to the cow and then follow that cow into the hands of C for the purposes of asserting whatever proprietary claims are available on the facts. Alternatively, however, A may approach X and ask him to transfer the title to the cow directly to C, in consideration for A's decision to transfer B's title to the llama to X. As Smith points out, the interposition of an intermediary makes no difference in principle to the status of the transaction as an unauthorized substitution of the title for the llama for the title to the cow. In both situations, A achieves the end he wishes to bring about—C's acquisition of title to a cow—by exploiting his control over B's asset, the title to the llama. The justification for tracing in the second case is as strong as in the first.

4.42 The most important practical application of this point is that it captures situations where a defendant confers assets on another, or pays for assets himself, via a payment system[91] that requires the interposition of an intermediary or several intermediaries, such as a bank or multiple banks. For example, suppose that A wishes to use B's bank account to buy a llama for himself. One possibility is that he manages to get the bank to reduce the credit balance of B's account and to give him cash in exchange; he might then physically hand this cash over to X, and she might convey her title to the llama to him. This is *Taylor v Plumer*, and we have seen that tracing from the title to the banknotes to the llama conveyed by X is straightforwardly possible.[92] However, it is equally possible that A will not bother with cash, but will instead instruct B's bank to reduce its indebtedness to B, and to bring about a corresponding increase in the indebtedness of X's bank to X instead. If B wishes to identify the llama as the traceable proceeds of the bank account controlled by A, then he needs to show that the increase in the credit balance of X's account with her bank—in consideration for which A obtained the llama—is transactionally linked to the decrease in the credit balance of her own bank account. This requires her to say that the decision of X's bank to increase the amount of the debt it owes to X can be shown to be a response to A's instruction to B's bank to reduce the amount of the debt owed to B.

4.43 Where X and B happen to share a bank, the analogy to other forms of unauthorized substitution via an intermediary is obvious. A will have instructed the bank to

[90] See L Smith, *The Law of Tracing* (Clarendon Press 1997) 244–47 for variations on the cow-llama example.

[91] See, generally, B Geva, *Bank Collections and Payment Transactions* (OUP 2001) 127–317 for an overview of national and international interbank payment systems.

[92] For another example of tracing from a bank account to cash, see *Lipkin Gorman v Karpnale Ltd* [1991] 2 AC 548.

increase its debt to X in consideration for its agreement to reduce the debt it owes B. This is formally identical to a case where A simply hands B's cash to the bank in exchange for its agreement to increase X's credit balance. In both cases, the relevant legal person—here, the bank—is conferring assets on one person (X) in exchange for a change in its legal relations with another (B), brought about by a third (A). Tracing ought to be possible whenever the person making the decision (A) to vary the rights of the claimant (B) is not at liberty to make that decision for her own ends, as where A has brought about an unauthorized reduction in the credit balance of B's account or has used cash stolen from him.

Where X and B do not share a bank, however, it becomes necessary to trace 4.44 through inter-bank transactions to show how A's initial instruction to reduce the credit balance of B's account with one bank brought about the increase in the credit balance of X's account with another bank. In *Agip (Africa) Ltd v Jackson*, for example, the claimant company's employee had issued an unauthorized instruction to its bank—the Banque du Sud in Tunis—to reduce the credit balance of its account with them, and to bring about a corresponding increase in the account of a company called Baker Oil Ltd with Lloyds Bank in London. Banque du Sud sent a telex to Lloyds Bank instructing it to credit Baker Oil's account accordingly, and sent another telex instructing its correspondent bank in New York to reimburse Lloyds Bank. Lloyds Bank complied with the instruction to increase the credit balance of Baker Oil's account on receipt of the instruction from Banque du Sud, and before it had, in fact, been reimbursed by the correspondent bank in New York.

In *Agip (Africa) Ltd v Jackson*,[93] it was said that it was impossible to trace through 4.45 these transactions to the Baker Oil account with Lloyds at common law, but that such tracing was possible in equity. At first instance, Millett J said that common law tracing was barred by the absence of a physical asset, like a cheque, passing from A's bank to B's bank.[94] This is difficult to reconcile with the earlier decision in *Banque Belge pour l'Etranger v Hambrouck*,[95] where money paid into an account with one bank was traced into the credit balance of an account with another, on the basis of a series of payment instructions that did not take the form of a cheque. Acknowledging this point, Fox LJ in the Court of Appeal said that common law tracing had become impossible because Lloyds Bank had taken a delivery risk by accepting the instruction to credit Baker Oil's account before actually being reimbursed by Banque du Sud's correspondent bank in New York.[96] On the other hand, this intermediate transaction made no difference to the possibility of tracing in equity.

We have seen that the supposed objection to tracing at common law is really 4.46 about problems that arise when asserting common law claims to intangible assets that appear to be vested in other people.[97] It is not, therefore, a problem about tracing but instead about the remedies that are available once the process of tracing is completed.[98] Once the supposed distinction between law and equity in this context

[93] [1990] Ch 265 (HC), affirmed at [1991] Ch 547 (CA).
[94] *Agip (Africa) Ltd* (HC) (n 93) 279 (Millett J).
[95] [1921] 1 KB 321.
[96] *Agip (Africa) Ltd* (CA) (n 93) 566.
[97] See Chapter 3, Section 3.3.2. this volume.
[98] See Chapter 8 this volume.

is set aside, then, the issue of tracing through the clearing system, in a case like *Agip (Africa) Ltd v Jackson*, becomes one of distinguishing between the order of payments and the order of transactions and of recognizing the possibility of tracing through transactions involving an intermediary.

4.47 What happened in *Agip (Africa) Ltd v Jackson* was that Banque du Sud conferred an immediate right on Lloyds Bank—a right to be reimbursed by it—in consideration for Lloyds Bank's decision to increase the amount of its debt to Baker Oil. Banque du Sud made the decision to confer this right on Lloyds Bank in consideration for Agip's employee's wrongful—but effective[99]—decision to reduce the debt that it owed to that company. Thus, the debt owed by Lloyds Bank to Baker Oil ultimately depended on the decision of Agip's employee to reduce the debt owed to it by Banque du Sud, and tracing was possible. It made no difference, from Agip's perspective, how and when the banks eventually settled[100] these debts between themselves. That Banque du Sud satisfied its debt by instructing its correspondent bank in New York to pay Lloyds Bank, and the timing of this payment, would have mattered only if Banque du Sud itself was seeking to trace the money that was used to pay off the debt.[101] It did not matter to Agip, because Agip was not tracing through Banque du Sud's dealings with its own assets, but rather through its decisions to vary Agip's rights against itself.[102]

4.3. Mixed Substitutions and Cherry-Picking

4.48 As we have seen, the fundamental question raised by a clean substitution is whether a defendant's decision to acquire an asset should be attributed to his control over the claimant's assets or, instead, to his control over other assets that he is entitled to exercise for his own benefit or the benefit of persons other than the claimant. Mixed substitutions complicate this binary distinction by permitting a single asset in the hands of a defendant—often an asset that he may undoubtedly have acquired for his own benefit prior to the misappropriation, such as a bank account in his own name—to be treated as a mixed fund for the purposes of tracing. The result is that the law must answer an additional set of questions, settling which assets can be treated as a mixed fund in the hands of the defendant and then attributing transactions drawing on the fund to the claimant or the defendant or both.

[99] *Agip (Africa) Ltd* (HC) (n 93) 283 (Millett J); *Agip (Africa) Ltd* (CA) (n 93) 561–62 (Fox LJ).

[100] For the importance of this distinction between settlement and clearing, in the context of tracing, see C Hare, 'Tracing value and the value of Tracing: three puzzles for the banking lawyer' (2013) 24 JBFLP 249.

[101] For example, if the instruction to the correspondent bank had been unauthorized by the bank itself, wrongfully reducing the New York bank's indebtedness to Banque du Sud, and the bank wished to trace through that transaction to the receipt by Lloyds Bank.

[102] See Smith, *The Law of Tracing* (n 90) 255: 'It would not matter if Bank A settled with Bank B by giving it £400 worth of kiwi fruit'.

4.3.1. Tracing into a mixed fund

4.49 A mixed substitution may sometimes take the form of the acquisition of a single new asset, using value belonging to both the claimant and the defendant. For example, A may buy a promissory note from X using £50 of his own money and £50 of B's money. In this situation, the law is prepared to treat the promissory note as a mixed fund[103] and to permit B to make claims, based on tracing, in respect of that note. Alternatively, a mixed substitution may take the form of a change in the content of an existing right held by the defendant. For example, suppose A has a bank account with X Bank with a credit balance of £50. He pays £50 of B's money to X bank, in consideration for which X Bank increases its indebtedness to him by a further £50, creating a credit balance of £100. In this situation, too, the law is prepared to treat the bank account as a mixed fund[104] and to permit B to make claims, based on tracing, in respect of that account.

4.3.1.1. Fund constituted by increasing the value of pre-existing rights

4.50 However, not every use of the claimant's money to increase the value of the defendant's existing assets will qualify as a mixed substitution. In *Re Diplock*,[105] some of the defendant charities had spent money mistakenly paid to them out of the testator's estate on carrying out physical improvements to their land, which increased the market value of the land. Thus, for example, the Leaf Homeopathic Hospital had spent £1,137 on improvements to its existing buildings while some of the other charities had built entirely new structures on their land. The Court of Appeal denied that these transactions qualified as mixed substitutions that could turn the charities' titles to the improved land into mixed funds for the purposes of tracing. They rejected the analogy between the use of money to increase the market value of one's pre-existing title to land and the payment of money into an existing bank account, increasing the credit balance of the account.

4.51 In the Court of Appeal decision in *Foskett v McKeown*,[106] Sir Richard Scott V-C and Hobhouse LJ considered the trustee's use of the trust money to pay his life insurance premiums to be more closely analogous to the maintenance or improvement of an existing asset, like a house, than to a mixed substitution; on this basis, they held, the beneficiaries could not claim a pro rata share of the rights under the life insurance policy, including the death benefit. In the House of Lords, Lord Browne-Wilkinson rejected the analogy between maintaining a house and paying the premiums on a life insurance policy. An increase in the value of a pre-existing title to a physical thing, like a house, could not be treated as similar to an increase in the credit balance of a pre-existing bank account and the case of the life insurance policy was closer to that of the bank account. Once an improvement to a physical thing has been made, he pointed out, the value of that improvement

[103] *Re Hallett's Estate* (1880) 13 Ch 696, 711 (Jessel MR).
[104] *Pennell v Deffell* (1853) 4 De G M & G 372, 43 ER 551.
[105] [1948] Ch 465.
[106] *Foskett* (CA) (n 80), 277–81 (Richard Scott V-C) and 289 (Hobhouse LJ).

cannot be separated out from the thing and treated as a freestanding asset. It is not possible to physically divide improved land 'into its separate constituent assets, ie the land and the money spent on it'.[107] He contrasted this with a mixed fund, the essence of which was its potential to be divided up into its constituent parts, pro rata, according to the contributions made to it.

4.52 Of course, a contractual claim to be paid a certain amount of money is not *physically* divisible into 'constituent parts', any more than land can be divided from the money spent on it. However, looked at from the perspective of a limitation on defendant autonomy, there is a plausible distinction between a pre-existing entitlement like a bank account, into which money has been paid, and a pre-existing title to land on which money has been spent in physical improvement. In the case of the bank account, its only function is in the context of exchange: what matters about a defendant's bank account is that it can be dealt with in exchange for other rights, not that it can be used in some other way. By contrast, a pre-existing title to land has a use value and a potential link to the personhood[108] of the defendant that would render it more of an intrusion on his autonomy to treat an increase in its value as a substitute asset to which another person might be entitled. The rights under the insurance policy in *Foskett v McKeown* could be seen as something of an intermediate case, involving a contractual right to be paid money—like a bank account—that was, however, contingent on a deeply personal event in the life of its holder, the trustee. Lord Millett, in the House of Lords, took the view that such a right should be thought of as essentially resembling a bank account,[109] while Sir Richard Scott V-C thought it should be thought of as resembling a title to a house.[110]

4.53 If we generalize from this reasoning, then, it seems to follow that the use of A's money to increase the value of B's pre-existing asset counts as a mixed substitution only when the process of 'unmixing' the value that has gone into that asset does not involve a significant intrusion on B's autonomy, by depriving him of a pre-existing right that is closely linked to his person. The core case of an unauthorized substitution—a clean substitution—involves the acquisition by the defendant of an assignable right, capable of being transferred to another without loss to the personhood of the defendant; the concept excludes those valuable benefits that are incapable of being separately transferred in this way, such as the benefit of services that increases the defendant's earning potential or the market value of land that he already owns. Similarly, mixed substitutions, where the claimant traces into the value of a pre-existing right already held by the defendant, can exist only where the right in question can easily be thought of as reducible to fungible units of value—that is, where requiring the defendant to give up that right, and take a share of

[107] *Foskett* (n 42) 109.

[108] A distinction that loosely mirrors Radin's distinction between fungible property and 'personal property': see M Radin, *Reinterpreting Property* (University of Chicago Press 1996). Cf J Penner, *The Idea of Property in Law* (OUP 1997) 130–32, drawing a distinction between 'personality-poor' choses in action—like bank accounts—and other rights against persons that are too 'personality-rich' to be treated as objects of proprietary protection. On this view, and using Penner's terminology, the majority of the Court of Appeal in *Foskett* differed from the majority of the House of Lords on the question whether rights under a life insurance contract were personality-rich or personality-poor.

[109] *Foskett* (n 42) 134.

[110] *Foskett* (CA) (n 80) 279.

money in exchange for it, would not involve a loss to some interest of the defendant other than money. A bank account is the paradigm case of such a right.

4.3.1.2. *Fund constituted by mixed contributions to acquisition of asset*

In holding that the payment of the insurance premiums could properly be understood as the improvement of a subsisting asset, the majority of the Court of Appeal in *Foskett v McKeown* also took the view that the trustee had acquired his rights under the insurance contract as soon as he entered into his agreement with Barclays Bank. The payments of insurance premiums were later events, only linked to the initial acquisition of the rights under the contract by their potential—in the event, unrealized—for increasing their value. Before these payments took place, the trustee's children had already obtained vested rights under the trusts of the insurance policy and the issue, in the Court of Appeal, was therefore framed in terms of whether it would be just to divest the children of their existing rights as a result of the misappropriation of the trust assets by their father. 4.54

By contrast, Lord Millett denied that the trustee had obtained anything that he could have vested in his children before he paid the first premium; the situation was analogous to the purchase of an asset by instalments, not the improvement of an existing asset.[111] James Penner has suggested that this aspect of the decision in *Foskett v McKeown* renders it an example of successful backwards tracing. If X transfers an asset to A in return for A's agreement to pay in instalments, the consideration for the transfer is A's promise to pay: that is, it is the incurring of a debt. If A then satisfies some part of his debt using B's money, and this is enough to turn the asset he has acquired into a mixed fund for the purposes of tracing, the implication is that B must have traced through the discharge of part of the debt to the asset acquired by incurring the debt.[112] 4.55

However, this characterization of the decision in *Foskett* depends on maintaining the idea—adopted by the majority of the Court of Appeal, but rejected in the House of Lords—that what the trustee had done in that case was to enter into a series of distinct transactions, each of which had to be independently assessed by reference to his intentions and the causal consequences of each transaction. That is, he first entered into the contract and purchased his rights under that contract, incurring a debt under the same transaction; then he used the claimants' money to discharge a series of debts to the insurance company; and it was because he had used their money to pay the debts that the claimants could obtain a proportionate share of the death benefit.[113] In fact, Lord Millett held that the payment of the premiums and the acquisition of rights under the contract represented the two sides of a single 4.56

[111] *Foskett* (n 42) 136–37.

[112] J Penner, 'Value, Property and Unjust Enrichment: Trusts of Traceable Proceeds' in R Chambers, C Mitchell, and J Penner (eds), *Philosophical Foundations of the Law of Unjust Enrichment* (OUP 2009) 306, 321.

[113] Thus, adopting this 'backwards tracing' analysis of the facts, Hobhouse LJ denied that tracing was possible on the authority of *Bishopsgate Investment Management Ltd* (n 81): *Foskett* (n 83) [1998] 289.

transaction. He emphasized the fact that the contract provided that the death benefit was payable only 'in consideration of the payment of the first premium already made *and of the further premiums payable*';[114] it was this which justified a decision that the bundle of rights acquired under the insurance policy represented the product of the premiums.

4.57 Despite Lord Millett's use of the language of an instalment purchase, therefore, the better analogy to the insurance contract in *Foskett v McKeown*—on his analysis of that contract—seems to be an acquisition of goods by hire purchase. A defendant may enter into a contract that entitles him to acquire an asset if, and only if, certain contingencies are met, including his payment of an agreed price by fixed instalments.[115] In such a case, his payment of some instalments using the claimant's money is simply a slower version of the scenario where he pays in full, and acquires title at once, using £50 of his own money and £50 of the claimant's money. Goods acquired in this way are a mixed fund. An instalment purchase, by contrast, involves immediate acquisition of the asset on credit, with the buyer agreeing to pay off his debt to the vendor in instalments. As has been argued, there is no general rule that permits tracing through the payment of a debt to an asset acquired by incurring the debt; tracing in such a case will depend on the intentions of the defendant at the time of entering into the contract to buy the asset.

4.3.2. Tracing out of a mixed fund: cherry-picking

4.58 We have seen[116] that the law treats a mixed substitution as broadly analogous to a physical mixture, as regards the attribution of dealings with the mixture as between the different contributors. Where the creation of the mixture was a wrong, the law applies a rule that subordinates the interests of the wrongdoer to that of the other contributor. This 'cherry picking'[117] rule permits the claimant to treat the valuable investments made drawing on the fund as acquired for her benefit, and to treat transactions that have no traceable proceeds as made using the defendant's money. It is limited only by the lowest intermediate balance rule that forbids the claimant to appropriate any subsequent contributions to the fund from the resources of the defendant or a third party, and to treat these contributions too as made for her benefit.

4.3.2.1. Availability of cherry-picking: breach of duty in mixing assets

4.59 In the context of tracing, the cherry-picking rule is sometimes explained on the basis that it represents an application of the rule that bars a fiduciary from profiting from his use of his principal's property.[118] This suggests, first, that the rule will

114 [2001] 1 AC 103, 133.
115 Cf *Helby v Matthews* [1895] AC 471. See also Consumer Credit Act 1974, s 189(1).
116 See Chapter 2, Section 2.2.1 this volume.
117 *Shalson v Russo* [2003] EWHC 1637, [144]–[143] (Rimer J).
118 Eg S Williston in 'The Right to Follow Trust Property when Confused with other Property' (1888) 2 Harvard Law Review 28, 29.

always apply to a case where a trustee or other fiduciary has mixed his principal's or beneficiary's assets with his own, and secondly that it will not apply where the person who has mixed the assets is not a fiduciary. Neither limitation is accurate. Rather the rule is that cherry-picking is available whenever the act of mixing the assets was a breach of a duty owed by the defendant to the claimant, and is not available where the defendant was at liberty to mix the assets with her own.

This is the best way to explain the difficult decision in *Re Tilley's Will Trusts*,[119] for example. In that case, Ungoed-Thomas J appears to have held that beneficiaries under a trust could not claim the most profitable investments made by a trustee, using a mixed account, because the trustee had not intended to acquire those assets for their benefit. Although the trustee was in fact in breach of trust, as she should not have paid the trust money into her personal bank account, it appears that Ungoed-Thomas J was influenced by the fact that she was not consciously in breach of trust and had had no intention of misappropriating the trust money.[120] In the rare situation[121] where a trustee or other fiduciary is not in breach of duty when she mixes her own assets with the assets of her principal—as where, for example, the principal has expressly authorized her to do so—the case is authority that cherry-picking does not apply to her transactions using the mixed fund. An innocent recipient, who is subject to proprietary claims in respect of the assets she has received, also does not commit a wrong by mixing her assets with the claimant's and is thus not subject to cherry-picking.[122] 4.60

Cherry-picking will also be available where the defendant has wrongfully mixed the claimant's assets with her own even though she is not a fiduciary. For example, in *Shalson v Russo*,[123] Rimer J held that the claimant had been swindled into parting with his money by one Mr Russo, that he had rescinded this transaction and revested a title in himself that was adequate to support a claim to the traceable proceeds of the money,[124] and that there was no fiduciary relationship between the claimant and Mr Russo.[125] Nevertheless, the proprietary claim generated by the decision to rescind the transfer was sufficient not only to permit a claim to traceable proceeds but also to permit tracing on a cherry-picking basis.[126] Thus, as Lord Millett's analysis in *Foskett v McKeown* suggests,[127] the principle of subordinating wrongdoers applies in any case where the defendant has knowingly and wrongfully made it impossible to distinguish the claimant's assets from his own. The principle that subordinates the interests of the innocent contributor to that of such a wrongdoer applies equally to wrongful physical mixtures, and does not depend on the status of the wrongdoer as a fiduciary owing the special fiduciary duties of loyalty. 4.61

[119] [1967] Ch 1179.

[120] See Smith, *The Law of Tracing* (n 90) 210–11 for this analysis of *Re Tilley's Will Trusts*.

[121] It will normally be a breach of trust for a trustee to pay his beneficiary's money into his personal bank account: *Massey v Banner* (1820) 1 Jac & W 241, 37 ER 367.

[122] *Re Diplock* (n 105). [123] *Shalson* (n 117). [124] *Shalson* (n 117) [121]–[127].

[125] *Shalson* (n 117) [133]–[132]. [126] *Shalson* (n 117) [143]–[146].

[127] See Chapter 2, Section 2.1.2 this volume.

4.3.2.2. Scope of cherry-picking: the requirement of a defined fund

4.62 The principle, however, is limited in scope; it captures only those transactions of the defendant that involve the actual mixed fund that he has created by his wrong. Where, for example, A has paid B's money into his account with X Bank, and happens to have another account with the same bank, B cannot invoke cherry-picking to consolidate the accounts and to treat profitable investments made using the second account as transactions involving his own assets.[128] It is perfectly possible, in such a situation, to distinguish the right that A holds for his own benefit from the right that he holds—thanks to his decision to mix assets—subject to the claims of the claimant. The principle of subordinating the wrongdoer in such a case will not stretch to confiscating assets that are no part of the mixed fund, and which the wrongdoer remains free to use to achieve his own ends.

[128] *Style Financial Services v Bank of Scotland* 1996 SLT 421; *Box v Barclays Bank* [1998] Lloyd's Rep 185; *Shalson* (n 117); *FHR European Ventures LLP v Mankarious* [2016] EWHC 359. In *Cooper v PRG Powerhouse Ltd (in liquidation)* [2008] EWHC 498 (Ch), Evans-Lombe J accepted that accounts with the same bank could be consolidated for the purpose of displacing the operation of the lowest intermediate balance rule. However, the relevant authorities were not cited and the decision in the case itself may be fully explained on the alternative ground that the relevant accounts were never actually overdrawn since the transactions in question were not final and were not ultimately accepted by the bank: see *Cooper v PRG Powerhouse Ltd (in liquidation)* [2008] EWHC 498 (Ch), [28]–[32].

5

Rules of Tracing II

Innocent Co-Contributors

It is a core principle of tracing that the intentions of a wrongdoing defendant are irrelevant to determining the consequences of transactions drawing on a mixed fund involving his own assets. This chapter argues that the courts have begun to move towards a similar general principle in the case where he is varying the rights of a third party contributor to the fund. In all contexts other than mixed bank accounts, they have traditionally applied a general principle of equal concern for each innocent contributor, with gains and losses allocated rateably between contributors; recent case law has adopted a similar approach to mixed bank accounts as well. 5.01

However, even as between innocent co-contributors, the principle is limited to contexts where the assets of the various contributors have been mixed so that it is impossible to tell whether the decision of the defendant involves a power affecting one claimant rather than another. Where a defendant has chosen to keep the assets of different contributors separate, his decisions are to be taken seriously; the principle of subordinating wrongdoers cannot be invoked by one innocent party to capture decisions affecting the assets of another, any more than it can be invoked to capture decisions by the defendant that involve only his own assets. 5.02

5.1. Bank Accounts: The Residual Role of the 'First In, First Out' Rule

The rule in *Clayton's Case*[1] is that, as between debtor and creditor, payments out of a running account are attributed to payments into the account in the chronological order in which payments were made. Thus, suppose A pays £100 into his account with X bank on Monday, pays £100 in on Tuesday, and pays £100 in on Wednesday. The effect of these transactions is that the bank came under an obligation to pay him £100 on Monday, an obligation to pay him £200 on Tuesday, and to pay him £300 on Wednesday. On Thursday, A draws £100 in cash from the bank, reducing its indebtedness to him from £300 to £200. In the absence of any intention to the contrary,[2] this first transaction is treated as having satisfied the earliest debt owed by the bank to A—that is, the £100 debt that was constituted by the first transaction 5.03

[1] (1816) 1 Mer 572, 35 ER 781.

[2] *Merriman v Ward* (1860) 1 J & H 371, 70 ER 790.

on Monday. The next £100 will be treated as having satisfied the next £100 of indebtedness and so on.

5.04 This is a rule that describes the legal relationship between a bank and its customer, and is intended to operate as a default rule as to their mutual intentions in the absence of contrary evidence. Thus, in *Clayton's Case* itself, Clayton was a customer of a firm of bankers, holding a current account with a credit balance of £453. He could not recover this debt in full from the then-partners in the bank because they were bankrupt. He sought, therefore, to instead recover the money from the estate of a former partner in the firm, Devaynes, who had died before the bankruptcy. He argued that the debt that was owed to him at Devaynes' death had not been satisfied by his subsequent drawings on the account, because these later debits had satisfied later credits, leaving the earlier debt unsatisfied and capable of being enforced against Devaynes' personal representative. Sir William Grant rejected this argument on the basis that the usual course of dealing with a running account was for debits to be appropriated to credits in their chronological order: first in, first out. If Clayton, as the customer, had wished to depart from this norm, it was incumbent on him to 'signify that such was his intention'.[3]

5.05 In *Pennell v Deffell*,[4] having held that it was possible to trace into a mixed bank account, the Court of Appeal held that payments out of such an account should be attributed—as between trustee and beneficiary who had contributed to the account—in accordance with this rule, in the absence of an express intention on the part of the account-holder to do something else. In *Re Hallett's Estate*,[5] *Pennell v Deffell* was overruled on this point. As between trustee and beneficiary, the trustee's intentions in dealing with the account were irrelevant. His drawings on the account were to be attributed, in accordance with the principle of subordination of wrongdoers, as best suited the beneficiary. It is important to note that this was not a displacement of *Clayton's Case*, in its usual context: as between the bank and the trustee as customer, the rule still describes the order in which the bank's payments to the trustee satisfy its indebtedness to him. Rather, it represented a rejection of the application of that rule in the context of an entirely different legal relationship—that between the trustee and the beneficiary—which does not depend on the intentions of the parties, but rather on the status of the defendant as a wrongdoer dealing with the assets of another.

5.06 As Sir William Grant MR said in *Clayton's Case* itself, a bank account is not a series of 'distinct insulated debts, between which a plain line of separation could be drawn';[6] rather, it is 'one blended fund, the parts of which no longer have a separate existence'.[7] When A pays £100 of his own money into the account on Monday, and pays £100 of B's money into it on Tuesday, he is not buying two distinct assets, a right to be paid £100, and then a different right to be paid a further £100; rather, he is simply increasing the value of a single asset, the bank's indivisible obligation

[3] *Clayton's Case* (n 1) 610; 793.

[4] (1853) 4 De G M & G 372, 43 ER 551. See also *Brown v Adams* (1869) LR 4 Ch App 764, where *Pennell v Deffell* was followed on this point.

[5] (1880) 13 Ch D 696. [6] *Clayton's Case* (n 3). [7] *Clayton's Case* (n 3).

to pay him the credit balance of the bank account. It is not true, therefore, to say that he has bought the first £100 with his money, and the second £100 with B's money; thus, it is not true that the principle of respect for defendant autonomy should apply to the asset he has bought with the first £100, while the principle of subordination of wrongdoers should apply only to the asset he has bought with the second. There is only one debt, a single asset obtained by indistinguishably blending the claimant's assets with the defendant's, and there is no reason why the intentions of the wrongdoer who has brought about the mixture should determine how subsequent payments out of it are allocated. The application of the rule in *Clayton's Case* as between a trustee and a beneficiary, therefore, cannot be justified on the grounds of the principles of tracing.

However, following *Re Hallett's Estate*, the logic of this position has not yet been 5.07 fully worked out in cases where the wrongdoer had not blended his own assets with the claimant's, but has instead blended assets of multiple innocent co-contributors. While *Clayton's Case* is not now applied as between wrongdoer and contributor, it is still applied as between such contributors as a default rule.[8] Thus, for example, suppose that A misappropriates £100 of B1's cash on Monday and £100 of B2's cash on Tuesday. He pays B1's cash into a new bank account in his own name on Monday, so that the bank becomes indebted to him by £100; on Tuesday, he pays B2's money into the same account, increasing the credit balance of the account to £200. As a result of his wrongdoing, it is no longer possible for B1 to point to any distinct asset in A's hands and say that it represents her money and her money alone. She cannot, as we have seen, say that the £100 debt owed by the bank to A on Monday is her money, while the £100 debt owed on Tuesday is B2's; the effect of the mixture has been to create a single asset, worth £200, and neither B1 nor B2 can identify some distinct part of this single asset as the separate subject matter of their separate rights. Suppose that, on Wednesday, A then decides to draw £100 from the account and spend it untraceably on food and drink that he consumes. On Thursday, he draws another £100 and spends it buying a title to a painting worth £1,000. As a result of the timing of A's decisions to deal with this asset that does not belong to him—the bank account he holds on trust for B1 and B2—B1 is obliged to accept that her money has been untraceably spent, while B2 can claim that the title to the painting is all hers.

In *Barlow Clowes International Ltd v Vaughan*,[9] the Court of Appeal sharply 5.08 criticized the arbitrariness of such an outcome in this type of situation. Legatt LJ noted that *Clayton's Case* is a rule of presumed intention, offering guidance on the intentions of banker and customer as to their mutual legal relations; he commented that applying *Clayton's Case* in the tracing context has the effect of equating the 'presumed intention of a person in relation to his banker with a beneficiary's intention in relation to his trustee, even though on the face of it they have nothing to do with each other'.[10] The Court held that, as a matter of authority, it was not open to it to reject the operation of the rule in this context. Nevertheless, Woolf LJ

[8] Eg *Re Stenning* [1895] 2 Ch 433; *Re Diplock* [1948] Ch 465; *Charity Commission for England and Wales v Framjee* [2014] EWHC 2507 (Ch).

[9] [1992] 4 All ER 22.

[10] *Barlow Clowes International Ltd* (n 9) 28.

said that the rule would not be applied where the effect of its application would be impractical, unjust, or too expensive;[11] nor would it apply where the intentions of the contributors were known. In *Russell-Cooke Trust Co v Prentis*,[12] Lindsay J said that the application of the rule would be displaced by even a 'slight counterweight',[13] and it has been displaced on the basis that it is too expensive to apply,[14] that it does not reflect the likely intentions of the contributors,[15] and that it would be unfair and arbitrary in its operation.[16]

5.2. Other Mixed Substitutions: Proportionate Shares or the Rolling Charge

5.09 Outside the context of bank accounts, and where *Clayton's Case* has been displaced, the courts have usually responded to mixed substitutions by treating the contributors to the fund equally *inter se*. In *Re Diplock*,[17] the Court of Appeal held that there was no justification for extending the rule in *Clayton's Case* beyond the context of bank accounts and held that contributors to any other kind of mixed fund ought to be treated rateably. In English law, this has conventionally meant proportionate sharing of the indistinguishable pool of assets,[18] and proportionate sharing of each asset obtained out of the fund.[19] However, where there have been differences in the timing of contributions to the mixed fund, proportionate sharing of each asset obtained out of the mixed fund at the end of the story may not, in fact, treat the different contributors rateably. It is in this context that the so-called 'rolling charge solution[20] might be thought to be preferable in principle.[21]

5.10 To illustrate the difference between the two scenarios, we might envisage a case where A misappropriates £100 from B1 on Monday, and misappropriates £100 from B2 on Tuesday, paying both sums into a single bank account. On any view, the effect is that the bank account, with its total credit balance of £200, is now held by A on trust for B1 and B2 as tenants in common in 50 per cent shares.[22] Suppose that A then withdraws £100 from the account on Wednesday, and uses it to buy a title to silver cup worth £1,000. *Clayton's Case* would tell us that all the money used to buy the cup is B1's. Proportionate sharing would suggest, instead, that half the money used to buy the cup is B1's and the other half is B2's. The distinction between

[11] *Barlow Clowes International Ltd* (n 9) 26.
[12] [2002] EWHC 2227 (Ch).
[13] *Russell-Cooke* (n 12) [55].
[14] Eg *Re Eastern Capital Futures Ltd (in liquidation)* [1989] BCLC 371.
[15] Eg *National Crime Agency v Robb* [2014] EWHC 4384 (Ch).
[16] Eg *Commerzbank AB v IMB Morgan plc* [2004] EWHC 2771 (Ch); *Charity Commission for England and Wales v Framjee* (n 8).
[17] [1948] 1 Ch 465.
[18] Eg *Murray v Pinkett* (1846) 8 ER 1612.
[19] Eg *Barlow Clowes International Ltd* (n 9).
[20] Which has been adopted in Canada and Australia: see *Re Ontario Securities Commission and Greymac Credit Corporation* (1986) 30 DLR (4th) 1 and *Re French Caledonia Travel Service Pty Ltd* (2003) NSWSC 1008.
[21] See *Barlow Clowes International Ltd* (n 9) 35 (Woolf LJ).
[22] *Re Hallett's Estate* (n 5).

this approach and a rolling charge solution becomes important if, on Thursday, A takes a further £100 from B2 and credits to the account. Now the contribution of B2 to the pool is £200, two-thirds of the total value. An approach based on net proportionate sharing would take this into account in relation to the purchase of the silver cup, so that B2 gets a two-thirds share even though his contribution at the date of acquisition of the cup was only 50 per cent. The rolling charge solution, by contrast, would distinguish transactions entered into before the additional injection of B2's money from transactions entered into afterwards.

The primary disadvantage of the rolling charge solution is in its complexity and, 5.11
thus, expensiveness. Where workable, however, its advantage is that it extends the principle of proportionate sharing only to cases where the assets of the claimant have in fact been rendered indistinguishable from the assets of a co-contributor at the date of a given transaction. Where £100 of B2's cash was, in fact, segregated from the fund at the date of a particular transaction, she is not allowed—or required—to say that a transaction at that date involved the use of that £100.

5.3. Requirement of a Defined Mixed Fund

In this sense, the rolling charge solution is the approach that is most consistent 5.12
with the law's refusal to treat all the assets of a set of claimants as a mixed fund even though they have, on the facts, been kept segregated by the wrongdoer. In *Russell-Cooke v Prentis*,[23] this provided the basis for rejecting the so-called 'common misfortune' approach, which would have set aside the wrongdoer's specific allocations of misappropriated funds[24] and treated all the assets obtained using misappropriated funds as single mixed fund, subject to proportionate sharing. Lindsay J accepted that the different contributors were 'so to speak, ... in the same boat' but said that this did not, in itself, 'require anyone to give up the life jacket which he [was] already plainly wearing'.[25] The principle is that the law will not permit the established rights of one person to a particular asset to be overridden by treating it as part of a mixed fund, in the absence of an specific act that creates such a fund by rendering her rights indistinguishable from that of another;[26] this parallels the rule requiring a defined fund that applies as between an innocent claimant and a wrongdoer.[27]

23 *Russell-Cooke* (n 12). 24 See also *Re Diplock* (n 8) at 562–63.

25 *Russell-Cooke* (n 12) [35].

26 *Russell-Cooke* (n 12) [44]: 'relatively clear property interests ... must be respected and cannot be altered by reference to some notion of common misfortune.'

27 See Chapter 4, Section 4.3.2.2 this volume.

6

Property Rights, Fiduciary Duties, and the Control of Assets

6.01 We have seen that the law of tracing works, in part, by distinguishing between transactions involving a variation of the claimant's existing legal rights and transactions that have no such effect; a claim to traceable proceeds is only available where the defendant has acquired the supposed proceeds by exercising a power of this kind over the claimant. This argument implies that the existence of a power–liability relationship between claimant and defendant is a precondition for tracing: a power cannot be exercised unless it exists. The concept of a power–liability relationship thus provides us with a starting point for understanding the case law in which courts have held that the claimant's right to the original asset, dealt with by the defendant, is or is not of a kind that entitles her to its traceable proceeds.

6.02 However, the best-known account of such power–liability relations—Hohfeld's—does not provide a satisfactory interpretation of that case law, for two reasons. First, on Hohfeld's account, the category of the power–liability relationship is very broad; it covers an enormously disparate range of legal relationships, including such relations as that between a tortfeasor and his potential victim and that between the state and a person who chooses to commit a crime. It is intrinsically unlikely that claims to traceable proceeds could arise whenever a power, in this sense, is exercised and the cases do not support any such conclusion. Secondly, there is a lack of fit between a focus on power–liability relations and the actual language of the cases that draw the boundaries of these claims. The judges do not talk about the presence or absence of powers when they explain the availability of claims to traceable proceeds; instead, they talk about the presence or absence of property rights or of fiduciary duties.

6.03 Yet it is also difficult to accept this judicial language at its face value. Not every holder of a conventional property right in a thing is entitled to the traceable proceeds of that thing; nor does every claim to traceable proceeds require the defendant to owe fiduciary duties to the claimant, in the strict sense of duties of fiduciary loyalty. While Hohfeld's category of power–liability relationship is over-inclusive, therefore, we cannot wholly dispense with the Hohfeldian language of powers, liabilities, claim-rights, and privileges, since the conventional language of property right or fiduciary duty is not precise enough to capture what is happening on the facts of the cases.

This chapter argues that claims to traceable proceeds arise where, and only where, there is a power–liability relationship of a special kind between claimant and defendant, which I call a relationship of 'control of assets'. This is a relationship where the defendant can, by entering into an intentional transaction, vary the rights of the claimant as against a third party, with respect to some assignable right ('asset'), and owes a duty to the claimant governing the exercise of that specific power. The key characteristic of this relationship is the existence of a gap between the scope of the power and the terms of the defendant's duty; it is this gap which renders it possible for the defendant to validly exercise the power, effectively varying the claimant's rights, in circumstances where the exercise of the power is a breach of a duty owed to the claimant. 6.04

6.1. The Language of the Cases: Trustees, Fiduciaries, and Owners

As we have seen,[1] the earliest cases to recognize claims to traceable proceeds involved transactions by trustees, executors, administrators, and agents. The language of trusteeship was frequently invoked in this early case law to explain why the claim was available. Thus, for example, in the early case of *Burdett v Willett*,[2] the claimant had employed the deceased, Willett, as his factor[3] to sell cloth. Willett had taken the cloth from the customs house and sold it to the first defendants, Wingfield and Bowater, for an agreed price of £115. Before Wingfield and Bowater had paid him, he died, insolvent.[4] The second defendant, Willett's widow, brought an action at common law to recover the amount of the debt from Wingfield and Bowater; she argued that the money should be paid to her as Willett's administrator and used to satisfy his debts, including the debt that he owed her personally under the terms of their marriage articles. The claimant then brought an action in equity, seeking an injunction to restrain Wingfield and Bowater from paying the money to the widow and ordering them to pay him instead. 6.05

[1] See Chapter 3, Section 3.1 this volume for a more detailed account of the early case law.

[2] (1708) 1 Eq Ca Ab 370; 23 ER 1017.

[3] That is, as an agent who has possession of his principal's goods, coupled with an authority to convey his principal's title to those goods to a third party in the ordinary course of his business. For this use of the term 'factor', see, for example, *Baring v Corrie* (1818) 2 Barn and Ald 137, 106 ER 319. Although the term 'factor' was used to describe a variety of different relationships in the seventeenth and eighteenth centuries, a common theme was the combination of possession of goods belonging to another coupled with an authority to sell those goods and, perhaps, to receive a commission on the sale: see, generally, R Munday, 'The Legal History of the Factor' (1977) 6 Anglo-Am Law Review 221.

[4] In the sense that the amount due on his debts exceeded the value of his assets at his death. It is not clear whether he could have qualified as a bankrupt, in the sense used in the bankruptcy legislation then in force, because the statute that explicitly extended the category of debtors capable of being bankrupted to include 'factors' was brought into force only ten years later, in 1718: see I Duffy, 'The English Bankrupt, 1571-1861' (1980) 24 Am Journal of Legal History 283, 292–95, discussing the impact of the statue (1718) 5 Geo I c 24. The statute (1624) 21 Jac I 19 had, however, extended the category to include persons who used 'the trade or profession of scrivener, receiving other men's monies or estates into their trust or custody' and this definition may have captured an agent to whom goods were consigned to be sold even before 1718: see, for example, *L'Apostre v Le Plaistrier* (1708) 2 Eq Ca Abr 113, 24 ER 406, also reported at Viner's Abr Tit Creditor and Bankrupt (T) 89.

6.06 The Lord Chancellor granted the injunction. He is reported to have justified this decision on the basis that 'the factor is in the nature of a trustee only; and although he has the right at law, yet he is in equity but a trustee'.[5] One could read this to mean that the factor *was* a trustee, collapsing the case of the factor into the case of the express trustee. The legal position, on this analysis, would be as follows: where a merchant consigned goods to a factor for sale, what happened was that the merchant assigned his[6] legal title to those goods to the factor outright, and the factor held that legal title on trust for the merchant up to the moment of the sale. On this view, the merchant's claim to the traceable proceeds of such chattels could be explained on exactly the same grounds as a claim by a beneficiary under an express trust to land bought using the trust money.

6.07 However, in a series of decisions over the course of the eighteenth century,[7] spurred on by the introduction of the new bankruptcy legislation,[8] the courts developed an account of the position of a factor that was more complicated than this. It was held in *L'Apostre v Le Plaistrier*[9] that, where the factor had *not* sold the original goods but retained possession of them up to the moment of his bankruptcy, the assignees in bankruptcy would be liable to the merchant in trover if they took possession of those goods and refused to give them up to the merchant at his demand. In *Tooke v Hollingworth*,[10] counsel for the assignees in bankruptcy sought to distinguish these cases, on the basis that they had been decided in the Court of Chancery, while the action of trover was 'founded on strict legal right'.[11] The court rejected this argument, holding that the merchant in *Tooke v Hollingworth* had the necessary title to sue in trover.

6.08 Given this line of authority, it seems inaccurate to say that the early factor cases involved express trusts of the title that was actually sold to the purchaser. If the principal retained his legal title to the original goods—which he must have done, if he was entitled to sue in trover at common law—it cannot also be said that the factor held that very title on trust for him. Rather, it seems that the factor was an agent with a power, at common law, to divest the principal of his legal title by carrying out an authorized sale. On this analysis, some of the earliest cases recognizing the existence of claims based on tracing, outside the context of transactions involving the purchase of land, were cases involving agents rather than trustees. Although the

[5] *Burdett* (n 2).

[6] It must have been the claimant's original legal title that was transferred to Wingfield and Bowater in any case; if they had only received the factor's possessory title, they would have been vulnerable to a claim in trover or detinue by the claimant with his superior title, and it is clear that no such claim was envisaged on the facts, even though Wingfield and Bowater were the defendants.

[7] *L'Apostre v Le Plaistrier* (n 4); *Whitecomb v Jacob* (1710) 1 Salk 160, 91 ER 149; *Copeman v Gallant* (1716) 1 P Wms 314, 24 ER 404; *Godfrey v Furzo* (1733) 3 P Wms 185, 24 ER 1022; *Paul v Birch* (1743) 2 Atk 621, 26 ER 776; *Ex parte Flynn* (1748) 1 Atk 185, 26 ER 120; *Ryall v Rolle* (1749) 1 Atk 165, 26 ER 107; *Ex parte Dumas* (1754) 1 Atk 232, 26 ER 149; *Kinloch v Craig* (1789) 3 TR 120; *Tooke v Hollingworth* (1793) 5 TR 215, 101 ER 121; *Collins v Martin* (1797) 1 Bos & Pul 648, 126 ER 1113 and *Ex parte Sayers* (1800) 5 Ves Jun 169, 31 ER 528.

[8] (1624) stat 21 Jac I c 19 and (1718) stat 5 Geo I c 24. [9] *L'Apostre* (n 4). [10] *Tooke* (n 7).

[11] *Tooke* (n 7) 224; 126.

analogy with trusteeship exerted a powerful influence, trusteeship as such was not necessary to support a claim to traceable proceeds.

In *Ex parte Dale*,[12] Fry J felt compelled by authority to distinguish between the case of a beneficiary tracing through the transactions of a trustee and a principal tracing through the transactions of an agent. *Pennell v Deffell*[13] had already decided that beneficiaries under trusts could trace into mixed bank accounts; Fry J considered that *Whitecomb v Jacob* and *Taylor v Plumer* compelled him to hold that a principal whose agent had paid his money into a mixed bank account could not do so. He did not, however, deny that a principal could claim the traceable proceeds of the transactions of his agent, even where the agent was not a trustee, and was critical of the distinction he felt obliged to draw between the two situations as to the tracing rules. In explaining why this distinction was problematic in principle, he invoked the language of the fiduciary relationship. A fiduciary relationship, he said, was one where 'if a wrong arise, the same remedy exists against the wrongdoer on behalf of the principal as would exist against a trustee on behalf of the cestui que trust'.[14] If the matter had been free from authority, therefore, he would have held that a principal could trace through his agent's dealings with his money in exactly in the same circumstances in which a beneficiary under a trust could trace through his trustee's transactions: it ought to make no difference, in his view, that 'instead of trustee and cestui que trust, it is a case of fiduciary relationship'.[15] 6.09

In *Re Hallett's Estate*,[16] Jessel MR affirmed Fry J's view that the two situations were identical in principle, and rejected his interpretation of the state of the authorities so far as the tracing rules were concerned. Overruling *Ex parte Dale*, he held that a bailee was in no different position from a trustee for the purposes of tracing into a mixed bank account. Although the bailor had a common law title to the bailed asset, this did not mean that he could not claim its traceable proceeds or invoke the equitable tracing rules to identify those proceeds. The assistance of the equitable rules was not only available to a person with an equitable interest in the asset substituted—like a beneficiary under a trust—but was also available to a holder of a common law title who was also the principal in a fiduciary relationship: 'the moment you establish the fiduciary relation, the modern rules of Equity, as regards following trust money, apply'.[17] 6.10

As explained in Chapter 3,[18] subsequent cases erroneously read these statements to mean that the 'modern rules of Equity' applied in cases where there was a fiduciary relationship, while cases where there was no fiduciary relationship were restricted by the old line of authority, deriving from *Whitecomb v Jacob* and *Taylor v Plumer*, forbidding the tracing of money into a mixed mass. The idea of a fiduciary relationship, which allowed a claimant to invoke 'the more refined doctrine of equity explained in *Re Hallett's Estate*',[19] therefore became important in the law of tracing. 6.11

12 (1879) LR 11 Ch D 772.
13 (1853) 4 De G M & G 372, 43 ER 551.
14 *Ex parte Dale* (n 12) 778.
15 *Ex parte Dale* (n 12) 777.
16 (1880) 13 Ch D 696.
17 *Re Hallett's Estate* (n 16) 710.
18 See Chapter 3, paras 3.82–3.118 this volume.
19 *Collins v Stimson* [1881–85] All ER Rep 382, 383 (Pollock B), distinguishing 'the principle in *Taylor v Plumer*' from 'the more refined doctrine of equity explained in *Re Hallett's Estate*'.

However, in *Re Hallett's Estate* itself, Jessel MR appeared to use the language of fiduciary relationship primarily as a kind of shorthand for 'beneficial ownership'. Thus, he said that the distinction between trustee–beneficiary relations and bailor–bailee relations had no foundation in principle *because* 'the beneficial ownership is the same, wherever the legal ownership may be'.[20] It was the claimant's status as the 'beneficial owner' of assets that justified her claim to the traceable proceeds of those assets. Both the beneficiary under a trust and the bailor with a common law title were beneficial owners in the relevant sense, and therefore entitled to claim the traceable proceeds of their assets, and to trace through mixed substitutions to identify those assets. This language of ownership was echoed by Lord Goff in *Lipkin Gorman v Karpnale Ltd*,[21] where *Taylor v Plumer* was cited as authority that 'a *legal* owner is entitled to trace his property into its product'.[22] In this view, ownership provides the unifying thread between claims to traceable proceeds at law and in equity. Although the applicable tracing rules may differ, so that it is harder for a legal owner to identify the proceeds of his asset than for a beneficial owner, the underlying justification for the claim to the proceeds is the same: ownership.

6.12 The problem then becomes one of determining who is—and is not—an owner for these purposes. In *Kirkham v Peel*,[23] this aspect of the decision in *Re Hallett's Estate* was at issue. The claimant, Kirkham, was a merchant in Manchester who had sent goods to the defendant firm, John Peel & Co, to be sold on by the branch of the firm which operated in Bombay. Under the terms of the arrangement between the parties, Kirkham would consign goods to John Peel & Co; John Peel & Co would normally make some advance to him on their value, and would then ship the goods to the Bombay branch of the firm to be sold. Once the Bombay branch had sold the goods, it was supposed to use the proceeds to buy more goods that were shipped back to London and sold by John Peel & Co, who then were supposed to account to Kirkham for the net proceeds of all goods sold.

6.13 In the accounts of the Bombay branch of the firm, Kirkham was credited with the net proceeds of sale of his goods and debited with the value—plus stamp duty and interest—of bills of exchange that had supposedly been sent to John Peel & Co on his behalf. On receiving the accounts, John Peel & Co would forward them on to Kirkham, credit him with the amount of the supposed bills of exchange and, having debited the money previously advanced to him and the commission they were owed, pay over the balance due. In fact, however, these bills of exchange were wholly fictitious. No bills of exchange were actually forwarded by the Bombay branch to John Peel & Co to be applied for Kirkham's benefit.

6.14 Having discovered that he had been wrongly charged stamp duty on these non-existent bills of exchange, Kirkham brought an action seeking an account of the dealings between himself and John Peel & Co as his agents, in respect of goods

[20] *Re Hallett's Estate* (n 16) 710. See A Televantos, 'Losing the Fiduciary Requirement for Equitable Tracing Claims' (2017) 133 LQR 492 for an account of this use of the term 'fiduciary' in its historic context.

[21] [1991] 2 AC 548. [22] [1991] 2 AC 548, 573 (emphasis added).

[23] (1880) 43 LT 171, affirmed by the Court of Appeal in (1880) 44 LT 195.

entrusted to them since 1 November 1875. By consent of the parties, Jessel MR ordered an account to be taken of all such dealings and transactions. The official referee directed an account not only of the transactions between Kirkham and John Peel & Co directly, but also of the application, by the Bombay branch of the firm, of the proceeds of sale of the claimant's goods in India, including the amount realized by the sale of the goods for which they had been exchanged. John Peel & Co objected to this direction, on the basis that it was not within the terms of Jessel MR's order and it was not 'a direction which the plaintiff was entitled to under the circumstances'. Counsel for Kirkham asserted that the defendants had 'bartered our goods instead of selling them, and we claim the value of the goods received in exchange', citing *Re Hallett's Estate* as authority.

Jessel MR rejected the view that *Re Hallett's Estate* had any application. He said that his 'observations in that case ... had nothing whatever to do with the case of a commission merchant or agent'.[24] *Re Hallett's Estate* had addressed the case of a 'bailee ordinarily called a factor, who sells single articles and whose duty it is to remit the necessary proceeds to his principal'.[25] *Kirkham v Peel*, by contrast, was a case of 'a totally different character'; Kirkham had treated his agents, John Peel & Co, simply as 'as creditor for his advances and interest and ... as a debtor for the amounts received and interest'.[26] No claim to the traceable proceeds of the goods sold in Bombay was, therefore, available. Although there was undoubtedly a principal–agent relationship on the facts of the case, it was not the kind of relationship that gave rise to a claim to traceable proceeds: it was a mere debtor–creditor relationship. This language—claims to traceable proceeds are available where the relationship between the parties is *not* a mere debtor–creditor relationship—frequently recurs in the cases,[27] and is used to define the distinction between cases where a claim to traceable proceeds is potentially available, and cases where no such claim is possible. 6.15

Thus, the courts use a range of concepts to explain why one type of claimant can successfully claim the traceable proceeds of assets while another type of claimant cannot: trusteeship, fiduciary duty, ownership, and the distinction between a mere debtor–creditor relationship and a relationship constituted by the retention of ownership. This language is clear enough at its extremes. At one extreme, it is clear that a beneficiary under an express trust can certainly assert a claim to the traceable proceeds of his trustee's transactions involving the trust asset. At the other extreme, it is equally certain that no such claim is available to a claimant who is owed a simple debt—a right to be paid an abstract sum of money—even where the debt happens to represent the value of assets that he has authorized the defendant to deal with on his account. Difficulties arise, however, in accounting for an intermediate range of cases. There are a number of cases where such claims have succeeded although the relationship cannot be easily characterized as one that gives rise to a trustee-like or fiduciary duty to account for specific proceeds; in these cases, the mere absence of a debtor–creditor relationship does not tell us everything we need to know about the 6.16

24 *Kirkham* (n 23) 172. 25 *Kirkham* (n 24). 26 *Kirkham* (n 24).

27 Eg *Re Stenning* [1895] 2 Ch 433; *King v Hutton* [1900] 2 QB 504; *Henry v Hammond* [1913] 2 KB 515; *Triffit Nurseries (A firm) v Salads Etcetera Ltd* [2001] 1 All ER (Comm) 737.

basis of the claim. The idea that the opposite of debt, in this context, is 'ownership'—so that the concept of the property right, or of the 'proprietary base', can explain the availability of such claims—is also problematic.

6.2. Difficulties with the Fiduciary Duty Analysis

6.17 It is notoriously difficult to offer a comprehensive abstract definition of a fiduciary relationship, either by reference to the type of situation that gives rise to fiduciary duties or by reference to the content of the duty itself.[28] However, it is generally accepted that a core feature of fiduciary relationships is that these relationships generate duties—or a duty—of 'loyalty'. In *Bristol and West Building Society v Mothew*, Millett LJ offered the following classic account of the origins and content of these duties:

> A fiduciary is someone who has undertaken to act for or on behalf of another in a particular matter in circumstances which give rise to a relationship of trust and confidence The distinguishing obligation of a fiduciary is the obligation of loyalty. … This core liability has several facets. A fiduciary must act in good faith; he must not make a profit out of his trust; he must not place himself in a position where his duty and his interest may conflict; he may not act for his own benefit or the benefit of a third person without the informed consent of his principal.[29]

6.18 As noted, the language of fiduciary relationship has been important in the context of tracing because *Re Hallett's Estate* has been seen as establishing special or distinctive rules of tracing that are more potent than the weaker rules available at common law, but that only apply where there is a fiduciary relationship. However, in reality, relationships with the characteristics defined by Millett LJ in *Mothew* have never been a necessity for invoking these equitable tracing rules and claiming traceable proceeds. In neither context is a genuine fiduciary relationship, of the kind described in *Mothew*, required.

6.19 Thus, claims to traceable proceeds are available in English law even where the relationship between claimant and defendant has not been consensually constituted by some undertaking on the part of the defendant. Fraudsters and recipients of misdirected assets, who may never have genuinely consented to act for or on behalf of the claimant, can nevertheless be subjected to this form of liability. *Gladstone v Hadwen*[30] is an early example. It will be recalled[31] that, in that case, Hadwen had transferred certain bills of exchange to a bankrupt, Sill, under a contract that he had been induced to enter into under the influence of a fraudulent misrepresentation. The contract was subsequently rescinded. Hadwen took possession both of the

[28] For recent perspectives on the problem of defining the circumstances in which a fiduciary relationship arises, see M Conaglen, *Fiduciary Loyalty: Protecting the Due Performance of Non-Fiduciary Duties* (Hart 2010) 245–54; T Frankel, *Fiduciary Law* (OUP 2011) 6–42; and, generally, AS Gold and PB Miller (eds), *Philosophical Foundations of Fiduciary Duties* (OUP 2014).

[29] [1998] Ch 1, 18. [30] (1813) 1 M & S 517, 105 ER 193.

[31] See Chapter 3, paras 3.92–3.93 this volume.

remaining bills of exchange and of certain banknotes for which some of the bills had been exchanged; Sill's assignees in bankruptcy brought an action in trover against him. Lord Ellenborough CJ held that, since the contract had been rescinded before the act of bankruptcy, title to the bills of exchange had never vested in the assignees in bankruptcy—neither, therefore, did title to the banknotes.[32] Hadwen was entitled to those banknotes, as the traceable proceeds of the bills of exchange he had transferred under the rescinded contract; the absence of any fiduciary relationship between himself and Sill, who had exchanged them for the banknotes, did not play any role at all in the reasoning. *Gladstone v Hadwen* was followed in *Small v Attwood*,[33] where the claimants had paid banknotes under a contract that was subsequently rescinded, and succeeded in tracing into a bank account into which the notes had been paid, and claiming stock that had been purchased using that bank account.

In *El Ajou v Dollar Land Holdings plc (No 1)*,[34] Millett J held that a claimant in this position, who had transferred assets under a contract subsequently rescinded, was not only entitled to claim the traceable proceeds of those assets but was entitled to invoke the aid of the equitable tracing rules in identifying the proceeds. He explained the availability of the equitable rules in terms that expressly ruled out the necessity of finding that there was any genuine fiduciary relationship between the parties. As he explained, in such cases, a claimant has been 'simply swindled'; 'no breach of any fiduciary obligation [is] involved'.[35] Nevertheless, once the transaction has been rescinded, the effect is to 'revest the equitable title to the purchase money in [the claimant], at least to the extent necessary to support an equitable tracing claim'.[36] The proprietary language of title, in this context, is not a mere proxy for the language of fiduciary duty—as the language of beneficial ownership might be—but is in contrast with it. A claimant who has been swindled into transferring his asset to someone else, and has subsequently rescinded the transfer, is not in a fiduciary relationship with the swindler. He is not relying on any special duty of loyalty that the swindler owes him. He is relying on his title. 6.20

6.3. Difficulties with the Proprietary Base Analysis

It seems clear, therefore, that the fiduciary model does not account for the current law governing claims to traceable proceeds. Instead, the concept of title, or of beneficial ownership of the thing or asset substituted, does the work. This analysis may suggest that claims to traceable proceeds are available to all holders of property rights in respect of the thing, or asset, substituted. This has sometimes been described as the requirement of a 'proprietary base'.[37] 6.21

[32] *Gladstone* (n 30) 527; 197.

[33] (1831–1832) You 407, 507, 159 ER 1051, 1092, reversed by the House of Lords on a different point in (1838) 7 ER 684.

[34] [1993] 3 All ER 717, reversed on a different point by the Court of Appeal at [1994] 2 All ER 685.

[35] *El Ajou* (n 34) 734. [36] *El Ajou* (n 35).

[37] P Birks, 'Establishing a Proprietary Base (*Re Goldcorp*)' [1995] RLR 83.

6.22 Like the concept of a fiduciary relationship, the concept of a 'property right' is deeply contested. This is so on two levels. First, there are debates about the nature of the legal relationship constituted by such a right and, in particular, whether it makes sense to envisage property rights as unitary relationships between persons and things.[38] Secondly, there are related debates about the extent to which it is accurate to describe certain classes of right as proprietary: intellectual property rights, equitable interests, including and especially beneficial interests under trusts, and choses in action. Nevertheless, despite these controversies, it is generally agreed that certain core categories of entitlement are members of the category 'property right', if that category has any content at all. These include titles to chattels, such as books, cars, watches, etc., leasehold and freehold titles to land, and certain non-possessory rights such as easements and profits *à prendre*.

6.23 Generalizing from these examples, the central case of the 'property right' concept is thus an assignable right, in respect of a tangible object—such as a book, a car, or a plot of land—which is also the object of direct trespassory protection.[39] A right is the object of direct trespassory protection if every subject of the legal system, barring the right-holder, is under a *prima facie* duty not to interfere with the thing that is the subject matter of the right; the exact scope of the duty in each case can be mapped out by reference to the law of torts, and is profoundly shaped by the physical character of the thing that is the locus of the right. Thus, for example, in relation to land, English law grants trespassory protection both to certain rights to possession (leasehold and fee simple titles) and to certain defined forms of non-possessory enjoyment (such as rights of way). Where A acquires one of these rights, she acquires a right that correlates to a *prima face* duty owed to her by every other subject of the legal system. Thus, for example, if she is granted a 'term of years absolute'—ie the right to exclusive possession of a plot of land for a certain term (a lease)—she can prevent any person from physically interfering with her possession of the land or, where such interference takes place, obtain damages from the person who has so interfered.[40] Similarly, if she acquires a more limited right, such as a right of way, she can prevent any person from disturbing her in her use of that right or obtain compensation for such a disturbance.[41] A right to exclusive possession of a chattel is similarly regarded and similarly protected.

6.24 If any one of these characteristics is removed, the description of the right as proprietary becomes a matter of doubt and controversy. Thus, if we take away the characteristic of assignability, and say that any right that correlates with a duty of non-interference with a physical object is a property right, it would be a reasonable

[38] Different perspectives are put forward by W Hohfeld, *Fundamental Legal Conceptions* (Yale University Press 1923); A Honoré, 'Ownership' in AG Guest (ed), *Oxford Essays in Jurisprudence* (Clarendon Press 1961) 104; J Penner, 'The "Bundle of Rights Picture of Property"' (1996) 43 UCLA Law Rev 711; K Gray, 'Property in Thin Air' (1991) 50 CLJ 252; and S Douglas and B McFarlane, 'Defining Property Rights' in J Penner and H E Smith (eds), *Philosophical Foundations of Property Law* (OUP 2013) 226.

[39] The terminology of 'trespassary protection', as a generic description for these duties of non-interference, is that of J Harris, *Property and Justice* (OUP 1996, 2003 reprint) 142.

[40] See, for example, *Lane v Dixon* (1847) 136 ER 311.

[41] See, for example, *Thorpe v Brumfitt* (1873) 8 Ch App 650.

extension of the term to say that a human body is the property of the person whose body we are discussing.[42] Since, absent slavery, the totality of one's rights to one's body cannot legally be assigned to another, it is controversial to say one 'owns' one's body as a matter of law.[43]

The extension of the term is equally controversial if we take away the idea of the physical object and take the view that any right that attracts trespassory protection and is assignable qualifies as 'property', whether or not it has tangible subject matter. Questions would then arise about intellectual property rights and about the extent to which—given the existence of the *Lumley v Gye*[44] tort of interference with contractual relations—an assignable right under a contract should be thought of as proprietary.[45] Finally, if we take away the idea of trespassory protection altogether, and focus exclusively on assignability, an even broader range of rights would be admitted to the category and the characterization of these rights as proprietary would again be dubious and controversial. 6.25

Thus, rights sharing the triple characteristics of assignability, association with a tangible object, and trespassory protection form the agreed-upon core of the category of 'property rights'. Although there is dispute about the proper analysis of the relationships created by such rights, no one doubts that, if the terminology of 'property rights' makes sense at all, it applies to them. In English law, common law titles to land and chattels are paradigmatic examples of rights of this kind. If, therefore, claims to traceable proceeds are available to holders of property rights, *qua* holders of property rights, we ought to be able to find many instances of situations where the holder of a common law title to land or a chattel has been able to assert a claim to the proceeds of someone else's transaction purely by virtue of his title, ie without standing in any other relationship to the person entering into the transaction other than that constituted by his title. 6.26

6.3.1. Absence of authority for the property right analysis

In fact, however, authorities indicating the existence of such a claim are sparse and unsatisfactory. If we exclude all those cases where the judge invokes the language of common law title but where there is no tangible thing at stake at all—cases where the claimant is complaining about what someone has done with a bank account,[46] stocks and shares,[47] or carbon emission licences[48]—there are only a few cases,[49] all of which are open to alternative interpretation. 6.27

[42] See, for an example of such an argument, T Keren-Paz, 'Poetic Justice: Why Sex-Slaves Should be Allowed to Sue Ignorant Clients in Conversion' (2010) 29 Law and Philosophy 307.

[43] See, generally, P Matthews, 'Whose Body? People as Property?' (1983) 36 Current Legal Problems 193; JW Harris, 'Who Owns my Body' (1996) 16 Oxford Journal of Legal Studies 55; R Hardcastle, *Law and the Human Body* (Hart Publishing 2007); and I Goold, K Greasley, and J Herring (eds), *Persons, Parts and Property* (OUP 2014).

[44] (1854) 3 El & Bl 114, 118 ER 1083.

[45] See *OBG v Allan* [2007] UKHL 21.

[46] Eg *Banque Belge pour l'Etranger v Hambrouck* [1921] 1 KB 321; *Re Leslie* [1976] 1 WLR 292; *Lipkin Gorman v Karpnale Ltd* [1991] 2 AC 548; *Trustee of FC Jones v Jones* [1997] Ch 159.

[47] Eg *Marsh v Keating* (1834) 1 Bing (NC) 198, 131 ER 1094.

[48] *Armstrong DLW GmbH v Winnington Networks Ltd* [2012] EWHC 10 (Ch).

[49] For a detailed and critical overview of these cases, see P Matthews, 'Limits of Common Law Tracing' in P Birks (ed), *Laundering and Tracing* (OUP 1995) 23.

6.28 The earliest case is *Golightly v Reynolds*.[50] One Ferguson had stolen a £50 banknote from the claimant, Golightly, and used it to acquire six silver tablespoons, two silver salts cellars, two silver salt-spoons, a £20 banknote, and ten gold guineas. The claimant had presented these things as evidence of the theft during Ferguson's trial at the Old Bailey; in the course of the prosecution, they had come into the possession of Reynolds, an officer of the state. After Ferguson's conviction for theft, the claimant demanded that these things be delivered to him and the defendant, Reynolds, refused to do so. The claimant brought an action in trover and succeeded. This action had a statutory basis; it had been enacted by Parliament that, where a victim of theft had been instrumental in securing the conviction of the thief, the judges were to have a power to award 'from time to time, writs of restitution for the said money, goods and chattels'.[51] Lord Mansfield's reported reasoning is extremely brief:

> There is no question . . . but some way, and to some extent, a plaintiff is entitled to restitution. But how are we to construe the restitution which should be made? Narrowly, for the very thing stolen? No: liberally, against so odious a prerogative.[52]

It is not clear, from this language, if the case turns on the scope of the citizen–state relation regulated by the statute or if the claimant would have been able to bring a successful action in trover against Ferguson himself, or private parties who had received the things from Ferguson. There is a suggestion that the claimant would have been entitled to bring trover *apart* from the statute—Lord Mansfield comments that the statute gives the claimant a new remedy but does not take away his existing remedies[53]—but his reference to the prerogative powers of the state suggests that the statutory context played a role in his reasoning.

6.29 In *Cattley v Loundes*,[54] the claimant, a former employee of the defendant,[55] sued him in conversion on the basis that she had left certain goods in his house, which he refused to return to her. According to one report of the case, these were clothes bought by the claimant for herself;[56] the other report indicates that she had also left behind some jewellery.[57] She failed in her action against the defendant because, as the two reports agree, she had purchased these things using cash she had dishonestly taken from the defendant's till. Although she had been acquitted of the criminal charge of theft,[58] the judges found as a fact, to the civil standard of proof, that she

[50] (1772) Lofft 88, 98 ER 547.
[51] (1529) stat 33 H 8 c 7.
[52] *Golightly* (n 50) 90, 549.
[53] *Golightly* (n 52): 'Since this statute, it gives him a particular remedy, but does not take away his other remedy'.
[54] (1885) 34 WR 139; also reported as *Cattley v Lowndes* in (1885) 2 TLR 136.
[55] The two reports of the case differ as to the precise nature of her employment. The Times Law Report describes her as a domestic servant employed by a victualler: *Cattley v Lowndes* (n 54). The Weekly Reporter describes her as a barmaid employed by an innkeeper: *Cattley v Loundes* (n 54).
[56] *Cattley v Lowndes* (n 54) 137.
[57] *Cattley v Loundes* (n 54).
[58] The Weekly Reporter states that this was on the 'technical ground' that her confession to the defendant was inadmissible in court, as she had made it in exchange for a promise that she would not be prosecuted.

had stolen the money and used it to buy the chattels left behind in the defendant's house; this was held to be a sufficient answer to her claim against the defendant.[59]

6.30 As Paul Matthews has pointed out, it is difficult to draw any general conclusions from this case.[60] It is poorly reported, so that important elements of the fact situation are unclear,[61] and the reported remarks of the judges are so brief that it cannot be determined exactly what principle justified the outcome in the case. The case is of interest in this context, however, because of the following brief exchange between A L Smith J and counsel for the claimant:

> Stolen money may doubtless be followed, but not if it be converted. [A L Smith J – If a thief steals a sovereign from me and then changes it for two half-sovereigns, cannot I claim them?] No. [A L Smith J – I think you are wrong.].[62]

No authority is cited for either of these abrupt statements, either by counsel or by the judge. The only reference to authority is introduced by the reporter, who adds a footnote to the judge's 'I think you are wrong', in which he cites a dictum of Willes J in *R v Bunkall*.[63] That case, and the dictum in the context of the facts of the case, shares some of the characteristics of *Cattley v Loundes*; it presents similar difficulties, and poses a similar question.

6.31 In *R v Bunkall*, the defendant had been charged with larceny as a bailee of a quantity of coal;[64] the issue was whether or not he had been a bailee for the victim at the time that he took the coal for his own use. The victim, a blacksmith, had entrusted the defendant with eight shillings and sixpence, and instructed him to buy half a ton of coal for him. Having bought coal at this price[65] from one Rix, the defendant delivered only part of it to the blacksmith, keeping the rest for himself. Counsel for the defendant argued that retention of the coal could not be larceny under the statute because, when the defendant initially received the coals from Rix, he received them as their absolute owner and not as a bailee. The court rejected this

[59] Matthew J is reported as saying that 'the property detained by the defendant was bought with money stolen from the till of the defendant' in the Weekly Reporter, while the Times has him saying 'that the goods stolen represented money stolen by the plaintiff from the defendant's till': *Cattley* (n 53); *Cattley v Lowndes* (n 54) 137. A L Smith J concurred.

[60] Matthews (n 49) 52.

[61] In particular, it is not clear whether the claimant was a domestic servant who had no right to touch the cash in the defendant's till or a barmaid who was authorized to take cash from the till for his purposes but had improperly taken it for her own. That is, it is not clear whether she is best characterized as a tortfeasor who had taken wrongful possession of a stranger's assets, or as an agent who had misappropriated her principal's assets in breach of duty.

[62] *Cattley v Loundes* (n 54).

[63] (1864) Le & Ca 372, 169 ER 1436.

[64] Under the Larceny Act 1861, s 3 (now repealed), which provided that 'whosoever, being a bailee of any chattel, money, or valuable security, shall fraudulently take or convert the same to his own use, or the use of any person other than the owner thereof... shall be guilty of larceny'.

[65] It is not clear, on the facts, whether the defendant had paid the very cash given to him by the victim's agent in exchange for the coal. According to Rix's evidence, the defendant bought coal worth the amount given to him the day after he received the money, but paid only eight shillings immediately, saying that he did not have sixpence with him but would pay later: *R v Bunkall* (n 63) 373. There is nothing in the report to indicate that the money paid was the particular money given to the defendant by the claimant's agent and it seems likely that the sixpence in any case was not the same, as it was paid later.

argument, holding that the blacksmith had acquired a title to the coal from the moment of the defendant's receipt of them from Rix, so that the defendant was in possession of them only as a bailee. The judges divided on the source of this title Some members of the court thought that use of the victim's money to buy the coal '*ipso facto* vested the property in the coals'[66] in him, while others thought that there needed to be a specific intention by the defendant to appropriate the coals to the victim and that he had manifested such an intention.[67]

6.32 Willes J took the view that the use of the victim's money automatically gave him a right to the coal. He cited *Taylor v Plumer*[68] as authority, again in the course of argument, and began by describing the ratio of that case narrowly: 'it was held the property of a principal entrusted by him to his factor for any special purpose belongs to the principal, notwithstanding any change which that property may have undergone in point of form'. He then explained the practical application of this principle in a brief example: 'if I give a man money to buy a horse for me, and he buys a cow for himself with it, the cow is mine'.[69]

6.33 Two points emerge from these cases. First, as in *R v Bunkall*, there is sometimes a pre-existing relation between claimant and defendant; the claimant is not relying purely and simply on his existing common law title to a thing, but rather on his act of entrusting that thing to the defendant. Secondly, they all involve money. There are a few dicta in which the courts have indicated that, where money has been stolen—and thus cannot be said to have been entrusted to the defendant—the victim can nevertheless trace through the transactions of the thief, either on the basis of his common law title to the stolen money[70] or because the theft gives rise to a trust of the thief's title to the money.[71] If *Golightly v Reynolds* is a common law action in trover, rather than a statutory action, it can be analysed as an instance of a claim to the traceable proceeds of stolen money, brought in reliance on a common law title to the money. It is difficult to find even dicta suggesting that a similar principle applies to land, or to chattels other than money.[72] What authority there is goes the other

[66] *R v Bunkall* (n 63) 373, 377; 1438 (Cockburn CJ).

[67] *R v Bunkall* (n 63) 378; 1438 (Cockburn CJ).

[68] (1815) 3 M & S 562, 105 ER 721.

[69] *R v Bunkall* (n 63) 373, 375–67; 1437. The example is very close to one put by counsel in *Taylor v Plumer* itself, which Lord Ellenborough CJ adopted at *Taylor* (n 68) 575; 726: 'The contention on the part of the defendant was represented by the plaintiff's counsel as pushed to what he conceived to be an extravagant length, in the defendant's counsel being obliged to contend, that "if A is trusted by B with money to purchase a horse for him, and he purchases a carriage with that money, that B is entitled to the carriage." And, indeed, if he be not so entitled, the case on the part of the defendant appears to be hardly sustainable in argument'.

[70] Eg *Re Hulton* (1891) 8 Morr 69, 39 WR 303; *Banque Belge pour l'Etranger v Hambrouck* [1921] 1 KB 321; *Trustee of FC Jones v Jones* [1997] Ch 159.

[71] *Westdeutsche Landesbank Girozentrale v Islington LBC* [1996] AC 669, 716 (Lord Browne-Wilkinson). For an overview of the competing perspectives on whether this ought to be the case in English law, as in Australian law, see R Chambers, 'Trust and Theft' in E Bant and M Harding (eds), *Exploring Private Law* (CUP 2010) 223; S Barkehall-Thomas, 'Thieves, Owners and the Problem of Title' (2011) 5 Journal of Equity 228 and (2012) 6 Journal of Equity 1; and J Tarrant, 'Thieves as Trustees: In Defence of the Theft Principle' (2009) 3 Journal of Equity 170.

[72] Compare *Hendy Lennox Ltd v Grahame Puttick Ltd* [1984] 1 WLR 485, in which Staughton J held that a seller's retention of legal title to goods did not—in the absence of a relationship such as agency or bailment with the buyer—automatically bring with it a right to the proceeds of those goods.

way. For example, in *Twentieth Century Fox v Harris*[73] Newey J held that a holder of copyright could not assert a proprietary claim to the proceeds of an infringement of the copyright. In rejecting the argument that an entitlement to such a claim flowed from a statutory provision that holders of copyright were entitled to 'all such relief . . . as is available in respect of the infringement of any other property right,'[74] he denied that claims to traceable proceeds were routinely available as a response to the infringement of property rights: 'a landowner has no proprietary claim to the fruits of a trespass.'[75]

6.3.2. Analytical problems with the property right analysis

This result can be seen to arise from the logic of tracing, which identifies an unauthorized substitution as an event involving the loss of *rights* on the part of the claimant. A thief of money has, in a sense, a power to deal with the rights of the claimant: because of the currency of money,[76] a transaction by the thief can have the effect of depriving the claimant of his title. A thief of a chattel that is not money or a negotiable instrument does not normally possess such a power. If A steals a book from B, for example, she may deliver the book to X under a purported sale, but this will not in itself have any effect on B's superior title. A will have sold her own possessory title to X, and B can still sue A or X, at his election, for their interference with the book, since his title to it is superior to theirs. This claim, in the tort of conversion, will normally entitle him to damages reflecting the value of the book;[77] sometimes, as where the book is a unique chattel, such as a signed first edition, he may be able to recover physical possession of the book itself.[78] Where A or X have obtained benefits from their use of the book, he may also be entitled to recover the amount of the benefit in the form of restitutionary damages.[79] This will be an abstract money award, reflecting the amount by which the defendants have gained as a result of their wrong. 6.34

If, instead, B decides that he would prefer instead to have the specific traceable proceeds of the book in the hands of A, we have seen that there is very little authority for such a claim. Apart from authority, it is also difficult to see why the law should respect such a preference as a matter of principle. B's title to his book entitles him to possession of the book, and to compensation or restitution from anyone who has violated that right to possession and benefited from that wrong. The duties owed to B are delineated by the legal system by reference to the physical thing that is the locus of his rights;[80] he has a right to be compensated for losses flowing from his loss of access 6.35

[73] [2013] EWHC 159. [74] Copyright, Designs and Patent Act 1988, s 96(2).

[75] *Twentieth Century Fox v Harris* (n 73) [17] (Newey J).

[76] *Miller v Race* (1758) 1 Burrow 452, 97 ER 398. See *Twentieth Century Fox v Harris* (n 73) [16] (Newey J), distinguishing the case of stolen coins from that of copyright infringement: 'While the owner of the coins will have lost title to the coins at law, the copyright owner will have retained title throughout both in equity and at law.'

[77] *Kuwait Airways v Iraq Airways Co* [2002] UKHL 19 (Lord Nicholls at [67]).

[78] Torts (Interference with Goods) Act 1977, s 3.

[79] Eg *Strand Electric and Engineering Co LD v Brisford Entertainments LD* [1952] 2 QB 246.

[80] For a detailed analysis of the way in which the duties are mediated through interactions with the physical thing, see Douglas and McFarlane (n 38) 226.

to that physical thing, and to restitution of gains made by exploitation of wrongful access to the thing. When B asserts that what A has done is enter into an unauthorized substitution, however, he is not confining his attention to what has been done with the particular physical thing that is the locus of his original right. Rather, he is arguing that A's decision to deal with her own possessory title to the book is the thing he is entitled to control. The standard structure of an entitlement to a tangible thing does not easily accommodate this shift from a focus on what has been done with the physical object to a focus on what has been done with the rights of a person.

6.36 Thus, for example, suppose that A sells her possessory title to the book to X, and receives money in exchange; she uses this money to buy a guitar from Y. In this situation, it is A's own possessory title to the book that she has chosen to swap for X's title to the money, and thus Y's title to the guitar. It is not clear why this decision on her part should be subordinated to B's ends in this scenario. If we substitute the *Foskett v McKeown* facts, so that B is now insisting that A's contract of life insurance should be treated as entered into for his benefit, the oddity of the argument becomes even clearer. The subordination of personal autonomy that arises from the operation of the tracing rules, with their focus on the transactions by persons rather than on the physical identity of things, cannot be justified on the basis of a principle of respect for property in things as such.

6.37 If, however, A has a power in this scenario capable of defeating B's title to the book, the situation changes. If A has sold B's book to C, and B's title to the book has been extinguished by that sale,[81] B's complaint is no longer about an interference with the book, but rather about the loss of his right to the book. His title to the book, which he was previously entitled to rely on and exchange for other things if he wished, is gone; the reason for this loss is that the legal system has given A the legal power to bring about the destruction of this title, which she has exercised to obtain cash on her own account. In this situation, it is precisely A's decision-making that B is concerned with. In the absence of the legal power, A would not have been able to make the decision to sell B's title to the book at all; her decision could only have affected her own possessory title to the book. The logic of B's claim that he is therefore entitled to treat A's decision as made for his benefit is thus more compelling in this example than in the case where A's decision to sell her possessory title, and to use the money to buy a guitar, has no effect on B's position as a holder of a title superior to A's.

6.4. Control of Assets and Other Power–Liability Relations

6.38 This idea of a legal power, therefore, tells us something about the availability of claims to traceable proceeds that the idea of the property right, or of the fiduciary duty, cannot. However, it does not follow that a claimant is entitled to the traceable proceeds of the defendant's transactions whenever those transactions involve an

[81] For example, because A is a seller in possession within the meaning of s 25 of the Sale of Goods Act 1979.

exercise of a legal power in Hohfeld's sense. The Hohfeldian conception of a legal power is too broad for this analysis to be plausible.

6.4.1. Hohfeld's powers

Hohfeld describes A as the holder of a legal power, correlative to a liability in B, in any situation where B's legal position would be altered in any way by the occurrence of some fact and A has 'volitional control'[82] over whether the fact occurs. On this view, A has exercised a power both when her voluntary act places B under the burden of a new duty and when her act has the effect of freeing B from a duty previously owed to A or another. **6.39**

His analysis of the law governing the abandonment of chattels is typical. By abandoning a chattel and so extinguishing my title to it, I remove the duty of non-interference that was previously owed to me by a stranger, so that the stranger commits no wrong in taking the chattel; in so freeing the stranger from a duty, Hohfeld says, I have exercised a power over him.[83] Conversely, a power–liability relationship also exists in any situation where one person has the ability to make any choice that will impose a new duty on another. Suppose, for example, A makes a contractual offer to B. The effect is of the offer is that B, 'by dropping a letter of acceptance in the box, has the power to impose a potential or inchoate *obligation ex contractu* on A and himself'.[84] B has the capacity, by his voluntary act of acceptance of the offer, to subject A to a new duty that he did not owe before. On the facts of *Carlill v Carbolic Smoke Ball Company*,[85] for example, this analysis implies the existence of a power–liability relationship between the company and every reader of the Pall Mall Gazette. When the newspaper published the company's advertisement promising £100 to any user of the carbolic smoke ball who contracted influenza, everyone who saw the advertisement gained a power over the company. By voluntarily buying the carbolic smoke ball, and using it according to the instructions over the prescribed period, a reader could impose a new contingent obligation to pay £100 on the company, albeit one that would only crystallize in the event that she contracted influenza. **6.40**

However, it could hardly be suggested that an exercise of power in either of these senses could qualify as 'unauthorized' in the sense relevant to claims to traceable proceeds. Suppose that A, the holder of a right of light over B's land, entered into a deed of release that extinguished the easement in consideration for a payment of £1,000 from B. The transaction would not only extinguish B's duty to avoid obstructing A's enjoyment of light, it would also remove the duty owed to A by others, such as B's tenants, licensees, and successors in title. In this scenario, it would be true that A had obtained a right—the £1,000—in consideration for altering the legal position of these third parties without their consent. However, they would hardly have grounds for complaining that the alteration was 'unauthorized' and **6.41**

[82] WN Hohfeld, *Fundamental Legal Conceptions as Applied in Judicial Reasoning* (D Campbell and P Thomas, eds, Ashgate Publishing Company 2001) 21.

[83] Hohfeld (n 82) 22.

[84] Hohfeld (n 82) 23.

[85] [1893] 1 QB 256.

demanding the proceeds of the transaction. It is possible to have a power to change someone else's legal position in a way that is beneficial to them, as in the case of the release of a duty, and a 'power' in this sense clearly does not generate the kind of vulnerability that is the concern of the judges who developed the tracing concept.

6.42 However, it is also improbable that the concept of want of authority could have any role to play even in some situations where the alteration is not beneficial—as in the case of a discharge of a duty—but involves the imposition of a new duty. For example, there might be situations where the acceptance of a contractual offer enables the acceptor to obtain a new right from a third party. Suppose that, on the facts of *Carlill v Carbolic Smoke Ball Co*, a rival company, with the aim of discrediting the claims of the Carbolic Smoke Ball Company, had promised a cash reward to anyone who fulfilled the terms of the advertisement and successfully sued the company. If Mrs Carlill had accepted this offer, and received the cash reward, she would in a sense have obtained her title to the cash in consideration for her decision to alter the legal position of the Carbolic Smoke Ball Company without its consent. Nevertheless, the company would have had no basis for arguing that the money represented the product of an unauthorized variation of its rights and therefore ought to be paid to it.

6.43 The language of authority or want of authority is inapplicable to these cases because in neither case is there any duty owed to the person affected by the exercise of the supposed power. If Mrs Carlill had the power to impose a new obligation on the Carbolic Smoke Ball Company by accepting its contractual offer, she was free to exercise that power as she saw fit for her own ends. If she did not have any such power—if, for example, the advertisement had been held not to comprise a genuine contractual offer but a 'mere puff'[86]—then her attempt to exercise it by accepting the supposed offer would simply have been a nullity. The concept of an *unauthorized* exercise of a power to subject another to a duty owed to oneself, or release him from such a duty, only makes sense if some other legal relationship between the parties[87] co-exists with the power–liability relationship.

6.44 On the face of it, and apart from his own examples, Hohfeld's definition also seems to capture the case where A has a choice as to whether to breach a duty to B, and in this sense to alter B's legal position by conferring a new right on B. The definition can even be extended to capture a person's ability to commit a criminal offence and thus to alter the legal position of the state and officials of the state. As MacCormick has pointed out,[88] if we define a legal power purely as an objective capacity to bring about any sort of legal consequence by one's voluntary

[86] *Carlill* (n 85) 261 (Lindley LJ).

[87] It is possible, of course, to imagine cases where A's power over B is governed by a duty owed to C. For example, a holder of an easement might have promised his mortgagee that he would not release the benefit of the easement without the consent of the mortgagee. In such a situation, however, the power–liability relationship is independent of the right–duty relationship: the same transaction is a breach of a duty owed to C and an exercise of a power over B, rather than an exercise of a power over B that is, simultaneously, a breach of a duty owed to B.

[88] In the context of his discussion of Hart's account of power-conferring rules: N MacCormick, *H.L.A Hart* (Stanford University Press 1981) 73–79.

act, this would compel us to accept 'the odd conclusion that among the powers conferred ... by law are powers to commit wrongs and so to make oneself liable to ... punishments'.[89]

In order to be liable in the tort of trespass, for example, the trespasser must intentionally or negligently intrude upon the land of the claimant.[90] Any subject of the legal system has 'volitional control' over the set of facts—the intrusion upon his neighbour's land—that would render him liable in trespass and thus vest a new legal right in his neighbour. On Hohfeld's account, therefore, every subject of the legal system has a power correlative to a liability in every landowner. In a similar vein, the commission of a criminal offence can be understood as the exercise of a Hohfeldian power correlative to a liability in the state: the criminal, by voluntarily committing the offence, confers new legal rights (such as the right to deprive him of his liberty) on the state.[91] Again, the implication is that every subject of the legal system stands in a power–liability relation to the state. 6.45

This leads us to the conclusion that, for Hohfeld, a power–liability relation exists wherever A owes B a duty that can be breached by a volitional act, with the exercise of the power being identical to the breach of the duty. Given this definition of a Hohfeldian power–liability relationship, it is implausible that every such relationship generates an entitlement to the proceeds of any wrongful exercise of the power. If this were true, it would mean that every wrong generated a proprietary claim to assets representing gains made in breach of duty. With the specific exception of the duty not to profit from one's position as a fiduciary,[92] this is not the law. A profit-making breach of contract may, exceptionally,[93] generate a claim to an account of profits, but it will not generate a proprietary claim to the specific asset representing the profit.[94] Similarly, although there is controversy regarding the exact range of situations in which a profit-stripping remedy will be available in response to a common law tort,[95] such remedies are not routinely available in the current state of the law.[96] An unauthorized substitution occurs when A wrongfully varies the legal, rather than the factual, position of B, as the tracing case law demonstrates, but this cannot mean that every case where A breaches a duty owed to B counts as a variation of legal rights of the relevant kind. 6.46

Thus, while the idea of the 'power–liability relation' in its Hohfeldian sense is necessary to our understanding of unauthorized substitution, it is not sufficient. The category is over-inclusive, capturing cases where the courts would undoubtedly reject the possibility of any claim based on unauthorized substitution. In order to make sense of the case law, and to identify the category of legal relations 6.47

[89] MacCormick (n 88) 74.

[90] *Smith v Stone* (1647) Sty 65, 82 ER 533.

[91] MacCormick (n 88) 75 and A Halpin, 'The Concept of a Legal Power' (1996) 16 OJLS 129, 143.

[92] *FHR European Ventures LLP v Cedar Capital Partners LLC* [2014] UKSC 45.

[93] In *Attorney-General v Blake* [2001] 1 AC 268, the majority describes the remedy of an account of profits in response to a breach of contract as 'exceptional' six times: 284, 285, and 286 (Lord Nicholls) and 292 (Lord Steyn).

[94] *Blake* (n 93) 288 (Lord Nicholls).

[95] Discussed, eg by C Rotherham, 'Gain-based Relief in Tort After *A-G v Blake*' (2010) 126 LQR 102.

[96] *Forsyth-Grant v Allan* [2008] EWCA Civ 505.

presupposed by a claim based on unauthorized substitution, it is necessary to carve out this category from the broad range of Hohfeldian power–liability relations. The doctrinal usage of the term 'power' in the context of English private law supplies a starting point.

6.4.2. Private powers in English law

6.48 By contrast with the sweeping Hohfeldian usage, English private lawyers conventionally use the term 'power' to denote a far more limited set of legal relations. The leading textbook on the subject, *Thomas on Powers*, offers the following definition:

> [I]n this book, the term 'power' … is used, in the main, to signify an authority or mandate conferred on, or reserved by, a person to deal with, as well as dispose of, property which he himself does not own. Thus, a power is distinct from the dominion that a man has over his own property.[97]

'Property' in this usage is not restricted to title to tangible things, but includes such rights as shares and bank accounts and other choses in action. The definition can be glossed, therefore, to mean that a power is an authority to deal with or dispose of any assignable right—that is, a right that can be 'dealt with or disposed of', so as to be separated from its holder by some consensual transaction. Private powers to deal with rights of this kind ('assets') are to be contrasted with that capacity to deal with an asset which is an incident of having the asset vested in oneself.

6.49 One reason why this definition is narrower than the Hohfeldian one is because it specifies the kind of change in legal position that the power-holder is able to bring about. It excludes those situations where A has the ability to alter the duties owed to herself by B, either by extinguishing a subsisting duty (as where she extinguishes her title to a chattel and so extinguishes B's duty of non-interference) or by creating a new duty (as where she accepts B's contractual offer). In these cases, A is only altering duties owed to herself by other subjects of the legal system and thus, by definition, dealing with rights that are vested in her and not in someone else. It also excludes cases where A alters B's legal position by breaching a duty and thus conferring a new set of claims on B; here, A is not 'dealing with or disposing of' B's pre-existing rights, which remain intact, but adding a new right to the number. Excluding these cases, then, it captures those situations where B has a pre-existing claim-right, which is correlative to a duty owed to him either by A or by some other person, C, and A has the capacity to extinguish or alter that claim-right by her voluntary act.

6.50 Uncontroversial examples of powers in this sense include equitable powers of appointment, powers of attorney, and the power of a company director to deal with the assets of the company. The terminology used by English lawyers to describe these relationships varies with context. For example, an agent is normally described as having an 'authority' to affect the rights of his 'principal', while the holder of a

[97] G Thomas, *Thomas on Powers* (2nd edn, OUP 2012) 2–3.

power of appointment is referred to as a 'donee' of the power, which enables him to alter the rights of its 'object'. For the sake of consistency, this book adopts a modified version of the terminology that is standard in the context of powers of appointment when speaking generally of private powers: the person who grants a power is its 'donor'; the person who holds the power is its 'donee'; and the person whose rights may be varied by its exercise is the 'object'.[98] In some cases, as with principal–agent relationships, the donor of the power is likely to be the same person as its object: the agent is empowered to alter the principal's rights by virtue of the authority granted to him by the principal himself. In other cases, as in the case of the trust, the donor and the object are likely to be different: the trustee is empowered to alter the beneficiaries' rights by virtue of the authority granted to him by the settlor, who need not be one of the beneficiaries under the trust.

Powers have been classified in several different ways, depending on the purpose of the classification.[99] Some[100] traditional classifications distinguish between powers based on their jurisdictional origin—law, equity, and statute[101]—as well as their scope (eg administrative and dispositive, special, and general) and the content of the duties constraining their exercise (eg fiduciary and non-fiduciary). 6.51

At first glance, the jurisdictional distinction between legal, equitable, and statutory might be thought to be a classification based on the source, as a matter of legal history, of the rule recognizing the existence of the power. As such, its relevance might be questioned on the basis that it reflects a purely historical and accidental distinction that is no longer of any analytical or normative significance in the modern law.[102] However, apart from the doubtfully relevant historical question, the question of jurisdictional origin can also be understood as a proxy for other questions that are undoubtedly important in the modern law. This is because the distinction between 'common law' and 'equity' does not only describe the historical origins of a given 6.52

[98] Describing the person whose subsisting rights are altered by the exercise of a power as its 'object' is a departure from the language conventionally used in the context of powers of appointment, where it is the class of persons who may be benefited by the exercise of the power who are described as its objects. The objects of a power of appointment, in the traditional sense, have no vested interest in the assets subject to the power until the power is exercised and therefore it cannot be said that the donee of the power has varied their subsisting rights by exercising the power: *Re Brooks Settlement Trusts* [1939] Ch 993, 997 (Farwell J). Rather it is the persons entitled in default of appointment whose rights are varied by the exercise of the power, and who are the 'objects' in the sense used here.

[99] See, generally, Thomas (n 97) 4–12.

[100] The other traditional classification, which is being ignored here, is the classification of powers by reference to the nature of the donee's own interest in the right in respect of which the power exists: see CJW Farwell, *A Concise Treatise on Powers* (3rd edn, Stevens & Sons 1916) 9–10 and E Sugden, *A Practical Treatise of Powers* (8th edn, H Sweet 1861) 46–49. Apart from a residual significance in relation to the capacity of minors to exercise powers, these distinctions are now 'of antiquarian interest only': *Mettoy Pension Trustees Ltd v Evans* [1990] 1 WLR 1587, 1613 (Warner J).

[101] Thomas (n 97) 6. In Farwell and Sugden, the distinction is between equitable powers, common law powers, and powers deriving their effect from the Statute of Uses: see Farwell (n 100) 1–4, and Sugden (n 100) 45–47. On powers deriving their effect from the Statute of Uses, see para 6.53 this chapter.

[102] For the view that it is a mistake to classify private law doctrines by reference to the jurisdictional distinction between law and equity, without more, see WJ Swadling, 'Snell's Equity' (2011) 127 LQR 638: 'a random collection of disconnected doctrines, confusing issues of substance and procedure, covering topics only connected by historical accident'.

body of doctrine; it also describes the characteristics of rights which are governed by substantively different legal rules in the modern law, since the location of a right in one or other of these categories can, in some circumstances, dictate the terms on which that right will be enforced.[103] As such, the terms denote a cluster of modern rules on the creation, transfer, and enforceability of rights.[104] It is in this doctrinal rather than historical, sense that the terms 'common law' and 'equitable' can be used to classify powers: a power to vary a legal right is a common law power, while a power to vary an equitable right is an equitable power. As such, the classification is one based on the consequences of an exercise of a power, rather than the jurisdictional source of that power.

6.53 The language of statutory powers is also often used to describe the consequences of the exercise of a power rather than its source: although, as Thomas notes, there are important equitable powers that are conferred by statute,[105] the term 'statutory power' is traditionally reserved for powers conferred by statute that can be said 'to authorise the creation or conveyance of a legal estate'.[106] This can be traced to Sugden and Farwell, who distinguished between common law powers, equitable powers, and powers made effective by the Statute of Uses. The Statute of Uses 1536 enabled the creation of a number of future legal estates in land that were previously unknown to the common law,[107] and also made it possible for landowners to vest powers to create such estates in others.[108] These powers were statutory in the sense that, but for the Statute of Uses, donors would have been unable to create them; they were not statutory in the sense that they were actually vested in donees by virtue of the statute.[109] On this basis, the characterization of a power as statutory also

[103] There is an ongoing debate regarding whether the historical terminology of common law versus equitable should be abandoned in favour of one which better reflects the work done by the distinction: see A Burrows, 'We Do This at Common Law and That in Equity' (2002) 22 OJLS 1, 4, arguing that 'the general rules of priority in relation to property cannot easily be replicated without using the law and equity labels'. Attempts to provide alternative labels have been made by, for example, Jaffey and McFarlane: P Jaffey, *Private Law and Property Claims* (Hart Publishing 2007) 111–28, B McFarlane, *The Structure of Property Law* (Hart Publishing 2008) 66–77. Since nothing turns on this labelling issue for present purposes, the orthodox terminology of common law and equitable rights is here retained, since it is the language most frequently used by commentators and courts in this jurisdiction.

[104] It is worth noting, in this context, that Parliament has sometimes deliberately re-classified formerly legal rights and powers as 'equitable', in order to ensure that their creation and exercise attract the consequences that follow from that classification: see the Law of Property Act 1925 (LPA), ss 1(3), 1(7). Along similar lines, the Law Commission has recently recommended the reverse strategy of replacing a formerly equitable right (the restrictive covenant) with a legal equivalent in order to arrive at the desired outcome: Law Commission, *Making Land Work: Easements, Covenants and Profits à Prendre* (Law Com No 327) 5.70. It cannot be said, as a matter of legal history, that the jurisdictional source of these rights is their recognition by the courts of equity; in such cases, the use of the label 'equitable' can only signify the modern rules that govern the right, not its historical origins.

[105] Eg powers of advancement and maintenance conferred on trustees by the Trustee Act 1925, ss 31 and 32.

[106] Thomas (n 97) 6.

[107] For the new future legal estates that were made possible by the Statute of Uses, see Goodhart and Hanbury (eds), *W S Holdsworth, A History of English Law: Volume 7* (2nd edn, Sweet & Maxwell 1937) 122–29. It is no longer possible to create these futures estates in land at common law: LPA 1925, s 1(1).

[108] For these powers, see JH Baker, *An Introduction to English Legal History* (4th edn, OUP 2007) 289.

[109] As Baker notes (n 108), they became an important part of the machinery of the traditional strict settlement, an elaborate structure for facilitating the intentions of a settlor.

represents a classification by reference to the potential consequences of its exercise, with statutory powers representing a sub-category of common law powers.[110]

However, the distinction between statutory and other powers could, with some modification, instead be generalized to a distinction based on causative event, allowing us to distinguish powers arising by operation of law from powers arising by the consent of some private person. This characterization is not plausible for those statutory powers that are implied into consensual transactions between private individuals and can be excluded, limited, or modified by the intentions of the parties to the transaction. An example of such a power is the mortgagee's power of sale under section 101 of the Law of Property Act 1925, which arises in response to a deed[111] and can be varied[112] or excluded[113] by express provision in the deed. The statutory grant of such a power can essentially be seen as 'a form of conveyancing shorthand designed to implement the ordinary expectations'[114] of the parties to the relevant transaction. Although the power does, in a sense, arise by operation of law, being implied into the agreement between the parties by statute, it will only do so when the parties have entered into such an agreement in the first place and have neglected to exclude or modify it. 6.54

Such powers are similar to powers that arise by the consent of private parties, and there is only a limited justification for distinguishing them from non-statutory powers that also arise in the context of consensual transactions. However, other statutory powers do genuinely arise by operation of law, in the sense that the event that gives rise to them is not a bargain or other consensual transaction, but rather some event that may take place without anyone's consent. For example, if a person dies intestate, section 33 of the Administration of Estates Act 1925 confers a power of sale on his personal representatives. Although the deceased can prevent the power from arising by choosing to make a will,[115] the power itself does not arise in response to any consensual act; dying intestate may sometimes be a choice, but it certainly does not need to be one. The power in this case is better understood as a default rule, applicable in the absence of any expressed intention by the deceased, rather than as directly intended to reflect his likely intentions. 6.55

Apart from such instances of the statutory grant of a power in default of the expression of a relevant intention, there are also stronger cases of statutory powers that arise by operation of law and cannot be excluded by anyone's choice. For example, a trustee in bankruptcy has a power of sale[116] in respect of the bankrupt's estate; this power arises by operation of law, has nothing to do with the consent of the bankrupt, and cannot be excluded by the decision of either the bankrupt or his creditors.[117] 6.56

[110] Under the LPA s 1(7), the only powers to create or transfer an estate in land which are now capable of existing at law are the mortgagee's power of sale and the rights of the person in whom that estate is vested (which may be exercised by himself or by his duly appointed agent on his behalf).

[111] LPA s 101(1). [112] LPA s 101(3). [113] LPA s 101(4).

[114] *Horsham Properties v Clark* [2008] EWHC 2327, [35] (Briggs J).

[115] Administration of Estates Act 1925, s 33(7).

[116] Insolvency Act 1986, s 314(1) and schedule 5, para 9.

[117] Although the trustee has an obligation to inform the creditors' committee of certain intended exercises of the power of sale, such as a sale to an associate of the bankrupt: Insolvency Act 1986, s 314(6).

Similarly, the powers of a life tenant under a strict settlement of land, governed by the Settled Land Act 1925, could not have been[118] excluded or modified by the intention of the settlor.[119] On this basis, the jurisdictional divide between statutory and other powers can sometimes refer to a distinction based on causative event: some powers arise in response to consent, while others arise by operation of law.

6.57 Private powers can, therefore, be seen from three distinct perspectives. First, they may be classified by reference to the potential consequences of an exercise of the power, with some powers enabling the donee to transfer or create common law rights and others applying to equitable rights. Secondly, powers may be distinguished from each other based on the terms of the duty attached to the exercise of the power. Some powers can be exercised freely, with no consideration for the interests of the object of the power; some impose stringent duties of fiduciary loyalty; others allow for a degree of self-interest in the decision to exercise the power. Finally, powers can be classified by causative event. While many powers arise in response to the consent of a donor, there are cases where the law confers a power on a donee on other grounds and without reference to anyone's consent.

6.58 This analysis presupposes a definition of a private power as the objective capacity to bring about a certain result: wherever A's transaction can deprive B of his subsisting rights, whether at law[120] or in equity,[121] a private power exists. It might be objected that this definition is unhelpful because it abandons the consent-based concepts of authority and mandate that are central to the traditional understanding of a private power. If a private power is not only an objective capacity to bring about a given result but is an *authority* to bring about that result, arising from a mandate, it is inaccurate to characterize situations where there has been no grant of authority by anyone as instances of private power. In addition, the explanatory force of even a consensually created power, understood as an authority, runs out when we are dealing with unauthorized transactions. On this view, we can explain the legal consequences of a transaction carried out by the donee of a power by reference to that power only where transaction is an authorized one. If the donee does something in purported exercise of the power, which is actually unauthorized by the initial mandate granted by the donor, this would not count as a genuine 'exercise' of the power: even if the transaction were effective in bringing about some consequence, that consequence would have to be explained by reference to some other principle than the principle of facilitating the donor's intentions which justifies the law's response to the authorized disposition.

6.59 For example, suppose a donee of a power of attorney is authorized to sell his donor's title to a painting, and then purports to sell that title to a third party. If the transaction is authorized, we can explain the legal consequence—title

[118] Under section 2(1) of the Trusts of Land and Appointment of Trustees Act 1996, it is no longer possible for a settlor to create a strict settlement governed by the Settled Land Act 1925. Any attempt to create such a settlement after 1 January 1997 will take effect as an ordinary trust of land, governed by the 1996 Act.

[119] Settled Land Act 1925, ss 106 and 108.

[120] See Chapter 8, Section 8.1 this volume for a more detailed analysis of common law powers in this context.

[121] See Chapter 7, Section 7.1 this volume for a more detailed analysis of equitable powers in this context.

is transferred from the donor of the power to the third party—by reference to donor intention. If, however, the donor had revoked the power of attorney the day before the sale, this explanation would no longer hold. Under section 5 of the Powers of Attorney Act 1971, the purported sale might[122] have identical[123] legal consequences to the authorized sale—title would pass to the third party who did not know of the revocation—but the consent of the donor would no longer entirely explain that consequence, since the donor would have withdrawn that consent. It could be argued, on this basis, that the transaction in this scenario does not count as an exercise of the (revoked) power of attorney: it is, instead, an occasion for the operation of a mandatory rule of law that has no connection to the idea of a power in its proper sense.

This argument, however, collapses the distinction between the justification for the existence of a power–liability relationship and the content of such a relationship, once it exists. In the example in para 6.59, it is true that the consent of the donor of the power supplies a complete justification for the transfer of title to the painting in the case of the authorized disposition and cannot do so in the case of the post-revocation disposition. If we are classifying legal relations by reference to the event to which they respond, the two power–liability relations (the one constituted by the initial grant of the power of attorney and the one constituted by the operation of section 5 of the 1971 Act) are fundamentally different: one falls into the 'consent' category and the other resides in the 'miscellaneous fourth column' of the Birks grid.[124] On the other hand, if we are classifying legal relations by reference to their content, the two cases are either very similar, or identical.[125] From the perspective of the third party dealing with the donee, the transaction is 'as valid as if the power had then been in existence';[126] as a corollary, the effect is the same for the object of the power, at least so far as her relationship with the third party is concerned. For whatever reason—whether by her consent or by the operation of a legal rule—the decision of the donee of the power will have changed her legal relationship with the third party, without her having any involvement in that particular decision. Thus, prior to the transaction, the donee of the power possessed the objective capacity—or power—to transfer the object's title to the third party, even in a situation where the initial grant of the power of attorney has been revoked. 6.60

Of course it is perfectly plausible to say, by definitional fiat, that such an objective capacity should not be described as a private power because the idea of a power is intrinsically linked to the idea of a mandate: that is, the idea of a private power is intrinsically linked to a particular causative event (ie the consent of some donor). Whether this definitional choice is apt depends on what it is we are trying to understand about power–liability relations. In the context of claims 6.61

[122] Depending on whether the third party knew of the revocation. Where the third party is a purchaser, and the transaction has taken place within twelve months of the initial grant of the power, there is a presumption that he did not know of the revocation: Powers of Attorney Act 1971, s 5(4).

[123] Where the donee of the power also does not know of the revocation, the effect is identical as he will not incur any personal liability for purportedly exercising the revoked power: Powers of Attorney Act 1971, s 5(1). Where he does know, but the third party does not, the effect of the transaction will differ as between donor and donee, but not as between donor and third party.

[124] P Birks, *Unjust Enrichment* (2nd edn, OUP 2005) 24.

[125] See para 6.59 this chapter.

[126] Powers of Attorney Act 1971, s 5(2).

to traceable proceeds, the primary puzzle is the nature of the power–liability relationship presupposed by the availability of the claim, rather than its origins It is clear that some claims based on unauthorized substitution arise where the initial relationship between the parties is constituted by consent, as in the case of an express trust.[127] However, this is not the fact unifying those cases: we know that there are relationships constituted by consent where such claims are not available,[128] and that there are cases where such claims seem to be available where the parties are effectively strangers to one another, as where a beneficiary under a trust traces through the transactions of a recipient from the trustee.[129]

6.4.3. Defining a relationship of control of assets: content of the power

6.62 Claims to traceable proceeds depend on the existence of private power, therefore, in the sense of an objective capacity to deal with another's assets held by a defendant; they do not require that the defendant have a private power in the sense of a mandate or authority consensually conferred on him by the claimant or some other right-holder in respect of the relevant assets. This might suggest that A has a power capable of generating claims to traceable proceeds whenever his act has the potential to be the immediate cause of B's loss of rights as against C. Such an account would capture, for example, any situation where B's rights are contingent on the continuation of some physical state of affairs and, unluckily for B, A has the factual ability to alter that state of affairs. For example, anyone who physically destroys a thing will, inevitably, have destroyed the vested rights of the person who previously had title to the thing. If A steals B's cake, and eats it, B will no longer be in a position to assert that C owes him a duty of non-interference with that particular cake. For all practical purposes, the cake has ceased to exist and therefore, no one can owe B the duties they owed him before its destruction, as those duties were shaped by the physical characteristics of the cake. As soon as a thing ceases to exist in its original form, 'the title to [it] simply disappear[s]'.[130]

6.63 In *Borden (UK) Ltd v Scottish Timber Products*,[131] the claimants had contracted to sell resin to the defendant company; the contract included a retention of title clause providing that title to the resin would not pass to the defendants until the purchase price had been paid in full. In the course of the defendant's manufacturing operations, the resin was mixed with various other things in an irreversible process that led to its incorporation within the chipboard manufactured by the defendants. The claimants argued that they could trace from their title to the resin into the chipboard and any proceeds of sale of the chipboard. One aspect of their argument was that there was an analogy between unauthorized substitution and what the defendants had done, such that they were entitled to trace the value of their lost resin into the chipboard. Bridge LJ accepted, in line with the long history of such

[127] Eg *Foskett v McKeown* [2001] 1 AC 102.

[128] Eg *Henry v Hammond* (n 27).

[129] Eg *Dudley v Champion* [1893] 1 Ch 101.

[130] *Borden (UK) Ltd v Scottish Timber Products* [1981] Ch 25, 35 (Bridge LJ).

[131] *Borden (UK) Ltd* (n 130).

analogies in English law,[132] that there is an analogy between tracing and physical mixture, but denied that there was any such analogy between tracing and a situation where the claimant's thing is simply destroyed:

> I can well see the force of that argument if the goods mixed are all of a homogenous character. ... But a mixture of heterogeneous goods in a manufacturing process wherein the original goods lose their character and what emerges is a wholly new product, is in my judgment something entirely different.[133]

It might be argued that a person who turns someone else's thing into a wholly new product, without his consent, is exercising a power over that person in destroying her rights without her consent. There is very little authority to suggest, however, that the owner who has lost her title in this way can claim the product, on the basis that it represents a right obtained in consideration for the destruction of her vested rights. According to Moore-Bick J in *Glencore International AG v Metro Trading International Inc*,[134] the claimant who wishes to claim her thing despite a physical change must show that it has *not* been so fundamentally altered as to extinguish her title. In such a situation, she can characterize what the defendant has done as a mixture and make claims in respect of the product. But this is so only insofar as the original materials can be identified. Once 'the goods can no longer be regarded as remaining in existence as a substantial component of the product' ... 'property in them must be considered to have passed to the [manufacturer] ... by accession'.[135]

The implication is that the kind of legal power presupposed by tracing differs fundamentally from a capacity to alter rights by altering physical things. There are two important differences, which illustrate the normatively distinct character of the kind of powers that are at issue in the tracing case law, as opposed to other capacities to act in a manner that has consequences for the rights of others. 6.64

First, taking the example of A destroying B's title to his cake by eating it, there is a distinction arising from the fact that A's ability to eat cake is not conferred on him by the legal system; that physical ability would exist even in the absence of any legal rules recognizing and regulating titles to cakes. It is true that the destructive effect on B's rights of A's decision to exercise a physical ability of this kind is, in a sense, a consequence of a choice made by the legal system. We can say that B's title to the cake has been destroyed by A's decision only in the context of a legal system that recognizes such titles to edible chattels in the first place. However, the destructive effects of A's actions on B's title, in this example, do not represent a freestanding choice made by the legal system. These effects are a logical corollary of the decision to allow B to enjoy rights that are contingent on the existence of physical objects in the world in the first place. If rights of this kind are to exist at all, their content will depend on features of the physical universe that the legal system cannot determine, but can only respond to. The only way to prevent B's losing his title to a piece of 6.65

[132] See Chapter 2, Section 2.1.2 this volume.
[133] *Borden (UK) Ltd* (n 130).
[134] [2001] 1 All ER (Comm) 103.
[135] *Glencore International AG* (n 134) 166.

cake, in the face of A's decision to eat the relevant piece, is to reject the possibility that anyone could have such a title in the first place.

6.66 By contrast, it is perfectly consonant with the logic of B's rights for those rights to survive an exchange transaction. Suppose that A, having stolen B's cake, advertises it for sale in his bakery and later sells it to X. While it would have been conceptually impossible to say that B could enforce his original title to the cake in the situation where it had been eaten by A, no such problem arises in this case. It makes as much sense to say that X must refrain from taking possession of B's cake as it did prior to the sale. If the law is nevertheless to refuse to allow B to enforce his title against X, on the grounds that A was a mercantile agent who sold the cake in the ordinary course of his business,[136] this is a positive choice to depart from the logic of B's original right. In this scenario, the destructive consequence of A's choice on B's rights results from a specific decision by the legal system, rather than responding to the logic of B's original rights.

6.67 Secondly, the two scenarios attribute a different significance to A's rational agency as a person. If, without meaning to, I accidentally destroy my neighbour's cake—for example, if it happens to be on the floor and I step on and smash it—the fact that I had no intention of destroying it (let alone doing anything to my neighbour's title to it) will have no bearing on the outcome. The destructive effect on her title would happen automatically in response to any chain of events leading to the destruction of the cake, even if no person were involved at all and the cake had been eaten by a cat or destroyed in an earthquake.

6.68 By contrast, whether a *nemo dat* exception like the currency of money operates in a given situation will normally depend on the character of the transaction purportedly engaging the exception: the status of a recipient as a 'purchaser' who has given 'value' ultimately depends on exactly what has been agreed between that purchaser and the person he is dealing with. If the transaction is void,[137] or was never intended to involve any transfer of legal rights,[138] it will not be effective in conferring a defence against the claims of the original right-holder. It is impossible to determine whether a transaction has these characteristics without reference to the intentions of the parties to it, in accordance with the ordinary rules for the interpretation of contracts. While the donee of the power need not have any conscious intention of depriving the object of her rights, he must have an objectively discernable intention to dispose of the object's asset in exchange for some consideration supplied by his counterparty. Absent such an intention, it would not be possible to characterize the transaction as a disposition for value in favour of the purchaser.

[136] Factors Act 1889, s 2.

[137] Eg *Clark v Shee and Johnson* (1774) 1 Cowp 197, 98 ER 1041; *Lipkin Gorman* (n 46).

[138] Eg *Worcester Works Finance Ltd v Cooden* [1972] 1 QB 210, a case concerned with the Sale of Goods Act 1893, s 25, the predecessor of s 24 of the 1979 Act. In holding that there had been a genuine 'disposition' within the meaning of the section, engaging the rule conferring title on the purchaser from the seller in possession, the court relied on the intentions of the seller as objectively understood by the purchaser: 'It is perfectly clear that at that time, when Mr Gillingham collected the car, it was understood that if they retook the car, the defendants would not attempt to pursue Griffiths in regard to the cheque; and it was on this basis that Griffiths cheerfully handed over the key and probably the log book as well' (Phillimore LJ at 219).

6.69 This characteristic of the powers at issue in the case law governing claims to traceable proceeds can be explained by reference to Raz's account of legal powers as 'normatively, not causally, effective'.[139] In his view, legal powers do not include all abilities to influence events in the world, such that some event takes place that the law recognizes as effecting a change in legal relations. A legal power must be the ability to act such that *one's own act* is the very event recognized by law as effecting the legal change. The distinction is illustrated by the difference between a factual ability to persuade A to make a gift of A's property rights to B and the legal power to convey one's own property rights to B.[140] Raz suggests that we can define the exercise of legal powers, as distinct from other acts that bring about a change in legal relations, on the basis that the law permits such actions to have this effect because they will 'standardly be performed only if the person concerned wants to secure these legal consequences'.[141] In other words, a person has a legal power only if his intentional act is not merely a cause for a change in the legal situation of another, but is treated by the law as a justification for that change.

6.70 However, paradoxically, he also argues that a legal power is not necessarily a sub-category of the class of 'rights' because there are situations in which one may have a power to act without also having a liberty to exercise the power at will (since one has a duty not to exercise the power in certain circumstances or unless certain conditions are met). Company directors and agents are the examples that he suggests; he also presents a thief, in a legal system that recognizes market overt,[142] as a person who 'has the power, but not the right, to sell stolen property in the open market'.[143] His argument is that people in this position are undoubtedly power-holders but their powers are not conferred upon them by the legal system in their own interest. As such, these powers are not properly characterized as rights, since the normative guidance which they provide (to their holders and to duty-bearers within the legal system) has nothing to do with the protection of the interests of the power-holder.[144]

6.71 This distinction between right and power, as explained by Raz,[145] captures the paradoxical character of the situation of such persons as the thief selling in market

[139] J Raz, 'Voluntary Obligations and Normative Powers' (1972) 42 Proceedings of the Aristotelian Society 79, 80.

[140] Raz (n 139): 'I may be able to bring it about that my wife will make a gift of all her property to me, but it is she, not I, who has the power to make a gift of her property.' The law may take account of the means of persuasion employed by the husband in these circumstances, in order to decide whether the wife has properly exercised her power to make the gift or if her exercise of that power is vitiated by undue influence or duress, but the ability to persuade is not itself a legal power although, at its boundaries, its consequences are regulated by law.

[141] Raz (n 139) 81.

[142] By the common law doctrine of market overt (codified in statutory form in the Sale of Goods Act 1893, s 22) the buyer of a stolen chattel in an open market, if purchased in accordance with the usages of that market, obtained a good title to the chattel provided that he was a good faith purchaser without notice of the defect in his vendor's title. The doctrine was abolished in England by the Sale of Goods (Amendment Act) 1994, s 1. For a historical survey of its operation in England, see PM Smith, 'Valediction to Market Overt' (1997) The American Journal of Legal History 225.

[143] Raz (n 139) 82.

[144] For Raz's general theory of rights as protective of interests, see J Raz, 'On the Nature of Rights' (1984) 93 Mind 194.

[145] Some authors may reject this definition of 'rights', but nothing turns on this debate for the purposes of the argument in the text: see M Kramer, N Simmonds, and H Steiner, *A Debate Over Rights* (OUP 1998).

overt. The donee, in this situation, is not at liberty to exercise a power for his own benefit (like the agent or the company director) or at all (like the thief in market overt); nevertheless, it is true to say he has that power and can validly exercise it in the forbidden circumstances. Even a person who has a legal duty *not* to exercise a power can, without contradiction, be said to have the power itself, because the law recognizes his decision to act in breach of duty as a valid justificatory reason why the rights of others should be altered.

6.72 The question that then arises is why the law takes the intentions of a wrongdoer seriously in this way. The primary reason, which seems to operate across the broad range of situations where these powers exist, is the protection of strangers to the relationship between the claimant and the defendant, especially purchasers for value. It is from the perspective of the stranger dealing with the wrongdoer, in a market context, that the objectively discernable intention of the donee of the power can be effective in depriving the claimant of rights. The donee of such a power, therefore, possesses a capacity to make legally significant decisions affecting the legal rights of the object for reasons that are extrinsic to the relationship between the donee and the object.[146] Such an alteration may occur in equity, when it may be said that the subject matter of the claimant's rights have been transferred,[147] or at law, when it may be said that the claimant's rights against a stranger have been directly varied.[148]

6.4.4. Defining a relationship of control of assets: content of the duty

6.73 A private power, then, may be defined as an objective capacity, however arising, to vary the vested rights of another person by one's own voluntary act. We have seen that such a power has a distinctive transactional character, with the law treating the objectively discernable intention of the donee as normatively relevant to the question whether the claimant's rights have been varied. In this sense, tracing can be contrasted with doctrines like accession and specification, which involve the destruction of rights by virtue of some event that may or may not be the result of human agency.

6.74 However, not all powers that have this transactional character give rise to claims to traceable proceeds. For example, it has been plausibly argued that the common law right to rescind a voidable contract for the sale of goods is best understood as a kind of legal power.[149] On this analysis, the vendor's title to the goods sold initially passes to the purchaser under the contract for sale;[150] the vendor, by rescinding the

[146] They may be justified by elements of the relationship between the object and the third party, as in cases where the donee's power exists because the object's conduct, from the perspective of the third party, estops her from denying the donee's capacity to bind her. This does not, however, alter the paradoxical character of the situation as between object and donee.

[147] See Chapter 7 this volume. [148] See Chapter 8 this volume.

[149] B Häcker, 'Proprietary Restitution After Impaired Consent Transfers: A Generalised Power Model' (2009) 68 CLJ 324, at 336.

[150] *Cundy v Lindsay* (1878) 3 App Cas 459, 464 (Lord Cairns LC), describing a voidable contract for sale of goods as a 'contract passing [the] property [in the goods], even although ... that contract might afterwards be open to a process of reduction, upon the ground of fraud'.

contract, also rescinds the transfer of title[151] and re-vests legal title in himself.[152] Prior to the decision to rescind, the seller can be said to have a legal power correlative to a liability in the buyer under the initial contract of sale, and this power shares the structure of other private powers. It is a capacity, by one's intentional act, to deprive another person (the buyer) of a right (the title obtained under the voidable contract of sale) that is already vested in him (this follows from the conclusion that the initial transfer of title was voidable rather than void, implying that title did pass to the buyer prior to the seller's decision to rescind). However, the purchaser under such a voidable contract obviously has no right to claim any asset acquired by the vendor in consideration for his exercise of this power. In *Car and Universal Finance v Caldwell*, for example, the claimant had rescinded a contract that he had been induced to enter into by fraud; if he had been paid a sum of money by a third party in consideration for his decision to rescind the contract,[153] it would hardly have been open to the fraudster to object to the transaction and to demand the money as a substitute for his lost title to the car. There is no duty owed to the object of the power, in such a case, and therefore no room for a claim to traceable proceeds.

Granting the obvious point that no claim will arise in a case like this—where the donee of a power holds that power for his own exclusive benefit and owes no duties at all to the object of that power—we need to know what kind of duty is necessary to justify a claim to traceable proceeds. Is it sufficient for a person to hold a power and simultaneously owe some duty to the object of that power, or must there be a closer connection between power and duty? Must the duty prescribe or proscribe some particular type or standard of conduct? 6.75

It seems that the mere existence of a duty to the claimant, which co-exists with the existence of a power over the claimant, is not enough to generate a claim to traceable proceeds. For example, in *Kirkham v Peel*,[154] it is arguable the claimant had retained his title to his goods but had transferred possession to the defendants, authorizing them as his agents to sell his title to the goods and remit the net proceeds obtained to him. If so, they possessed a common law power to deprive him of his title to those goods by selling them. In addition, they owed him a duty to account to him for their transactions, which they breached by adding false items to the accounts that they remitted to him. Nevertheless, as has been explained, his claim to the traceable proceeds of the goods that they had sold failed. Jessel MR denied the claim on the basis that the defendants' duty, which they had breached, had nothing to do with the sales that the claimant authorized them to carry out. They were not in the same position as a factor 'who sells single articles and whose duty it is to remit the necessary proceeds to his principal'.[155] Similarly, in both *Henry v Hammond*[156] and 6.76

[151] For criticism of this analysis as conflating the rules of contract-formation with the rules for the passing of title to goods, see W Swadling, 'Rescission, Property and the Common Law' (2005) 121 LQR 123.

[152] *Car and Universal Finance v Caldwell* [1965] 1 QB 525.

[153] For example, if he had contracted to sell his title to the car to a third person once he recovered it, and had received the purchase price in advance.

[154] *Kirkham* (n 23). The facts are discussed at paras 6.13–6.15 this chapter.

[155] See para 6.15 this chapter.

[156] *Henry* (n 27).

King v Hutton,[157] the claim failed because the agent or stockbroker did not owe a duty to segregate the proceeds of the transactions affecting the claimant's rights. Thus, it seems the power to deal with the assets of the claimant must be coupled with a duty that relates in some way to the specific asset sold, and to its proceeds.

6.77 It is also not enough for the defendant to hold a power to deal with the claimant's asset, coupled with a duty to the claimant that relates to that asset in some way. For example, every equitable interest in land is susceptible to a *nemo dat* defence under the Land Registration Act 2002 (registered land),[158] the Land Charges Act 1972 (some equitable interests in unregistered land),[159] or the doctrine of notice (equitable interests in unregistered land that are not registrable land charges). In the context of registered land, certain legal interests, such as some easements arising by prescription or implication,[160] are also subject to the same defences. In a sense, then, it might be said that every registered proprietor of a title to land has a power to destroy the rights of the holders of these lesser interests on a conveyance. Such a registered proprietor will also owe these right-holders duties that relate in some way to the land: to comply with the requirements of a restrictive covenant, for example, or not to interfere with the exercise of a prescriptively acquired easement. However, it is implausible to suppose that every time a right of this kind is destroyed by such a conveyance, the right-holder is entitled to the traceable proceeds of the conveyance. Suppose that when A sells his land to X, a restrictive covenant over the land held by B ceases to be enforceable because X has a defence. There is no authority that suggests that B can demand a share of the purchase price of the land from A, on the basis that this purchase price was obtained in consideration for a transaction destructive of B's rights. The simple answer to such an argument, at the level of principle, is that selling land affected by a restrictive covenant is not, in itself, necessarily a breach of the covenant. The duty owed by the landowner to the holder of the covenant concerns his use of the physical land but not his powers of disposition as a landowner, which he is free to exercise entirely for his own ends and without taking any account whatsoever of the interests of the holder of the restrictive covenant. For this reason, the holder of the restrictive covenant has no right to insist that the decision to transfer or assign the landowner's title be treated as entered into for his benefit, even when the transfer or assignment has a destructive effect on his rights.

6.78 Contrast *Buhr v Barclays Bank*,[161] where a claimant did succeed in claiming the traceable proceeds of a conveyance on the grounds that, as a result of the operation of a *nemo dat* defence, the conveyance had destroyed its rights. In 1989, Barclays Bank had been granted a second mortgage over unregistered land. Such a mortgage is a class C land charge,[162] which must be registered on the land charges register to bind a purchaser for value of the relevant land.[163] By mistake, the bank registered its charge against the wrong address, so that the registration had no effect for the purposes of the statute. The mortgagors, Mr and Mrs Buhr, subsequently sold their

157 *King* (n 27).
158 Land Registration Act 2002, s 29.
159 Land Charges Act 1972, s 4.
160 Land Registration Act 2002, sch 3, para 3.
161 [2001] EWCA Civ 1223.
162 Land Charges Act 1972, s 2(4)(i).
163 Land Charges Act 1972, s 4(5).

title to the land, and the purchase price was paid into their solicitors' client bank account. The effect of the sale was to destroy the bank's mortgage; by the operation of the Land Charges Act 1972, the purchasers took the Buhrs' title to the land free from Barclays' right to possession of that land, and its power to sell that title in the event of the Buhrs' default on their debt. The Court of Appeal held that Barclays had a proprietary claim to the money that had been paid into the solicitors' client account, on the grounds that the money represented the traceable proceeds of their mortgage. Arden LJ held that such a claim would arise 'automatically and as a matter of law' whenever a 'mortgagor makes a disposition of the mortgaged property in a manner which destroys the mortgagee's estate in the mortgaged property'.[164] As this reasoning suggests, the destructive effect of a transaction on the rights of the claimant mortgagee is one important reason why the mortgagee should be entitled to the proceeds of that transaction. However, it is not the only reason: if it were, the reasoning would equally apply to the case where land subject to an unregistered restrictive covenant is sold, with the effect of destroying the rights under the covenant. In explaining why the principle applied in favour of the mortgagee, Arden LJ emphasized that a mortgagor could be said to owe a 'fiduciary'[165] duty to a mortgagee. She also characterized the sale by the Buhrs as 'unauthorised'; since the transaction was unauthorized, the bank 'could adopt ... [the] transaction and thus retrospectively make the Buhrs its agent.'[166] This analysis implies that the mortgagors' legal power to sell the legal estate in the circumstances of the case was one that could be rightly exercised only with the consent or authority of the mortgagee. The mortgagors' duty to the mortgagee does not relate merely to the physical land, but also captures their decisions to deal with the mortgaged title in a manner prejudicial to the interests of the mortgagee.[167]

If we compare *Buhr* to cases like *Kirkham v Peel*, the character of the link between power and duty that is necessary becomes clear. Claims based to traceable proceeds arise when the defendant holds a power to vary the rights of the claimant against a third party *and* owes the claimant a duty as to his decision to exercise that very power. In *Kirkham v Peel*, the agents had the power to sell the principal's goods and also, separately, had a duty to pay him an abstract amount of money equivalent to the proceeds of sale of the goods. They did not owe him a duty to account for the proceeds of each individual sale of his goods, ie each individual exercise of their power to vary his rights. Like the landowner bound by a restrictive covenant that could be extinguished by a transfer, they held a power over, and owed a duty to, the same person, but this was not enough to entitle him to claim the proceeds of their exercise of power when they breached the unrelated duty. By contrast, in *Buhr v Barclays Bank*, the Buhrs owed the bank, as their mortgagee, a specific duty not to destroy its security by conveying the mortgaged title without its consent. The duty 6.79

164 *Buhr* (n 161) [45]. 165 *Buhr* (n 161) [47]. See para 6.80 this chapter.
166 *Buhr* (n 161) [49].
167 Compare *Hughes v Howard* (1858) 25 Beav 575 (surrender of a mortgaged lease by a mortgagor) and *Leigh v Burnett* (1885) 29 Ch D 231 (renewal of a mortgaged lease by a mortgagor).

governed the exercise of the particular power, which the mortgagors could not be said to have held free from any duty to their mortgagee.

6.80 This structure of a duty that affects the exercise of a particular power is often linked to the idea of fiduciary relationship.[168] Fiduciary relationships, in turn, are often associated with certain paradigmatic obligations owed by trustees and agents,[169] like the duty not to profit from one's position and the duty to avoid conflicts of interest. However, as Arden LJ's description of a mortgagor as a fiduciary in *Buhr v Barclays Bank*[170] suggests, the existence of a fiduciary duty in this second sense is not a condition for the availability of a claim. A mortgagor is under no duty to promote the interests of the mortgagee when exercising her power to convey the mortgaged estate. If she has obtained the consent of the mortgagee to a sale that will effectively destroy the mortgagee's security—for example, because the proceeds of sale will be adequate to discharge the debt owed to the mortgagee—it is no objection to the transaction that the mortgagor will realize a surplus for her personal benefit and has chosen the purchaser for this reason. Thus, the fact that the donee of a power may have a liberty to exercise that power for his own self-interest, and to profit from his position as power-holder, is no obstacle to claiming the proceeds of his transactions when he exercises the power in breach of some other duty governing when or if he exercises the power.

6.81 In *Ex parte Kingston*,[171] for example, the defendant was a county treasurer, a statutory office that authorized him to receive public money for various purposes, including the payment of the local police. He opened separate bank accounts for the purpose of receiving this money and using it for the public purposes, but then began to draw on one of the accounts in order to make payments into his personal account, which was held at the same bank. He became overdrawn on his personal bank account, partly as a result of restoring the credit balance of the accounts he held in his public capacity to what they ought to have been, and eventually became bankrupt. His banker sought to appropriate the credit balance of all his accounts, including the ones labelled public, to pay off the indebtedness on the overdrawn personal account, but it was argued that the public money could be traced into the various accounts and they were, therefore, held on trust for the county. One of the arguments made by counsel for the bank was that Kingston could not be a trustee or a fiduciary, because he was free to profit from his position as a public official. Mellish LJ accepted that Kingston did not owe any duty not to make a profit out of his office, but held that this made no difference to the claim based to traceable proceeds. The credit balance of the account counted as the proceeds of the public money, and 'the mere circumstance of the treasurer being allowed to make a profit from them'[172] did not provide an argument to the contrary.

6.82 Thus, it is the existence of a duty relating to the actual transactions undertaken in the particular circumstances that is central to the claim to traceable proceeds. It encompasses cases where the duty of the donee of the power is not to exercise it at

[168] Eg P Miller, 'Justifying Fiduciary Duties' (2013) McGill Law Journal 58.
[169] See para 6.20 this chapter.
[170] *Buhr* (n 161) [47].
[171] (1871) LR 6 Ch App 632.
[172] *Ex parte Kingston* (n 171) 639.

all, as where he is a recipient under a contract that has been rescinded in equity,[173] or a thief of cash. It also includes cases where the donee is entitled to exercise the power for his own ends, but only for a limited purpose; thus, a mortgagee is obliged to account to the mortgagor for the surplus proceeds obtained in the exercise of its power of sale[174] and the same is true for a pledgee.[175] These are duties that vary considerably in their content, in terms of the standard of concern for the interests of the claimant that they mandate, but they share the common characteristic of being particular to a specific power to deal with a third person in a manner that varies the rights of the claimant. It seems, therefore, that it is a duty that is linked to the decision to exercise a power that is required for the claim to be available; the actual content of the duty, while relevant for many purposes, has no bearing on whether the claimant is entitled to claim the proceeds of an exercise of a power of this kind in breach of duty.

6.5. Conclusions: Identifying a Relationship of Control of Assets

We have seen that claims to traceable proceeds are available in a wide range of situations that are unified by the formal structure of the legal relationship between claimant and defendant: the fact that the defendant has a legal power to deal with or dispose of rights vested in the claimant, coupled with a duty governing the exercise of the power in some circumstances. Despite their differences, these relationships share a normative character that is reflected in their formal structure. In each case, the defendant's power has been conferred on him for ends that are neither his own nor that of the claimant; the power is conferred on him for instrumental reasons, with the aim of protecting third parties and facilitating goals of the legal system that are not particular to the ends of either claimant and defendant. The defendant's loss of autonomy in the tracing context is thus accounted for by the instrumental character of the powers that he is exercising when entering into a transaction captured by the tracing rules—a justification that holds regardless of the factual context of his relationship to the claimant. 6.83

We can identify the existence of a relationship of control of assets, therefore, in any case where the claimant has a legal power to vary the rights of the claimant in relation to some asset, owes the claimant a duty not to exercise that power in some circumstances, and is able to validly exercise the power even where this represents a breach of the relevant duty. This account of the law allows us to determine whether or not a claim to traceable proceeds is available in some situation by reference to a two-stage inquiry. Is there a power to vary the claimant's rights in relation to some particular asset? Is there a duty governing the exercise of that very power, which is owed to the claimant? This two-stage inquiry offers a more focused guide to determining when claims based to traceable proceeds should be available rather 6.84

173 *El Ajou* (n 34). 174 Law of Property Act 1925, s 105.
175 *Mathew v T M Sutton Ltd* [1994] 1 WLR 1455.

than the more contested concepts of fiduciary duties or property rights. Unlike these concepts, it allows us to isolate the elements in the fact situation that justify the subordination of the defendant's decision-making to the claimant that ultimately underpins the tracing concept. Chapters 7 and 8 briefly analyse the circumstances in which these relationships have been recognized to exist, at law and in equity.

7

Control of Assets in Equity

A beneficiary under an express trust is the paradigm case of the person with an equitable claim to traceable proceeds. The courts have always characterized such a beneficiary as vulnerable to another's power to deal with his assets, and thus as entitled to claim the traceable proceeds of a transaction that involves a wrongful exercise of that power. 7.01

A beneficiary may be vulnerable to exercises of power by an express trustee in a double sense. First, as the holder of the trust asset, a trustee has inherent powers to deal with that asset, varying the legal position of the beneficiary as against third parties so far as that asset is concerned. Secondly, an express trustee may have been given various equitable powers to deal directly with the equitable rights of the beneficiary, extinguishing or varying these rights by an exercise of these powers. 7.02

This chapter argues that it is the inherent powers of an express trustee to deal with the trust asset—not his equitable powers to vary the beneficial interest—that explain the availability of claims to the traceable proceeds of his transactions. This structure—the claimant has the benefit of an equitable interest in respect of some asset, and another person has a power to deal with that asset—is then shown to justify tracing in a number of contexts where equitable powers are non-existent or irrelevant but where the holder of the power is not at liberty to exercise the legal power as he or she pleases. The requirement that the holder of the power be under obligations that relate to her exercise of that particular power also explains why there are some equitable rights in respect of assets that do not generate any claims to the traceable proceeds of those assets. 7.03

7.1. The Nature of Equitable Powers

The traditional definitions of equitable powers reflect the long-standing controversy as to the proper analysis of equitable rights, as giving rise to either obligations with unusual features[1] or property rights with unusual features.[2] Thus, Sugden defines an equitable power in the language of obligation, as a capacity to create duties binding on particular persons: he calls them 'declarations or decisions operating only on the conscience of the person in whom the legal interest is vested'.[3] Farwell, on the other 7.04

[1] Eg FW Maitland, *Equity* (Cambridge 1909).
[2] Eg AW Scott, 'The Nature of the Rights of the Cestui que Trust' (1917) 17 Columbia L Rev 269.
[3] E Sugden, *A Practical Treatise of Powers* (8th edn, H Sweet 1861) 45.

hand, uses the language of property. He says that equitable powers 'are such as affect the equitable, not the legal, estate or interest: i.e., where the legal interest is properly vested in one or more, but the power of disposing of the beneficial interest is in some other person'.[4]

7.05 As both definitions make clear, in their different ways, the fact that the subject matter of an equitable right is itself usually a legal[5] right[6] complicates our understanding of what an equitable power is and does. The holder of an equitable interest in some asset has a right that is immediately enforceable against another person in that other's capacity as the holder of the relevant asset; he normally[7] gains similar rights against other people only if they themselves acquire the asset in question or other rights derivative from it.[8] As a result, an additional layer of legal relations is introduced into the picture of the private power as a capacity to deal with the rights of someone else. In the case of an equitable power, the object of the power has rights in respect of some asset, and that asset itself is necessarily vested in a different person, who may well be the donee of the power (as where he is a trustee). The donee of the power, in this scenario, has inherent power to deal with the assets because they are vested in him; in addition, he may well have further powers to deal with the rights of the objects of the power directly.

7.06 Put in Hohfeldian terms, the standard case is one where T has a claim-right correlative to a duty owed to him by X, and himself owes B a duty as to his exercise of this right against X. This is the situation where, for example, there is a trust of a bank account that is in credit. The trustee (T) is owed a debt by the bank (X), and owes his beneficiary (B) a duty as to whether he undertakes any transactions that reduce, increase, or extinguish the debt. The same analysis holds in relation to a trust of a title to a tangible thing, such as land; the trustee (T) is owed a duty of non-interference with the thing by every subject of the legal system (X), and owes the beneficiary (B) duties as to whether he enforces, varies, or extinguishes those duties (for example, by granting a lease of the land to one member of class X and thus, inter alia, extinguishing X's pre-existing duty of non-interference with the land).[9]

[4] See CJW Farwell, *A Concise Treatise on Powers* (3rd edn, Stevens & Sons 1916) 3.

[5] In the broad sense of a right recognized by the legal system. It need not be a legal right in the narrow sense of a common law rather than equitable right.

[6] For the 'right to a right' conception of equitable interests, see B McFarlane and R Stevens, 'The Nature of Equitable Property' (2010) 4 Journal of Equity 1. Although the significance of this feature of equitable interests has been contested, it is generally accepted that they do have it: see, eg, J Penner, 'The (True) Nature of the Beneficiary's Equitable Proprietary Interest Under a Trust' (2014) 27 Canadian Journal of Law and Jurisprudence 473, 475.

[7] An exception is the restrictive covenant which, although an equitable interest, does not bind only the original covenantor and his successors in title but also affects any stranger who makes use of the land in breach of the terms of the covenant: *Re Nisbet and Potts Contract* [1906] 1 Ch 386.

[8] *Burgess v Wheate* (1759) 96 ER 67; *MCC Proceeds Inc v Lehman Brothers International Ltd (Europe)* [1998] 4 All ER 675. Penner characterizes this element of third party liability as reflecting a 'successor' rather than a 'trespassory' conception of rights in rem: J Penner, 'Duty and Liability in Respect of Funds' in J Lowry and L Mistelis (eds), *Commercial Law: Perspectives and Practice* (LexisNexis Butterworths 2006) 215.

[9] See S Douglas and B McFarlane, 'Defining Property Rights' in J Penner and HE Smith (eds), *Philosophical Foundations of Property Law* (OUP 2013) 226.

7.07 The term 'equitable power' usually refers to a power to alter the T–B relationship, altering or extinguishing T's duty to B. The exercise of such a power, in itself, leaves the T–X relationship unaltered, although it will often produce a duty or a liberty to alter that relationship[10] and—where the trustee is the holder of the equitable power—may coincide with his decision to do so. Examples include powers of appointment, which may be held either by trustees or by third parties, and powers of sale or investment, which are conventionally held by trustees themselves. However, quite apart from the existence of such powers, T will necessarily possess the legal capacity to alter the T–X relationship, by virtue of his status as the person holding the right correlative to X's duty. Such an alteration will have inevitable legal consequences for B, producing a double sense in which it could be said that a power exists in equity.

7.08 The point can be illustrated by comparing a donee of a common law power, such as an agent, with the paradigm donee of equitable powers, the trustee. A common law power exists, for example, in a case where P, the principal, holds a legal title to Blackacre and authorizes his agent, A, to deal with or dispose of that title. A trustee, T, who holds his title to Whiteacre on trust for B may have various equitable powers to deal with or dispose of B's beneficial interest: for example, he may hold his title on trust for B and her husband for their joint lives, with a power to appoint the remainder to one or more of B's children at his discretion, and with the survivor of B and her husband taking the remainder in default of appointment. In addition to such dispositive powers, he may also have administrative powers in equity. For example, the terms of the settlement may authorize T to grant short leases of Whiteacre, but not to grant any long leases or mortgages.[11]

7.09 In the case of the common law power, A's attempt to exercise the power—for example, by mortgaging P's title to Blackacre to Bank M—could have one of two possible consequences, so far as P's legal relations to Bank M are concerned. Either the exercise of power will be effective,[12] and Bank M will gain a new set of rights and remedies directly enforceable against P, or it will be ineffective and nothing will happen; Bank M will think it has obtained a mortgage of P's title to Blackacre and will be mistaken. The same analysis would hold if A had been authorized to draw on P's bank account with Bank D. Either the attempt to make such a withdrawal from the account would reduce Bank D's debt, owed to P, or it would not. The supposed exercise of a common law power either directly intervenes in the legal relations between the object of the power and a third party, or it is a nullity.[13]

[10] See Sugden (n 3) cited in *Re Brown* (1886) 32 Ch D 597, 601 (Fay J): 'The legal interest is not divested by the execution of the power, but equity will compel the person seised of it to clothe the estate created with the legal right'.

[11] In the absence of express provision in the trust instrument, restricting his powers, T would be authorized to exercise 'all the powers of an absolute owner' for the purpose of performing his trust functions; see Trusts of Land and Appointment of Trustees Act 1996, ss 6 and 8.

[12] Whether because it is authorized or because, for example, Bank M was entitled to rely on A's ostensible authority to enter into the transaction: *Freeman & Lockyer v Buckhurst Park Properties Ltd* [1964] 2 QB 480.

[13] As between the object of the power and the third party. It is likely that the third party would have remedies against the wrongdoing agent personally in such a case: for example, via the tort of deceit or by exercising its power to rescind the transaction and recovering any funds transferred to the agent under it.

7.10 In the case where T is a trustee of title to Whiteacre or the bank account, the situation is more complex. By virtue of his status as a trustee—a holder of the very rights held on trust—T's dealings with his title to Whiteacre will never be a complete nullity.[14] This will be true whether or not he has any specific powers to vary B's beneficial interest, which he intends to exercise when embarking on a transaction. For example, suppose T were to mortgage his title to Whiteacre to Bank M. Assuming T's own consent was genuine and that he complied with all the necessary steps for the creation of such a right, the transaction would be effective at law and would give rise to the mortgage in favour of Bank M. This would be so even where T lacks the equitable power to mortgage his title to Whiteacre, so that his decision to do so constituted a breach of trust.

7.11 It might be argued that, in the absence of an equitable power to enter into such a transaction, held by T, the creation of this mortgage will be irrelevant to B. Her beneficial interest under the trust of T's title to Whiteacre will remain and, unless Bank M has a defence, B can enforce her rights against it as a successor in title to the trustee. However, this in itself represents a change in B's legal relations with a third person: Bank M. Rather than relying on her rights against T, and insisting that T enforce his rights in respect of Whiteacre against any interfering strangers, like Bank M, B is now obliged to deal with Bank M herself if she wants title to Whiteacre to continue to be used for her benefit.

7.12 So, for example, if Bank M seeks an order for possession of Whiteacre, B can no longer demand that T resist the order on the basis of his superior common law title; she will, instead, have to ask the court to refuse the order on the basis that she herself is in possession, or is entitled to possession, and the mortgagee's right is not enforceable against her.[15] If Bank M exercises its power of sale, and transfers T's title to Whiteacre to a purchaser, this transaction will not be a nullity from B's perspective. Although the sale in exercise of the mortgagee's power of sale will not, in itself, overreach her interest under the trust,[16] the purchasers from the mortgagee may have a freestanding defence against her claim.[17] Even if they do not have such a defence, the mortgagee will nevertheless have brought her into a new legal relationship with yet another person—the purchaser—against whom she must enforce any claims she has in respect of the title to Whiteacre.

7.13 These conclusions would flow from the trustee's decision to mortgage his title to Whiteacre even in a situation where Bank M has no defence and B's right is binding

[14] Assuming that the transaction is not void for some freestanding reason, such as the operation of the *non est factum* doctrine.

[15] *Williams & Glyn's Bank v Boland* [1981] AC 487.

[16] Under the Law of Property Act 1925, s 2(1)(ii), a conveyance by a mortgagee in the exercise of its exercise of its power of sale will overreach 'any equitable interest . . . capable of being overreached by such conveyance'. This includes the equity of redemption of the mortgagor and any interests derivative of the equity of redemption, but not a right that takes priority over the equity of redemption. See M Conaglen, 'Mortgagee Powers Rhetoric' (2006) 69 MLR 583, and the Law of Property Act 1925, s 104(1).

[17] Either because they are a bona fide purchaser for value without notice of her equitable interest (unregistered land), or because the transaction in their favour is a registered disposition for value (registered land) and her interest did not have overriding status at the date of the disposition: Land Registration Act 2002, s 29(1) and schedule 3, para 2.

on it as successor in title to the trustee. The grant of a new right in respect of the trust asset, or its outright transfer to a third person, is thus a non-trivial change in the legal position of a beneficiary under a trust even where her right is binding on the transferee. She stands in a new legal relation to the transferee, which does not exactly mirror her relationship to the trustee,[18] and which leaves her rights vulnerable to the decisions of a new person or set of persons.

In addition, of course, her right might not bind a transferee in the first place. Bank M may have a defence which effectively extinguishes B's rights in respect of title to Whiteacre as against the bank and its successors in title. In the context of registered land, a purchaser may rely on the completion by registration of a registered disposition for value.[19] In any other context, where the trust asset is unregistered land[20] or title to a chattel or a chose in action,[21] a purchaser may have the defence of bona fide purchase for value of a legal interest without notice of the equitable interest. Whether one of these defences operates has nothing to do with any specific power to deal with the equitable interest, or vary the terms of the trustee–beneficiary relationship. Title passes to the mortgagee because the trustee has exercised his powers as the holder of legal title to Whiteacre; the extinction of the equitable interest happens by operation of law, as a result of the rule favouring a bona fide purchaser for value of a legal estate (or a purchaser of a registered estate where the land is registered).[22] 7.14

7.2. Control of Assets in Equity: Power to Deal With the Asset, Not the Interest

At the level of principle, therefore, any trustee has a level of control over the trust assets that justifies a claim to traceable proceeds on the part of the beneficiary. This 7.15

[18] In particular, a transferee who is bound by a trust may not be personally liable, as the original trustee would be, for dealing with the trust asset and untraceably spending the proceeds: *Re Montagu's Settlement Trusts* [1987] Ch 264. The transferee would only be liable to the beneficiary for the value of the lost assets if she knew, or ought to have known, that she had received the trust assets in breach of trust: *BCCI (Overseas) Ltd v Akindele* [2001] Ch 437.

[19] Under the Land Registration Act 2002, s 29(1). Unless B was in actual occupation of the land, the mortgagee's legal charge would take priority over her beneficial interest once the registration requirements for creation of a charge were met: Land Registration Act 2002, s 29, and schedule 3, para 2.

[20] *Kingsnorth Finance Co Ltd v Tizard* [1986] 1 WLR 793.

[21] *Macmillan Inc v Bishopsgate Investment Trust plc* [1995] 1 WLR 978.

[22] Contrast the effect of an overreaching transaction, which will occur for assets other than titles to land only when the transaction is within the scope of the equitable powers of the trustee: see D Fox, 'Overreaching' in P Birks and A Pretto (eds), *Breach of Trust* (Hart Publishing 2002) 95 and C Harpum, 'Overreaching, Trustees' Powers and the Reform of the 1925 Legislation' (1990) 49 CLJ 277. In relation to land, s 2 of the Law of Property Act 1925 now provides that a conveyance by two trustees or a trust corporation will have overreaching effect. It is a controversial question whether this section depends on other statutory provisions that widen the powers of trustees of land: for the rival views on this question, see G Ferris and G Battersby, 'The General Principles of Overreaching and the Modern Legislative Reforms 1996-2002' (2003) 119 LQR 94; M Dixon, 'Overreaching and the Trusts of Land and Appointment of Trustees Act 1996' [2000] Conv 267; and N Jackon, 'Overreaching in Registered Land Law' (2006) 69 MLR 214.

is true whether or not that trustee also has any specific equitable powers that directly affect the beneficiary's equitable rights. As a matter of authority, this is reflected by the fact that beneficiaries under trusts are able to trace through the transactions of any defendant who has the power to deal with the trust asset, whether or not the defendant also has any power to deal with their equitable interests in that asset. There are a number of cases in which beneficiaries have succeeded in tracing through the transactions of someone who has no power to vary their equitable interests, but who has been authorized by the trustee to deal with the trust asset directly.

7.16 In *Lane v Dighton*,[23] for example, Dighton was the life tenant under a marriage settlement. He had 'prevailed upon the trustees to let him have £4010, 10s of the trust money',[24] which he then used to buy land.[25] More specifically, he had gained control of the trust assets—shares in the South Sea Company—by virtue of a power of attorney granted to him by the trustees. This power of attorney gave him the legal capacity to deal with the shares, but did *not* give him any power to alter the equitable interests of his wife and children under the terms of the marriage settlement.[26] Their claim to trace through his transactions rested purely on his status as a person with the legal power to deal with the assets held on trust for them, and not his status as a donee of a specifically equitable power.

7.17 In a number of these cases,[27] where the substituting transactions were carried out by agents of trustees, the trustees themselves brought the claim to recover the proceeds. Nevertheless, the judicial language in these cases makes it clear that the trustees were able to do so qua trustees—on behalf of the beneficiaries—as well as in their own capacity as principals in an agency relationship. This was so regardless of whether, under the terms of the trust, it was permissible for the trustees to authorize the particular transaction undertaken by the agent.

7.18 For example, in *Trench v Harrison*,[28] another marriage settlement case, the trust instrument stipulated that the trust money could be used to purchase only certain types of investment: in the case of land, the trustees were authorized to purchase only leasehold estates or heritable estates, which might be either freehold or copyhold. In addition, they were authorized to exercise the power of investment only with the consent of both husband and wife. The life tenant, Harrison, a solicitor, proposed to the trustees that he invest the trust money in a copyhold estate in Cornwall. Without the consent of his wife, the trustees granted Harrison a power of attorney to sell some of the trust consols for this purpose. Having done so, he used the proceeds of sale to get himself admitted to the copyhold, which, rather than being a heritable estate, was for a term of lives. This transaction was outside the scope of the trustees'

[23] (1762) Amb 409, 27 ER 274. [24] *Lane* (n 23).

[25] In fact, he first used the money to buy bank annuities and then declared a trust of these annuities in favour of persons nominated by the vendor of land who, in consideration for this declaration of trust, conveyed title to the land to him. See Chapter 4 this volume, para 4.07.

[26] The settlement did grant the survivor of the marriage, or the couple jointly, a power of appointment among their children, but Dighton had died by the date of the litigation, survived by his widow, and so was never in a position to exercise that power.

[27] Eg *Price v Blakemore* (1843) 6 Beav 507, 49 ER 922; *Trench v Harrison* (1849) 17 Simons 111, 60 ER 1070; *Re Strachan* (1876) 4 Ch D 123; *Birt v Burt* (1877) 11 Ch D 773.

[28] *Trench* (n 27).

powers under the marriage settlement, both because it had been entered into without the consent of the wife, and because the wrong sort of copyhold had been purchased. The Master, having investigated the facts and found that the purchase price of the copyhold represented the proceeds of sale of the trust consols, reported that 'Harrison, in making the purchase ... was to be deemed and considered as an agent acting for and on behalf of the Petitioners *in their character of trustees of the settlement*'.[29]

Counsel for Harrison's creditors, who sought to have the copyhold sold to pay his debts after his death, argued that he could not have purchased it on behalf of the trustees of the settlement because such a purchase was beyond the scope of their powers as trustees. The Vice-Chancellor held that this was irrelevant as between Harrison and the trustees. While he considered that 'questions may hereafter arise between Mrs Harrison and the trustees', on the grounds that the purchase of the copyhold represented a breach of trust, this did not mean that 'as between Harrison and the trustees, he must not be considered to have purchased the copyholds for them'.[30] In itself, this seems to suggest that the trustees were simply bringing a claim against Harrison on their own account, as the donee of a power of attorney and thus as their agent, rather than on account of the beneficiaries and against Harrison as a person dealing with trust assets. However, the Master's opinion suggests that they were relying on their status as trustees, rather than merely as principals, and were bringing their claim on behalf of the beneficiaries. 7.19

In the later case of *Re Strachan*,[31] the Court of Appeal clearly distinguished these two types of claim (the trustee claiming qua principal, in his own right, and the trustee claiming qua trustee, on behalf of his beneficiaries). The trustee in that case, Cooke, had authorized Strachan, a stockbroker, to sell trust consols and invest the proceeds in railway stock. Strachan sold the consols and received a cheque as their price, which he paid into his own bank account. He then became a bankrupt. The Court of Appeal unanimously held that the trustee was entitled to recover as much of the credit balance of the bank account as was attributable to the sale of the trust consols. James LJ and Bramwell JA, citing *Taylor v Plumer*,[32] considered that, even if Cooke had not been a trustee, he would have been able to recover the money on the basis that Strachan was his agent dealing with his cheque. Baggallay JA, although 'much impressed' by *Taylor v Plumer*,[33] did not take a view on what would have happened if the money had not been trust money. However, because it was trust money, all three judges agreed that it was recoverable on the facts. Bramwell JA said that 'if the whole of the money had remained in the hands of the bankers without being drawn out, I think it clear that *the cestui que trust could have claimed it as trust money* traced into their hands, and if on properly attributing the payments any part of it is found to remain there, the same rule must apply to what so remains'.[34] 7.20

[29] *Trench* (n 27) 116; 1073 (emphasis added).
[30] *Trench* (n 27) 119; 1074.
[31] *In Re Strachan* (n 27).
[32] (1815) 3 M & S 562, 105 ER 721, cited by James LJ at *In Re Strachan* (n 27) 127 and by Bramwell JA at 129.
[33] *In Re Strachan* (n 27).
[34] *In Re Strachan* (n 27) 128 (emphasis added).

7.21 The claim, therefore, runs directly between the beneficiary and the trustee's agent. The agent, in such a case, clearly does not have any power to vary the particular equitable interests of the beneficiaries: that is, he has not been authorized to change the content of the duty owed to the beneficiaries by the trustees, or the identity of the beneficiaries to whom the duty is owed. All he has is the capacity, obtained from the trustee, to transfer the subject matter of the trust—for example, the shares in the South Sea company in *Lane v Dighton*—to a third person. This is sufficient power to generate the right to trace through his transactions.

7.22 On this analysis, a relationship of control of assets may potentially exist wherever an equitable right is recognized. This is because, by the very structure of such rights, the power to dispose of the subject-matter of the equitable right will always be vested in some person other than the right-holder. Since all such rights are susceptible to defences that protect purchasers, all such power-holders have the capacity to destroy the equitable right by a transaction. However, the existence of a power of this kind is not enough to generate a claim to the traceable proceeds of its exercise, even where it has the effect of destroying the claimant's equitable right. It is also necessary to show that the power-holder was not at liberty to exercise that power in the circumstances. This requirement of a duty that is linked to the specific power exercised by the defendant explains why many—but not all—equitable rights generate claims to traceable proceeds.

7.3. Vendor–Purchaser 'Constructive Trusts'

7.23 It has been held that, where a vendor has entered into a specifically enforceable contract to sell an asset to a purchaser and then sells that asset to another, in breach of contract, the purchaser under the initial contract may claim the traceable proceeds of the wrongful sale.[35] In such a case, the vendor has the inherent power to convey the asset in question, as its owner, but is under a direct contractual obligation not to exercise the power except in favour of the purchaser. This obligation fetters the specific power of conveyance, such that the purchaser is entitled to insist on injunctive relief to prevent the power from being exercised; this gives rise to a proprietary interest under a 'constructive trust'[36] that entitles the purchaser to claim the proceeds of a sale destructive of that interest.

7.24 Contrast the situation where a landowner enters into a specifically enforceable contract to grant a derivative estate or interest out of his own estate, such as a lease or an easement. Here, too, an equitable interest—an equitable lease[37] or equitable easement[38]—will arise in response to the specifically enforceable contract. However,

[35] *Lake v Bayliss* [1974] 1 WLR 1073, following a dictum of Lord Eldon LC in *Daniels v Davison* (1809) 16 Ves Jun 249, 33 ER 978; *Luxe Holding Ltd v Midland Resources Holding Ltd* [2010] EWHC 1399.

[36] For the view that the purchaser's interest in such a case is not properly characterized as a trust at all; see WJ Swadling, 'The Vendor-Purchaser Constructive Trust' in S Degeling and James Edelman (eds), *Equity in Commercial Law* (Lawbook 2005) Ch 18.

[37] *Walsh v Lonsdale* (1882) LR 21 Ch D 9.

[38] Eg *Celsteel and Others v Alton House Holdings and Another* [1985] 1 WLR 204, overruled on a different point by the Court of Appeal [1986] 1 WLR 512.

there is no authority that, in such a case, the holder of the equitable lease or easement will have any claims to the traceable proceeds of a subsequent sale of the landowner's estate in land, even if he sells it to a purchaser who takes free of the equitable interest. At the level of principle, no such claim should be available. The landowner in such a case has not placed himself under any obligations—specifically enforceable or otherwise—that affect his powers to convey the legal estate. He may have placed himself under a specifically enforceable obligation to grant an easement or a lease, but this obligation does not relate in any way to the power exercised by a conveyance of the legal estate to someone else.

7.4. Recipients of Misdirected Assets

An analysis based on a combination of power and duty raises questions about the position of innocent recipients of misdirected assets. An innocent recipient of trust assets can be made liable to give them up if she still has them when demanded by the beneficiary, but is under no personal obligation to account for their value if she has dissipated them prior to discovering the trust.[39] It is arguable, therefore, that an innocent recipient does not owe any duties to the beneficiary until she discovers that the assets under her control are trust assets; nevertheless, the beneficiary can claim the traceable proceeds of transactions entered into by such a recipient, using the trust assets.[40] 7.25

In this context, the duty to account for the abstract value of assets must be distinguished from the duty to account for specific transactions entered into using those assets. In her capacity as a recipient of the trust asset, such a recipient acquires the inherent power to dispose of that asset to third parties. She is not at liberty to exercise this specific power for her own benefit; the beneficiary is entitled to demand that she exercise the power only to convey the asset to him and she is under a negative duty not to keep the assets for her own benefit in the face of such a demand. When she instead exercises the power to acquire specific assets for her own benefit, therefore, she comes under a similar negative duty in respect of those assets; she must not keep those assets for her own benefit in the face of a demand from the beneficiary. However, as an innocent recipient, she is under no obligation to actively preserve the value of the assets for the benefit of the beneficiary. If the beneficiary cannot point to any specific asset she has obtained by exercising the power to deal with his assets, as where the assets have been untraceably dissipated, he has no grounds for complaint. Her duty, linked to her power to deal with trust assets, disappears when she loses the power by innocently and untraceably disposing of those assets. 7.26

[39] *Re Montagu's ST* [1987] Ch 264.

[40] Eg *Wilson v Foreman* (1782) Dickens 593, 21 ER 402; *Dudley v Champion* [1893] 1 Ch 101; *Barclays Bank v Kalamohan* [2010] EWHC 1383 (Ch).

7.5. Recipients Under Rescinded Transactions

7.27 The distinction between a duty that fetters a specific power, and a duty that does not have any such effect, also explains why a claimant may trace through the transactions of a person who received assets from him under a voidable disposition *after* that disposition has been avoided,[41] but not before.[42]

7.28 Suppose, for example, that B transfers his title to £100 in banknotes to A under the influence of a fraudulent misrepresentation, or undue influence. The effect of this transaction is that B's own title to the £100 is transferred to A, and B gets a power to rescind the transaction instead.[43] While A's title to the £100 is vulnerable to B's exercise of this power of rescission—if B exercises the power, he can obtain an equitable interest in the money—this liability to be divested of a right by the exercise of a power is not the same as a duty governing one's exercise of the right itself. Until the transaction is rescinded, A is at liberty to deal with the title to the money as she pleases; if B chooses not to rescind the transaction, A can point to B's intentional act as a reason why she should be entitled to use the money to pursue her own ends. Once B's power of rescission has been exercised, however, this changes. B gets an equitable interest in the title to the money that, like other equitable interests, is vulnerable to destruction by a conveyance to a bona fide purchaser for value without notice of her equitable interest. A, meanwhile, comes under a new obligation to restore the specific £100 to B. When, instead of doing this, she uses that title to obtain assets for herself, she is now exploiting her control over B's assets and it is unsurprising that a claim to the proceeds of her transactions is available.

[41] Eg *Gladstone v Hadwen* (1813) 1 M & S 517, 105 ER 193; *Small v Attwood* (1831–1832) You 407, 507; 159 ER 1051, 1092; *El Ajou v Dollar Land Holdings plc (No 1)* [1993] 3 All ER 717; *Beverley v Pearce* [2013] EWHC 2627 (Ch); *Bainbridge v Bainbridge* [2016] EWHC 898 (Ch).

[42] *Halifax Building Society v Thomas* [1996] Ch 217; *Box v Barclays Bank* [1998] Lloyd's Rep 185; *Ciro Citterio Menswear plc v Thakrar* [2002] EWHC 662.

[43] See generally B Häcker, 'Proprietary Restitution after Impaired Consent Transfers: a Generalised Power Model' (2009) 68 CLJ 324.

8

Control of Assets at Law

As explained, the concept and significance of 'common law tracing' has been a major source of doubt and discussion in recent years. Questions have been raised[1] about the traditional interpretation of the supposed leading case, *Taylor v Plumer*,[2] and it has been argued that the whole idea of tracing at common law, as opposed to in equity, has been an unfortunate historical misunderstanding that badly distorts our understanding of the general distinction between common law and equitable rights.[3] 8.01

There are three elements of the traditional account of *Taylor v Plumer* that have been challenged on these grounds. The traditional story is that Sir Thomas Plumer once had a common law title to a cheque. By virtue of this title, he obtained a common law title to some gold bullion and share certificates purchased by a person in possession of the cheque and its cash proceeds, Walsh. In order to show that the gold and share certificates were, in fact, the product of his initial cheque, however, he was obliged to rely on the stringent common law tracing rules, which he was luckily able to do because Walsh never paid the cash into a mixed bank account. 8.02

It has been objected that none of these claims are true on an accurate interpretation of the case. First, it is arguable that Walsh was a trustee of his title either to the cheque or to the banknotes obtained in exchange for it,[4] and that Sir Thomas' right to traceable proceeds depended on his status as a beneficiary under this trust, rather than any common law title. Secondly, whatever the status of his right to the original asset, there was no need for him to assert a common law title to the substitute assets in the litigation in the Court of King's Bench, and, in fact, he did not do so: in defending himself against the claim in trover brought by Walsh's assignees in bankruptcy, he could rely on the argument that Walsh had held his title to them on trust for him,[5] which would prevent that title from vesting in assignees in bankruptcy. Finally, given that the case involved a beneficiary under a trust asserting that substitute assets were also held on trust for him, Lord Ellenborough CJ's dicta about the impossibility of tracing into a mixed fund had nothing to do with any distinctive common law principles.[6] Instead, they reflected his understanding of the 8.03

[1] Eg L Smith, 'Tracing in *Taylor v Plumer*: Equity in the Court of King's Bench' [1995] LMCLQ 240.
[2] (1815) 3 M & S 562, 105 ER 721.
[3] S Khurshid and P Matthews, 'Tracing Confusion' (1979) 95 LQR 75.
[4] Khurshid and Matthews (n 3). [5] Smith (n 1).
[6] L Smith, *The Law of Tracing* (OUP 1997) 5.

tracing concept in general—an understanding that was decisively rejected by the Court of Appeal in *Re Hallett's Estate*.[7]

8.04 In *Trustee of FC Jones v Jones*,[8] Millett LJ dismissed these arguments based on the historical facts as irrelevant to the modern law, given that later authoritative decisions[9] had relied on the traditional interpretation of *Taylor v Plumer* in recognizing common law claims based on unauthorized substitution. He said that the authority of these cases could not be undermined by their misunderstanding of an earlier case, since 'that is not how the English doctrine of stare decisis operates'.[10] It is true that the purely historical questions—what actually did happen on the facts of *Taylor v Plumer*, and what Lord Ellenborough CJ thought he was deciding at the time—are of doubtful relevance to the modern law. If, over the next two centuries, the courts had consistently applied *Taylor v Plumer* on the basis of a clear, if factually mistaken, understanding of the principle that justified that decision, that principle would then have a sound footing in English law as a matter of authority. It would make little difference if it turned out, on detailed investigation, that all the later judges had been wrong about the principle operative in Lord Ellenborough CJ's own mind on the facts of the case actually before him; their own decisions would have been sufficient to support the principle that they thought *Taylor v Plumer* supported.

8.05 The problem, however, is that the later authorities are much less clear cut than this: it is as difficult to understand these later cases as it is to interpret *Taylor v Plumer*. The difficulty is not due to a lack of historical data, but instead because of conceptual problems with the traditional accounts based on common law title.[11] It is these conceptual problems that have produced the search for a reading of *Taylor v Plumer*, and the cases following it, that 'does [the least] violence to established doctrines of property and title in English law'.[12]

8.06 This chapter considers what it means for a relationship of control of assets to exist at law, as opposed to in equity, and whether the common law version has distinctive features that justify a distinctive tracing regime and a distinctive remedial response. It argues that a common law right to an asset can justify the availability of a claim to the traceable proceeds of that asset, in circumstances when someone else has the power to deal with or dispose of that right and owes a duty not to exercise the power. This structure explains the wide range of cases where the language of fiduciary relationship has been used to justify the invocation of tracing by a claimant with a common law right, as well the handful of authorities that support the idea of a unique common law claim to traceable proceeds where no fiduciary relationship has been said to exist. It goes on to argue that there is no justification for the theory that such a common law claim requires any special form of tracing or any special type of remedial response. The equitable tracing rules are already available in a number of situations where the claimant is relying on a common law title, and there

[7] (1880) 13 Ch D 696. [8] [1997] Ch 159.

[9] *Banque Belge pour l'Etranger v Hambrouck* [1921] 1 KB 321 (Court of Appeal) and *Lipkin Gorman v Karpnale Ltd* [1991] 2 AC 548 (House of Lords).

[10] *Trustee of FC Jones* (n 8) 169. [11] As discussed in Chapter 6 this volume, Section 6.3.2.

[12] Khurshid and Matthews (n 3) 94.

is no principled reason for restricting their availability to these situations. Rather, as explained in Chapter 3,[13] the restrictive account of the common law tracing rules derives from the mistaken idea that there is a special remedial response to common law tracing—a common law title, of some kind, to the substitute asset. This idea has limited support as a matter of authority and creates serious conceptual difficulties that can be avoided by permitting all common law claimants, and not just some, to make equitable claims to substitute assets.

8.1. The Nature of Common Law Powers

Common law powers have been defined as powers to create or convey a legal estate vested in someone else;[14] by extension, they can be said to include powers to enter into transactions which create or transfer other rights recognized by the courts of the common law. Thus, they include the powers to transfer title to chattels belonging to others, as well as to create or assign choses in action, such as rights to sue under contracts. 8.07

A prototypical example of such a power could be found in the medieval English law in the context of devises of land. In those parts of England where, prior to the Statute of Wills 1540,[15] local custom allowed estates in land to be devised away from a man's heirs, he was also allowed to give his executors a power to sell his estate. In this situation, the estate itself was vested in the heirs until the moment of sale, while the executors had only the ability to convey that estate to the purchaser. The effect of the exercise of the power was to transfer the very rights vested in the heirs directly to the purchaser, without those rights ever being vested in the executors themselves: 8.08

> And this is an amazing proposition in law, but it seems to that it is the nature of a devise and devises have always been used in that way. Thus may a man lawfully acquire a freehold from someone who has nothing, in the same way as a man can get fire from a flintstone even though there is no fire inside the flint.[16]

While such powers to transfer land no longer exist in English law,[17] Babington CJ's dictum captures the distinctive characteristic of those common law powers 8.09

[13] See Chapter 3, Section 3.3.2.1 this volume.

[14] G Thomas, *Thomas on Powers* (2nd edn, OUP 2012) 6.

[15] Before the Statute of Wills, legal title to freehold land in England could not be alienated by will but descended automatically, on death, to the heir of the freeholder. However, title to land held according to the customs of the boroughs of England could be alienated by will, 'like a chattel', even before the Statute of Wills: see Pollock and Maitland, *A History of English Law Before the Time of Edward I* (2nd edn, CUP 1968) 645, and M de W Hemmeon, 'Burgage Tenure in Medieval England III' (1911) 27 LQR 43.

[16] *Farynton v Darell* (1431) YB Trin 9 Hen VI, fo 23, pl 19; translation from J Baker, *Baker and Milsom, Sources of English Legal History: Private Law to 1750* (2nd edn, OUP 2010) 80, 83 (Babington CJ).

[17] Since the Land Transfer Act 1897, the real property of a deceased person has vested directly in his personal representatives (that is, his executors or administrators), rather than in his heirs: see now the Administration of Estates Act 1925, s 1(1). The executor's power to transfer those rights in accordance with the testamentary dispositions of the deceased are not, therefore, powers to transfer rights that are vested in someone else.

that do survive in the modern law. Examples include powers of attorney,[18] a security-holder's power, on default, to sell the right on which the debt is secured,[19] and the authority of an agent to contract with third parties on behalf of his principal,[20] as well as to transfer the principal's legal property rights to third parties.[21] In each of these cases, the effect of an exercise of the power is to directly alter the relationships between the object of the power and other subjects of the legal system. Thus, for example, where an agent acts within the scope of his authority to enter into a contract with a third party on behalf of a person disclosed to be his principal, the new contractual relationship arises between, and only between, the principal and the third party: the obligations created by the contract bind and benefit the principal himself and, unless the circumstances fall within one of a defined set of exceptions to the general rule,[22] the agent can neither sue or be sued on the contract.[23] Similarly, an agent acting within the scope of his authority may directly transfer his principal's legal title to a chattel to a third party: as a result of this transaction, the third party will not have committed any tort in respect of the chattel by taking possession of it, and the duties formerly owed by other subjects of the legal system to the principal will now be owed to the third party.

8.10 As Babington CJ notes, there is something 'amazing' about the effect of these powers. From the perspective of the third party, the valid exercise of the power can enable him to acquire a right by dealing with someone other than the person who is normally able to create that right. From the perspective of the object of the power, the exercise of the power can result in him being deprived of a right, or subjected to an obligation, otherwise than by his own personal act. Both effects may be called amazing because they involve a sharp departure from the *prima facie* rules which govern the transmission and creation of rights in English law: that is, the rule that only a person in whom a right is vested can transfer that right[24] and the rule that only a person who himself enters into a contract can be bound by its terms.[25] The donee of the power, like the flintstone in Babington CJ's simile, is able to give what he himself does not have.

[18] Aldridge defines a power of attorney as 'a document by which one person ("donor") gives another person ("attorney") the power to act on his behalf and in his name': T Aldridge, *Powers of Attorney* (10th edn, Sweet & Maxwell 2007) 1. As this definition suggests, the defining characteristic of such a power is not what the power itself enables the donee to do (which may be very general or highly specific) but the formalities necessary for its creation: Powers of Attorney Act 1971, s 1(1). A power created by these means can be considered simply as an instance of an authority vested in an agent, but is distinctive in that the instrument creating it is subject to special rules of interpretation which do not apply to documents (or spoken words) creating other forms of consensual agency: see P Watts (ed), *Bowstead & Reynolds on Agency* (20th edn, Sweet & Maxwell 2016) paras 3-010 to 3-012.

[19] For the power of sale of a pledgee of a chattel, see *In Re Morritt* (1886) 18 QBD 222; for the mortgagee's power of sale in respect of land, see the Law of Property Act 1925, s 101(1)(i).

[20] See Watts (n 18) para 8-001. [21] Watts (n 18) para 8-126. [22] Watts (n 21).

[23] *Montgomerie v United Kingdom Mutual Steamship Association* [1891] 1 QB 370, 371 (Wright J).

[24] In accordance with the maxim *nemo dat quod non habet* (nobody gives what he does not have).

[25] This follows from the doctrine of privity of contract which, in relation to the burden of contractual obligations, has been regarded as 'so obvious that it hardly needs to be stated: if a contract between A and B provided that C was to pay £100 to A, no-one would suppose that this contract could oblige C to make the payment': H Beale (ed), *Chitty on Contracts* (30th edn, Sweet & Maxwell 2008) paras 18–33.

If we turn this on its head, so that any person able to give what he himself does not have is defined as the donee of a common law power, we are led to the various exceptions to the principle *nemo dat quod non habet* recognized by English law.[26] For example, a seller in possession of goods is able to transfer his buyer's title to those goods by delivering them to a purchaser in good faith without notice of the prior sale.[27] Any person in possession of cash is able to extinguish a superior title by paying the money to a bona fide recipient who has given value for it.[28] The same is true for a negotiable instrument.[29] In all such cases, it might be said that a common law power exists in an the objective sense. The seller in possession or the thief of cash is effectively able to do something very like what the agent of a principal can do by an authorized act: alter the rights of the object of the power against a third party by a particular transaction, without the personal involvement of the object in that transaction. The doctrine of apparent authority also lends a similar power to agents[30] or company directors[31] acting outside the scope of their authority in some circumstances. 8.11

The existence of a power–liability relationship of this kind, coupled with a duty not to exercise the power in the circumstances of the particular transaction, explains a number of the cases where a claimant relies on a common law title to an asset to claim the traceable proceeds of an unauthorized transaction involving that asset. It explains, for example, the claim of a principal to the traceable proceeds of his agent's unauthorized transactions;[32] that of a bailor of assets against a bailee;[33] that of a company against its directors;[34] and that of a mortgagee against a mortgagor.[35] 8.12

In some of these cases, there is a genuine fiduciary relationship between the claimant and defendant. Thus, a company director undoubtedly owes the company fiduciary duties of loyalty in his exercise of his powers to deal with the company's assets, and the same is true for an agent dealing with his principal's assets. In this sense, the claimants in all these cases have equitable rights; the right correlative to a fiduciary duty is certainly one that has historically been recognized by the courts of equity. However, this is not the same as holding an equitable interest in the *assets* 8.13

[26] For an overview of both common law and statutory exceptions to the principle, with a particular focus on security interests, see L Gullifer (ed), *Goode on Legal Problems of Credit and Security* (5th edn, Sweet & Maxwell 2013) 175–89.

[27] Sale of Goods Act 1979, s 24: 'the delivery or transfer . . . has the same effect as if the person making the delivery or transfer were expressly authorized by the owner of the goods to make the same'.

[28] *Miller v Race* (1758) 1 Burr 452, 97 ER 398. See D Fox, 'Bona Fide Purchase and the Currency of Money' (1996) 55 CLJ 547 and *Property Rights in Money* (CUP 2008) 265–303.

[29] *The London Joint Stock Co v Simmons* [1893] AC 201.

[30] Eg *Freeman & Lockyer v Buckhurst Park Properties Ltd* [1964] 2 QB 480.

[31] Eg *Royal British Bank v Turquand* (1856) 6 El & Bl 327, 119 ER 886.

[32] Eg *Burdett v Willett* (1708) 1 Eq Ca Ab 370; 23 ER 1017; *Scott v Surman* (1742–3) Willes 400, 125 ER 1235; *Taylor v Plumer* (1815) 3 M & S 562, 105 ER 721; *Hopper v Conyers* (1866) LR 2 Eq 549; *Re Strachan* (1876) 4 Ch D 123.

[33] *Re Hallett's Estate* (1880) 13 Ch D 696.

[34] Eg *Ernest v Croysdill* (1860) 2 De G F & J 175, 45 ER 589; *Ex parte Oriental Bank* (1870) LR 5 Ch App 358; *Great Eastern Railway v Turner* (1872) LR 8 Ch App 149; *Re Leslie* [1976] 1 WLR 292; *Dyson Ltd v Curtis* [2010] EWHC 3289 (Ch); *Access Bank v Akingbola* [2012] EWHC 2148 (Comm); *Goldspan Ltd v Patel* [2012] EWHC 1447 (Ch); *Templeton Insurance Ltd v Brunswick* [2012] EWHC 1522.

[35] *Buhr v Barclays Bank* [2001] EWCA Civ 1223; *Dick v Harper* [2006] BPIR 20.

that have been dealt with by the wrongdoing fiduciary. A company, for example, is the common law owner of its own assets and its director has fiduciary powers over those assets, but does not hold them as a trustee.[36] These cases demonstrate that a common law power to deal with assets vested in another, at least when coupled with a fiduciary duty to exercise that power only in the interests of that other, is sufficient to generate a claim to traceable proceeds. A claimant in this situation is undoubtedly entitled to rely on the equitable tracing rules, and claim an equitable interest, such as a charge or a beneficial interest under a trust, over the proceeds.[37]

8.14 However, we have seen that a fiduciary relationship, in the strict sense of a duty of loyalty, is not necessary for all claims to traceable proceeds. A transferor of assets under a contract that has been rescinded, in equity, is entitled to claim the traceable proceeds of those assets on the basis of his equitable interest in those assets.[38] Nor is it the case that a claimant must either hold an equitable interest in assets or stand in a genuine fiduciary relationship with the defendant in order to make such claims. In *Buhr v Barclays Bank*, for example, the mortgagee's claim was brought in reliance on a legal mortgage, not an equitable one. Nevertheless, it succeeded in tracing into a mixed bank account and claiming a proportionate share of that bank account under a constructive trust.[39] Although Arden LJ characterized the mortgagor as a 'fiduciary' for certain limited purposes,[40] this cannot mean that a mortgagor is a fiduciary for the mortgagee in the sense that a company director is a fiduciary for the company. A mortgagor does not owe her mortgagee any duty to promote its interests over her own, although she may be prevented from entering into certain transactions that prejudice the position of the mortgagee. The existence of the mortgagors' power to destroy the mortgagee's security, coupled with a duty not to exercise that power, was sufficient to generate the claim.[41]

8.15 These cases provide the background, therefore, to the handful of difficult cases where the judges have expressly said that a claimant is entitled to traceable proceeds based on his common law rights, even though there is no fiduciary relationship between the claimant and the person dealing with those rights. These fall into two categories: dicta concerning stolen chattels, which ultimately focus only on stolen money, and cases where the facts are so complex that they are difficult to generalize from. The core elements of a relationship of control of assets—a private power, coupled with a duty not to exercise that power—can be found in each of these scenarios.

8.2. Money

8.16 A few cases offer limited authority, and forceful dicta, in favour of a claim to the traceable proceeds of stolen money. In *Re Hulton*,[42] for example, the bankrupt

[36] Cf *Templeton Insurance Ltd* (n 34) [74] (HHJ Simon Baker QC).
[37] As was decided in *Re Hallett's Estate* (n 33).
[38] See Chapter 7, Section 7.5 this volume.
[39] *Buhr* (n 35) [44] (Arden LJ).
[40] *Buhr* (n 35) [47] (Arden LJ).
[41] See Chapter 6, paras 6.78–6.79 this volume.
[42] (1891) 8 Morr 69, 39 WR 303.

was a cashier employed by the claimant bank who had stolen fifteen £100 notes that were sent to his branch in Oldham by the head office in Manchester. He had used these notes[43] to buy shares in a gold mine from a stockbroker in London. On his bankruptcy, the claimants sought a declaration that the shares were 'the property' of the bank and an order that the trustee in bankruptcy deliver up the share certificates and 'other documents of title' to the bank. In the county court at Oldham, HHJ Jones refused to grant this relief, holding that the bank must come in as an ordinary creditor in the bankruptcy to recover its losses; the decision was overturned by the Queen's Bench Division of the High Court on appeal. Counsel for the bank did argue that Hulton had received the money in his capacity as a servant of the bank and 'held them in a fiduciary relation', but Cave J did not comment on this aspect of the argument in his judgment, treating the money as simply stolen. He said:

> It is admitted that if the clerk had simply stolen the fifteen notes and retained them, the trustee must have been ordered to give them up; but it is said that since the notes were exchanged into shares, something was thereby effected so as to enable the trustee to keep the proceeds. In my opinion it is impossible to find any authority for such a contention.[44]

This argument obviously invokes the familiar fiction of persistence of rights through changes of subject matter. Setting the fiction aside, the reality is that something was effected by the exchange of the notes into shares: the London stockbrokers, who had received the notes and sold Hulton the shares in exchange, were likely to have gained an indefeasible title to the notes, leaving the bank with no remedy except its claims against Hulton. The judicial intuition in favour of tracing into the proceeds of stolen money, which does not appear in the case of stolen chattels that do not have the status of money,[45] can be explained on the basis of this legal consequence. The *nemo dat* exception of the currency of money operates to deprive a claimant of his rights, even where the person undertaking the transaction is a thief, rather than a trustee or a fiduciary.

8.3. Hard Cases

The person in unauthorized possession of money belonging to another is the paradigmatic example of the person who, without being a fiduciary, undoubtedly has a power to destroy the rights of a common law claimant and a duty not to do so. However, the traditional interpretation of *Taylor v Plumer*,[46] as adopted in *Lipkin Gorman v Karpnale Ltd*,[47] is framed in broader terms and seems to use the language of property in a wider sense. 8.17

[43] The report says the notes received by the stockbroker were 'identical in amounts, dates and numbers to those sent to the bankrupt from the head office'.
[44] *Re Hulton* (n 42). [45] See Chapter 6, Section 6.3.1 this volume.
[46] *Taylor* (n 2). [47] *Lipkin Gorman* (n 9).

8.18 In *Lipkin Gorman v Karpnale Ltd*, a partner in the claimant firm, Cass, had drawn on the firm's client account with Lloyds Bank, receiving banknotes that he then gave[48] to the defendant gambling club. Lord Goff acknowledged that, in these circumstances, Cass would have received his title to the banknotes as a trustee for the claimants. However, because the claimants were not arguing that the defendants were knowing recipients of trust property, but were instead bringing the common law action for money had and received, the argument that there was a trust was irrelevant: in his view, the claimants were seeking to show 'that the money in question was their property at common law.'[49] In order for them to do this, they did not need to show that Cass was their fiduciary or their trustee, but only that they were entitled at common law to the chose in action represented by the bank account with Lloyds; they could then trace from this chose of action into the cash received by Cass from Lloyds.[50]

8.19 On the facts of *Lipkin Gorman v Karpnale Ltd* itself, Cass's control over the assets of the firm can be derived from his status as one of the partners in the firm and his apparent authority to draw on the bank account. As the Court of Appeal decided,[51] on the terms of the banking contract between Lipkin Gorman and the bank, Cass's transaction was effective in reducing the debt owed to them without their consent. However, Lord Goff's dicta in the case are broader, and suggest—on the authority of *Taylor v Plumer*—that claims to traceable proceeds will arise whenever the claimant's thing is wrongly exchanged for something else.[52] He went to say that the firm's bank account was a chose in action, and thus 'a species of property'; since the debt they were owed by the bank was a legal debt, 'the chose in action was legal property belonging to the solicitors at common law',[53] and entitled them to its traceable proceeds. This analysis in the language of property is complicated by the fact that, as we have seen, the assets that are most conventionally described as property rights in English law—common law titles to land and chattels—do not generate any such claims.[54] Such claims have succeeded, however, in a handful of cases involving intangible assets, like bank accounts. The complex facts of these cases are best understood through the lens of the power–liability and right–duty relationships between the claimant and the person whose transactions are at issue. The language of property, as applied to these intangible assets, is only a proxy for describing these instances of relationships of control over the assets of another.

8.3.1. *Banque Belge pour l'Etranger v Hambrouck*

8.20 The difficult case[55] of *Banque Belge pour l'Etranger v Hambrouck*[56] is best understood from this perspective. In that case, Hambrouck had forged[57] the signature of his

[48] The House of Lords held that the transaction was equivalent to a gift, since gambling contracts were rendered void by the Gaming Act 1845, s 18.

[49] *Lipkin Gorman* (n 9) 572.

[50] *Lipkin Gorman* (n 9) 574.

[51] *Lipkin Gorman v Karpnale Ltd* [1989] 1 WLR 1340 (CA).

[52] *Lipkin Gorman* (n 9) 573.

[53] *Lipkin Gorman* (n 52).

[54] See Chapter 6, Section 6.3.1 this volume.

[55] See Millett J's comments on the case at first instance in *Agip (Africa) Ltd v Jackson* [1990] Ch 265 at 287: 'It is not easy to know what that case decided.'

[56] *Banque Belge pour l'Etranger* (n 9).

[57] *Banque Belge pour l'Etranger* (n 9) 331 (Atkin LJ).

employer, who had an account with the claimant bank, on cheques payable to himself. The cheques were crossed cheques, meaning that they could not be directly exchanged for cash at the employer's bank, but could only be collected via another bank.[58] Hambrouck, therefore, opened a new bank account with Farrow's Bank, who obtained the amount due from the claimants, through the clearing system,[59] and credited it to Hambrouck's account with them. The bank claimed that it could trace into the credit balance of this account, and its proceeds in the hands of the recipient from Hambrouck, and succeeded.

All three judges treated the clearing system as a mechanism under which the claimant bank had paid cash to Hambrouck directly. Thus, Atkin LJ spoke of Hambrouck's void or voidable title to 'the cash which under the operations of the clearing house they must be taken to have paid to the collecting bank'.[60] Scutton LJ did not mention the existence of Farrow's Bank as the collector of the cheque; in his version of the facts, Hambrouck first received cash from the claimant bank *and then* paid it into his account with Farrow's.[61] Bankes LJ mentioned the process by which Hambrouck's account came to be credited with the amount debited from his employer's account with the claimants, but also treated the bank as having dealt directly with Hambrouck himself, receiving the cheques from him and transferring possession to cash to him in consideration for the cheques authorizing them to debit their customer's account.[62] 8.21

The case must, therefore, be looked at from two perspectives: first, on the actual facts and, secondly, as a judicial account of the law's response to a direct transfer of title to money, or possession of money, under a void or voidable disposition. In terms of the effect of Hambrouck's actual transactions, it seems that his actions, via his agent, Farrow's Bank,[63] brought about a change in the legal relations of the claimant bank with the London and Southwest Bank, and perhaps other banks, within the clearing system. Hambrouck obtained his own rights against Farrow's in consideration for authorizing them to collect on the cheque, which transaction was effective in varying the claimant's rights against other banks within the clearing system. This is a somewhat tenuous basis on which to hold that the claimants had a right in respect of Hambrouck's bank account, however, since the exact chain of transactions within the clearing system is unknown and it is not clear how the bank's settlements of its various debts within that system eventually generated the debt due 8.22

58 Bills of Exchange Act 1882, s 77.

59 According to Atkin LJ, it did not deal directly with the claimant bank but collected via the London and South Western Bank, who then collected from the claimants.

60 *Banque Belge pour l'Etranger* (n 9) 332.

61 'The defence is that … payment into Hambrouck's bank, and his drawing out other money in satisfaction, had changed its identity': *Banque Belge pour l'Etranger* (n 9) 329–30.

62 'Whatever the position of the plaintiff Bank may have been in relation to their customer … in the event of the Bank being unable to recover the moneys which they had paid out when the cheques were presented to them for payment, it is I think clear that the moneys which were so paid out were the moneys of the plaintiff Bank which they were entitled to recover if they could': *Banque Belge pour l'Etranger* (n 9) 324–25.

63 A bank collecting on a cheque is an agent for its customer: *Capital and Counties Bank Ltd v Gordon* [1903] AC 240.

to Hambrouck. Nevertheless, it is difficult to see on what other basis they could have made a claim in respect of the account, since there is nothing else that Hambrouck did which could qualify as something he did to them, as opposed to his employer, from whom he took the physical cheques and the credit balance of whose account he succeeded in reducing.

8.23 The alternative seems to be the *Re Hulton* model of the facts, in which Hambrouck is seen as someone who has wrongfully possessed himself of cash belonging to the bank and used it to buy a new chose in action, like a bank account or shares in a gold mine. If the case is understood in this way, in the light of the Court of Appeal's invocation of cash payments, the issues seem clearer. On Hambrouck's payment of cash to Farrow's, the bank would have lost whatever title it had to that cash because Farrow's, not having any knowledge of Hambrouck's fraud, would have received it as currency. The strength of the analogy, therefore, depends on the judges seeing Hambrouck's transactions as effective in altering the legal position of the claimant as against Farrow's bank or someone else: the objection to the idea that 'their money' 'lost its identity' on payment to Farrow's seems to depend on the idea that, when the payment to Farrow's was made, some right of theirs was lost or altered.

8.3.2. *Marsh v Keating*

8.24 *Marsh v Keating*[64] is another difficult case from the perspective of defining what it is, exactly, that the claimant says has been done to her by another person in order to justify her claim to the proceeds of his transactions. The claimant, Mrs Keating, held certain stock in the Bank of England; that is, the Bank owed her £12,000 in 3 per cent annuities. She also held a bank account with the defendants' firm, Marsh & Co, into which the dividends due to her from the Bank of England were always paid. One of the partners in the firm, Henry Fauntleroy, used a forged power of attorney to purportedly authorize his stockbroker to transfer some of her stock to a third party (a Mr Tarbutt). In reliance on that forged power, an entry was made in the 'transfer-book' of the Bank of England, stating that the claimant transferred £9,000 of her share in the stock to Tarbutt; in reliance on this entry in the transfer-book, that sum was debited from her account and credited to his account in the 'ledger book' at the Bank. Tarbutt paid the purchase price to the stockbroker who, having deducted his usual commission, gave a cheque payable to the defendants to Fauntleroy, who paid it into the defendants' bank account. Tarbutt then entered into many transactions with other parties by which shares in the same stock were transferred to him and by him. As a result of these transactions, according to the special verdict in the case,

> ... in the books kept by the said Governor and Company [of the Bank of England] the said sum of £9000 reduced 3 per cent annuities had become blended and mixed with other stocks standing in the said ledgers in the said W. B. Tarbutt's name ... [and] it was not possible to

[64] (1834) 1 Bing (NC) 198, 131 ER 1094.

distinguish the account to the credit of which the said 9000l reduced 3 per cent annuities stood.[65]

After his various forgeries were discovered, Fauntleroy was arrested, tried, and executed; the remaining partners of Marsh & Co, the defendants, became bankrupt. The claimant, having discovered the forgery, informed the Bank of England but did not seek to have criminal proceedings brought in respect of that forgery. After the bankruptcy, she wrote to the Bank of England asking for her stock to be replaced. The Bank agreed to replace the stock and pay the dividends that would have been due on it if it had not been transferred, provided that she agreed to attempt a recovery of the proceeds of the sale of her stock in the defendants' bankruptcy. Having received the dividends from the Bank, she duly claimed the value of the cheque as money had and received by the defendants to her use and succeeded in this claim.

The problem with this case, from the perspective of understanding the power–liability relationship between Henry Fauntleroy and Mrs Keating, is that he seems not to have done anything to her rights. In *Davies v Bank of England*,[66] the Court of Common Pleas had held that a purported transfer of stock in the Bank of England books, under a forged power of attorney, did not affect the Bank's liability to the holder of that stock: the claimant in that case, whose stock had been purportedly transferred to a third party, had sued the Bank of England for dividends due on the stock and had succeeded in the claim. If this is right, then it seems that Mrs Keating still had her right to dividends against the Bank of England and Henry Fauntleroy's supposed transfer of the stock to Tarbutt was a nullity from her perspective. However, Park J emphasized that this did not mean that the transaction had no effect on her at all: 8.25

If the Plaintiff below ... were to apply to receive payment of the dividends, or to sell the stock, she would be met with a difficulty, insuperable in fact: although the stock may, in contemplation of law, still be vested in her, it is certain that she could not either receive the dividend or sell the stock, until she had first compelled the Bank to purchase, de novo, in her name, an equal quantity of the same stock.[67]

The reason for this was that the Bank of England could not simply deny that Fauntleroy's transfer to Tarbutt and Tarbutt's subsequent transactions with purchasers had been effective. As Park J said, Tarbutt and those who had purchased from him had, as against the Bank of England, 'the right to insist upon the payment of the dividend'.[68] This right arose simply by virtue of the entry of Tarbutt's name in the Bank's books, which estopped the Bank from denying his title to the stock. In *Davis v Bank of England*, Best CJ expressly said that the decision that the original holder of the stock could sue for the dividend did not mean that the Bank of England could deny the right of the purchaser of the stock to also be paid a dividend:

If the bank should say to such subsequent purchasers, the persons of whom you bought were not legally possessed of the stocks they sold you, the answer would be, the bank, in the books

65 *Marsh* (n 64) 202; 1096.
66 (1824) 2 Bing 391, 130 ER 357.
67 *Marsh* (n 64) 215; 1100.
68 *Marsh* (n 67).

which the law requires them to keep, and for the keeping which they receive a remuneration from the public, have registered these persons as the owners of these stocks, and the bank cannot be permitted to say that such persons were not the owners.[69]

It is because the Bank of England could not simply cancel Fauntleroy's transaction with Tarbutt and all Tarbutt's transactions with third parties that there was any practical difficulty involved in Mrs Keating asserting her rights, and that such an assertion of rights would ultimately have involved the Bank altering its books to add to its own liabilities by purchasing stock in Mrs Keating's name.

8.26 This leaves us with a number of possible interpretations of *Marsh v Keating*. First, we might take Park J's statement to mean that, where A's transaction renders it very difficult for B to exercise his rights, this is equivalent to depriving B of those rights and entitles B to claim the traceable proceeds of A's transaction. This is a very broad proposition, the scope of which is difficult to define, and which is unsupported by other authority. Alternatively, the facts of *Marsh v Keating*, understood in the context of the surrounding litigation, are susceptible to two other possible explanations.

8.27 First, at the time of the decision in *Marsh v Keating* it was not absolutely clear, as a matter of authority, that Mrs Keating still had her stock, after the transfer to Tarbutt. The judgment of the Court of Common Pleas in *Davis v Bank of England* had been reversed two years later, on a writ of error,[70] on the basis that the claimant could not have his dividends because he had not pleaded that the Government had issued any dividends on his stock. In *Marsh v Keating*, counsel argued that this decision must have meant that Davis did not own the stock after all:

How could the stock, which was as it were the tree, be treated differently from the dividends, which was the fruit?[71]

8.28 In *Stracy v Bank of England*,[72] another case arising out of Fauntleroy's forgeries, the claimants had attempted to sell the stock they still, supposedly, held after Fauntleroy's forged transfer of their stock to the third party. The Bank of England refused to alter its books to reflect this sale and the claimants brought an action seeking damages for the Bank's breach of its duty to make such a transfer at the request of a holder of the stock. Like Mrs Keating, the claimants had entered into an agreement with the Bank under which it promised to replace their stock provided that they came in as creditors in the bankruptcy of the defendant firm and then assigned their rights to the Bank. They had failed to do this, but counsel argued that this made no difference to their right to assign the stock, which, according to *Davis v Bank of England*, they still had. It was also argued that the contract was not binding in any case, because the Bank of England's promise to replace the claimant's stock was not good consideration: if, as was contended, the claimants still had their original stock, unaffected by the fraudulent transfer, the Bank's promise was of no benefit to them. The court, without taking a view on the correctness of *Davis*, rejected this argument:

[69] *Davis v Bank of England* (n 66) 407–08; 363.
[70] (1826) 5 & C 185, 108 ER 69.
[71] This remark is not reported in the Bingham report, but appears in the Clark & Finelly report of the arguments in *Marsh v Keating*: (1834) 2 Cl & F 250, 277; 6 ER 1149, 1159.
[72] (1830) 6 Bing 754, 130 ER 1471.

It was at that time a question of great nicety and difficulty, whether the Bank was by law liable to make good this loss: so that the engagement of the Bank to replace this stock without any litigation on their part, was of itself a very valuable and important concession.

If this is right, it seems that Fauntleroy did significantly alter Mrs Keating's legal position: the standard incidents of her original right, such as the right to recover dividends and to sell the stock held in her name, were no longer enforceable as of right against the Bank. Although she did receive dividends, this was after she had promised to prove in the insolvency of the defendant firm and this suggests that the Bank no longer acknowledged that she was entitled to these dividends as of right.

The other argument is that, on the realities of the case, Mrs Keating was actually suing as a proxy for the Bank of England and the decision of the court in her favour could be explained as a response to Fauntleroy's exercise of a power to radically alter the legal position of the Bank of England by multiplying its liabilities. The Bank was unable to unravel the transactions that had taken place, and was obliged to pay dividends to all the purchasers whose names it had entered in its books in reliance on Fauntleroy's forged powers of attorney; in addition, if *Davis v Bank of England* was right, it was obliged to pay the equivalent dividends to all the defrauded original holders of stock. It is plausible to argue that the decision in *Marsh v Keating* was ultimately aimed at allowing the Bank to recover some of its losses, given that Mrs Keating had agreed to assign her claims against the bankrupt firm to it. If so, the case is unique on its facts and one from which it is difficult to generalize. 8.29

8.3.3. *Armstrong DLW GmBH v Winnington Networks Ltd*

Regardless of the view taken, an important element of the situation in *Marsh v Keating* arises out of the fact that Fauntleroy succeeded in persuading the Bank of England to change what its books said. It was not the forged power of attorney, or the supposed contract of sale between Mrs Keating and Tarbutt, which gave Tarbutt his rights: rather, he gained those rights against the Bank of England, and perhaps against Mrs Keating, because the bank had 'registered [him] as owner of the stocks' in 'the books which the law require[d] them to keep'. The role of such a public registration system, in allowing fraudsters to alter rights by acts which would otherwise constitute nullities, also explains the decision in *Armstrong DLW GmBH v Winnington Networks Ltd*.[73] 8.30

That case concerned European Union Allowances (EUAs), which are essentially carbon emission licences that permit the holder to emit a specified amount of carbon dioxide within a specified period without incurring a penalty.[74] Under the scheme of the Directive, each member state has a national registry of EUAs, and individuals and companies may open accounts in this registry and acquire and trade in EUAs within the system. Account holders are able, via nominated individuals, to alter the register themselves; the national registry issues usernames and passwords that 8.31

[73] [2012] EWHC 10 (Ch).

[74] Established under Council Directive 2003/87/EC of 13 October 2003 establishing a scheme for greenhouse gas emission allowance trading within the Community [2003] OJ L275/32.

allow access to the system, and, subject to additional security requirements that vary across member states, anyone with the relevant access may alter the register. A fraudster, purporting to represent a company called Zen Holdings Ltd, gained access to the claimant company's username and password via an email fraud. They then used these details to transfer 21,000 EUAs from the claimant's account to that of the defendant, Winnington Networks Ltd, in consideration for a payment by the defendant of €267,645. On the same day, the defendants transferred these EUAs[75] to a third-party purchaser, and obtained €272,500 as their price. The claimants sought to recover the money from the defendants, and succeeded on the basis that the money represented the traceable proceeds of their EUAs. The power–liability relationship between claimant and defendant can be explained on the basis of a bona fide purchaser defence available to any purchaser from Winnington Networks Ltd the defendants. Stephen Morris QC said, obiter, that such a defence was generally available where the claimant was asserting his subsisting legal rights in an intangible asset against a third-party recipient.[76] The idea of a legal right to an intangible asset held by someone else is a doubtful one, however, and the power–liability relationship between the parties on the particular facts may be better explained by features of the EUA system and its rules governing transferability. Article 37(4) of the relevant Regulations provide that:

> A purchaser and holder of an allowance or Kyoto unit acting in good faith shall acquire title to an allowance or Kyoto unit free of any defects in the title of the transferor.[77]

The fraudster who gained access to the claimant's passwords was, therefore, in a position to divest the claimant of its EUAs and thus to vary its legal position against the state, by reducing the amount of carbon it could emit without penalty. In fact, because the defendants were not in good faith, the transaction did not have the effect of destroying the claimant's title to the EUAs; the subsequent sale of the EUAs by the defendant to a third party would be likely to have had this effect. However, Stephen Morris QC said that the claimants could trace through the transactions of the defendants because they were recipients of trust property, rather than because they had this power to vary the claimants' rights as against the state.

8.32 He took the view that, prior to the transfer of the EUAs from claimant to defendant, the fraudster had become a constructive trustee. This analysis raises the problem of identifying the subject matter of the trust. It could not have been the EUAs themselves, since these remained registered in the name of the claimants until the fraudster executed a direct transfer to the defendants; there was no moment in time when the EUAs were vested in the fraudster himself. Instead, Stephen Morris QC said that the fraudster held his *control* over the EUAs on trust for the claimants:

[75] It was known that these were the same EUAs, because each one had a unique reference number incorporating a reference to the national registry of origin.

[76] *Armstrong DLW GmBH* (n 73) at [94].

[77] Commission Regulation 1193/2011 of 19 November 2011 [2011] OJ L315/1.

Some time between 0745 and 1130 on 28 January 2010, the third party fraudster gained de facto ministerial control over the EUAs lying in Armstrong's account. ... To the extent that the fraudster had obtained ministerial control, he was to be regarded as, at least, in possession of the EUAs. He was in a position such that he could offer to sell them to strangers, such as Winnington, and subsequently effect their transfer away.[78]

It is unclear what it means to be a trustee of a de facto ministerial control over the rights of another person. Where the person with the correlative liability and the beneficiary under the trust are different people, it is possible to understand this structure in the orthodox terminology of the trust: the trustee has a power over X, and he owes Y a duty to exercise the power and alter X's legal position in accordance with Y's best interests. However, it is not clear what this type of analysis would add in a situation where X and Y are the same person: in such a case, the distinctive double layer of legal relations found in the case of the trust is missing, and there is a single legal relationship involving both a power and a duty not to exercise that power. This structure is itself sufficient to give rise to claims to traceable proceeds when the power is wrongfully exercised, and an invocation of the trust concept is not necessary in these circumstances.

8.4. No Special Rules of Common Law Tracing

The equitable rules that permit tracing into and through mixed substitutions have been shown to be available to a range of claimants whose assets have been wrongly dealt with by defendants who have control over those assets. These include claimants who have an equitable interest in assets, and to whom a fiduciary duty is owed by the defendant;[79] claimants who have an equitable interest in assets, but to whom no fiduciary duty is owed by the defendant;[80] claimants who have a common law right to assets, and to whom a fiduciary duty is owed;[81] and claimants who have a common law right to assets, to whom no fiduciary duty is owed.[82] At the level of principle, therefore, it is difficult to justify a rule that only one limited category of common law claimants, such as victims of a theft of money, should not be entitled to invoke these rules. The authority of the dicta in *Foskett v McKeown* to the effect that it is unprincipled to distinguish between tracing at law and tracing in equity[83] is reinforced by the fact that the current distinction does not reflect any kind of principled distinction, either in terms of the source of the relationship between claimant and defendant or in its content. 8.33

[78] *Armstrong DLW GmBH* (n 73) [276].

[79] Such as a beneficiary under a trust: *Pennell v Deffel* (1853) 4 De G M & G 372, 43 ER 551.

[80] Such as a recipient of assets under a rescinded transaction: *El Ajou v Dollar Land Holdings plc (No 1)* [1993] 3 All ER 717.

[81] Such as a bailee: *Re Hallett's Estate* (n 33).

[82] Such as a mortgagee: *Buhr v Barclays Bank* (n 35).

[83] [2001] 1 AC 102, 128 (Lord Millett).

8.5. No Common Law Titles to Substitute Assets

8.34 As a matter of authority, we have also seen that the origin of this restriction on tracing into mixed substitutions arose from the view that a common law claimant obtained a common law title to the substitute asset—a conclusion that would lead to problematic consequences where the substitute asset is either a mixed fund of intangible assets or a chose in action.[84] There is, however, limited authority that a common law claimant is either entitled to, or obliged to, assert common law rights in respect of substitute assets. The strongest authority in favour of such an option is the decision in *Lipkin Gorman v Karpnale Ltd* that the claimant firm was entitled to bring the common law action in money had and received against the defendant club, and the dictum in the case that a common law title was necessary to support this common law cause of action. However, as Lionel Smith has shown,[85] the availability of this cause of action on the facts could be supported on the basis that the cash received by the defendant club was held on trust for the claimant firm. One advantage of this analysis, as Smith argues, is that it allows us to dispense with the difficult concept of a previously unknown innominate common law title—not quite a trust, but not quite a full-fledged possessory title imposing duties of non-interference on all the world—that can exist in respect of chattels. Another is that it avoids the difficulties that would arise if tracing into mixed funds of intangible assets was permitted at common law. Unlike the equitable constructs of the charge or trust, a common law claim to such a fund would require the law to effectively confiscate the defendant's assets and assign them to the claimant,[86] distorting the core principle of respect for defendant autonomy that underpins the requirement of tracing and prejudicing the position of third parties affected by such an involuntary assignment of rights by operation of law.

8.35 Thus the remedial resources of equity—which enable us to say that a right-holder holds his rights subject to duties owed to someone else, without confiscating those rights entirely—are necessary to facilitate the possibility of tracing into mixed funds. It does not follow that a claimant must have an equitable right at the outset to take advantage of these equitable remedies, or that common law causes of action cannot be invoked by such a claimant. Claims to traceable proceeds are available to all claimants who are vulnerable to the exploitation of power by private parties; such vulnerabilities exist both at law and in equity, and the law's principled response draws on the resources of both jurisdictions.

84 See Chapter 3, Section 3.3.2.1 this volume.
85 L Smith, 'Simplifying Claims to Traceable Proceeds' (2009) 125 LQR 338.
86 See Chapter 3, paras 3.116–3.117 this volume.

Index

The manufacturer's authorised representative in the EU for product
safety is Oxford University Press España S.A. of El Parque Empresarial
San Fernando de Henares, Avenida de Castilla, 2 - 28830 Madrid
(www.oup.es/en or product.safety@oup.com). OUP España S.A. also acts
as importer into Spain of products made by the manufacturer.
Printed and bound by CPI Group (UK) Ltd, Croydon, CR0 4YY
12/09/2026
02215930-0003